STUDIES OF T

edit(

Maxine]
Institute for the St
Universit
School of A

Titles in this series are multidisciplinary studies of aspects ~~or the sout~~
hemisphere, particularly in the areas of politics, economics, history, anthropology,
sociology, and the environment. The series covers a comparative perspective across
the Americas, including Canada and the Caribbean as well as the United States and
Latin America.

Titles in this series published by Palgrave Macmillan:

Cuba's Military 1990-2005: Revolutionary Soldiers during
Counter-Revolutionary Times
    By Hal Klepak

The Judicialization of Politics in Latin America
    Edited by Rachel Sieder, Line Schjolden, and Alan Angell

Latin America: A New Interpretation
    By Laurence Whitehead

Appropriation as Practice: Art and Identity in Argentina
    By Arnd Schneider

America and Enlightenment Constitutionalism
    Edited by Gary L. McDowell and Johnathan O'Neill

Vargas and Brazil: New Perspectives
    Edited by Jens R. Hentschke

When Was Latin America Modern?
    Edited by Nicola Miller and Stephen Hart

Debating Cuban Exceptionalism
    Edited by Bert Hoffman and Laurence Whitehead

Caribbean Land and Development Revisited
    Edited by Jean Besson and Janet Momsen

Cultures of the Lusophone Black Atlantic
    Edited by Nancy Priscilla Naro, Roger Sansi-Roca, and David H. Treece

Democratization, Development, and Legality: Chile, 1831-1973
    By Julio Faundez

The Hispanic World and American Intellectual Life, 1820-1880
    By Iván Jaksić

The Role of Mexico's Plural *in Latin American Literary and Political Culture:*
From Tlatelolco to the "Philanthropic Ogre"
    By John King

Faith and Impiety in Revolutionary Mexico
    Edited by Matthew Butler

History and Language in the Andes

Edited by

Paul Heggarty and
Adrian J. Pearce

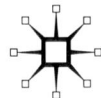

HISTORY AND LANGUAGE IN THE ANDES
Copyright © Paul Heggarty and Adrian J. Pearce, 2011.

All rights reserved.

First published in 2011 by
PALGRAVE MACMILLAN®
in the United States—a division of St. Martin's Press LLC,
175 Fifth Avenue, New York, NY 10010.

Where this book is distributed in the UK, Europe and the rest of the world,
this is by Palgrave Macmillan, a division of Macmillan Publishers Limited,
registered in England, company number 785998, of Houndmills,
Basingstoke, Hampshire RG21 6XS.

Palgrave Macmillan is the global academic imprint of the above companies
and has companies and representatives throughout the world.

Palgrave® and Macmillan® are registered trademarks in the United States,
the United Kingdom, Europe and other countries.

ISBN: 978–0–230–10014–5

Library of Congress Cataloging-in-Publication Data

History and language in the Andes / edited by Paul Heggarty and
Adrian J. Pearce.
    p. cm.—(Studies of the Americas)
Includes bibliographical references and index.
ISBN 978–0–230–10014–5 (hardback)
    1. Indians of South America—Andes Region—Languages. 2. Language
and languages—Andes Region. 3. Linguistic geography—Andes Region—
History. 4. Quechua language—History. 5. Aymara language—History.
6. Andes Region—Languages. I. Heggarty, Paul, 1967– II. Pearce, Adrian J.

PM5100.H57 2011
498—dc22   2011014997

A catalogue record of the book is available from the British Library.

Design by Newgen Imaging Systems (P) Ltd., Chennai, India.

First edition: November 2011

10 9 8 7 6 5 4 3 2 1

Printed and bound in Great Britain by
CPI Antony Rowe, Chippenham and Eastbourne

Adrian dedicates this book to the Tansley family:
Katherine, Robert, Lucy, Eddie, and Marmy

Contents

Part I   The Colonial Era

Figures and Tables

Figures

Tables

Contributors

Kenneth J. Andrien is Humanities Distinguished Professor in History at the Ohio State University. He received his B.A. at Trinity College and his M.A. and Ph.D. degrees from Duke University. He has written or edited several books and numerous articles dealing with Colonial Latin America, focusing primarily on the Andean region. He is currently completing a book (with Allan Kuethe of Texas Tech University) entitled *War and Reform in the Spanish Atlantic World, 1700–1796,* and another book-length study on church-state relations in Bourbon Peru.

Alan Durston is an associate professor in the History Department at York University in Toronto, where he teaches Latin American history. His research focuses on the history of Quechua as a written language and on the discourses and politics surrounding Quechua in colonial and modern Peru. He is the author of *Pastoral Quechua: the History of Christian Translation in Colonial Peru, 1550–1650* (University of Notre Dame Press, 2007). His current research concerns the place of Quechua letters in nation-building and modernization processes in twentieth-century Peru.

Sue Grosboll is the director of the University of Northern Iowa Museums and adjunct professor of archaeology at UNI. Her archaeological research within the Andes has focused on the correlation of architectural remains with early colonial documentation. Using various sixteenth-century *visitas,* her studies have analyzed the demographic changes that occurred during the late prehistoric and early colonial periods and the cultural impact of those changes.

Paul Heggarty is a researcher in the Linguistics Department of the *Max Planck Institute for Evolutionary Anthropology* in Leipzig, Germany. His focus is on language history and prehistory, aiming to ensure that the perspective from linguistics is better understood outside that field, to contribute towards a more coherent, cross-disciplinary vision of the human past. To that end he works closely with historians, archaeologists, and geneticists. Within interests that range worldwide, his specialism is in the indigenous languages of the Andes, particularly the divergence history of the Quechua and Aymara families. He was the lead convener of the series of interdisciplinary conferences on the Andean past that led to this volume, and its companion on the pre-Columbian period, *Archaeology and Language in the Andes*, co-edited with Andean archaeologist David Beresford-Jones (British Academy/Oxford University Press).

Rosaleen Howard, chair of Hispanic Studies in the School of Modern Languages at Newcastle University, is a sociolinguist who works on Quechua-speaking areas of Ecuador, Peru, and Bolivia. She has published widely on Quechua language and oral culture; multilingualism, language and identity; language, education, and indigenous social movements; and other topics. Her most recent book is *Por los linderos de la lengua. Ideologías lingüísticas en los Andes* (Instituto de Estudios Peruanos, Lima, 2007). She is currently working on a British Academy Latin American/Caribbean Link project on "Paradigms of Cultural Diversity and Social Cohesion," looking at language and education rights, policy, and planning for indigenous populations in the Andes and Mexico.

César Itier is a philologist and specialist in the Quechua language, which he teaches at the Institut National des Langues et Civilisations Orientales (INALCO) in Paris. At the intersection of linguistics, history, and ethnology, his research focuses on oral and written literature in Quechua, as well as on the internal and external history of the language from the sixteenth to the twentieth centuries. Among his most notable works are a study of modern Quechua theatre in Cuzco, in two volumes (*El teatro quechua en el Cuzco*, 1995 and 2000), another on the oral literature of the Cuzco region (*El hijo del oso. La literatura oral quechua de la región del Cuzco*, 2007), an edition, translation, and study of a seventeenth-century Quechua play (*El robo de Proserpina y sueño de Endimión* by Juan de Espinosa Medrano, Lima, 2010) and a Quechua-French dictionary (Paris, 2011).

Tim Marr is a sociolinguist with a particular interest in language use in Peru; he lived in Lima for several years. He is currently Principal Lecturer in Applied Linguistics at London Metropolitan University, where he teaches mainly postgraduate courses in sociolinguistics.

Adrian J. Pearce is a historian of Latin America, with research interests principally in the political, economic, and cultural history of the eighteenth and nineteenth centuries. He was co-organizer, with Paul Heggarty, of the symposium from which this volume originated, held at the Institute for the Study of the Americas in London in September 2008. He is currently completing a book on Spanish imperial policies in the viceroyalty of Peru during the early eighteenth century, while his new project looks at the phenomenon of reindigenization in the nineteenth-century Andes. He teaches at King's College, London, in both the Department of History and the Department of Spanish, Portuguese, and Latin American Studies.

Gabriela Ramos is a lecturer in Latin American History at the University of Cambridge. She is the author of *Death and Conversion in the Andes: Lima and Cuzco, 1532–1670* (2010).

Frank Salomon is the John V. Murra Professor of Anthropology at the University of Wisconsin-Madison. An ethnographer and ethnohistorian of the Andes, he is the author of *Native Lords of Quito in the Age of the Incas* (1986), *The Huarochiri Manuscript, a Testament of Ancient and Colonial Andean Religion* (1991), the *Cambridge History of the Native Peoples of the Americas—South America* (1999), and *the Cord Keepers* (2004) as well as articles on indigenous media and language including "Names and Peoples in Post-Incaic Quito" (1986). His current researches concern the survival into modernity of the Andean knotted-cord script, the quipu (or more correctly, in Quechua *khipu*).

Acknowledgments

Our recognition goes first to the British Academy, for the lion's share of funding that made possible at all the wide-ranging scholarly enterprise that has become this book. Our series of cross-disciplinary symposia on the Andean past, and the ensuing publications of which this book is one, are thanks directly to the generous funding of the Academy's far-sighted UK-Latin American/Caribbean Link Programme.

This volume arises directly from our symposium on *History and Linguistics in the Andes*, held in September 2008 at the Institute for the Study of the Americas of the University of London. We thank, in particular, its director Maxine Molyneux, who not only threw her support behind the symposium in the form of further institutional funding, but also accepted the book proposal as Series Editor for Palgrave Macmillan's *Studies of the Americas*. For administrative prowess at the Institute, meanwhile, our thanks go to Olga Jimenez. And for many a fine pisco sour and sundry gastronomic treats from the Andes, we are most grateful to the then Peruvian ambassador in London, H.E. Ricardo Luna, for hosting a reception in his residency to mark the occasion of our symposia.

Within our wider program of cross-disciplinary research into the Andean past, our London symposium followed hot on the heels of a sister event on the pre-Columbian period, *viz. Archaeology and Linguistics in the Andes.* This was hosted by the McDonald Institute for Archaeological Research at the University of Cambridge, two of whose members we must single out for their own crucial contributions. Colin Renfrew has long been a key player at the intersection of the disciplines that seek to illuminate our past; it is to his intellectual inspiration that our own enterprise in the Andes is so deeply indebted. David Beresford-Jones, meanwhile, our fellow Andeanist musketeer from the perspective of archaeology, co-organized with us our whole interdisciplinary project.

Many contributors, too, took part equally in both symposia: so if their chapter is not to be found here, then readers should look instead among the pages of its sister volume, *Archaeology and Language in the Andes*, co-edited by Paul with David Beresford-Jones (British Academy/Oxford University Press, 2012). May we make special mention also of the willingness and enthusiasm of Luis Miguel Glave, and of the late Olivia Harris, a great loss to our field.

Chuck Walker and Rebecca Earle generously commented on our book proposal or on sections of the typescript, and we thank also the anonymous reader for our publisher for further support and valuable comments. Since then, making this book a reality has called upon the professionalism of Palgrave Macmillan and Newgen, in particular Robyn Curtis and Rohini Krishnan.

The wheels of our own editorial work were oiled by our current institutions. Adrian thanks the History Department at King's College, London, and its Head Dr Paul Readman, for the sabbatical in 2010–2011 that enabled him to complete his share. From Paul, thanks go to the Linguistics Department at the Max Planck Institute for Evolutionary Anthropology in Leipzig, particularly to its director, Bernard Comrie. His support has long been crucial to our multidisciplinary enterprise, from our original British Academy application to the funding and hosting of the following symposium on *Population Prehistory of the Andes*, held in Leipzig in November 2011.

There are many people, then, without whom this book would not have seen the light of day. But to close we move on to heavier debts still, owed to whom else but our long-suffering other halves, Céline and Coni, for forbearance beyond the call of duty through the many moons of this book's gestation. And naturally, the very last words in all our heartfelt thanks must go one by one to each of our contributing authors. It is their compendious experience, and their collective insights into the Andean past, that we now invite you to explore.

A Note on Spellings of Terms in Indigenous Languages

Inca or *Inka*? *Quipu* or *khipu*? *Mita* or *mit'a*? No scholar of the Andean past can fail to notice countless variant spellings of hundreds of personal names, toponyms and other terms taken from indigenous languages such as Quechua and Aymara. For publishers wishing to apply consistency in spellings—especially, as in this book, between many contributing authors from different disciplinary backgrounds—this is a veritable minefield.

In practice, full consistency is impossible to achieve, short of wholesale "indigenisation" to write, for example, *Wankawillka*, *Wankayu(q)*, and *Qusqu* in place of *Huancavelica*, *Huancayo*, and *Cuzco*. Nor does sticking to Spanish spelling solve the problem, for it too is highly inconsistent (for example in usage of *gua-* versus *hua-*), not least because it is very poorly suited to representing the native sound systems of Andean languages.

Traditional Spanish spellings of such words as *quipu*, *mita*, or *Inca* remains the strong majority usage in works on Andean history, and the preference of most of our contributors here. For these reasons alone we have chosen in this volume to apply consistency in favor of those traditional spellings. Feelings can get rather strong on this question, however, and some contributors to this book have their own good reasons for preferring alternative spellings, which the publisher's policy for consistency has thus had to override. We therefore feel that we should take this opportunity to clarify this vexed and long-standing question, hoping to make some contribution towards progress on it.

On the one hand, many of the strong feelings aroused actually go back to some over-simplistic assumptions about indigenous languages. Advocates of the spelling *Inka* typically protest that the word "should" be spelt with a *k* precisely to get away from Spanish *c*, that is, "out of respect for indigenous languages." The superficial logic here is that in standard Quechua orthography *Inka* is spelt with a *k*. And certainly, *k* is frequent in Quechua spelling, while *c* does not even exist in the alphabet for native Quechua words (other than within the combination *ch*).

At first sight that may seem all very well; but as any Andean linguist is aware, such assumptions are simplistic, and indeed thereby themselves very Eurocentric. All too often, enthusiasts adopt "pseudo–indigenous" spellings that in fact only demonstrate a *lack* of knowledge and true respect for several of the most fundamental aspects of the sound systems of indigenous Andean languages, which are far too rich to be subsumed under just "Spanish *c* = indigenous *k*." In fact, Spanish *c* represents indiscriminately any of six different sounds and spellings in Aymara or in Cuzco–Bolivian Quechua: *k, kh, k', q, qh, q'*. Assuming that Spanish *c* necessarily equates to Quechua *k*, then, is more likely than not to be wrong. In many cases, ignorance in practice does *more* disrespect and violence to indigenous languages than do the original Spanish forms.

Take, for example, the popular but deeply erroneous spelling *kero* for the type of wooden Inca vase. In this case, the *k* is—by any standards whatever—the wrong letter, for the wrong sound. This is no idiosyncratic linguist's dictate; it follows from the very pronunciation of the word itself. The misplaced popular confidence that *k* can safely be used here goes back to native speakers of English and Spanish being unaware of how the word is pronounced in the first place; indeed the sound at the start of this word does not exist in their languages. In languages that do have that sound, meanwhile, in no spelling system that we are aware of is it represented by the letter *k*, which always denotes a quite different sound instead.

Those who do not know the sound system of Quechua, then, should be under no illusions as to how basic this error is. To spell *kero* with initial *k* (rather than correct *q*) is every bit as erroneous as somebody who speaks no English deciding that the words *sank* and *tank*, for instance, can both safely be respelled *thank*, under some impression that the spelling *th* "looks more distinctively and natively English," and confident only because of their ignorance that all three words are *not* actually pronounced the same. An analogy in Spanish would be to spell *ñoche* and *lluego* [sic], for example, on similarly naïve grounds that *ñ* and *ll* "look more distinctively and natively Spanish" than *n* or *l*.[1]

One also finds *Pikillacta*, for instance, a mish-mash where Spanish *qu* has been changed to *k* (luckily, in this case, actually correct), but

Spanish *c* left in (it should be *q* in this case); or spellings like *curaka*, likewise erroneous and self-contradictory. Finally, note too the title of a paper by the distinguished Peruvian linguist Rodolfo Cerrón-Palomino: "Cuzco y no Cusco, ni menos Qosqo."[2]

Cerrón-Palomino is himself the one authority who has done most to draw up modern official spelling systems that at last faithfully reflect the native sound systems of Andean languages;[3] and he is at the same time the leading expert on indigenous etymologies.[4] It is worth reflecting on his own perspective and policy on the question of spellings. This is to use indigenous spellings *within texts written in indigenous languages*; but in texts written in Spanish or in English, to use conventional spellings where they are already established in those languages. There is nobody who has greater respect for indigenous languages than Rodolfo, nor greater erudition both as to how words in those languages are to be spelt, and as to the reasons and origins behind whatever variant spellings do exist. It is indicative, then, that his own judgement, more fully reasoned and justified in print than anyone's, is to keep to established spellings such as *Inca*, *Tiahuanaco*, and *Cuzco* when writing texts *in Spanish or English*.

Certainly in the case of *Inca*, then, this spelling has been established within the English language for centuries; it is effectively an English word now, as well as a Quechua one. Moreover, it respects the traditional spelling rule *in English*, which (for good historical reasons) is that *k* is generally used before a following *e* or *i*, but *c* before other vowels, notably *a*. Hence, many readers' perceptions of *Inka* as a wilfully "marked" spelling, to make a point in favor of indigenous spelling. But if *Inka* is so used, then why do those same authors then go on to ignore—as without fail they do—indigenous spellings for so many other native words?

That said, English is not Spanish, and as our contributor Frank Salomon points out, there is no good reason why English spellings need to be borrowed through those of Spanish, rather than directly from the indigenous source language itself. Hence his own preferred usage of *khipu*, which we have reluctantly changed here to traditional (Spanish) *quipu*, but only to ensure consistency across our contributors. The correct spelling in modern standard orthography for Southern Quechua itself is certainly *khipu*. Spanish *quipu* conspicuously fails to show that this word starts with an aspirate *kh*, rather than one of the other five different sounds that Spanish spelling *c* or *qu* fails to distinguish, but which are critical differences for the Quechua sound system.

Many supporters of using Spanish spellings like *quipu* in English too argue that they are preferable because they look less alien to English-speaking readers than do indigenous spellings. English, like Spanish, does not natively use *kh* or *k'*, for instance, or indeed *q* before any vowel other than *u*. Firstly, though, whether this helps English readers get any closer to the indigenous pronunciation is entirely debatable. A natural English reading of written *qui-* is not [ki] as in Spanish *quince* (fifteen) but as [kwɪ] with a [w] sound, as in English *quick*. Such differences between Spanish and English spelling rules, then, can actually take English speakers further away from the correct indigenous pronunciation, in this case [kʰi].[5]

Secondly, the original claim is only half true at best. Often, the English and modern indigenous spellings systems are in fact closer to each other than either is to Spanish, especially in their use of *h* and *w*. Spanish spellings *hu-* and *gu-* are thus highly susceptible of being misread if one follows English spelling rules, that is, actually pronouncing [h] and [g] sounds. *Guatemala* and *Guayaquil*, for example, never originally began with [gw], but just a simple [w] sound. Spanish *hu-* and *gu-* spellings were only ever used in the first place in imperfect attempts to represent this native [w] sound, by Spaniards for whom the written letter *w* was not traditionally in use. English always has used *w*, however, so the *hu-* and *gu-* devices are entirely unnecessary for English speakers. A spelling like *Wari* is, in principle, a simpler and unambiguous fit between English and Quechua spelling systems; while *Huari* is but an idiosyncratic Spanish diversion.

Much depends, however, on whether one considers that a word like *quipu* already exists as an "established" English spelling in any case—a subjective judgement. Moreover, upon those who advocate using indigenous spellings like *khipu* it is incumbent to explain and justify how far that policy should be taken. Should we really convert all place names to indigenous spellings too, such as changing *Huancavelica* to *Wankawillka*, or even respelling *Guatemala*? Anglophones in the United Kingdom, United States, and Australia do not "correct" their spellings of Celtic, Amerindian or Aboriginal toponyms in their own countries; although in India *Mumbai* is indeed promoted to replace *Bombay*, for example (not to mention *Hindu* for old *Hindoo*).

Clearly, then, there are arguments on both sides, and in practice there is no ideal solution. Here we have simply followed majority tradition in works on Andean history published hitherto. But we are only too well aware that there are good arguments why it might be high time for at least some of that tradition to change.

Notes

1. To be rigorous, *full* respect for the native sound system of Quechua, rather than that of Spanish or English, in fact requires that the word be spelt *qiru* — and that readers accept the basics of the Quechua pronunciation system if they wish to pronounce it reasonably correctly. Scholars typically do accept that Spanish cannot correctly be pronounced, written or read like English, and make this effort; but not for Quechua. Indeed, the battle for the respect of Quechua is so far from being won that even many a Quechua dictionary itself still spells the language's vowels according to traditional, Spanish-influenced norms, i.e. in this case as *qero* rather than preferable *qiru*. That linguistic battle is not one to be fought here, however. For our purposes, what remains is a separate issue: that spelling *kero* with *k* is simply wrong on any measure and alphabet, and greatly to be deprecated. To anyone who takes the least trouble to inquire as to the most basic facts of the sounds of Quechua, that much will become immediately apparent.

2. Rodolfo Cerrón-Palomino, "El Diccionario quechua de los académicos: Cuestiones lexicográficas, normativas y etimológicas," *Revista Andina* 29 (1997), pp. 151–205.

3. E.g. Rodolfo Cerrón-Palomino, *Quechua Sureño: Diccionario Unificado* (Lima: Biblioteca Nacional del Perú, 1994:).

4. E.g. Rodolfo Cerrón-Palomino, *Voces del Ande: Ensayos Sobre Onomástica Andina* (Lima: Fondo Editorial de la PUCP, 2008).

5. Transcriptions given within [ ] parentheses use the standard symbols used in linguistics, those of the International Phonetic Alphabet.

Introduction

History, Linguistics, and the Andean Past: A Much-Needed Conversation

Adrian J. Pearce and Paul Heggarty

Since there is scarcely any co-operation between the different disciplines working in the Andes, and since linguists, ethnologists, ethnohistorians and archaeologists proceed unaware of each other, there has been no attempt to establish an overarching vision that might help us better evaluate the import of isolated discoveries in any particular domain.

Gerald Taylor, *À la recherche des "proto-quechuas"* [1]

There is little clearer explanation of the rationale behind this book than the citation above. Scholars of various stripes all seek to uncover the "same" Andean past, each with their different data sources and methods that in principle should richly complement each other; yet the lack of co-operation between them is flagrant. This volume targets linguists and historians specifically, for the period since Columbus—or rather, Pizarro. A similar cross-disciplinary conversation on the pre-Columbian era can be found in our companion volume: *Archaeology and Language in the Andes* (see below).

Taylor's point is not just that it is a disappointment in principle that scholars with such common goals have not engaged with one another more. Most seriously, it limits how far any one of our disciplines can progress toward our shared end of a richer and more coherent understanding of the past. Or to put it in a more optimistic light: the potential gain from cooperating is all the greater, for the cross-disciplinary whole should be greater than the sum of its isolated disciplinary parts. We hope that this book will provide the proof of that simple, win-win arithmetic.

The contributions here open in similar vein to Taylor. Gabriela Ramos, herself a historian of her native Peru, effectively restates the case for this book, and in no uncertain terms:

Historians have paid scant attention to so significant a question as the relationship between language and society. [D]espite the understandings

gained [in many other fields of historical inquiry], the thorny problem
of language and intercultural communication has been addressed only
in the most general of terms. There is a paradox in how as historians
we so rarely imagine the people we are concerned with in our research
actually partaking in the basic act of communicating with each other...
[W]ork on this [the relationship between language and society] by historians themselves is still almost entirely lacking.

This shows not only admirable self-appraisal of one's own discipline, but
keen cross-disciplinary perspicacity with it. For Ramos here is putting
words on the key lament among *linguists* of the Andes, who do indeed
wonder at their peers in other disciplines. How is it that they do not
with much greater insistence ask themselves a question so central to the
identity of the people they study as what language(s) they actually spoke?
Nowhere more so than in the post-Columbian Andes, surely, has language tracked through both time and geographical space the impacts
and interactions of Spaniards and Native Americans. To this day, language serves as a bellwether of identity and indeed aspirations, as Tim
Marr so strikingly puts it in his contribution here.

Andean linguists are all but dismayed, likewise, by how little awareness
there seems to be outside their field of even some of the most fundamental and long-standing findings of their discipline, and the scale of the
repercussions that they should hold for others, if only they were recognized. Beguiling simplicities die hard, it would seem. For many, Quechua
is a monolith that can safely be explained away in just a line or two, in
terms as plain as John Howland Rowe's: "the Inca...impose[d] their own
language...in the whole extent of their dominions."[2] Yet it is entirely
unrealistic to imagine all Quechua as simply the Incas' *fiat;* witness the
failure of the similar colonial decrees in favor of Spanish centuries later
(Ken Andrien, this volume). It is anachronistic, too, for much of the spread
of Quechua dates back to long before the Incas, indeed to times when it
was not even yet spoken in Cuzco. Nothing is more at fault here than the
hopelessly misleading term "dialects," so easily dismissed by non–linguists
as a detail beneath their concerns. Which historian of Europe would ignore
as trivial the differences between Portuguese, Spanish, Catalan, French,
and Italian (and whether and where they spread across the Americas and
Africa), or confuse, in seeking to explain them, the impact of Rome with
that of Charles V? Failing to perceive the true nature of Quechua as a
whole family of *languages* (plural), akin to the collection of Romance languages in Europe, glosses over and does violence to an entire repository of
rich data on the past—origins, differences, and patterns throughout the
Andes—that lie precisely in Quechua's very diversity.

Perhaps, though, linguists have themselves as much to blame, for
remaining too cozily within the familiar bounds of their own discipline,

and failing to reach out more, and more accessibly, to publication venues where scholars of other disciplines might most hear what their rich record of the past has to say. Indeed lest our conversation become a *dialogue de sourds*, linguists more than most need to step outside the comfort of their in-house terminology, to distil from their detailed data the messages that can speak to other scholars of the past. This interdisciplinary challenge is necessarily far from an easy one: a difficult balance to strike between ensuring accessibility to non–specialists and at the same time also providing the detail and precision necessary if one's work is to be judged by one's colleagues in a specialist discipline such as linguistics.

As Ramos likewise reminds us, the fault, if fault there is, cuts both ways. Her own, historian's lament is how "the very actors who stand in the midst of the changes that we seek to understand" are conspicuous by their absence from most historical linguistic study, where "it is processes and trends that predominate, while the groups and individuals within a particular context are imperceptible."

There are, of course, notable exceptions to the stand-off between the disciplines, whose names help populate our author list here. César Itier's contribution here is rooted in the expertise and perspectives of the historian, but at the same time in a command of Quechua linguistic analysis the equal of any specialist in the discipline, recruited in his case particularly to colonial texts in the language, and for what they tell us of the historical context that spawned them. Our companion pre-Columbian volume, meanwhile, features an exemplary cross-disciplinary essay on language contact scenarios by the specialist Pieter Muysken, for whom Ramos's "actors" are anything but absent. An alternative approach, which we hope that this volume will duly encourage in the long run, is the one that as editors we have endeavored to illustrate here ourselves: a co-authored cross-disciplinary chapter. We have sought to bring together the very different (but thus complementary) data and methods of linguistic and historical inquiry, to bear on the same conundrum in the Andean past, that we might both understand it more fully.

Another brighter note, as we struggle to counsel across the disciplinary divorce, is that it was not always thus, as Richard Burger[3] well points out in our companion volume. The first great modern scholars of the Andean past, though we might now dub them "cross-disciplinary," were nothing if not model anthropologists of the broad school of their times. Archaeologists of the Andes might today instantly acclaim Max Uhle and Julio C. Tello as among the founders of *their* discipline; yet to the former we owe also our earliest records of the Uru-Chipaya language family, from the 1890s;[4] and to the latter our most extensive early research on Jaqaru/Kawki (alias the "Central" branch of the Aymara family).[5]

This volume would be grossly remiss if it did not salute one group of scholars who have indeed striven to keep true to the broad foundations of the tradition of anthropology in the Americas. Witness Bruce Mannheim's *The Language of the Inka Since the European Invasion;*[6] or more recently, the voluminous *Anthropological History of an Aymara Confederation*, by Tristan Platt, Thérèse Bouysse-Cassagne, and the late Olivia Harris,[7] whose tragic death robbed this volume of her own contribution. It is useful here to contrast anthropology in the narrower European sense, as a discipline in its own right, and a sister to archaeology, ethnohistory, and linguistics, rather than as a broad family to which they all belong, as per the more encompassing North American "four-field" tradition.

If we mention the distinction here, it is to help explain the nature of this book, by setting it more precisely in its particular disciplinary context. For from the perspective of the career anthropologist of this stamp, it might seem overstated to claim that a cross-disciplinary conversation is so sorely needed. For them, there was scarcely any need to begin a dialogue with either linguists or historians of the Andes, for it has never really ended, as attested by works like those just cited, by Mannheim and by Platt, Bouysse-Cassagne, and Harris.

Certainly, neither Taylor nor Ramos points a finger at anthropologists in this narrower sense (in which we shall use the term henceforth). Not that the problem thus goes away; rather, it pinpoints more accurately those disciplines between which it has remained. As Ramos makes clear, it lies more with career historians and linguists; and, we might add, with scholars within each discipline who would not see themselves as of explicitly anthropological inclination. It is specifically between linguists and historians proper, then, that we saw such a need to foment a meeting of minds, and it is above all that audience that this volume seeks to target. This explains why those seeking the anthropologist's particular conception of the post-Columbian Andes will not find it so fully displayed here; but only because that interest is already relatively well served.

Not that we sought to deprive this volume of the perspectives of anthropologists; of course not. Frank Salomon and Sue Grosboll represent the quintessential anthropologists, though their contribution here is also firmly within our focus on the relationship between language and history. Rosaleen Howard contributes too, though in this case particularly in her capacity as a sociolinguist, with her expertise in the period that brings this volume right up to the present date. Gary Urton and Anne-Marie Hocquenghem's chosen contributions to our enterprise, meanwhile, apply rather more to times before than after Pizarro, and therefore appear within our *Archaeology and Language in the Andes* volume instead.

Nonetheless, it was clear to us that a specifically anthropological vision should not too much dominate here, lest it detract from the specific and rather different task at hand: to encourage career linguists and historians to reflect on, hear from, and speak to each other, on their complementary perspectives on the Andean past.

*   *   *

This volume emerges from an interdisciplinary symposium to that same end, entitled "History and Linguistics in the Andes," and hosted at the Institute for the Study of the Americas of the University of London on September 15, 2008. That meeting was co-organized by the editors, and funded principally by an award from the British Academy, with further support from the institute itself. It brought together, by invitation, some 20 leading specialists from a range of disciplinary perspectives, from Latin America, the United States and Europe, for a groundbreaking, explicitly interdisciplinary look at the Andean past.

Given the relatively little interaction hitherto, and thus the need to stimulate debate, our symposium's aim was best served by adopting a novel structure: not lengthy formal papers pre-prepared by speakers, but discussion sessions on a series of major topics of historical or (in some cases) contemporary interest. Each session was launched by brief synopses presented by those participants with particular expertise in that issue and period; the synopses were to be given from each discipline's own perspective, but in terms meaningful to representatives of the other. Thus both a linguist and a historian spoke briefly to our sequence of topics, providing the basis for open debate among all scholars present.

Though perhaps unconventional, this format did succeed in spurring vigorous debate, irrespective of the disciplinary divide. It has also ensured that these written contributions arisen from it have been able to draw fully on, and have duly been shaped by, discussions and feedback at the symposium, rather than being prepared beforehand without such benefit. They are thus necessarily somewhat innovative in their approaches, since to our knowledge there has been no previous attempt to make history and linguistics speak to each other in this direct way. Together they provide, in balanced cross-disciplinary perspective, a continuous survey of the key determiners of the histories and ultimate fates of indigenous languages in the Central Andes from the Spanish Conquest to the present day, and of what those trajectories mean for our understanding of the contexts that shaped them.

In broader context, our symposium fitted into an overall interdisciplinary program that ranged over the whole of the Andean past, either side of the watershed of European conquest. Its sister symposium was "Archaeology and Linguistics in the Andes," held the preceding week at the McDonald Institute for Archaeological Research of the University of Cambridge. From that event too has arisen a companion volume, to appear concurrently with this one. *Archaeology and Language in the Andes* is published by our main sponsor, the British Academy (with Oxford University Press), and edited by the organizers of the respective symposium, namely Paul Heggarty and David Beresford-Jones, an Andean archaeologist.

The split between the two symposia and volumes is articulated around the fateful meeting of Pizarro with Atawallpa, but many issues, sources, and interpretations do of course straddle that divide. It goes without saying that the volumes do not exclude, but complement each other. Indeed, it can only help the balance and broad perspective of each that many of the leading scholars, including all who contribute to this one, took part in both symposia.

The two symposia together, and a day of public lectures on the Andean past at the British Museum, formed the first phase of a larger UK-Peruvian program that continued into 2009 with a full-scale conference and lecture series in the Andean countries themselves, principally at our partner institution, the Department of Humanities at the Pontificia Universidad Católica del Perú (PUCP) in Lima. From that conference will duly emerge a third volume, *Lenguas y Sociedades en el Antiguo Perú*, to appear as volume 14 of the *Boletín de Arqueología pucp* series, published by the PUCP's own press.

*   *   *

In sum, this book serves to explore how historians and linguists might inform and enrich each other's understanding of the Andean past. Indeed with that process now under way, it also provides a platform for presenting the first outputs of research in this explicitly cross-disciplinary approach.

How, then, is this interdisciplinary discussion developed in these pages? What are the main fruits of our dialogue between historians and linguists regarding the half-millennium elapsed in the Andes since the Spanish Conquest? The first four chapters constitute a distinct section, devoted mainly to the early and middle colonial periods: the sixteenth and seventeenth centuries.

The volume opens with a wide-ranging essay by Gabriela Ramos on language and society in Peru, mainly up to the mid-1600s. She begins by taking both of our disciplines to task—first, historians, for their scant or (indeed) "almost nonexistent" studies of relations between language and society in the early colony. Linguists are criticized for employing evidence and analyses that do not always seem convincing to historians, or for showing limited concern with the *agents* of language history— the people who stood behind broader trends and processes. For these reasons, having summarized research by historical linguists on major questions of native language history both prior and subsequent to the Conquest, Ramos's own contribution aims primarily at introducing some of these agents, in two contrasting contexts: Lima and the Rímac valley; and Cuzco and its surrounding region. She first examines the phenomena that underlay contact between different language communities (and perhaps also language diffusion), notably between the central and northern coasts, based on maritime trade, exchange of population through *mitimae* colonies, and long-distance marriage alliances between native leaders or even fisherfolk. For Cuzco, Ramos focuses upon large-scale migration to the Inca capital, whether under the Incas or during the turbulent post-Conquest decades to the mid-1500s, which she suggests may actually have strengthened the use of Quechua in the region as the viable lingua franca. The final section of the essay—which Ramos herself considers its major contribution—focuses especially on the neglected role of early colonial interpreters between Spanish and native tongues. In Lima, Ramos argues that these interpreters "played a substantial role in shaping the political culture of the colony." In Cuzco, meanwhile, the "confluence of interests, cultural origins, administrative practices, prejudices, and means by which to establish social networks" that grew up around the many interpreters all came to "foster the use of Quechua" still further—even after 1600, by which time most interpreters were mestizos.

The second essay, by Frank Salomon and Sue Grosboll, exploits a linguistic data-set to shed light on the social and spiritual world of people of the Pacific slopes of the Central Andes in the late sixteenth century. The essay focuses upon the settlement of Sisicaya in Huarochirí province, a key locus of commercial, cultural, and linguistic exchange between the highlands and the coastal lowlands. Sisicaya's population was divided between highlanders and *yunka* lowlanders, mythically linked respectively with the male and female *huacas*, Paria Caca and Chaupi Ñamca. The Huarochirí manuscript (composed ca. 1608) contains a parallel list of male and female names, derived from these *huacas*, ideally prescribed for children of either sex by birth order, and establishing a hierarchy of precedence among them. Salomon and Grosboll test this naming system against the real names recorded for males and females in Sisicaya during a *revisita*, a detailed administrative inspection undertaken by the Spanish colonial authorities some 20 years earlier, in 1588. The authors demonstrate that the "mythical" birth-order names recorded in the manuscript were indeed common among children born in Sisicaya since at least the 1530s—and also that this practice was growing rather than declining in popularity. They thus show that, more than half a century after the Conquest, Sisicaya remained "a place where symbolically female-like Yunka people and their cults...were articulated with...highland-based complements with affiliation to male deities."

But they also show that too few females were recorded in the 1588 inspection, in proportion to the total population, and that these females were given birth-order names less frequently than men, and at lower "ranks." They relate these facts to the post-Conquest demographic crisis in Huarochirí, and on this basis conclude that the image presented in the 1608 manuscript is that of a "damaged society"—one reflecting a "harsh and timely realism" within the late sixteenth-century Andean world they inhabited. The broader methodological point, then, and the key contribution of Salomon and Grosboll's work to our project here, is that "archives can also be seen as accumulations of verbal, that is, linguistic, data." These data can "reveal patterns of change—sometimes in elusive areas of cultural habit," and in this way yield "subtle and yet verifiable indices revealing how societies reproduced and changed themselves."

In the third chapter, César Itier addresses a major question: the nature of the *lengua general* ("general language") not of the Inca period, but under colonial rule. Itier's primary concern is with the controversial issue of whether or not this was a spoken language, or essentially only a written medium, developed primarily for purposes of evangelization. Against majority opinion among historical linguists, but defending a position first advanced by Gerald Taylor in the 1980s, Itier argues not only that the *lengua general* was indeed a spoken tongue, but also that it was both widespread and had a lasting impact on the Quechua spoken today. In making this argument, he first reviews the characteristics of the language evident in the majority of texts in Quechua to survive from colonial times (including the celebrated Huarochirí manuscript), particularly in its morphology (word structure), but also in lexis and syntax. He then reviews the historical circumstances in which this language emerged, as a dominant "koine" dialect used as a lingua franca, forged above all in the colonial cities and "semi-urban network" of the *reducciones* (villages where Indians were forced to resettle). The *lengua general*, then, was formed—or reinforced, since its origins remain in dispute—in contexts where great numbers of displaced Indians were thrown into close contact with Spaniards. This context explains both the Spanish influences, and the tendency to morphological simplification, apparent in its surviving texts. Finally, Itier detects the influence of the "general language" in several Quechua variants spoken to this day, particularly in the southern regions of the Collao and Charcas. His work, then, goes to the very heart of the relationship between language and society in the early colonial period, over a vast region.

In the final essay of the opening section, Adrian Pearce and Paul Heggarty further seek to exemplify the merits of the cross-disciplinary discussion, by applying historical data to the resolution of an important linguistic enigma. This enigma consists of the only sharp demarcation internal to Quechua throughout its "Continuous Zone," from Ancash to the Lake Titicaca region: the frontier between the variants spoken in Huancayo in the Central Andes, and in Huancavelica a short distance to the south. In the first section of their essay, the authors review the traditional classification of the Quechua languages, based on supposed "branches" dubbed "QI" and "QII," and which meet (within the Continuous Zone) precisely in this central region. They note problems and inconsistencies within this traditional classification, which have brought it under increasing assault in recent years. They suggest, in fact, that Quechua rather displays the characteristics of a *dialect continuum* throughout the Continuous Zone; for the very substance of the Huancayo-Huancavelica frontier is susceptible to challenge, depending on the linguistic criteria on which it is judged. Nevertheless, on a considerable number of criteria, this frontier remains an anomaly, and one which "cries out to be accounted for." Alfredo Torero, the principal architect of the QI~QII model, sought such an explanation in a deep-time split of Quechua into two variants, which expanded and were then brought back into contact in the Huancayo-Huancavelica region by migrations occurring over an extended period of time. Pearce and Heggarty, by contrast, argue that an original dialect continuum in this region was disrupted by much later processes, thus creating a relatively sharp frontier within Quechua where no clear boundary had previously existed. They date this process to the colonial period, and identify its source as the great labor draft or *mita* established from the 1570s to supply Huancavelica with workers for its mercury mine—a pillar of the colonial economy, since mercury was the key catalyst in the production of silver (mostly at Potosí). They show that the *mita* not only drew sufficient numbers of people into Huancavelica to effect permanent language change there, but that these people came from the "right" regions (more southerly ones) to produce the linguistic scenario evident today. The essay thus aspires to contribute to a recasting of our whole vision of Quechua divergence history and dialect classification. More generally, and like César Itier's chapter, it demonstrates the capacity of colonial state and society to impact powerfully upon the very languages spoken by native Andeans.

The following section shifts the discussion onward in time, with three essays devoted to the late colonial and early republican periods: the eighteenth and nineteenth centuries. They open with a piece on the implications for native languages of late-colonial reforms in the Spanish empire and the Independence era, by historian Kenneth Andrien. Having first discussed early royal policies toward language in the Andes, Andrien reviews the major processes most often considered to have impacted upon native languages in the 1700s and early 1800s. He concludes, in unequivocal terms, that "none of the historical events of the eighteenth and early nineteenth centuries appear fundamental turning points in the spread or contraction of indigenous languages." Thus, for example, there is little hard evidence that the "regalist" assault on the Church, with the secularization of native parishes or the expulsion of the Jesuit order, had much impact on preaching in native tongues. The stringent measures directed against native culture and languages following the Great Rebellion of the early 1780s, meanwhile, had limited real impact at most. And even the brief hegemony of political liberalism in the aftermath of independence, and consequent measures aimed at abolishing the caste status of Indians and traditional chiefdoms or *cacicazgos*, had little practical impact on any rise of Spanish or decline of native languages. It may be worth emphasizing that we suspect the majority of historians will fully support these important conclusions—though they may prove more surprising to linguists and others, for whom it is therefore all the more important that they should be so explicitly stated and grounded here. Andrien then goes on to discuss the profound socioeconomic and political changes that gave rise to the formation of new ethnic identities in the Andes by the late colonial period, including forced and free migration, the loosening of ties with traditional native communities, the actions of the Catholic Church, and the rise and role of *indios ladinos*—those conversant in both native and Spanish cultures. He emphasizes that all these processes left an abundant documentary record, unquestionably capable of revealing much about the use and distribution of indigenous tongues, but to date little exploited by scholars to that end.

The following essay, by Adrian Pearce, moves the discussion firmly into the "long nineteenth century." Pearce explores the relationship between native languages in the Andes and the phenomenon known as "reindigenization," a striking feature of recent historical research on the early republican era. Reindigenization in Peru was first conceived of in demographic terms, when the decades following independence were identified as the only period since the Spanish Conquest during which the native population not only increased in absolute terms, but even recovered slightly as a proportion of the whole. More recently, the concept has been extended to embrace the broader conditions in which the native peoples lived from the 1820s until at least the 1870s; conditions that developed in the context of the crisis of both the creole state apparatus and the economy, themselves the products of chronic political instability and isolation from international markets. During this period, for example, native economies and markets appear to have experienced a reflorescence, evident most strikingly in control of the rich wool industry of the southern highlands. Native peoples also now enjoyed relatively favorable political conditions, given the weakness of the early republican state and its ongoing dependence on Indian tribute and manpower. In the first attempt to probe the relationship between reindigenization and native languages, then, Pearce suggests two significant conclusions for the language history of the Andes. First, the deepest roots of the modern decline of Quechua lie not, as some scholars have argued, in the decades ending in 1850, a period which in truth is likely to have witnessed a reinforcement of native language use in the region. Rather, the social prestige of Quechua and other native tongues was dealt a first blow during the half-century from the 1870s, when reindigenization was reversed, and native peoples themselves experienced widespread loss of lands, impoverishment, and political disenfranchisement. The second conclusion is that reindigenization helps explain the enigmatic early death of all native languages bar Quechua in northern Peru—because its absence there implied a process of *mestizaje* that overwhelmed native populations at an unusually early date.

A further essay by Alan Durston continues the focus on the nineteenth century, with research on Quechua political literature in Peru between 1810 and 1876. Durston presents the first survey of the known examples of such literature, and in doing so, contributes both to Quechua language history and the political history of early republican Peru. His essay discusses three "moments" in the development of native political writings: manifestos and propaganda from the wars of independence, panegyric texts addressed to warlords during the "Age of Caudillos" that followed, and translations of laws affecting the indigenous population from the 1860s and 1870s. As linguistic sources, the texts discussed by Durston have singular importance, whether as the earliest known documentation of Central (QI) Quechua, or as testaments to the development of "literary Cuzqueño"—"an ornate, archaizing register" that developed in the eighteenth century and remained influential into the twentieth. For the early republican history of Peru, the writings discussed by Durston speak centrally to the recruitment of Quechua into Peruvian national politics, both as a symbol and as a practical means of communication. Thus, during the independence era, a veritable war of propaganda developed between royalists and patriots, as both sides vied for the allegiance of the majority native population. During the caudillo age, national politics was dominated by men of highland origin, many of whom were speakers of native languages, and all of whom relied on alliances with the indigenous peasantry for their political and military strength. The 1860s and 1870s, meanwhile, were characterized by "a significant Quechuist boom," when Quechua was "invoked in…scholarly projects of national self-awareness," and referred to—in some elite quarters, at least—as the "national" or "Peruvian" language. The first significant works on Quechua by Peruvians to be published since independence appeared in the early 1870s. Nevertheless, Durston concludes that ultimately, elite interest in Quechua during the early republic was sporadic and "marginal to nation-building efforts that were increasingly centered on the coast"—an impression only reinforced by the bizarre and often unintelligible Quechua of José de Anchorena, among this period's leading "authorities" in the language.

The final section of the book addresses the twentieth century, a period marked by the historic decline of native languages in the Andes, evident especially from the mid-century onward. The first contribution, by anthropologist and sociolinguist Rosaleen Howard, deploys a "hybrid methodology" combining statistical analysis, interviews and other data, to present a lucid overview of the current state of Quechua and the complexity of its sociolinguistic circumstances in Ecuador, Bolivia and Peru. An opening section reviews data on language use contained in recent population censuses, inevitably concluding that "in percentage terms the community of speakers is clearly on the decline"— even where rapid population growth has actually boosted the total numbers of speakers. Twentieth-century globalizing processes in the Andes, especially urban migration and increasingly universal education, have often proven strongly adverse to native language maintenance. In a second section, Howard then reviews official policies developed in the three countries since the 1990s, ostensibly designed to safeguard or even sustain native language use. These include both legal declarations on the status of native tongues, whether in national constitutions or other legislation, and policies on bilingual education. The impact of bilingual education programs has varied by country: broadly positive in Ecuador, less so in Peru, while in Bolivia, ironically, since 2005 the presidency of Evo Morales (whose origins lie in the Aymara-speaking community) has in practice created a "legislative hiatus with pedagogical consequences." A third and final section exploits selected interview data to put flesh on the bare statistical bones of census materials, demonstrating how Quechua-speaking is actually lived in different social and geographical contexts, from Cañar to Cochabamba. Howard concludes with an assessment of the prospects for Quechua and other indigenous languages, emphasizing that a less puristic attitude toward language, and an expansion of the functions of Quechua "to spheres of activity associated with the modern and globalizing world," may help to ensure its ongoing vitality. Meanwhile, a recent trend toward the reinforcement of indigenous identity, even while native languages decline, "may constitute the necessary condition for eventual language revitalization in subsequent generations."

Approaching a similar topic from a rather different perspective is the concluding essay. Tim Marr explores the phenomenon of mass language-shift away from Quechua and toward Spanish in contemporary Peru, based primarily on sociolinguistic research among migrants to Lima. He begins with a section on migration and urbanization, which emphasizes the indisputable point that in Peruvian cities—in the provinces as well as the capital—"Spanish is effectively the only game in town." In the main body of the essay Marr then ponders why this might be so, starting from theoretical discussion of the extent to which language shift represents a "free choice" on the part of the speaker. Against a significant trend within the sociolinguistic and anthropological literature, he argues that the abandonment of indigenous languages in urban contexts in Peru does indeed represent an act of will, and to the speakers themselves is perhaps even "a positive and empowering process." He then goes on to review the factors underlying the shift to Spanish, including the association of Quechua with the past, elderly speakers, and a lack of social mobility and economic opportunity. The words of Marr's informants in this section provide the clearest possible sense of the processes that lie behind Quechua's present decline, and the (frankly formidable) obstacles to its survival in the twenty-first century. There then follows a section devoted specifically to the self-image of the modern Peruvian migrant, which Marr argues is based on pragmatism, opportunism, and an unsentimental attitude toward what might be regarded as his or her roots or traditional culture. Rather than abandoning Quechua out of a sense of "shame," then, as is often argued, Marr concludes persuasively that "they do not use it for it no longer fits their identity: their sense of who they are, or who they want to be." In this sense, language shift can even be interpreted as resistance, "a defiant appropriation by migrants" of the *langue légitime* and "an assertion that it belongs to them as much as to anybody"—and with it so too does Peruvian nationhood. Throughout the piece, Marr thus places language shift in Peru firmly in a contemporary global context, as an intrinsic aspect of "modernity." As a result, he concludes that efforts at Quechua maintenance, if they are to be successful, face a clear, though hugely challenging task: "To find ways of being modern in and through Quechua."

To conclude: the essays collected in this volume have as their core concerns the place of language in society, and society's impact on language; the linguistic sources for Andean history; and the application of historical data to conundrums in historical linguistics. Taken together, they survey the entire trajectory of the native tongues of the Andes since the Spanish Conquest and into the twenty-first century. For the early colony, relations between language and society are explored directly through the protagonists and processes of language history. During the late colony and early republic, logically the perspective shifts to state policies on native language use, and indeed the retreat of that state apparatus soon after independence, with all the linguistic implications of "reindigenization." By the twentieth century, the focus turns inexorably to the trends behind the modern decline of Quechua and other

languages, as well as state-based gestures and efforts toward maintenance or revival. For three of the contributors here, relations between
language and society take on very specific linguistic form, embodied
in the development of the *lengua general* during colonial rule, and of
the Huancayo-Huancavelica Quechua frontier through the *mita* labor
draft. The latter demonstrates the potential in applying historical data
to problems of historical linguistics; as does Pearce's attempt to trace
the origins of the modern decline of Quechua, or to explain the deaths
of the native tongues of northern Peru. Conversely, linguistic source
materials hold out similar promise for historical studies, as apparent in
how a name list from the Huarochirí manuscript helps explore changes
in indigenous people's social and spiritual world during the early colony,
and how nineteenth-century Quechua texts can enrich our understanding of the political life of the early republic in Peru. Many of the chapters
here draw attention to the abundant historical sources extant for native
language history, such as the documents arising from the powerful processes that brought about ethnogenesis in the Andes—from migrations,
forced or free, to the actions of the church. Finally, all the essays speak
of the long and chequered career of the languages of the Andes over the
past five centuries, closing with a contemporary focus on the Quechua
family as it embarks upon surely the most challenging century in its
remarkable history.

We trust that the benefits of our interdisciplinary dialogue stand
amply proven by the essays that have resulted from it. A conversation
of the type attempted here—between linguists and historians of the
Andes—was indeed, we feel, much needed; and long may it continue. We
shall end, then, conventionally, by hoping that this volume proves to be
far from the last word on its subject, but merely an early chapter.

Notes

1. Gerald Taylor, "A la recherche des 'proto-quechuas'," *Mémoires de la
   Société de Linguistique de Paris*, Nouvelle Série vol. I: 91–102. (Paris:
   Klincksieck, 1990), 97. Our translation is of the original text:
   comme il n'y a pratiquement pas de collaboration entre les dif-
   férentes disciplines qui travaillent dans le domaine andin et
   que linguistes, ethnologues, ethnohistoriens et archéologues
   s'ignorent, il n'existe aucun essai d'établissement d'une vision
   d'ensemble qui pourrait aider à mieux évaluer la portée des
   découvertes isolées dans un domaine précis.
2. John Howland Rowe, "Inca culture at the time of the Spanish
   conquest". *In Handbook of South American Indians*, vol. 2 (Washington,
   DC, Smithsonian Institution, Bureau of American Ethnology, 1946,
   pp. 183–330). See pp. 185, 272, 273.

3. Richard Burger, "Central Andean Language Expansion and the Chavìn Sphere of Interaction", in P. Heggarty and D. Beresford-Jones (eds.), *Archaeology and Language in the Andes* (London: British Academy / Oxford University Press, forthcoming).

4. Rodolfo Cerròn-Palomino, "Reconstrucciòn del proto-uro: fonologìa," *Lexis* 31 (2007), pp. 47–104, see p. 53.

5. Rodolfo Cerrón-Palomino, *Lingüística Aimara* (Lima: Centro de Estudios Regionales Andinos "Bartolomé de las Casas,", 2000), pp. 49–50.

6. Bruce Mannheim, *The Language of the Inka Since the European Invasion* (Austin: University of Texas Press, 1991).

7. *Qaraqara-Charka: Mallku, Inka y Rey en la Provincia de Charcas, Siglos XV–XVII*, Travaux de l'Institut Français d'Études Andines, 174 (La Paz: Institut Français d'Études Andines, 2006).

Figure 0.1 Present-day distribution of the two major language families of the Andes: Quechua and Aymara.

Part I

The Colonial Era

Chapter 1

Language and Society in Early Colonial Peru

Gabriela Ramos

Historians have neglected the study of how language and society related to each other in the early colonial Andes. This chapter examines the possible reasons for this significant gap in the historiography, and discusses the contributions that linguists have made over the past decades to a greater understanding of the history of Andean languages and their speakers both before and after the Spanish Conquest. I consider some avenues by which historical research could enrich our knowledge about the field, which involves identifying the speakers of Andean languages and reconstructing the context in which they lived. To this end, and using ethnohistorical information from published sources and my own archival research, I discuss two examples that linguists have studied or hypothesized on. The first concerns the central coast of Peru, the spread of Quechua, and the possible relations between speakers of various Andean languages in the area, particularly the Lima valley. The second case involves the problem of what were the boundaries of Quechua in the Cuzco region, which I investigate by examining evidence of resettlement policies under the Inca, which to an extent continued for a few decades after the Spanish Conquest. The final part of this chapter discusses how the indigenous population of the cities of Lima and Cuzco related to the Spanish language. I examine the conditions—particularly those involving population composition and governmental decisions—that led to the waning of Quechua in Lima, and its strengthening in Cuzco. The point of this final part is to offer some pointers to understanding the dynamics that lead to the spread of a specific language in a multilingual society.

* * *

Historians have paid scant attention to so significant a question as the relationship between language and society. Over the last two decades, ethnohistorical studies have broadened considerably our knowledge of the changes undergone by Andean societies in the wake of the Spanish invasion, among them: the demographic crisis and migrations; transformations in land ownership structures and in labor systems; new forms of association in urban contexts; and debates on evangelization policies. We can with confidence state that we are now able to conceive of the history of Andean societies not according to the standard set of oppositions that have dominated historiography for so long, that is, in terms of colonizers versus colonized, or the struggle between opposing forces of resistance (or continuity) and change; instead we can conceive of the Andean past as a realm full of complexities. Yet despite the understandings gained, the thorny problem of language and intercultural communication has been addressed only in the most general of terms. There is a paradox in how, as historians, we so rarely imagine the people we are concerned with in our research actually partaking in the basic act of communicating with each other. To imagine them actually speaking complicates the task of reflecting on them, when we have only just found the evidence that they even existed at all.

Here I would like to raise, from the historian's perspective, a number of issues in the study of the relationship between language and society in early colonial Peru. Since work on this by historians themselves is still almost entirely lacking for this period, I shall first discuss the impact of a number of studies by linguists—though without of course aspiring to completeness, or claiming competence in a discipline that is not my own. Second, I shall analyze some illustrations of the relationships between speakers of various Andean languages on the central coast of Peru and in Cuzco, immediately before and after the Spanish Conquest. The third and final section examines relationships between the speakers of Andean languages and Spanish, using examples taken from my own research on two major colonial centers, the cities of Lima and Cuzco and their respective hinterlands. It is in this last section that I hope to make a contribution of my own: the cases I present might be used to expand upon some of linguists' own proposals on the history of Andean languages, and the changes they underwent due to conquest and colonization.

Language and Society in the Early Colonial Period: Historians and the Linguistic Contribution

Linguists have opened up paths to the study of the historical links between language and society that do seem attractive, but to historians far too adventurous, given some understandable methodological and heuristic differences. The starting points, evidence and types of analyses employed appear largely, if not entirely, unfamiliar, and too general; the proposals are quite suggestive, certainly, but hard to substantiate. The *longue durée* of the historical linguist's purview sets a number of serious limitations on the contribution that historians might make to an understanding of the development of Andean languages.[1] Another aspect of the study of these languages' histories that historians view with skepticism has to do with the role of the very actors who stand in the midst of the changes that we seek to understand. In historical linguistics, it is in the nature of the data, and the methods used to analyze them, that the historical agent is usually nowhere to be seen: in the image presented to us, it is processes and trends that predominate, while the groups and individuals within a particular context are imperceptible. Linguistic research has provided us with maps that broadly sketch the interactions between the languages of the region and its inhabitants, both indigenous and outsiders. Much remains to be established, though. Displacements arose that spread particular languages through the Andes—but under what conditions, for what reasons, and in which ways? And what political circumstances might explain the presence of a frontier between, say, Quechua and the Yunga language, or between Aru and Quechua?

Hypotheses on the origins, dispersal, and divergence of Andean languages have focused on Quechua. In the last few decades, the combined research of Alfredo Torero,[2] Gary Parker,[3] Rodolfo Cerrón-Palomino[4] and Willem Adelaar[5] has proven fundamental in furthering the pioneering proposals on the history of Andean languages set out in the early twentieth century, both by historians like José de la Riva-Agüero and Manuel González de la Rosa, and by archaeologists like Max Uhle.[6] Some of their most valuable contributions have questioned established beliefs, fiercely defended by certain scholars and politicians with regionalist inclinations. For instance, contrary to the belief that the origins of Quechua lay in Cuzco and with the Incas, Alfredo Torero argued instead, in several studies, that it must have originated in the Central Andes, perhaps even on the central coast, whence it would have then spread throughout the region.[7] While the first of those hypotheses is widely accepted, the suggestion that Quechua originated on the Peruvian coast now enjoys less support. The Incas adopted Quechua for practical reasons that facilitated their political expansion and—except in their colonization of Cochabamba—did not spread it as some civilizing device, as some of their descendants reported to the chroniclers. Besides broadening the study of the various forms of Quechua in the Central Andes, Rodolfo Cerrón-Palomino has also contributed to systematically undermining the thesis that claims Cuzco and Inca origins for Quechua, by positing that the Incas were originally Puquina speakers, who then later adopted Aymara. The putative use of Aymara among the Incas, hypothesized by Manuel González de la Rosa in the late nineteenth and early twentieth centuries, and restated years later by Torero, is based on the evidence of the language's former deep-rooted presence across a considerable expanse of the Andes. To these studies one must add research by Willem Adelaar and Gerald Taylor on other Andean languages, such as Culle, and more highly localized and even extinct variants of Quechua, such as those spoken in Pacaraos, Yauyos, Chachapoyas, and Ferreñafe. Historians of early colonial Peru would do well to reflect on how these contributions might be put to most profitable use.

Linguistic research over recent decades has likewise shown that the prestige of Quechua and its hold on some regions were enhanced during Spanish colonial domination, albeit without uniform results. Hypotheses have been aired on developments in the years immediately after the Conquest, but little has yet been done to test them. To explain the survival of regional variants of Quechua in a number of parts of Peru, for instance, Torero claimed that "many of the inland regions [of Peru] suffered socio-economic isolation."[8] This claim is based on a deeply rooted belief in the social sciences that in the Andes the Indian population lived in a world of its own, a view now called into question by historical research.[9] For historians, the persistence of regional dialects throughout the colonial period is of particular interest. Well might we ask how valid it is to imagine that some regions could have remained apart from the changes that altered the economic and social framework of the Andes once the colonial system was in place. If isolation is not the only explanation for the survival and even strengthening of some regional variants of Quechua, then how else might we account for it?

Torero's research on the so-called Chinchaysuyu language—based on books of sermons by clerics (among them Hernando de Avendaño) based in Lima, and whose careers were in part spent traveling through the highlands and plains of their archdiocese—attests to how some *criollo* and mestizo priests fought to establish primacy for the southern variant of Quechua, even in the central highlands. Cerrón-Palomino likewise makes reference to this trend, fairly widespread among the higher clergy in the colony.[10] Gerald Taylor's study of colonial writings in Quechua, meanwhile, particularly the Huarochirí manuscript, has progressively refined our understanding of the variety of Quechua spoken by its author.[11] Mannheim's research on southern Quechua, and Durston's on the repertoire of "Pastoral Quechua" texts, reveal how the variant of Quechua dubbed "Cuzqueño" by the priests and intellectuals of the colony progressively gained ground as the main working language of the Andes, to the detriment of the languages originally spoken in central Peru.[12]

The vitality of the "general language" (*lengua general*, i.e., Quechua) was only relative, however, for we know that Spanish progressed rapidly in the spheres of government and administration. If we are to gain a detailed understanding of the path taken by colonial Andean society, and the political and cultural dynamics that guided it, it is essential to clarify the nature of the relationships between the vernacular languages of the Andes, and Spanish. Explanations offered thus far still need much refining, and again it is historical research that may provide pointers to take us beyond visions that remain overly schematic. Torero on this point judged that it was Quechua-Spanish bilingualism on the part of Indian officials that led to the *lengua general* being displaced from large swathes of the Andes.[13] But on what evidence might we validate this proposal? More to the point: If we were to confirm it, what new insights might it bring us on the power exercised by the *curacas* (chiefs) in colonial society? Mannheim, meanwhile, posits that the Spanish invasion brought about a far-reaching transformation in the sociopolitical geography of Quechua in the Andes.[14] The fragmented linguistic panorama of the Andes moved inexorably toward homogenization and the sociolinguistic stratification that came to characterize both colonial and modern Peru. Mannheim suggests that the stigmatization of Quechua, and the development of a small Spanish-speaking minority wielding power over a majority speaking only a native language, were processes that proceeded hand in hand, and almost from first contact gave rise to a Quechua/Spanish opposition, a bellwether of the wider structural conflict of Indians/Spaniards, or oppressed/oppressors.

Torero and Mannheim sketch in broad strokes the unequal relationship between Spanish and the Andean languages, which so starkly echoes sociocultural contrasts within Peru. It is essential that we enrich and refine those claims with further ethnohistorical research, if we are fully to understand the relationship between these languages and the real people who spoke them. There is scope here for fruitful collaboration between historians and linguists. The former's contribution would be to identify who the agents of communication actually were, that we might understand the contexts in which they lived, the direction and rationale behind their movements, and the reach of the cultural influences that they exerted, and were exposed to themselves.[15]

Andean Languages and Society before and after the Conquest in the Lima Valley and in Cuzco

How did speakers of different Andean languages interact before and after the Spanish Conquest? Torero's hypothesis on the use of the so-called *lengua general*, and how Quechua may have spread from the central coast to other parts of the Andes (with coastal trade as one possible means), has long enjoyed considerable support, at least until recently. But were there other, more lasting forms of exchange that may have left a mark on Andean languages? A study of the migrations and political strategies followed by Andean chiefdoms should shed new light on issues such as contacts between speakers of the languages of the central coast and the peoples of the north coast. We might thus uncover explanations for why the frontiers between different Andean languages survived, notwithstanding the long histories of interaction indicated by administrative sources.

In 1573 the *visitador* (inspector) Rodrigo Cantos de Andrade summoned the *curacas* of the Pachacamac Valley to question them on the condition of their subjects: their resources, what tribute they rendered, how and how frequently they received religious instruction, and how they were being treated by their *encomenderos* (the beneficiary of *encomienda*, a grant of native laborers in exchange for religious instruction).[16] The most serious problem they faced was in paying their tribute, given how markedly the local population had declined as a result of the Conquest. Don Luis Luyan, one of the *curacas*, pointed out that some ten years earlier one of the valley's Indian *principales* (headmen) had fled to Trujillo, along with some of his subordinates. The Indian authorities and their people then had to face the consequence that they had still to keep paying to the *encomenderos* the tribute owed by those who had fled.

As the major ceremonial center on the Peruvian coast, the Pachacamac Valley, some 18 kilometres from the city of Lima, had since ancient times been a dynamic place of symbolic and material exchange between various populations of the Central Andes.[17] The valley was home to a large population divided into several *curacazgos* (chiefdoms), which at the time of Spanish Conquest had formed a confederation—known to archaeologists and ethnohistorians as the Yschma *señorío*—which in the early sixteenth century had acknowledged the political supremacy of the Inca.[18] Thanks to its religious prestige, large numbers of travelers continuously visited Pachacamac from various parts of the Andes.

Scholars have stressed the role of Pachacamac and the central coast in promoting cultural transfer. Based on references in the chronicles and research by Rostworowski, Torero posited that it was trade which before the Spanish Conquest brought the central coast into contact with the lands to the north and south: a flow of goods and people from the central coast that contributed to Quechua spreading northward as far as modern-day Ecuador. These exchanges along the coast would presumably, Torero adds, have continued into the colonial period, albeit with some restrictions.[19]

It has been questioned, however, whether sea-borne trade along the Peruvian coast was so frequent and effective as to have enabled commerce and language dispersal; and it has been argued instead that movement from the central coast northward was essentially by land, on routes following the inter-Andean valleys. This argument is based on colonial descriptions of coastal trade, and on the fact that newly arriving viceroys and their entourages usually disembarked in the northern port of Paita and travelled on to Lima by land, since currents made it all but impossible to continue southward by sea. It may be, too, that some scholars take trade to be a somewhat sporadic activity, unconvincing as a vehicle for the spread of language spread. Nonetheless, I suggest that these observations should not have us simply reject coastal trade as a driver of major cultural exchanges, in favor of such links being mediated exclusively along the highland routes. The possibilities are far too numerous to be narrowed down so crudely.

How frequent was such contact between coastal peoples? There are other hints besides the sources cited by Rostworowski and Torero—such as the responses given by the *curacas* of Pachacamac to the *visitador* Cantos de Andrade, as cited above—to suggest that the peoples of the central coast had more sustained links with their northern neighbors than trade alone might lead us to think. We may surmise that the "flight" to Trujillo on the part of the *principal* of Pachacamac and his men was no chance event, much less an escape to an unknown land. Rather, it may be explained by long-established kinship links and political alliances that would have afforded sustenance and shelter on the north coast to both officials and people of Pachacamac and the central coast.[20] A number of illustrative sources corroborate that Indians did continue to sail along the coast throughout the colonial period, a practice built upon skills mastered before the Spanish Conquest; and that ethnic authorities on the central coast formed alliances preferentially—or even exclusively—with their counterparts on the north coast. In the first case there are, besides the data cited by Torero,[21] indications that some on the central Peruvian coast had both the resources (in vessels and manpower) and skills to combine their fishing with trade and shipping. These fishermen were no group living and operating in isolation, as some have suggested,[22] but worked with people of various origins; their services as sailors were even required by the colonial government itself, probably because their small craft were able to sail closer in to shore and thus with fewer difficulties. A very detailed example appears in the will and *relación de bienes* (list of possessions) of one Juan de Mondragón, a native of the port of Huanchaco, close to the city of Trujillo, who lived in Lima in the early seventeenth century. This document, dated 1631 in Lima, reveals the connections between fishermen in various settlements near the colonial capital (Surco, Ancón, Cañete) and the activities they performed besides fishing (transport of salt, flour, maize, and coal). Mondragón claimed to have sailed one of his ships from Lima to Panama and back, bearing messages on behalf of the government; evidence that these Indian fishermen did not sail only short distances, but continued plying the ancient routes of pre-Hispanic merchants.[23] There is abundant evidence of continuous sea-borne trade in consumable goods throughout the early colonial period.[24] Although challenging, a study of human activities on the central coast throughout the colonial period would add data on how frequently they traveled, what networks they established to conduct their business deals, and whether they did so in ways that either emulated or distanced them from their predecessors.

Besides the indications left to us by activities such as fishing and sailing, other data too illustrate relationships established before the Spanish Conquest between the people of the central coast and groups arriving from elsewhere. Witness the significant numbers here of specialist workers and their ethnic officials from the north coast (speakers of Mochica, Quingnam or the so-called Yunga language?) and from Chincha (Quechua speakers?), *mitimaes* (draft laborers) relocated by the Incas to the valleys of the central coast.[25] Burial contexts yield ceramics that clearly attest to cultural transfers brought about by these movements.[26] Such transfers may also have been underway on the linguistic level. Marriage alliances between families on the central and northern coasts appear not entirely unconnected to these interactions. Rostworowski noted that in the years following the Spanish Conquest, women from fishing settlements like Quilcay, in the Pachacamac Valley, married men from neighboring coastal towns or from places to the north as far removed from Lima as Santiago de Cao.[27] Other sources indicate that the indigenous elite in the valleys around Lima opted for similar marriage strategies. These families established links with others of similar social standing from neighboring towns or from the north, for example, Huaura, described by Calancha and Cobo as a frontier zone with the Quingnam-speaking region,[28] and Olmos, where both Calancha and Cabello Valboa report a specific local language.[29] For reasons still unclear, families from highland *curacazgos* were excluded from these alliances (which must have predated the Spanish Conquest).[30] The surnames of some *curacas* in the Lima Valley are clearly of Mochica and Quingnam ancestry and tell of the links they forged with northerners.[31] This strategy adopted by coastal peoples may be in some way connected with the presence in parts of northern Peru of groups of Quechua speakers from the central coast,[32] a local strategy that may have been part and parcel of the Inca policy of relocating *mitimaes* to a region once they had incorporated it into their empire.[33]

Cuzco and its surroundings present some significant contrasts with the central coast, and pose historians other problems too. As Cerrón-Palomino, Torero, and Mannheim have all pointed out, the region was linguistically very diverse.[34] It has been stressed how the main languages in contact here were Quechua and Aymara, and that although by the height of the Inca expansion the city itself had adopted Quechua, it had remained surrounded by Aymara-speaking populations both toward Collao to the south, and to the south-east, as suggested by toponymy and by certain of the accounts in the *Relaciones Geográficas de Indias*.[35] The sources that tell of the changes that the Incas wrought upon the region in the decades prior to the Spanish Conquest reveal an even more complex picture, for the frontiers separating Quechua from other languages were none too clear.

It is oft repeated that one of the pillars of Inca policy as their conquests advanced was to transfer loyal populations and *mitimaes* to areas far removed from the heart of the empire; population movements that are claimed to have contributed to the spread of Quechua to regions such as what is now northern Peru. Rather less attention has been paid to how the Incas also moved outsiders into the city of Cuzco and its environs, as can be deduced from the data collected on the orders of Viceroy Toledo in Cuzco in 1570–1571.[36] This strategy presumably served to consolidate Inca control over populations close to Cuzco but only recently annexed and potentially rebellious.[37] The *mitma* populations and their respective leaders performed various duties, from herding to agriculture, weaving, construction, security, and administration. Although they preserved the memory of their origins, and of whichever Inca had ordered their resettlement in Cuzco, they were integrated into local societies in various ways, depending on the Incas' objectives: either they were put under the orders of the local population, or they kept their own chiefs and distinctions, interacted closely with the locals, and put down roots in the region.[38] The officials and elders questioned by Toledo's inspectors included natives of Cañaris,[39] Chachapoyas,[40] Huaylas, Lurin Guanca,[41] Collaguas,[42] and other subject provinces.

These migrations mandated by the Incas must have helped strengthen the *lengua general* in Cuzco, which served as a lingua franca to enable those of different origins to communicate. To judge from the data collected by Toledo's officials, the resettlement of *mitimaes* in Cuzco intensified as the Inca Empire entered its period of greatest expansion, during the rule of Topa Ynga Yupangui—whose successors maintained the policy, so these same sources relate. What remains unclear is quite how fast Quechua spread, and particularly how it managed to take root among sectors other than the elite.

Nor was this flow of immigrants stemmed by the Spanish Conquest. Cuzco and its environs continued to receive groups arriving from provinces such as Cañaris, Chachapoyas, Yauyos, Xauxa, Hanan and Lurin Guanca, and Huánuco.[43] It may be that the inflow of newcomers to Cuzco, spurred by the troop movements and chaos that followed in the conquistadors' wake, abated only when the Spaniards' own civil wars came to an end. The people of Cuzco, mostly Indians, continued to use Quechua. Bearing in mind how ethnically diverse the region was, and that access to learning the language was limited by gender and by social hierarchy, the survival and even spread of Quechua during the colonial period cannot be understood as simply a natural process determined essentially by population density.[44] Nor can it be wholly or even largely explained as a result of religious instruction, which did not begin in any

organized way until after the region had attained some political stability
in the 1560s. To see it as a form of popular resistance is likewise insufficient, for it is a claim that typically makes no attempt at historical analysis,
substituting it with ideology instead, and ruling out any detailed study of
society. Any assessment of the sociopolitical circumstances that favored
the spread of the *lengua general* needs to consider not just the church,
but also those groups who took over the reins of power, those who acted
as intermediaries between the Indian population and the colonial government, and the strategies by which individuals or groups within the
Indian population adjusted to the new circumstances of the colony.

One way to shed light on some of the factors that determined whether
or not indigenous languages survived in urban contexts is to compare
how Indian populations related to the language of the Spaniards in Lima
and in Cuzco during the colonial era.

The Andean Languages and Spanish, in Two Colonial Cities

The contrast between the Indian populations of the two major colonial urban centers, Lima and Cuzco, was a rather stark one. The ethnic
composition of the Indian population and its rate of growth were very
specific to each city, so the study of how speakers of the native languages
related to Spanish offers us some leads on the links between language
and society.

In the Lima valley the native population suffered particularly gravely
in the demographic crisis unleashed upon Spanish Conquest. Alongside
that precipitous collapse, however, Lima served as a magnet for sustained
immigration throughout the colonial period. Cook maintains that it was
these migrations that ensured that the city was home to a population of
Andean origin at all, for its natural growth was almost nil due because of
low fertility and high mortality rates.[45] The census taken in 1613 on the
orders of Viceroy Montesclaros shows an Indian population of very varied origins, though mostly migrants from the central highlands.[46] This
was a multilingual community, from a very early stage under great pressure to adopt Spanish, probably due to its low level of self-organization
and its minority position vis-à-vis the Spanish and African populations.[47]
Various factors encouraged the switch from indigenous languages to
Spanish: most migrants came to Lima from a position of isolation, which
only continued when they arrived; many entered the service of Spaniards
from an early age;[48] and the colonial authorities increasingly favored the
use of Spanish in most aspects of daily life. It is on this last point that I
wish to present some data, and raise some questions. Without the space
here to discuss in depth those various facets that might illustrate attitudes to the use of Spanish on the part of the colonial authorities, I shall
approach the issue through the role of interpreters.

Documentation on the role of interpreters in the various sections of colonial administration is scarce, and little is known of their identities and professional lives. Various individuals appear as interpreters in Lima at relatively early dates—in the 1560s and 1570s—in sources such as administrative *visitas* or the issuing of legal documents. This indicates that there were in Lima a number of people, both men and women, who did not speak Spanish (or at least not well enough), but also that there was a willingness on the part of the state that they be free to express themselves in their own language in official contexts. *Corregidores* (Spanish provincial governors and magistrates) and notaries would therefore summon some person who spoke the *lengua general* and was held to be reliable enough to act as an interpreter. These people were usually Indians, a fact that in itself would be unremarkable had the colonial authorities not repeatedly stated, in various forms and on multiple occasions, that it was Spaniards who were to act as interpreters, given the little confidence to be placed in any Indian to make a trustworthy translation. More importantly still, perhaps, at early dates we also find "professional" Indian interpreters, that is, in salaried posts as such. These were first employed by the city's *cabildo* (city council),[49] and in the late 1570s Viceroy Toledo appointed an Indian interpreter to the Real Audiencia in the *lengua general*. Historians unhesitatingly rank Toledo among the most uncompromising of the viceroys, who energetically pursued policies aimed at subduing the Indian population and furthering the interests of the Crown; yet in appointing an Indian to so significant a post—the Real Audiencia was the supreme court of the viceroyalty—Toledo was contradicting the widely held official judgement that doubted any Indian's suitability for such a role.[50] The successor to the post, the second interpreter in the *lengua general*, was likewise an Indian. Three questions immediately spring to mind. Who were these interpreters? Which form of Quechua did they speak? And, bearing in mind the great linguistic diversity of the public they served, how did they cope with multiple variants of Quechua, and with the task of expressing the content of their statements in Spanish?

As so often with people of indigenous origin in the early decades of Spanish occupation, reconstructing these interpreters' biographies is no easy task. Like most of Lima's Indian population, the interpreters to the Real Audiencia in the *lengua general* were migrants, hence the difficulty in establishing their backgrounds. The high social status that some of these interpreters enjoyed accrued from the services they rendered to the colonial government rather than their ancestry. The *curacas* and some of the Indian population may even have seen them as parvenus. At all events, their presence and activities played a substantial role in shaping the political culture of the colony. Don Pedro Mayz, the Indian interpreter appointed by Toledo, is a case in point. Elucidating his origins is not easy, for we do not have his will, and his surname gives no clue. In the records his name appears out of the blue upon his appointment to his post. Shortly afterward, when the Viceroy decreed the *repartimiento* (distribution) of *mita* (draft labor) Indians among Lima's *vecinos* (citizens), Mayz was the only Indian accorded this privilege—a clear indication of his exceptional status.[51] He married Doña María Pasña, a Lima-born woman whose parents hailed from Quito. On her death, Mayz wedded Doña Constanza Caxachumbe, the only daughter of a powerful cacique in the province of Chinchaycocha, in the central highlands of Peru. Don Pedro appears as interpreter for the Indians native to the Lima Valley in the deeds they issued before notaries in the city up to the late 1570s.[52] Don Diego Solsol, his successor, was a native of Chachapoyas and cacique of Chasmal, a *repartimiento* with a very small population, which probably explains why he preferred to abandon his position and settle in Lima.[53] Besides succeeding Mayz as interpreter, Solsol also married his widow. These data give us a better grasp of the importance that this position held in the capital of the viceroyalty. The interpreter of the *lengua general* was doubtless one of the most influential individuals among the local Indian population: his role entailed not just translating, but also instructing his clients in the ways of the bureaucracy and judicial system. That Mayz and Solsol both married Doña Constanza Caxachumbe indicates that provincial *curacas* like those from Chinchaycocha recognized the "strategic" importance that these officials enjoyed, and by marriage alliances sought to gain access to the prestige and benefits that came with their position. By studying networks of the type that these *curacas* were seeking to establish we might also understand how an indigenous culture arose within the colonial context, by linking together individuals and groups from different regions, and by devising mechanisms through which to further their own interests.

In which language did people from such varied origins communicate? Was it the same *lengua general* as was adopted for evangelization? To what extent and under what circumstances did they feel forced to adopt Spanish? A study of lawsuits filed by Indians before the Real Audiencia might shed light upon the trend visible likewise in notary records: growing pressure on the Indian population to use Spanish as its main means of communication. Services to enable those who spoke no Spanish to deal with the government (and officialdom more generally) were very limited, where they existed at all: while there was just one official interpreter to the Real Audiencia in the *lengua general*, no evidence has been found that any of the notaries working in Lima knew the language.[54] Interpreters gradually fade out of the deeds and other documents issued by Indians as of the 1630s, by which time notaries with Indian clients often describe them as "*ladinos* [competent] in the Spanish language."[55] By 1650 Spanish had grown so strong that the position of Quechua interpreter to the Real Audiencia was in decline: that same year Diego de Ávila, the Indian in post at the time, requested of the Viceroy permission to resign and move to Chuquisaca.[56]

In Cuzco circumstances were significantly different. Here the Indian population was in the majority and the social fabric did not suffer the calamity experienced in the Lima Valley—even if the Spanish Conquest, colonial administration, and a prolonged period of acute instability did conspire to weaken, modify, and in some cases even put an end to the tenure of a number of local political authorities.[57] As we have seen, long-range migrations were numerous and significant in the early years of the Conquest, but by the late sixteenth century had tailed off. On the other hand, population movements from neighboring areas continued into the following decades. Any language differences were probably resolved by means of the *lengua general.*

Cuzco was one of the main hubs of debate on the implications of using either Spanish or the *lengua general* to evangelize the native population. We know that some, like Garcilaso de la Vega, rejected the suggestions of those who in the sixteenth century asked whether the Indians were not capable of learning Spanish, and whether it would not be better for them to forget their own language and learn that of the colonizer.[58] Simpler, argued Garcilaso, would be to address and instruct them in the doctrine in their own language. The mestizos could serve as intermediaries, for they knew both Quechua and Spanish, as well as Indian culture. With few exceptions,[59] Garcilaso's declarations have not been scrutinized sufficiently closely, especially as regards contexts other than evangelization.

Indian notaries active in Cuzco between 1560 and 1570 likewise acted as interpreters,[60] but unlike the Mexican *tlacuilos* did not write in native languages, for in the Andes the colonial government only recognized documents and transactions drawn up in Spanish. Given that their potential clients were much more numerous, and that the city had neither a court of law nor an *audiencia* as Lima did, the bilingual scribes and interpreters of Cuzco make for a significant contrast with their peers in Lima.

Interpreters active in Cuzco formed a large group which initially was neither compact nor homogeneous. Of the 40 or so I have identified in the period 1559–1650, few appear regularly in deeds certified by notaries. In the sixteenth century, Indian interpreters alternated or shared their positions with mestizos and even Spaniards,[61] but by the seventeenth, the position of *intérprete general de los naturales* came under the control of a group of mestizos. Some of them, well aware of the tremendous significance and political advantages that this position entailed, endeavored to keep it within their family circles: Lucas Gutiérrez de Melo, who held the post as early as 1612,[62] married one of his daughters to Juan Maldonado Cornejo, also an interpreter, possibly in the late

1630s. In 1657 Maldonado Cornejo then passed the post on to none other than Gutiérrez de Melo's nephew.[63] The latter had previously taken out a *censo*—somewhat akin to a mortgage—on the position. Also among the interpreters of Cuzco were other, less Hispanicized mestizos. Francisco Díaz, for instance, decided against wedlock, perhaps because to do so would have meant marrying into a less favored social group. He nonetheless fathered many children, and by the time of his death had woven dense networks of connections with ethnic leaders and Indian commoners in the provinces of Cuzco.[64]

Interpreters were a permanent presence in Cuzco, even when those calling on the notaries' services claimed to speak Spanish. Women, and in general all who appeared before the notary in Indian attire, were immediately taken to be monolinguals who therefore required interpreters. Besides, in the deeds issued by their Indian clients some mestizo notaries recorded that they had also acted as interpreters, for as natives of Cuzco they knew the "lengua de yndio."[65] This confluence of interests, cultural origins, administrative practices, prejudices, and means by which to establish social networks, all came together to foster the use of Quechua. This was not necessarily because interpreters and notaries sought to preserve native culture, much less to help resist the colonial order; but because it made possible a form of social exclusion that would duly prove as long lasting as it was effective.

Conclusion

Differences in method, time-scale and use of evidence should not deter historians from reflecting on the insights that linguists can offer for the study of Andean societies. Dialogue between the disciplines is not easy, but once engaged in, its results can prove promising. It can lead historians to an understanding of aspects of Andean history as yet little explored. Linguists, meanwhile, once apprised of local diversity, of how significant is the role of historical agents, and of the differences between the social sciences in the time-scales at which they operate, may well be able to fine-tune their own perspective on the history of the Andes.

Notes

1. In order to trace the development of Andean languages and come to a chronology for Quechua, pioneering studies such as those of Alfredo Torero looked on the one hand to archaeology, and on the other, to lexicostatistical analysis. As we shall see, what Torero took from history was less significant and far more open to criticism. It is a mark of how linguistics has developed and grown in complexity that some of Torero's ideas have recently been subjected to in-depth

critique, and the methods he applied even discarded entirely. See the critique of Torero's approach by Rodolfo Cerrón-Palomino: *Lingüística quechua* (Cuzco: Centro de Estudios Regionales Andinos "Bartolomé de las Casas," 1987), p. 332. For recent contributions to the study of Quechua, see Paul Heggarty, "Enigmas en el origen de las lenguas andinas: Aplicando nuevas técnicas a las incógnitas por resolver," *Revista Andina* 40 (2005), 9–57, 70–80, and "Linguistics for Archaeologists: Principles, Methods, and the Case of the Incas," *Cambridge Archaeological Journal* 17:3 (2007), 311–40.

2. Alfredo Torero, *El quechua y la historia social andina* (Lima: Universidad Ricardo Palma, 1974); and *Idiomas de los Andes. Lingüística e historia*, 2nd ed. (Lima: Instituto Francés de Estudios Andinos / Horizonte, 2005).

3. Gary J. Parker, "Falacias y verdades acerca del quechua," in Alberto Escobar (ed.), *El reto del multilingüismo en el Perú* (Lima: Instituto de Estudios Peruanos, 1972), pp. 111–21.

4. Cerrón-Palomino, *Lingüística quechua*; *La lengua de Naimlap. Reconstrucción y obsolescencia del mochica* (Lima: Pontificia Universidad Católica del Perú, 1995); and "Tras las huellas del aimara cuzqueño," *Revista Andina* 33 (1999), 137–61.

5. Willem F. H. Adelaar, with Pieter C. Muysken, *The Languages of the Andes* (Cambridge and New York: Cambridge University Press, 2004).

6. Waldemar Espinoza Soriano, "Los fundamentos lingüísticos de la etnohistoria andina y comentarios en torno al Anónimo de Charcas de 1604," in Rodolfo Cerrón-Palomino (ed.), *Aula quechua* (Lima: Signo, 1982), pp. 163–202.

7. Torero, *El quechua y la historia social andina; Idiomas de los Andes.*

8. Torero, *Idiomas de los Andes*, p. 90.

9. Juan Carlos Estenssoro Fuchs, *Del paganismo a la santidad. La incorporación de los indios del Perú al catolicismo, 1532–1750* (Lima: Instituto Francés de Estudios Andinos / Pontificia Universidad Católica del Perú / Instituto Riva-Agüero, 2003); Gabriela Ramos, *Death and Conversion in the Andes. Lima and Cuzco, 1532–1670* (Notre Dame, IN: Notre Dame University Press, 2010).

10. Cerrón-Palomino, *Lingüística quechua*, p. 35.

11. Gerald Taylor (ed.), *Ritos y tradiciones de Huarochirí*, second revised ed. (Lima: Instituto Francés de Estudios Andinos / Banco Central de Reserva del Perú / Universidad Particular Ricardo Palma, 1999); and "Camac, camay y camasca en el manuscrito quechua de Huarochirí," in Gerald Taylor, *Camac, camay y camasca y otros ensayos sobre Huarochirí y Yauyos* (Lima: Instituto Francés de Estudios Andinos, 2000), pp. 1–17.

12. Bruce Mannheim, *The Language of the Inka since the European Invasion* (Austin: University of Texas Press, 1991); Alan Durston, *Pastoral Quechua: The History of Christian Translation in Colonial*

Peru, 1550–1650 (Notre Dame, IN: University of Notre Dame Press, 2007).

13. Torero, *Idiomas de los Andes*, p. 90.
14. Mannheim, *The Language of the Inka*, p. 35.
15. Cerrón-Palomino made similar proposals in his *Lingüística quechua*, p. 44.
16. María Rostworowski (ed.), *El señorío de Pachacamac: El informe de Rodrigo Cantos de Andrade de 1573* (Lima: Instituto de Estudios Peruanos / Banco Central de Reserva del Perú, 1999).
17. María Rostworowski, *Pachacamac* (Lima: Instituto de Estudios Peruanos, 2002).
18. Izumi Shimada, *Pachacamac Archaeology: Retrospect and Prospect* (Philadelphia, PA: University Museum Press, 1991); Peter Eeckhout, *Pachacamac durant l'Intermédiaire récent. Étude d'un site monumental préhispanique de la côte centrale du Pérou* (Oxford: BAR International Series, 1999); Rostworowski, *Pachacamac*.
19. Torero, *Idiomas de los Andes*, pp. 96–97.
20. Not that the *principal* in question had not severed his links with Pachacamac, for he returned to the valley months later and recovered his position. He appears as one of the deponents in the inquest by Cantos de Andrade in 1573: Rostworowski (ed.), *El señorío de Pachacamac*.
21. Torero, *Idiomas de los Andes*, p. 96.
22. Torero, *Idiomas de los Andes*; Alberto Flores Galindo, *Aristocracia y plebe: Lima, 1760–1830* (Lima: Mosca Azul, 1984).
23. Archivo General de la Nación (Lima, Peru, henceforth AGN), Protocolos Notariales, Antonio de Tamayo #1854, f. 1565. Francisco de Guascuanquiche, a native of Mansiche, near Trujillo, is an earlier example (1583) of an individual considerably less affluent, but with connections similar to Mondragón's (in Callao, Pachacamac, and Surco). See AGN, Protocolos Notariales, Rodrigo Gómez de Baeza #43, f. 262.
24. An example is the trade in agricultural produce and textiles all along the coast of Peru in the seventeenth century: Gabriela Ramos, "Diezmos, comercio y conflictos sociales a inicios del siglo XVII (Arzobispado de Lima): 1600–1630," in Gabriela Ramos (ed.), *La venida del reino: religión, evangelización y cultura en América, siglos XVI–XX* (Cuzco: Centro de Estudios Regionales Andinos "Bartolomé de las Casas," 1994), pp. 229–81.
25. Adelaar with Muysken, *The Languages of the Andes*.
26. Miguel Antonio Cornejo Guerrero, "Pachacamac y el canal de Guatca en el Bajo Rímac," *Bulletin de l'Institut Français d'Études Andines* 33:3 (2004), 783–814. A significant number of the burial contexts studied by Guillermo Cock at the Inca site of Puruchuco (Lima) have pottery with characteristics of both the central and northern coasts.
27. Rostworowski, *Pachacamac*.

28. Cerrón-Palomino, *Lingüística quechua*, p. 62.
29. Antonio de la Calancha, *Corónica moralizada del orden de San Agustín* 6 vols. (1638; Lima: Ignacio Prado Pastor, 1974); Miguel Cabello Valboa, *Miscelánea Antártica. Una historia del Perú antiguo* (Lima: Universidad Nacional Mayor de San Marcos, 1951), p. 219; Torero, *Idiomas de los Andes*, pp. 218–21.
30. There are sufficient grounds to support this hypothesis. Genealogies of Indian noble families from the Lima Valley consistently show that marriage alliances were arranged between the families of neighbouring chiefdoms (*señoríos*), who had been brought together after the conquest into towns such as Surco, Magdalena, Pachacamac, and Callao: Paul Charney, *Indian Society in the Valley of Lima, Peru, 1532–1824* (Lanham, MD: University Press of America, 2001). In some cases, families from these towns established connections with others in various places along the coast. We know, for instance, that Don Martín Canchomacan, one of the *curacas* of Pachacamac who appears in the inspection by Rodrigo Cantos de Andrade, married a woman from Huaura, a coastal town north of Lima (AGN, Protocolos Notariales, Francisco Hernández 823, f. 1351). The *curacas* of Callao and their descendants were similarly related to the ruling families of the chiefdoms of Maranga and Surco. In the seventeenth century the sole descendant of the Callao *curacas* married the *curaca principal* of the town of Magdalena, and on his death she was then remarried to the governor of the northern town of Olmos (AGN, Protocolos Notariales, Gaspar de Monzón 1153, registro 6, f. 1039v; Alonso Durán Vicentelo 422, n.p.; Gaspar de Monzón 1156, f. 66v).
31. Among examples one might cite is Doña Ana Quipan, daughter of Don Diego Chayavilca, *curaca* of Maranga. The mother of Doña Ana Quipan was Doña Ana Ñacam, whose name also appears as Doña Lucía Nacam. Her brothers were Don Pedro Chumbichanam and Alonso Channam; the former was *curaca* of the neighbouring town of Guadca in the late sixteenth and early seventeenth centuries. AGN, Protocolos Notariales, siglo XVI, Rodrigo Gómez de Baeza 49, f. 1017. See AGN, Protocolos Notariales, siglo XVII, Rodríguez de Torquemada 1673, f. 539. On Quingnam names, see Adelaar with Muysken, *The Languages of the Andes*. For a study of the Mochica language, see Cerrón-Palomino, *La lengua de Naimlap*. On the ruling families of the *curacazgos* of the Lima Valley see also Charney, *Indian Society in the Valley of Lima*.
32. Torero, *Idiomas de los Andes*.
33. Waldemar Espinoza Soriano, "Los mitmas yungas de Collique en Cajamarca, siglos XVI y XVII," *Revista del Museo Nacional* 36 (1970), pp. 9–57; Cerrón-Palomino, *Lingüística quechua*, p. 62.
34. Cerrón-Palomino, *Lingüística quechua*, pp. 334; Torero, *Idiomas de los Andes*; Mannheim, *The Language of the Inka*.

35. Marcos Jiménez de la Espada, *Relaciones Geográficas de Indias. Perú* 3 vols. (Madrid: Ediciones Atlas, 1965).

36. Roberto Levillier, *Don Francisco de Toledo, supremo organizador del Perú. Su vida, su obra, 1515–1582* (Madrid: Espasa-Calpe, 1935).

37. R. Alan Covey, *How the Incas Built Their Heartland: State Formation and the Innovation of Imperial Strategies in the Sacred Valley, Peru* (Ann Arbor: University of Michigan Press, 2006). Also R. Alan Covey and Christina M. Elson, "Ethnicity, Demography, and Estate Management in Sixteenth-Century Yucay," *Ethnohistory* 54:2 (Spring 2007), 303–35.

38. Gabriela Ramos, "Los tejidos y la sociedad colonial andina," *Colonial Latin American Review* 19:1 (Apr. 2010), 115–49.

39. Among a group of elders and officials summoned to make statements to the inquest held in Cuzco in March 1571 appears one Don Juan Çuaytunba, a "Cañar principal" who claimed to "descend from other Cañares" brought to Cuzco from Quito by Topa Ynga Yupangui: Levillier, *Don Francisco de Toledo*, vol. 2, p. 78.

40. Others summoned on the same occasion as just noted included: Don Gonzalo Guacanqui, "who declared that he was of the lineage of Capac Yupanqui"; Don Felipe Uscamayta Ynga; and Martín Vilca, a native of Chachapoyas, who testified that "Guainacapac [had] brought him from Chachapoyas to these lands around Cuzco": Levillier, *Don Francisco de Toledo*, vol. 2, p. 86.

41. Among those questioned in the Yucay Valley between March and July 1571 were: Don Pedro Cochachi, "who declared that he was from the Yucay Valley, in the *parcialidad* of Chuquipata"; Cristóbal Curimay, "who declared that he was of the lineage of the Ynga"; and Domingo Achimec, *curaca* of the *parcialidad* of Checo. Cochachi and Achimec declared that Topa Ynga Yupanqui, once his conquests were complete, had taken their forefathers ["abuelos"] from the provinces of "Guaylas and Luringuanca, where they were born, to the Yucay valley, where these witnesses are now [living]…". It was the Inca himself, they claimed, who had appointed them *curacas*: Levillier, *Don Francisco de Toledo*, vol. 2, pp. 101–2.

42. At this same inquest a certain Gómez Condori, a native of Collaguas who lived in Chinchaypuquio, explained that his father had been brought to Cuzco as a retainer to Amaro Topa Ynga, brother of Topa Ynga Yupangui. Gómez Condori had in turn served Huayna Capac: Levillier, *Don Francisco de Toledo*, vol. 2, pp. 113–14.

43. Sources such as notary records provide evidence of this process. Especially from 1560 to 1570, a number of men and women making wills in Cuzco stated they had been born in the former Inca province of Chinchaysuyo. In 1566, for instance, Francisca Auatanta, daughter of Guari Puma and Ñauintanta, and who was then living near the convent of San Francisco, stated that she had been born in Xauxa (Archivo Histórico del Cuzco, henceforth AHC, Protocolos

Notariales, siglo XVI, Antonio Sánchez 16, f. 357). Domingo Pariguana, a *yanacona* to several Spaniards, stated in his will in 1571 that he was the son of Alonso Asto and María Ponchauac, Indians from Chinchaysuyo (AHC, Protocolos Notariales, siglo XVI, 19, f. 1307). In 1590 Don Gonzalo Guanuco Quispe, a native of Huánuco and son of Lliuyacguaman and Pamo Yllacsa, explained in his will that he had arrived in Cuzco together with Francisco Pizarro's troops. In Cuzco he acted as cacique to a hundred Indians in the parish of the Indian hospital (AHC, Protocolos Notariales, siglo XVI, Pedro de la Carrera Ron 4, f. 880). Ramos, *Death and Conversion in the Andes.*

44. On the population of Cuzco in the early colonial period, see Noble David Cook, *Demographic Collapse: Indian Peru, 1520–1620* (Cambridge: Cambridge University Press, 1981), and particularly Ann Wightman, *Indigenous Migration and Social Change: The Forasteros of Cuzco, 1570–1720* (Durham, NC: Duke University Press, 1990).

45. Cook, *Demographic Collapse.*

46. Miguel de Contreras (Noble David Cook, ed.), *Padrón de los indios de Lima en 1613* (Lima: Universidad Nacional Mayor de San Marcos, 1968).

47. Frederick P. Bowser, *The African Slave in Colonial Peru, 1524–1650* (Stanford: Stanford University Press, 1974); Claude Mazet, "Population et société à Lima aux XVIe et XVIIe siècles: La paroisse San Sebastián (1562–1689)," *Cahiers des Amériques Latines* 13–14 (1976), 53–100.

48. In census records many men and women alike stated that they had arrived in Lima alone, or had been brought by a Spaniard in whose service they were engaged. Many of those who worked independently as artisans or day labourers lived in the houses of Spaniards or people of African origin: Contreras (Noble David Cook, ed.), *Padrón de los indios de Lima.*

49. Enrique Torres Saldamando, Pablo Patrón, and Nicanor Boloña (eds.), *Libro primero de cabildos de Lima* 3 vols. (Paris: Paul Dupont, 1888); Juan Bromley (ed.), *Libros de Cabildo de Lima* 23 vols. (Lima: Imprenta Torres Aguirre, 1935–64).

50. Emilio Lissón Chávez, *La Iglesia de España en el Perú. Colección de documentos para la historia de la iglesia en el Perú* 5 vols. (Seville: Católica Española, 1943–56), vol. 1, n. 3, pp. 112–13; Diego de Esquivel y Navia (Félix Denegri Luna, ed.), *Noticias Cronológicas de la Gran Ciudad del Cuzco* 2 vols. (Lima: Fundación Augusto N. Wiese, 1980), vol. 2, p. 9.

51. Francisco de Toledo (María Justina Sarabia Viejo, ed.), *Disposiciones gubernativas para el virreinato del Perú*, 2 vols. (1569–1580; Seville: Escuela de Estudios Hispanoamericanos, 1986–89), vol. 2, p. 336.

52. In 1577, for instance, Mayz acted as interpreter in drawing up the will of one Don Bartolomé Guamac Chumbi, cacique of Guanchallay

(Guanchoguaylas, to the east of the city of Lima). The notary indicated that Don Pedro acted as interpreter "as someone knowledgeable in the language of said Don Bartolomé" (AGN, PN, Marcos Franco de Esquivel 33, f. 730).

53. On Chasmal see José de la Puente Brunke, *Encomiendas y encomenderos en el Perú. Estudio social y político de una institución colonial* (Seville: Excelentísima Diputación Provincial de Sevilla, 1992), p. 479; and on his background, see AGN, PN, Gómez de Baeza 740, f. 711.

54. It may be that notaries in places such as the Indian precinct of El Cercado, or the towns surrounding the city, were Indians who simultaneously acted as interpreters, at least in early times; but their records are lost. Those notary records (AGN, Testamentos de Indios) that are still extant are mostly of late (eighteenth century) date, and suggest that both the notaries and the Indians issuing the deeds communicated exclusively in Spanish.

55. Only a few of the many notaries in Lima served Indians, or others who lived in migrant neighbourhoods like San Lázaro.

56. AGN, PN, Fernando García 682, f. 404.

57. It is worth bearing in mind the statements by Indian officials and elders recorded for Toledo's *visita*, in Levillier, *Don Francisco de Toledo*. A number of them stated that since the conquest, and because of the disorder it had unleashed, their former subjects would no longer take orders from them.

58. Inca Garcilaso de la Vega (A. Rosenblat, ed.), *Comentarios Reales de los Incas* 2 vols. (1609; Buenos Aires: Emecé, 1945), vol. 2, book. 7, chap. 3, pp. 92–93.

59. Berta Ares Queija, "'Un borracho de chicha y vino'. La construcción social del mestizo (Perú, s. XVI)," in Gregorio Salinero (ed.), *Mezclado y sospechoso. Movilidad e identidades, España y América (siglos XVI–XVIII)* (Madrid: Casa de Velázquez, 2005), pp. 121–44.

60. The one Indian notary who has left us the richest traces of his activities in Cuzco is Pedro Quispe, whose deeds appear within the records of scribe Pedro de la Carrera Ron. Quispe served as interpreter in the parish of the Indian hospital.

61. The latter's presence is suggested by the Spanish names that some of them went by. Unlike in Mexico, Indian surnames remained in constant use in the Andes, particularly in the Cuzco region and in the highlands generally.

62. AHC, PN, Juan de Olave 244 [1610–11], f. 216.

63. AHC, PN, Juan Flores de Bastidas 98 [1657–59], f. 266.

64. AHC, PN, Martín López de Paredes 147 [1665], f. 74.

65. AHC, PN, Beltrán Luzero 6 [1639], f. 208; Juan Flores de Bastidas 94, f. 468

Chapter 2

A Visit to the Children of Chaupi Ñamca: From Myth to History via Onomastics and Demography

Frank Salomon and Sue Grosboll

Often, our sources for languages of the past are mythic and prescriptive rather than empirical and descriptive ones: narratives of gods, laws, and so on. As much as we treasure them for linguistic and cultural reasons, for historical and archaeological purposes we would also like to know whether practice actually matched ideals. This chapter presents a method for getting from sacred norms to social history. It concerns the only known book that presents the pre-Christian mythology of an Andean society in an Andean language, namely the Quechua manuscript of Huarochirí (1608). In the segmented Huarochirí society, birth rank was a central principle of hierarchy. An idealized system for naming persons by birth rank is explained. But at the time when the mythology was compiled, was birth-order hierarchy just a cultural memory, or was it contemporary social practice "on the ground"? A 1588 *visita* or tribute-roll inspection yields a large database concerning the same population from which the text arose. By statistical and probabilistic methods, we show that the Andean birth-rank onomasticon (an onomasticon is a vocabulary or ordered list of proper names) was in fact a wide social practice, not a memory from pre-Hispanic antiquity. But to talk of practice is to also to talk of historic change: in the disastrous early colonial decades leading up to the composition of the Quechua text, name usage was shifting. Analysis of linguistic practices over time gives historical sources subtle but precise meanings never manifested on their textual surfaces.

* * *

Andean sources often present verbal schemes for hierarchies, such as the common threefold classification of descent groups (*collana, payan, cayao*) or Guaman Poma's ranked brackets of makers of the knotted-cord records called *quipu* (or to be correct in modern Quechua orthography, *khipu*), noble ladies, and so on. How can we tell whether such schemes prescribe ideal categories of myth, ritual, and ideology, or describe social practice?

For example, the Quechua manuscript of Huarochirí (probably 1608) details many hierarchies, but it speaks in the idiom of myth. Do its rankings allegorize real social practice at the time of writing? Or do the "gods and men of Huarochirí" represent a scheme of pre-Columbian culture that was only a memory in the post-Toledan setting of forced resettlement villages? How can we tell when categories like *ayllu* are old lexical bottles holding new semantic wine,[1] and when they express ongoing continuities?

This essay illustrates one way to connect mythic representations with practices. Using a new source, we will analyze one paradigm of rank and identity in Huarochirí, namely hierarchy within gender complementarity, as expressed in an onomasticon. Statistical analysis and onomastic study can wring new kinds of information from an important document genre, the *visita* or tribute inspection.[2]

Methodologically, the point is general and not just Andean. The *Annales* school taught historians how to elicit from accumulations of economic data systematic patterns of societal change that the writers themselves could hardly see. Archives can also be seen as accumulations of verbal, that is, linguistic, data. As we find similarly systematic means to follow linguistic traits, these too reveal patterns of change—sometimes in elusive areas of cultural habit. The point is to treat the linguistic attributes of historical sources (in this case, lexical ones) as parts of their historical testimony, rather than simply as less or more transparent media. Linguistically linked historiography may yield subtle and yet verifiable indices revealing how societies reproduced and changed themselves by deploying devices of discourse.

The Ideology of Highland/Valley Complementarity and Its Gender Metaphor

Societies on the Pacific slope of the Central Andes saw themselves as partnerships between lineages of highland pastoralist origin, identified with male *huacas* (revered object or place) incarnated in snowcaps, and lineages of valley-based agriculturalists, identified with valley-based female fertility *huacas*. (The term *huaca* is a Spanish rendering of a Quechua word denoting any place or object held to embody a superhuman being.) In the Huarochirí province and adjoining areas,[3] dialectical union connecting the powers of the heights (storm and water) with those of the valleys (soil and vegetation) was often mythicized as a sexual union or sibling pairing between invading male water deities and deep-seated, unmoving female earth-deities. These polities understood the union as a ritualized, institutionalized, and sexualized structure of antagonistic interdependence uniting dissimilar peoples. In Huarochirí, the former pole was associated with *puna*-rooted people affiliated to the snowcap Paria Caca as male deity, and the latter with *yunka*-rooted people affiliated to the valley shrine of Chaupi Ñamca as female deity.

The political hinges of such articulation were the prized mid-valley coca-growing villages where outliers of highland populations lived enclaved together with Yunka people.[4] Such sites could be apples of discord,[5] and their management understandably was a focus of ideology. Thanks to Rostworowski's ethnohistoric studies of conflicts over coca fields in the middle Chillón Valley, we possess detailed testimony showing what an unstable and contentious interethnic relationship underlay the idealization expressed as the wedding of peoples and elements.[6] Such was the case in Sisicaya (department of Lima, Province of Huarochirí), the case we will analyze.

A good deal of research, notably by Spalding and Espinoza Soriano, restores nonmythic context to this social and economic complex.[7] On the linguistic side, it is now clear that our scene was a linguistic contact zone where an Aymara-like vernacular coexisted, in decline, with Quechua and with another vernacular peculiar to coastal and lower valley groups.[8] But for the truly detailed, field-research level, we have had little to work with. This impedes reconstructing the social reality which the myths allegorize. Rostworowski found one summary of early Huarochirí field records, a regional synthesis of six Inka "thousands" for 1577.[9] Here, we will concentrate on a more detailed administrative inspection (*revisita*) made 11 years later—but still 20 years before the compilation of the Quechua testimonies. The 1588 *revisita* of Sisicaya is preserved in the Archivo General de la Nación, Buenos Aires. It remained unrecognized as Huarochirí material because of a confusion with Sicasica in Alto Perú (later Bolivia).[10] Thanks for identifying it are due to a sharp-eyed Bolivianist, Tom Abercrombie. Because this soon-to-be-published source includes a person-by-person, house-by-house description of sociopolitical order, it allows us to tell how far Chaupi Ñamca's prescribed order was actually being implemented among the population that later told her legend to the anonymous Quechua writer. The *revisita* was organized by a man actually mentioned in the Quechua text, the *curaca* (colonial ethnic lord) Don Diego Chauca Guaman of San Francisco de Sisicaya.[11]

Sisicaya, Its Goddesses, and Its Curaca in the Quechua Manuscript of 1608(?) and in the 1588 Revisita

In Inka times three major ethnic sectors dwelled on sites overlooking the riverbank oasis of Sisicaya: highland, Yunka, and Inka.[12] A lifetime later, at the time of the Quechua source, forced resettlement had concentrated all three together onto the valley floor.[13] But Spanish supervision failed to break Sisicaya's links with the female and coastal-oriented superhuman Chaupi Ñamca.

In Chapter 13 of the Huarochirí manuscript, titled "Mama,"[14] an apparently Checa narrator (that is, a member of a descent group or *ayllu* seated much higher up, near San Damián, and belonging to a putatively invasive upland lineage) talks at length about the cults affiliated to Chaupi Ñamca. This teller sees the snowcapped mountain deity Paria Caca as "our father" and Chaupi Ñamca of the valley as "our mother." Passages of Chapter 13 spotlight a cluster of shrines considered as her alter egos. These include Llacsa Huato and her "sister" Mira Huato, who held cults at or near Sisicaya. Probably because Sisicaya was seen as a Yunka-Checa contact zone, the Sisicaya deities had both Yunka and Checa names, which the narrator sporadically collates.

The biethnic cultic system articulating "our father" Paria Caca and his male instantiations with "our mother" Chaupi Ñamca and her female instantiations endured into the colonial era as cultural contraband. The 1608 Quechua source twice reminds us that Sisicaya's Don Diego Chauca Guaman had protected the latter's cults, and this pagan indulgence might have continued had he not been replaced by his purportedly more Christian son Don Martin.[15] From 1608 a female *huaca* priesthood of "our mother" persisted.[16]

At *revisita* time, 20 years earlier, the lord Don Diego Chauca Guaman, then 42 years of age, was ruling. He was too young to remember pre-Hispanic times. He wrote Spanish with a practiced hand (f.2v). Like many native lords of the Toledan era, he brokered between *quipu* information bases and alphabetic scribal work, for in the *revisita* (f.8r) he speaks of data "which I gave the said corregidor by quipes" [*sic*][17], that is by *quipu* or knotted-cord records.

Sisicaya and Ritual Organization in the Huarochirí Manuscript

The Quechua manuscript makes two main points about Sisicaya's cultic standing. The first is that Sisicaya was the very hinge of organization between montane and valley powers. This is stated mythically in the following fashion. Checa informants from upslope San Damián claimed their hero-ancestor, Paria Caca's son or avatar Tutay Quiri, had swept down the "Sici Caya" (i.e., Lurín) and "Mama" (i.e., Rímac) rivers,[18] until his westward and seaward conquests stopped near Sisicaya. The resulting frontier was to be a line of interaction, not of segregation. Coca producers of Sisicaya (and other mid-to-lower valley natives) were to perennially honor the invaders' "father" Paria Caca by bringing coca to a deity (shrine) he stationed at the limit of invasion. Moreover lowlanders were even to make the annual pilgrimage up to Paria Caca Mountain, high in the cordillera. The politico-economic imperative these arrangements encoded was highlanders' need for Sisicaya's main product: coca leaf.

The second point is that, at Sisicaya, worshippers could come peculiarly close to female divinity. Highland-based worshippers trooped down to visit female deities, as Yunkas trooped up to Paria Caca. Two of Chaupi Ñamca's component personages lived within the Sisicaya parish: Llacsa Huato, called Copacha by the Checa, and Mira Huato, whose Checa name was transcribed as Ampuche or Ampuxi . Their cult is explained in fascinating ethnographic detail.[19]

The Birth-Order Onomasticon in Sisicaya Village and in the Huarochirí Manuscript

It is in context of Chaupi Ñamca's cult that the Quechua text minutely explains ideals of both male-female and highland-lowland complementarity.

The Quechua manuscript pervasively emphasizes one template for inequality: a sib of descent groups ranked by birth order among their founding ancestors. The list of founders in seniority order becomes a ranked onomasticon. Birth-order naming, not necessarily with reference to focalized ancestors, occurs in a wide variety of cultural systems including Japanese, certain Papua-New Guinean peoples,[20] Ho-Chunk or Winnebago Siouans,[21] Delaware Algonkians in Oklahoma,[22] Ilongot of the Philippines,[23] Hausa,[24] as well as Dogon and Kanuri Africans,[25] and (vestigially) classical Romans. In Huarochirí as in many of these societies, birth-order naming squares the circle of solidarity-with-inequality; while emphasizing likeness of substance (shared birth) it also provides a criterion for discrimination. The rank correlated to birth, however, primarily concerns *precedence* among commensurate segments of society. Only when colonial legalism equated it to European primogeniture could it serve to *exclude* the junior groups' interests.

The birth-order onomasticon is stated in a partly Spanish marginal note to the Huarochirí manuscript.[26] It consists of a pair of parallel male and female hierarchies. The context, as we will see below, is a mention of two names which a reader (possibly P. Francisco de Avila, who sponsored the compilation of the text) saw as needing clarification.

hijo
curaca o ancacha el 1º
chauca el 2º

lluncu el 3°
sullca el 4°
llata el 5°
ami el 6°[27]
hijas
paltacha o cochucha[28] la 1ª
coba pacha la 2ª
ampuche[29] la 3ª
sullcacha la 4ª
ecancha la 5ª[30]
anacha anasi

Was the name-rank scheme in fact implemented in nonritual contexts? Was it implemented differently between valley folk and highlanders? Was it used equitably between the sexes? Did the strikingly female-centered cultic complex that gave Sisicaya its ideological identity have a counterpart in secular practice?

Sisicaya's Ayllu Organization in 1588 and Its Relevance to the Quechua Manuscript

In 1588, as in 1577, Sisicaya was the smallest (f.62v) of the Huarochirí "thousands." The Sisicaya "thousand" in turn was made up of ten *ayllus* or corporate descent groups (see Table 2.1).

This sociological pattern of *ayllus* reflects two major historic facts. The first is that social segments were ethnically differentiated. The first four *ayllus* are Yunka, native to Sisicaya. The rest are enclaves, or "islands" in Murra's terminology. These six are outliers of highland-based populations, sent to exploit the mid-valley coca oasis. The second fact is the disturbance of this pattern by forced resettlement, which was an accomplished fact by 1588.

Three of four Yunka *ayllus* (Andapocro, Chillaco, and Çiçicaya) correspond to place names in the immediate Sisicaya area. The four Yunka *ayllus* constituted by far the majority of Sisicaya tributary households (77.3 percent) and persons (74.9 percent in 1579, 76.7 percent in 1588). They were probably the ones cultically in charge of the female-oriented shrines of Llacsahuato and Mirahuato.

By contrast, five of the six last-named *ayllus* are tiny eponyms of much larger and higher upriver villages.[31] The *revisita* identifies the *principales* (*ayllu* heads) to whom the six groups were subject. Three of them are independently known to have had political seats in highland villages.[32]

Thus, in the youth of the manuscript's makers, Sisicaya was a far-reaching "multiethnic formation." Some of the highland villages that controlled

Table 2.1   The *Ayllus* of Sisicaya and Their Tributary Populations, 1579 and 1588[1]

Ayllu	Persons, 1579[2]	Households*, 1588	Persons, 1588
Ayllu Chillaco	62	17/23	60
Ayllu Andapocro	30	4/6	19
Ayllu Llangaçapa	217	48/70	177
Ayllu Cicicaya	254	57/83	235
Ayllu Checa	63	11/21	48
Ayllu Lupo	12	1/3	5
Ayllu Quinti	20	4/7	17
Ayllu Papano	86	19/29	71
Ayllu Yampilla	6	1/1	3
Ayllu Chaucarima	7	1/2	5
TOTAL	757	163/245	640**

*The two figures under the column "Households" refer to: (1) tributary households; and (2) tributary households plus households of widowers, widows, singles, and orphans. The 1579 and 1588 population figures in the table include members of all household types.
**Table 2.1 summarizes the tributary Indians only. To arrive at the total 1588 population one must add in one exempt household, that of the "Cacique Principal," and its seven members, yielding 647 persons in 246 households.
1. For each *ayllu* the *visitador* wrote separate listings of complete households, of widowers and male orphans, of widows and female orphans, of those whose deaths since the last *visita* were documented by parish register entries, and of those allegedly dead but undocumented.
2. The inspector Xuárez de Angulo was charged with updating a 1579 *visita*. He did not copy the findings of the 1579 inspector by *ayllus* but it is possible to reconstruct them by the following steps: (population in 1588) + (adult deaths since 1579)—(children born since 1579, still alive) + (children born before 1579, now dead, estimated). Cristóbal Xuárez de Angulo, Revisita de Sisicaya, Archivo General de la Nación, Buenos Aires (AGN/BA) Padrones de La Paz (PLP) 13–17–5-1.

"islands" were not seated in the Lurín basin at all, but belonged to the Rímac and Mala drainages, representing at least four of the "thousands" of Huarochirí. This shows that resettlement had not as of 1588 demolished the Inka-era multivalley "vertical archipelago" that the 1608 myths allegorized. In sum, the Sisicaya of 1588 was a place where symbolically female-like Yunka people and their cults, embodied in four land-endowed social segments, were articulated with six highland-based complements with affiliation to male deities. How were the male and female name series associated with this dyad actually applied among humans?

The Application of the Birth-Order Onomasticon in Sisicaya ca. 1588

Let us consider the names in rank order.

Male name 1, Curaca or Ancacha: Curaca seems derived (perhaps under Aymara morphological influence) from Quechua *kuraq*, "first-born"; its use as an Inka and colonial title for local customary rulers is a typical political extension of the birth-rank principle. The 1608 Quechua manuscript uses the word *curaca* 15 times in this sense.

In the *revisita* this name and its variants (mentioned for both living and dead members) are extremely common: there are 75 cases, namely Curacacha (9)[33], Curacache (15), Curacaxe (4), Curaca Poma (2), and Curaca (45). It occurs in all *ayllu*s with no obvious disproportion to population. The name Ancacha, which the informant equated to Curaca, occurs with some variation four times, three in Checa *ayllu* (f.79v).

Male name 2, Chauca: The Huarochirí manuscript uses this element connoting "secondborn male" in seven instances: in the names of two local collectivities,[34] once in the name of a second-ranking lineage,[35] twice in names of ancestors,[36] and twice in names of contemporary men.[37] The former of the two is none other than Diego Chauca Guaman, the organizer of the 1588 *revisita*.

The element Chauca was extremely common in Sisicaya in 1588. Of the men, 75 were named Chauca. Additional variant names included Chaucacha (2), Chaucalla (1), Chaucalivia (1), Chaucacolque (1), Chauca Cancho (1), Chauca Guaman (2), Chauca Paico (1), Cara Chauca (1), Caxa Chauca (1), Casa Chauca (1), Chumbi Chauca (1), Colque Chauca (2), and Tello Chauca (1). In total, 91 men bore the name. This name occurred in all *ayllu*s with no obvious disproportion to population.

Male name 3, Lluncu: The Huarochirí manuscript uses the element connoting "thirdborn male" sparingly. It occurs in the name of the priest or calendrical expert Macoy Lluncu[38] or Macoy Llenco.[39] The name of the female *huaca* Lluncuhuachac[40] or Llunchu Huachac[41] may mean "Gives birth to Lluncu," perhaps indicating she was the deity and oracle of a third-ranking group.

Lluncu was quite common in Sisicaya, with 50 instances. The *revisita* listed Llunco (3), Llungo (11), Llongo (17), Llongucha (2), Lungo (1), Lungucha (2), Lluncuchi (1), Lluncomisa (1) Llonga Yauri (1), Calevai Lungo (1), Caxa Llongo (1), Caxa Llungo (1), Chumbi Llongo (2), Chumbi Llungo (2) Anche Llungo (1), Poma Llongo (2), and Sirve Llongo (1). Lluncu names occur in all *ayllu*s proportionally, except for a slightly higher than expected occurrence in Llangaçapa.

Male name 4, Sullca: The Huarochirí manuscript uses this term connoting "fourth-born male" in the names of a *huaca*, but crosses it out.[42] It also uses it as, probably, an *ayllu* name.[43]

In Sisicaya in 1579 and 1588, Sullca and its variants were common, with 44 instances: Julca (27), Sulca (1), Xulca (5), Julca Caxa (1), Julca Chumbi (2), Julca Yauri (2), Julcacha (3), Tanta Julca (1), Tanta Xulca (1), and Tello Julca (1). It occurs in all *ayllu*s without obvious disproportion to population.

Male name 5, Llata: At this point the Yunka/highlander contrast comes into play. The reason for marginally explaining the onomasticon in the first place was to clarify an enigmatic passage about "Ami and Llata." The passage is as follows. Paria Caca promised a disconsolate worshiper of the ancient cannibal-*huaca* Huallallo Carhuincho, that if he were to worship Paria Caca instead, he would not have to sacrifice his son to Huallallo. The worshiper was worried that Huallallo would retaliate for losing his sacrifice.

> "Let him get angry!" [replied Paria Caca.] "He won't be able to do a thing to you. And what's more I will bring people into being, males under the care of Ami and Llata and females under that of Añasi, one as the male and one as the female, that is how I will have them live." And while he was speaking his breath came out of his mouth like bluish smoke.[44]

The Quechua wording *camasac amiyocta llatayocta*, in a translation closer to morphemic structure, would be "I will make them as possessors of Ami and Llata." This could signify that the future humans would enjoy the protection of *huaca*s called Llata and Ami. But as will be seen later, this interpretation may be complemented by the idea of "having Llatas and Amis" in a more down-to-earth social organizational sense.

Up to this point the sense of the story seems to be that Paria Caca promised the Huallallo-worshiper a better future insofar as there would later be people having Llata and Ami. Why would that be a better future? A native audience, familiar with the scheme, would understand that a world with Llata and Ami meant a world in which Paria Caca's protegés would have younger siblings to stand as subordinates. That is the point which the marginal list clarified for nonlocal readers.

Ami and Llata reappear three chapters later. The context is the story of how the Checa ancestor-hero Tutay Quiri, a "son" of Paria Caca, led a victorious invasion down the Lurín ("Sisicaya") and Rímac ("Mama") valleys. Since the Yunkas there waited to pay him homage, he forbore to sweep them away. Instead he ordained that they should stay on with the conquerors. These valley people would address the victors saying, "We are your Amicha, we are your Llatacha."[45]

Thus Paria Caca's earlier prophesy was made good: The Yunka aborigines not only form fraternal links with the invaders, but also subordinate themselves by adopting the ritual status of younger brothers. It is this ritual junior brotherhood which the two names connote.

But why did the specific names Llata and Ami become bywords for a specific type of political subordination, namely one in which defeated Yunka groups were classified as junior members of a larger sib? The Huarochirí manuscript generally speaks of human categories in terms of *huaca*s which are their symbolic eponyms, without ever descending to any sociological level of description. The text therefore refers to a pantheon of sibling-superhumans who stand for the whole ideal order of society. In the priestly or ritual discourse that dominates the Quechua source, the kinship of the superhumans is presented as a cosmic given, of which human practice is the mere consequence.

But myths are often sociological models standing on their heads. The paradigm of sibling-*huaca*s, though presented as the cause of human practice, might be taken as a distillate of observations about practice at human level. We know from an independent case that the tellers of the Huarochirí texts scrutinized different groups' respective birth-order naming practices as index traits, suitable for classifying them as like or unlike each other. In Chapter 26 of the Huarochirí manuscript, a teller explains that two groups (Pihcca Marca and Allauca) belong together because both have the custom of calling their firstborns Canricha.[46] In the case of the Llatas, too, the utterance of Paria Caca might be an etiological myth explaining observed interethnic differences still visible in the lifetime of the manuscript's makers. In tellers' eyes, what sort of people called their sons Llata?

In 1588, Llata was a name which members of the local Yunka *ayllu*s of Sisicaya gave to some of their male offspring, but which members of the highland *ayllu*s generally did not. The *revisita* shows 19 instances of the name: 17 Llatas, 1 Llatacha, and 1 Llatache. Of the 19, 18 (94.7 percent) occur in Yunka *ayllu*s. This suggests that as of 1588 the custom of naming some boys Llata may well have looked to highlanders in Sisicaya like a distinctively Yunka one. In this sense people "who have Llata(s)," (*llatayoc*) might mean "the sort of people who call their sons Llata," that is, "Yunkas."

There may be an additional layer of meaning to the use of "possessors of Llata(s)" as a byword for ritually subordinated Yunka groups. The males bearing names with the element Llata in 1588 tended overwhelmingly to be to be underage or dependent, not able-bodied tributaries. 13 of the 19 Llatas (68.4 percent) were underage and 10 (52.6 percent) were children.

So being called Llata went together with being Yunka, junior in birth order, and young. The term may, then, not only mean Yunka, but Yunka in a dependent status. Perhaps, by extension, the Yunka name for a dependent was used to mean the Yunkas, collectively, in their status as dependents. Paria Caca's prophecy would then have meant "The Yunkas collectively will be to the invaders, as the Yunkas' own lastborn are, individually, to their siblings."

Male name 6, Ami: Ami is used in parallel to Llata in the Huarochirí manuscript. Its incidence in the *revisita* of 1588 follows the same distribution as Llata but with somewhat less clarity. Sisicaya had seven Amis: Ami (1), Amicha (4), Amiche (1), and Aumycha (1). Six of the seven (85.7 percent) were of the Yunka *ayllu* which made up three-fourths of the village. However in the case of Ami there is no noticeable demographic association between the name and underage status. We do not know whether or why an Ami would typically be a subordinate person.

We turn now to the female naming series. Much as the numbered *huaca*s of the male set were identified as parts of the overarching Paria Caca cult, myth-tellers explained the female series (in more detail) as the array of *huaca*s making up the Chaupi Ñamca cult. And, as in the male case, *revisita* respondents showed this series to be a real-life component of their village's naming pool.

Female name 1, Paltacha or Cochucha: In Chapter 13 these names connoting "firstborn female" are equated to Chaupi Ñamca herself,[47] as one might expect from the normal Andean tendency to use the first member of a set as the eponym of the whole set. The name Paltacha occurred only twice in the 1588 *revisita*. The Checa synonym Cochucha was not found.

Female name 2, Cobapacha: This name connoting "secondborn female" was equated to the names Copacha and Llacsa Huato among the Checa. Coba Pacha was attached to the cult described in Chapter 13 as one of the Chaupi Ñamca-affiliated *huaca*s resident in Chillaco (adjacent to Sisicaya).[48] It was her cult and female priesthood which Don Diego Chauca Guaman allegedly protected. In 1588 only one woman named Copacha was found.

Female name 3, Ampuche: The thirdborn female *huaca* Ampuche is also called Ampuxi and Mira Huato in Chapter 13.[49] This chapter groups her with Copacha/Llacsa Huato as one of the shrines worshiped by people seeking remedies for illness.

Variants of this name were quite common in Sisicaya in 1588: the *revisita* found 33 women bearing them (1 Ampo, 1 Anbo, 25 Ambos, 2 Ambochas, 2 Amboches, 1 Anpucha, and 1 Ambucha). Only five (15.2 percent) were of highland *ayllu*s. Since 23.3 percent of the people in Sisicaya were of highland *ayllu*s, the name was weighted in favor of Yunkas by a modest margin.

Female name 4, Sullcacha: Sullcacha, also called Xullca Paya and, in the Checa onomasticon, Lluncho Huachac in Chapter 13,[50] was said to reside at a shrine in a remote part of Huarochirí Province, near Canta. So it is not surprising that only one woman of Sisicaya bore her name.

Female name 5, Ecancha: Ecancha (or Ecacha),[51] the "fifthborn female" whose position parallels that of Llata on the male side, is not detailed in the explanation of Chaupi Ñamca's shrines as understood in Checa (Chapter 13), nor did she have any namesakes in Sisicaya.

Female name 6, Añacha or Añasi: The tellers of Chapter 13 took a considerable interest in the sixthborn female *huaca* whose position paralleled the male Ami.[52] She was equated with Cahui Llaca, the female *huaca* whom Cuni Raya impregnated in Chapter 2.[53] She is said to live in the sea. Her physical body may have been one of the guano islands in the Pacific near the mouth of the Lurín. Añacha had 12 namesakes in Sisicaya in 1588. Ten (83.3 percent) were of Yunka *ayllu*s.

Conclusions about the Birth-Order Onomasticon

Pulling together these findings about birth-order names and adding in observations based on the ages of those who bore them, yields several conclusions.

First, the superhuman birth-order onomasticon captured in 1608 had indeed been in common use for naming human beings since at least 1530. In fact, 38 percent of all the people living or dead mentioned in the *revisita*, had names using its elements.

Second, such naming was in 1588 a thriving, not disappearing practice. In fact, beginning in 1538, in the early years of the Spanish invasion, birth-order naming steadily rose. For males aged 50 or more, only about 37 percent had birth-order names. But by 1576, 68 percent of the male children had been given birth-order names. The sharpest rise in naming practice seems to have occurred around 1538. Though the birth-order naming of females cannot be tracked with the same precision because of the absence in the *revisita* of ages for females, a similar pattern of increased usage also is evident between female adults and female children.

The trend would seem to indicate that the synthesis of *huaca*s from the coast all the way up to the sierra into a unified scheme homologous with intra-family hierarchy, was in the ascendant—perhaps even a popular novelty—during Inka and post-Inka times.

Third, the use of birth-order names was markedly gender-unequal, with a heavy tilt toward males. Many more males than females had birth-order names, and the names males bore signaled higher birth rank than those females bore. In other words, to signal birth rank for girls, and especially senior birth rank, was apparently considered less desirable than to do so for boys.

Fourth, the birth onomasticon was predominantly a Yunka custom, but highland *ayllu*s also used it to some degree. Its acceptance may be an example of "Yauyo" highlanders' eagerness to absorb prestigious Yunka social forms as part of their terms of complementarity.

A fifth point concerns how firmly use of these names really reflects birth order. (After all, it is possible that birth-order names stayed in circulation after losing their original denotation.) This is hard to ascertain because the *revisita* only tells us about living children. The issue was addressed by analyzing birth-order names with demographic reconstruction methods that assign a birth order to male and female children based on their known ages, average spacing of births, and the age of their father. The results reveal a strong covariance between a birth-order name and a child's actual birth order, with some differences among *ayllus*. The Quechua source leaves doubt as to whether birth order means rank within gender (e.g., thirdborn among the sons) or across gender (thirdborn of all children, a son). Statistical analysis favors the latter reading, with qualifications.[54]

Sixth and last, the total name pool is much bigger for adults than children. Girls had only 89 different names while women had 254. Boys had only 130, while men had almost three times as many (361). Was the rise in birth-order naming, along with the assignment of Spanish given names, depleting over time a pool of native names? Or was there some tendency for people to stop using their birth-order names later in the life cycle, perhaps because they had ritually received other names? Ritual bestowal of names on persons is mentioned three times, as well as twice for groups, and twice even for llamas.[55]

Gender Imbalance and the Birth-Order Onomasticon

We turn now to a closer study of observation three, namely the gender-skewed usage of birth-order names.

Taken simply as a structure, the birth-order onomasticon reflects a clear ideology of gender symmetry. If its actual implementation were also gender-symmetrical, one would expect to find similar frequencies across sex for the first rank, for the second, and so forth, with declining absolute frequencies as rank declines (because there are at any given time more first children than sixth, and so on). Demography belies this prediction.

Unexpectedly, the birth-order name set was applied to males much more than to females. Table 2.2 shows their incidence among those living in 1588. Of the living males, 214 had birth-order names, and 47 females, so only 18 percent of people with names from the divine paradigm were female. The pattern changes little if one includes the named dead.

In a later section we will explore why an ideally symmetrical matrix was applied so asymmmetrically.

Naming anomalies go together with other, similar irregularities. These irregularities are similar insofar as they bring together parallelism and symmetry in gender *structures*, with *numbers* that call in question equitable implementation.

First of all, there are simply not enough females. The 1588 *revisita* underreports females in a variety of ways. Female ages are not given for either adults or children. Women's deaths were grossly underreported (only 25 percent of the attested dead being female).

Table 2.2 Incidence of the birth-order onomasticon by sex among living persons in **Sisicaya** in 1588

Rank of name	Number of males	Number of females
1	60	1
2	65	1
3	38	31
4	32	2
5	13	0
6	6	12

A striking disparity occurs in the ratio of male to female children. One would normally expect to see an approximate 50/50 split between the children of any age. The Sisicaya ayllus show 59 percent of living children male and 41 percent female. The adult population was 53 percent male to 47 percent female, also substantially abnormal because in normal adult population, females, not males, hold a majority (by about 3 percent).

The scarcity of females with names suggesting firstborn or second-born status thus occurs together with a shortage of females overall and especially young ones. Were girls born early in the family cycle being hidden, done to death in some way, or sent or taken away? N.D. Cook (personal communication) points out that the practice of putting young females out to work as domestic servants or to become laborers in the *mita de plaza* subtracted many females from Huarochirí's resident native population.[56] But then one wonders why such girls and women were not mentioned among absentees. In a society both depopulating and inclined to endogamy, it is hard to imagine girls being married out or given for adoption. Perhaps some daughters were hidden.

What is clear is that, ca. 1588, Sisicaya society combined gender-parallel cultural structures with major sex inequalities in acknowledged population. If the females missing from the record were missing in fact, some demographic trend was specifically prejudicial to female survival within the community.

While (mostly male) birth-rank naming increased after 1570, girls were becoming scarcer or at least less commonly resident at home, and received lower birth-rank names. Apparently Sisicaya households de facto favored family strategies with elder sons conspicuously positioned to defend hereditary rights in the "man's world" of colonial society. Perhaps a colonial bias in favor of male primogeniture was making high-birth-rank female names less useful. The picture as a whole reminds us that a "shrinking web"[57] of kin-based society was the real-life setting of mythic discourse toward 1600.

The Names of the Ancient Progenitor-Deities:
A Countertendency and an Enigma

How do birth-order names compare with other kinds of names? The contrast is striking.

Among female names, the most common one by an enormous margin was Maclla, which has no place in the birth-order onomasticon; 23.6 percent of girls and 24.8 percent of women had this name. Maclla does however have a very important place in the Huarochirí manuscript. In explaining the cult of Chaupi Ñamca, the first point the narrator saw fit to make is that Hanan Maclla, which means "High" or "Upper Maclla," was a primordial *huaca*: the Sun's wife.[58] She gave birth to both Paria Caca and Chaupi Ñamca. That is, she was the mother of both of the two apical deities who frame the whole mythology.

Maclla's name was about equally popular among Yunka and highland sectors. Unlike the colonially growing birth-order names, Maclla names were already popular in 1530 and remained steadily popular. About 14 percent of the 84 Macllas were first or secondborn.

Does anything parallel exist on the male side? The Sun, Hanan Maclla's mate, has well-known Quechua cultic names (Punchao and Inti in colonial spellings). These were not given to humans in Sisicaya. We do find a conspicuously Aymara name, Vilca, which Bertonio mentions as meaning "sun...among the ancients."[59] Given the known prevalence of Aymara-related language among highlanders, we can take this name as a solar allusion. But Vilca's name is nowhere near as common as his consort's. Of the males, living or dead, 30 names contained the morpheme Vilca. Though this makes Vilca a strikingly popular name, its incidence in the male population is only about one-third as great as that of Maclla among females. Like Maclla, Vilca occurs about evenly across age groups. Unlike it, it occurs unevenly across *ayllus*. About half of Vilcas were of highland *ayllu*s, while these groups made up a scant quarter of population, suggesting a persistent Aymara tilt in upland onomasticon. And, also interestingly, Vilca contrasts with Maclla in its relation to birth order. Not one Vilca was first or secondborn.

Maclla's superior popularity on the female side, then, suggests that Maclla's standing as the mother of the mythic totality, the female emblem of overarching cosmological unity, was very salient in the imagination of Yunka-dwelling people including those with highland affiliations.

It is as if the population were reluctant to assign girls names high in the birth order of the cultically active *huacas* and more ready to do this for boys, yet had opposite feelings regarding the names of the ancient progenitive powers. They gave more girls than boys a name evoking the remote source of all divinity. And they gave such names to higher-ranking girls.

Some Concluding Inferences

The Sisicaya *revisita* of 1588 describes the mid-Yunka coca village to which the Quechua narrator(s) of the 1608 (?) Huarochirí manuscript paid closest attention. Sisicaya in ca. 1588 had been a basically Yunka village of four *ayllu*s into which six small *ayllu*s of highland origin were inserted. The latter were affiliated to upland villages, which in turn belonged to four Inka "thousands." Within the mythic-ritual schema that dramatized this constellation, Sisicaya Yunkas were seen as connected to the female apex (Chaupi Ñamca) of a male-and-female pantheon. The mythological image of a far-reaching integration between highlanders and Yunkas does find confirmation insofar as the *revisita* shows Yunka *ayllu*s and those derived from highland invaders using heavily overlapping pools of personal names. A fund of shared culture was still in voluntary practice ca. 1588. The common onomastic pool seems all the more significant as an indicator of shared ritual culture, because the local peoples had different linguistic heritages.[60] People of the region especially considered birth-order names as ethnic shibboleths. That they shared the system indicates overlapping identities. When the time comes for a more concertedly linguistic study of the above dataset, it should be possible to trace morphological interference effects among the coexisting languages (as Cerrón-Palomino has done with the supposedly Inka but latently Aymara triad *collana—payan—cayao*).[61] This would yield a clearer idea of just how the commonalities had taken shape before 1588.

Although birth-order naming underlined a pervasive cultural concern with gender parallelism, toward 1588 the scheme was not applied equitably. Many more males than females had birth-order names. Females hardly ever received names implying high birth rank.

This fact is related to demographic disaster, as the 1608 myth-tellers knew when they said "*yuncacuna collon*" ("the Yunkas are perishing").[62] For brevity, we omit analysis of demographic change in Sisicaya. One finding is that the period leading up to the composition of the Huarochirí manuscript saw relatively bearable losses for Repartimiento Huarochirí as a whole, but within this picture the Yunka village of Sisicaya village suffered a fearsomely steep rate of loss. Sisicaya had lost 15.6 percent of its people between 1579 and 1588 (compared to 2.14 percent of tributary population for Huarochirí as a whole). Adjustment for female underreporting reveals a loss of 22.5 percent in not even ten years. Don Diego Chauca Guaman, later a protagonist in the Huarochirí Quechua text, said no more than the truth when he wrote that "being Yunka Indians, we are quickly diminishing day by day" (f.19r-v).

The self-image that the Huarochirí Quechua text expresses is that of a damaged society. Huarochirí still saw itself as based on articulation of invader-descended groups with aboriginal Yunka groups. But the actual places at which this articulation remained the daily work of politics—that is, *chaupi yunkas*[63] like Sisicaya—had been tranformed by demographic, social, and economic disaster.

As of 1588, then, a stark contrast separated cultural schemata of gender symmetry from an organizational reality that was anything but symmetrical. The Yunkas, the symbolically female part of society, were disproportionately dying off; female demographic losses were disproportionately high within Yunka losses; and of those females who survived, disproportionately few were given high-ranking names.

Yet although Sisicaya from the conquest to the 1580s gave few of its daughters names marking high *sibling* rank, it did give an enormous number of them a name reflecting high *maternal* rank. It did so by conferring the name of Maclla on nearly a quarter of its females. The immense popularity of this female name—far outstripping any of the female names in the birth-order paradigm—suggests that females were deeply associated with a primordial state of the world rather than with actuality. The female side of divinity seems to have been associated with *illud tempus*—with remote, ancient, original genesis, a time prior to current distinctions of rank, and prior to the collapse of the female side of society.

An enigmatic detail is that 72 percent of adult Macllas were married to men with birth-order names—about twice as many as one would expect given the ratio of male birth-order names compared to all male names. When the gender-symmetrical paradigm lost cogency as a model for practice, was primordial female legitimacy considered an alternative complement to male eminence?

Or could Maclla-naming have expressed a colonial reinterpretation of female *huaca*s? Did "High Maclla," mother of *huaca*s, retain her popularity because she could be cast as "mother of God[s]" in response to the burgeoning of Marianism? Among *yndios* as well as Spaniards the later sixteenth century saw a flowering of cults to Christendom's mother-goddess. Maclla might have seemed a pre-Hispanic analogue to María, similar even in pronunciation. (In Quechua, the Virgin's name has initial stress: *Márya*.) This might reflect a Huarochirí instance of the common heterodox belief that biblical history had taken a parallel course in pre-Hispanic America.

From this exercise we draw a clearer and more nuanced idea of what people were talking about when they explained their society in terms of its huacas. At the turn of the seventeenth century, the gender-pairing of *huaca*s still expressed a template for ideal biethnic structures. But it was expressed at a moment when the practical balance of biethnic, gendered complementarity was failing. Tellers poignantly adored the mystique of fertility while fertility collapsed, especially among the Yunkas. They voiced reverence for femaleness while females disappeared. Once one knows this, one knows that the myth-tellers were talking about themselves in quite a pointed way. Although the Quechua stories unfold in a glittering realm of heroes and miracles, they also implicitly reflect a harsh and timely realism.

Notes

1. William H. Isbell, *Mummies and Mortuary Monuments. A Postprocessual Prehistory of Central Andean Social Organization* (Austin: University of Texas Press, 1997).

2. Frank Salomon and Sue Grosboll, "Names and Peoples in Incaic Quito: Retrieving Undocumented Historic Processes through Anthroponymy and Statistics," *American Anthropologist* 88:2 (June 1986), 387–99.

3. Pierre Duviols, "Huari y Llacuaz: Agricultores y pastores, un dualismo prehispánico de oposición y complementariedad," *Revista del Museo Nacional* 39 (1973), 153–91; Duviols, "Sumaq T'ika. La Princesse du village sans eau," *Journal de la Société des Américanistes* 63 (1974–76), 153–98.

4. Joyce Marcus and Jorge E. Silva, "The Chillón Valley 'Coca Lands': Archaeological Background and Environmental Context," in María Rostworowski de Diez Canseco (ed.), *Conflicts over Coca Fields in XVIth-Century Peru* (Ann Arbor: University of Michigan, 1988), pp. 1–32; Elías Mujica, *"Altiplano-*Coast Relationships in the South-Central Andes: From Indirect to Direct Complementarity," in Izumi Shimada, Craig Morris and Shozo Masuda (eds.), *Andean Ecology and Civilization: An Interdisciplinary Perspective on Andean Ecological Complementarity* (Tokyo: University of Tokyo Press, 1985), pp. 103–40; John V. Murra, "El control vertical de un máximo de pisos ecológicos en la economía de las sociedades andinas," in John V. Murra, *Formaciones económicas y políticas del mundo andino* (Lima: Instituto de Estudios Peruanos, 1975), pp. 59–115; Yoshio Onuki, "The *Yunga* Zone in the Prehistory of the Central Andes: Vertical and Horizontal Dimensions in Andean Ecological and Cultural Processes," in Izumi Shimada, Craig Morris, and Shozo Masuda (eds.), *Andean Ecology and Civilization: An Interdisciplinary Perspective on Andean Ecological Complementarity* (Tokyo: University of Tokyo Press, 1985), pp. 339–56.

5. María Rostworowski de Diez Canseco, "El avance de los Yauyos hacia la costa en tiempos míticos," in Maria Rostworowski de Diez Canseco, *Señoríos indígenas de Lima y Canta* (Lima: Instituto de Estudios Peruanos, 1978), pp. 31–44; Rostworowski de Diez Canseco, "Los Yauyos coloniales y el nexo con el mito," in Maria

Rostworowski de Diez Canseco, *Señoríos indígenas de Lima y Canta* (Lima: Instituto de Estudios Peruanos, 1978), pp.109–22; Alfredo Torero, *El quechua y la historia social andina* (Lima: Universidad Ricardo Palma, 1974).

6. María Rostworowski de Diez Canseco, "Plantaciones prehispánicas de coca en la vertiente del pacífico," in Maria Rostworowski de Diez Canseco, *Etnía y sociedad: Costa peruana prehispánica* (Lima: Instituto de Estudios Peruanos, 1977), pp. 155–95; Rostworowski de Diez Canseco (ed.), *Conflicts over Coca Fields in XVIth-Century Peru* (Ann Arbor: University of Michigan, 1988), pp. 53–81.

7. Karen Spalding, *Huarochirí: An Andean Society under Inca and Spanish Rule* (Stanford: Stanford University Press, 1984); Waldemar Espinoza Soriano, "Agua y riego en tres ayllus de Huarochirí, siglo XV y XVI, " *Actas y memorias del XXXIV Congreso Internacional de Americanistas* (Lima: Pontificia Universidad Católica del Perú, 1981), vol. 3, pp. 147–66; Espinoza Soriano, "Los señoríos de Yaucha y Picoy en el abra del medio y alto Rímac. Siglos XV y XVI. El testimonio de la etnohistoria," *Revista Histórica* 34 (1984), pp. 157–279; Espinoza Soriano, "Huarochirí y el Estado Inca," in V. Thatar A. (ed.), *Huarochirí: Ocho mil años de historia* (Santa Eulalia: Municipalidad de Santa Eulalia de Acopaya, 1992), vol. 1, pp. 117–94. (1981, 1983–84, 1992).

8. Gerald Taylor, "Lengua general y lenguas particulares en la antigua provincia de Yauyos (Perú)," *Revista de Indias* 43:171 (1983), 265–89.

9. Retasa del repartimiento de Guarochiri por Rodrigo de Cantos de Andrada, 1577. Museo Nacional de Historia, Lima (MNH/L). Sin sigla.

10. Padrones de La Paz 13–17–5-1. Revisita de Sisicaya, 1588, henceforward AGN/BA PLP 13–17–5-1. For collaboration in transcribing this document we thank Lorena Toledo and Roberto Matos P. as well as Richard and Shirley Flint, who prepared the final transcription. It is to be published by the Pontificia Universidad Católica del Perú in its series in its series on archaeological studies of the Lurín River basin.

11. Also written Sisicaya, Siçi or Çiçicaya, Zizicaya, Saçi Caya, Çizicaya, and other ways. In the *revisita* it is called Çiçicaya or Sisicaya, and we standardize to the latter form (still in use). Sisicaya village is located at 950 m. over sea level on the bank of the middle Lurín River.

12. Rostworowski identifies the Inka "thousand" of Sisicaya as a population pre-Hispanically affiliated with the supreme coastal shrine complex of Pachacámac and its polity Ychma: *Conflicts over Coca Fields*, p. 72. Patricia Feltham reports an Inka *tambo* at Sisicaya, reflecting its salient position astride an Inka transport route to the shrine: "The

Lurín Valley Project. Some Results for the Late Intermediate and
Late Horizon," in A. Kendall (ed.), *Current Archaeological Projects
in the Central Andes* (Oxford: British Archaeological Reports,
International Series 210, 1984), pp. 45–73, see p. 57. Miguel
Cornejo believes Sisicaya's diversity of mortuary forms reflects the
coexistence of Inka, Yunka, and Yauyo highland populations there,
as does an abundance of local "sanctuaries" with offerings of clearly
Inka ceramics: "Arqueología de santuarios inkas en la Guaranga de
Sisicaya, valle de Lurín," *Tawantinsuyu: Una revista internacional de
estudios inkas* 1 (1995), pp. 18–28, see pp. 22, 25–26.

13. Diego Dávila Brizeño, "Descripción y relación de la provincia de los
    yauyos [1586]," in Marcos Jiménez de la Espada (ed.), *Relaciones
    Geográficas de Indias* (Madrid: Ediciones Atlas, 1965), vol. 1, pp.
    155–65, see p. 160.
14. San Pedro de Mama was a *reducción* village at the site of modern
    Ricardo Palma, in the lower Rímac Valley near Lima.
15. Frank Salomon and George Urioste (ed. and trans.), *The Huarochirí
    Manuscript, a Testament of Ancient and Colonial Andean Religion*
    (Austin: University of Texas Press, 1991), 85/188. In notes to the
    Salomon-Urioste edition of the Huarochirí manuscript, the slash
    separates translation from original text.
16. Ibid., 85/189.
17. que por quipes e dado/ a el dicho coregi*d*or
18. Salomon and Urioste, *The Huarochirí Manuscript*, 80/184.
19. Salomon and Urioste, *The Huarochirí Manuscript*, 85–87/189–91.
20. Chris Pearson, "Birth-order Names in Japan and Papua New Guinea,"
    Far Outliers blog, March 15, 2007, at http://faroutliers.wordpress.
    com/2007/03/15/birth-order-names-in-japan-and-papua-new-
    guinea/
21. Paul Radin, *The Winnebago Tribe* (1923; Lincoln: University of
    Nebraska Press, 1970), pp. 79, 185, 203–4.
22. Jay Miller, "Delaware Personhood," *Northeast Anthropology* 42 (Fall
    1991), 17–27, see 20.
23. Renato Rosaldo, "Ilongot Naming: The Play of Associations," in
    E. Tooker and H. Conklin (eds.), *Naming Systems* (Washington, DC:
    American Ethnological Society, 1984), pp. 11–24.
24. Susan Benson, "Injurious Names: Naming, Disavowal, and
    Recuperation in Contexts of Slavery and Emancipation," in Gabriele
    Vom Bruck and Barbara Bodenhorn (eds.), *The Anthropology of
    Names and Naming* (Cambridge: Cambridge University Press, 2006),
    pp. 178–99, see p. 182.
25. Ronald Cohen, *The Kanuri of Bornu* (New York: Holt, Rinehart and
    Winston 1967), p. 57; Walter E. A. Van Beek, "Becoming Human in
    Dogon, Mali," in Göran Aijmer (ed.), *Coming Into Existence: Birth
    and Metaphors of Birth* (Gothenberg: University of Gothenberg,
    1992), pp. 47–70, see p. 54.

26. Salomon and Urioste, *The Huarochirí Manuscript*, 67/174.
27. At this point, Gerald Taylor (ed.), *Ritos y tradiciones de Huarochirí*, second revised ed. (Lima: Instituto Francés de Estudios Andinos / Banco Central de Reserva del Perú / Universidad Particular Ricardo Palma, 1999), interprets two letters, ys, as "Aydolos (?)". Alternatively, they might mean y[ndia]s.
28. Taylor, *Ritos y tradiciones de Huarochirí*, p. 204, gives as alternate reading "cŏchucha (?)".
29. Ibid., p. 204, gives as alternate reading "(āpuche(?) = ampuche)".
30. Ibid., p. 204, gives "ecacha".
31. Checa *ayllu* bears the name of an Inka "thousand" "reduced" into San Damián and Surco parishes; Lupo that of a group "reduced" in Santa María Jesús de Huarochirí; Quinti that of San Lorenzo de Quinti; Yampilla that of another component of Santa María Jesús de Huarochirí; and Chaucarima that of Santa Ana de Chaucarima, centre of the Inka "thousand" of Chaucarima. The sixth, Papano, was also said in the *revisita* to consist of "serranos" but Papano is not the name of any extant village.
32. As follows: Ayllu Checa in Sisicaya served Don Gerónimo Cancho Guaman (f.32v). He is mentioned three times in Chapter 20 of the Huarochirí manuscript as the father of Don Cristóbal Choque Casa and as *curaca* of the Checa of San Damián. His reputation extending into the Yunka valleys is firmly attested (Espinoza Soriano 1983–84:266–68). Ayllu Quinti in Sisicaya served Don Pedro Llaxa Chari (f.33v). This man is known through 1621 testimonies in a lawsuit from San Lorenzo de Quinti to have been a Toledan "cacique prinçipal" of the Quinti "thousand": Miguel Huaman Chata, cacique, et al., Causas sobre el cacicazgo del pueblo de Quinti, 1596, 23 de agosto –1626, 13 de marzo, Lilly Library Latin American Manuscripts [unnumbered]. He acceded to rule between 1577 and 1579. Ayllu Yampilla in Sisicaya served "Don Sebastián" (f.36r). The man in question is probably Don Sebastián Quispe Ninavilca, paramount chief of the region and the lord of the *reducción* which controlled the highland hamlet of Yampilla, namely, Santa María Jesús de Huarochirí. He is mentioned in Chapters 7 and 19 of the manuscript as a bireligious native ruler.
33. Taylor persuasively suggests that the suffix-*cha* (or, frequently in 1588, -*che* e.g., Curacache) is in most instances an Aymara morpheme (i.e., in the local Jaqaru branch of the wider Aymara language family) and not the Quechua diminutive. It occurs in names of mature people about as frequently as in children.
34. Salomon and Urioste, *The Huarochirí Manuscript*, 75/180 and 74/179.
35. Ibid., 143/243.
36. Ibid., 118/216, 137/234.

37. Ibid., 85/188, 138/236.
38. Taylor, *Ritos y tradiciones de Huarochirí*, pp. 45–47.
39. Salomon and Urioste, *The Huarochirí Manuscript*, 150/248.
40. Taylor, *Ritos y tradiciones de Huarochirí*, pp. 188–89, 190–91.
41. Salomon and Urioste, *The Huarochirí Manuscript*, 86/190.
42. Ibid., 69/175, 91/194.
43. Ibid., 117/216, 119/218, 123/222.
44. Ibid., 67/174.
45. Ibid., 80/184.
46. Ibid., 128/226.
47. Ibid., 85/188.
48. Ibid., 85/188.
49. Ibid., 85/189.
50. Taylor, *Ritos y tradiciones de Huarochirí*, pp. 188–89.
51. In Ibid., pp. 106–7.
52. Salomon and Urioste, *The Huarochirí Manuscript*, 86/190.
53. Ibid., 47/158.
54. For Sisicaya as a whole, names from the birth-order onomasticon correlate slightly better with natural birth order than they do with order-within-sex. But it is likely that birth-order naming was being practiced in slightly different ways among the different *ayllus*. For instance, Llangaçapa's pattern conforms better to order-within-sex while the patterns of Chillaco and Sisicaya ayllus link most closely to natural birth order. As with the increased use of birth-order names after 1538, such variability may reflect societal adaptations to colonial circumstances.
55. Salomon and Urioste, *The Huarochirí Manuscript*, 72, 79, 95, 118, 124, 149.
56. Miguel de Contreras (Noble David Cook, ed.), *Padrón de los indios de Lima en 1613* (Lima: Universidad Nacional Mayor de San Marcos, 1968).
57. Spalding, *Huarochirí*, pp. 168–208.
58. Salomon and Urioste, *The Huarochirí Manuscript*, 84/188.
59. Ludovico Bertonio, *Vocabulario de la lengua Aymara* (1612; Cochabamba: Centro de Estudios de la Realidad Económica y Social, 1984), p. 435.
60. Willem F. H. Adelaar, "La procedencia dialectal del manuscrito de Huarochirí en base a sus características lingüísticas," *Revista Andina* 12:1 (1994), 137–54.
61. Rodolfo Cerrón-Palomino, "Collana, Payan, y Cayao: Los clasificadores de los ceques," in *Voces del Ande. Ensayos sobre onomástica andina* (Lima: Pontificia Universidad Católica del Perú, 2008), pp. 245–59.

62. Salomon and Urioste, *The Huarochirí Manuscript*, 76/181; see also Noble David Cook, *Demographic Collapse: Indian Peru, 1520–1620* (Cambridge: Cambridge University Press, 1981), pp. 145–46.

63. *Chaupi yunka* landscapes are valley bottoms from c. 1,000 or 1,200 meters above sea level. At such middling (Quechua *chawpi*) altitudes, irrigable land combined with a mild climate yields fruit, coca leaf, and many other crops.

Chapter 3

What Was the *Lengua General* of Colonial Peru?

César Itier

In historical sources, the term *lengua general* is applied to what in reality are several different concepts: in some cases, to the entire Quechua language family; in others, to the specific dialect that served as the lingua franca of Tawantinsuyu; in others still, to a collection of dialects that seems to coincide with what modern classifications call "Quechua IIc," to follow the nomenclature coined by Alfredo Torero. This set brings together what are today the dialects of Ayacucho, Cuzco, Collao, the center and south of Bolivia, and Santiago del Estero. Among these uses of the term *lengua general* we might distinguish, then, one "historical" sense (the lingua franca of Tawantinsuyu), and two "modern" ones: the one broad (the entire Quechua family), the other narrow (one dialect, or at most just one set of dialects). Most sources use *lengua general* in this narrow sense.

I shall be concerned here not with what was the lingua franca of the Inca Empire but with the reasons that brought many observers of the language situation in colonial times to identify one particular dialect or set of dialects within the Quechua language family as a *lengua general*. As will become clear, the career of this term as applied to southern Quechua reflects how one of its varieties came to serve, as a result of colonization, as the language of communication both between indigenous populations speaking many different native tongues, and between them and the Spaniards. This inter-ethnic speech community existed above all in the urban and semi-urban network woven by Spanish towns, large and small, and by the *reducciones*. It was by taking on a role of lingua franca that this form of Quechua spread to new regions in the sixteenth and seventeenth centuries. The linguistic innovations that this role brought with it left greater or lesser imprints on the dialects that resulted from this process. Henceforth, I shall use the expression *lengua general* to refer specifically to that variety of southern Quechua II that served as a lingua franca during the colonial period.

Specialists in the languages of the Andes have made various judgements on the nature or very existence of a *lengua general* in the colonial period. For Alfredo Torero "el Quechua General" existed exclusively as the language of Christian proselytism and for promulgating colonial ordinances among Indians who spoke no Spanish.[1]. In 1985, Gerald Taylor proposed that the *lengua general* was actually spoken by Indians associated with the colonial administration, and that the establishment of the *reducciones* even encouraged the language's spread among the bulk of the Indian populace, and thus their adoption of the "mestizo" culture that came with it. Taylor also observes that the language in which the Huarochirí manuscript is composed is the same *lengua general* as is reflected in all pastoral texts of the sixteenth century. Two years later, Rodolfo Cerrón-Palomino made clear his reluctance to concede that the *lengua general* could really have been employed by sectors of indigenous society: once the Incas' administrative and political apparatus had broken down, the lingua franca of Tawantinsuyu would have dissolved and local Quechua languages would have gone back to developing independently, "free of any remodelling" by a lingua franca.[2] In parallel, the clergy had restored a Cuzco-based *lengua general* as the language of evangelization. Yet this must have been an artificial construct, codified "on the basis of abstractions away from both regional dialect diversity and certain registers and sociolects proper to the Cuzco variety."[3] In 2000 and 2001, I presented a number of pointers in favor of the thesis put forward by Gerald Taylor, arguing that the *lengua general* was no artificial language but was indeed widely spoken among the Indians, leaving a deep imprint on southern Quechua dialects.[4] It would appear that the case I set out in those two papers was not well supported enough to convince, for in his monumental study on pastoral Quechua literature, Alan Durston expresses the doubt that the language of the documents composed by Indians could reflect a variety they actually spoke, seeing it more as the outcome of their learning of the standard language developed by the clergy.[5] I shall here present new evidence that a lingua franca of widespread use did indeed exist in colonial Peru.

1. Defining Characteristics of the *Lengua General*

Until the mid-1980s, our knowledge of the state of the language in the sixteenth and seventeenth centuries was limited to pastoral literature (some few thousand pages, of which historians and linguists have made all too little use), dictionaries and grammars that codify the language in which that literature is written, the famous Huarochirí manuscript, and the short Quechua texts included in a few chronicles such as those by Huaman Poma or Pachacuti Yamqui. In recent years this corpus has been enriched thanks to the discovery and publication of texts of another type, generally referred to as "mundane" writings, and composed by Indians or mestizo scribes.[6] From a linguistic perspective, these documents, the Huarochirí manuscript, and much of the pastoral literature of the sixteenth and especially seventeenth centuries are characterized by a series of innovations; but no modern dialect presents all or even most of them. These common innovations appear to me to demonstrate that all of these documents, despite revealing traces of different substrates, reflect a single linguistic tradition; that is, the same variety of Quechua. I shall endeavor to show that this variety resulted from a process of "koineization"[7] among various distinct Quechua dialects or speech forms in urban contexts (Huancavelica, Huamanga, Potosí) that brought together populations of diverse origins.

On the level of sound structure ("phonology"), this variety seems not to have retained the contrast between the two sibilants (roughly, *s* and *sh*) that central Quechua dialects, more conservative in this respect, do still show.[8] Texts composed by Indians never represent this contrast in spelling. Texts written by more learned clerics, such as Francisco de Ávila, a native of Cuzco, in his *Tratado de los Evangelios* (1646–1648), do attempt to represent it, albeit inconsistently, suggesting that it had already dropped out of the spoken language by the mid-seventeenth century. Only a few texts, such as those produced by the Third Lima Council in 1584 and 1585, manage to transcribe this contrast consistently, apparently sticking to a conservative Cuzco norm otherwise already falling out of use. It is more difficult to determine whether one or other variety of the *lengua general* retained the similar contrast between affricates (the simple and retroflex pronunciations of *ch*), since colonial texts never habitually represent it, for lack of any form equivalent to the retroflex form in Spanish.[9] Since no Quechua II dialect, north or south, retains it today, it is probable that it did not exist in the *lengua general* either. In the examples I transcribe below, then, I represent neither of these phonological contrasts. In any case, it is in word structure ("morphology") and lexicon that the *lengua general* takes on its most salient characteristics, as we shall now see.[10]

1.1 Morphology (Word Structure)

(a) A connector suffix *-ri* was created out of the question topic suffix *-ri*, the original use retained in Cuzco-Bolivian Quechua today.[11] In colonial texts, this suffix was equated with the Spanish conjunction *y* ("and") as used to mark the topic of a sentence, and tended to replace the native Quechua system of "discourse tracking.". That is, native Quechua has a fuller set of techniques by which sentences are linked to each other in sequence within a longer discourse: using particles such as *chaymi, chaysi, chayqa, hinaspa* and *hinaptin*; or repeating the verb from the previous sentence in the gerund form:

> *Llama urqukunari hinataq runakta ña qatirirqan*[12]
> **And** the male llamas likewise started to chase the men.

> *Chay qilqapiri allinta ñirqayki...*[13]
> **And** in that letter I told you correctly...

> *Chay wakchari achka mit'ataq ñiq karqan...*[14]
> **And** the poor man used to say time after time...

In the Huarochirí manuscript, *-ri* is often used in combination with the native Quechua discourse tracking system:

> ***Chaysi*** *payri ancha yachaq tukuspa [...] ancha achka runakunakta llullaspa kawsarqan.*[15]

> **So / And** he, by pretending he was some great sage, [...] spent his life tricking so many people.

(b) The *-rayku* suffix was equated with the Spanish causal conjunction *porque* ("because"), whereas in native Quechua *-rayku* denotes specifically the goal for which an action is performed. As it lost its original sense of goal, in the *lengua general -rayku* came to be associated frequently with the perfective nominalizing suffix *-sqa* that denotes an action as already accomplished (in part equivalent to the English *-ed* or other past participle suffixes). This is most unusual in modern dialects, which combine *-rayku* instead with the potential nominalizing suffix *-na*, for actions still to be accomplished.

> *Allqukta kananqa mikuchun runa mikusqan***rayku**.[16]
> (As punishment) **For** having eaten people, now let him eat dogs!

> *Chika uillacos kasqallayki***raykum** *pleytospi kawsasun.*[17]
> We'll always be having disputes **because** you are such rogues.

> *Wakcha uskakuqri alli runa kasqan***rayku** *samaypaq kusikuypaq rirqan.*[18]
> And the poor beggar, **because** he was a righteous man, went off to rest and to be content.

(c) When a verb of motion is accompanied by a second verb to show the goal of that movement, the latter is marked by the infinitive suffix *-y* combined with the benefactive suffix *-paq* (whereas in native

Quechua the second verb would be nominalized by the agent suffix
-q instead, and *-paq* would not be used). This structure is a calque
on Spanish *para* + infinitive.

*Mulaykikta upyachiy**paq** aysanki.*[19]
You take your mule **to** drink.

*Chayman riq karqanku tapukuy**paq**.*[20]
They used to go [to those two huacas] **to** ask them.

(d) The verb suffixes *-yku-* "toward the inside" or "completely" and
-rqu- "suddenly" are rarely used.[21] In the Huarochirí manuscript
the former is generally limited to spatial contexts, in its basic meaning of "into" or "down," and is seldom used in its intensifying
"completely" sense. The *-rqu-* suffix, meanwhile, does not appear
at all in the Huarochirí manuscript, despite being extremely common in modern Peruvian dialects, both central and southern. In
the manuscript, as in many other texts in the general language, the
aspectual value of suddenness is typically expressed by the adverb
tuylla, formed from the phonetically motivated particle *tuy* plus the
limiting suffix *-lla*, probably a creation of the *lengua general* given
that the form does not, to my knowledge, exist in modern dialects.
Here too we have an approach calqued on Spanish.

*Chaysi **tuylla** mancharispa manaña qispinanpas yachakuptin chay
ukumantaqa qayamurqan "yayanchikmi qayasunki" ñispa.*[22]

So **straight away** he got scared, [but] since he could no longer
escape, they called him from inside [the house], telling him: "Our
father is calling you."

*Angelkunari **t'uyllam** kayta ruranqa, hunt'achinqa.*[23]
And **straight away** the Angels will do this, and they will bring it
to pass **at once**.

(e) In all Peruvian dialects except for Collao Quechua the vowel *u* in
the verb suffixes *-kU-*, *-ykU-*, and *-rqU-* systematically changes (dis-
similates) to *a* when followed by any of the other suffixes *-mu-*, *-pu-*,
and *-chi-*; thus for example *-kU-* + *-mu-* → *-ka-mu-*, not **-ku-mu-*.
(By convention these suffixes are cited with *U* in upper case to indicate that the vowel changes in such circumstances.) In most colonial
Quechua texts the vowel undergoes no such change.

ñañaykunawanraq willanakumusaq.[24]
First I'll go to check with my sisters.

taça faltaykita apakumuy qulqipi.[25]
bring it in money, the tax that you're still to pay

Modern dialects would change the *-kU-* to *-ka-* in such cases, to use *willanakamusaq* and *apakamuy*. This vowel dissimilation reflects a need to clarify what are often complex combinations of suffixes within verbs. It is highly improbable that the *lengua general* could be retaining some archaic trait in the Quechua language family here, for to my knowledge all modern dialects of central and central-northern Peru do have recourse to vowel dissimilation. More likely is that the lack of vowel dissimilation in the *lengua general* is an innovation, probably as a result of the morphological impoverishment described in (c): as combinations of multiple verb suffixes became less frequent, vowel dissimilation would have been left as an irregularity that no longer served any purpose. And regularization is of course a typical characteristic of *lingue franche* and koineization.

1.2   Lexicon

(f)   The disjunctive conjunction *manañispa* was created out of the negative particle *mana* and the verb *ñi-* "say" in its gerund form *ñispa*: literally, "not saying," that is, "otherwise said, in other words." Within texts, *manañispa* is used to signal alternatives among various phrases within a sentence, as is Spanish *o* or *o sino* ("or," "or if not," "or otherwise"), where modern Quechua dialects would simply juxtapose the alternative phrases without any such conjunction.

> *Chaysi   maypachach   chay   unanchasqa   pirqanman   chayan chayqa, "kanmi* **manañispari** *"qayam" nispapas "risun" ñin runakunakta.*[26]
> When [the sun] reaches the wall in question, they tell the people that the day has come **or** [that they have to wait] until the morrow.

> *"Manam kawsariy kanchu" ñiqqa wak'amuch'aqmi* **manañispari** *eregem, ninapi ruphachinam.*[27]
> And otherwise whoever denies the resurrection or is an idolater **or** a heretic is to be burnt in fire.

> *Hiq'ipaway paywan huklla /* **manañişpa** *rikuchiway*[28]
> (Either) Drown me with him now / **or otherwise**, let me see him.

(g)   A true adverb *ña* "already" was created out of the particle *ña*, which in modern dialects only ever appears to anticipate and reinforce the suffix *-ña*, used to express the aspectual value of completion. Usage of *ña* in the *lengua general* represents a calque on Spanish *ya* ("already"):

> *Ñam chuquisusup rarqakta pichan.*[29]
> They've **already** cleaned the *Chuquisuso* irrigation canal.

Ñam iskay runa wañun.[30]
Two people have **already** died.

(h) The adverb *ñataq* was created out of the particle *ña* plus the contrastive suffix *-taq*, as a semantic equivalent of Spanish *de nuevo* ("anew," "again") and *otra vez* ("once more," "again"). In modern dialects this combination does not appear as a free-standing word, but only as a sequence of suffixes.[31] Yet the free-standing adverb is found 374 times in Ávila's *Tratado*.

> *Chaysi chay warmiqa **ñataq** ancha nanaqta waqakurqan chaykunakta rikuspa.*[32]
> So when she saw these things, the woman began to weep grievously **again**.

> ***Ñataq** huk mita vacata huk killa waqaychani.*[33]
> **Again** I went back to looking after cows for a month.

(i) The adverb *ñañispa* "sometimes" was created out of the particle *ña* and the verb *ñi-* "say" in its gerund form *ñi-spa* (literally "already saying").

> *Chay pukyus kanan chaypi runakuna chayaptinqa **ñañispa** chinkachin, **ñañispa** locotapas ruran.*[34]
> When people reach this place **sometimes** it makes them disappear, **sometimes** it makes them go mad.

> *suwasqakta maskaspari **ñañispa** tarinki **ñañispari** manataq.*[35]
> and when you look for the stolen goods **sometimes** you find them, but **other times** you don't.

(j) The particle *ichaqa*—which in modern dialects marks a contrast or a warning—is equated with the Spanish adversative conjunction *pero* ("but"); while the suffix *-taq*, the native Quechua technique for marking a contrast between one phrase and another, is dropped. This then opens up the option of using *-taq within* an individual phrase instead, as observed in innovation (h) and in the combination of *-taq* with *huk* to mean (or translate) Spanish *otro* ("other")—see below. *Ichaqa* occurs 208 times in Ávila's *Tratado*, always with the exact meaning of *pero* / "but."

> *Hinataqmi musyasqa tukuy hinantin llaqtakunapipas ruranku. **Ichaqa** kananqa ña qunqan.*[36]
> Confounded [by the devil] they do these things in all the communities. **But** now people are forgetting them.

(k) The conjunction *maypacha* (literally "which moment") was created to introduce subordinate time clauses, on the model of Spanish *cuando* ("when"). Modern Quechua dialects prefer other subordination strategies: the verb is nominalized, for example, using the gerund suffixes *-spa* and *-pti-*; or the two clauses are juxtaposed around an intervening demonstrative *chay* "this," to which a suffix is added to indicate the relationship between them.

> ***Maypacham*** *chay* Mullococha *ñisqanchikta* Churapa Pariacaca*p huqin yaykuspa quchaman tukuchirqan, chaypachas chaymanta* Huallalloqa *pisquhina pawamurqan.*[37]

> **When** *Churapa*, one of the [ones born with] *Pariacaca*, went into *Mullococha* and transformed it into a lake, then *Huallallo*, turned into a bird, flew up and away from there.

> ***Maypacham*** *qam* trigo*kta apt'arispa t'akarinki, saraktapas tarpunki huk'uchap pisquppas ichach mikhunanpaq.*[38]

> **When** you scatter the *grain* over the earth in fistfuls, and sow the maize, you do so at the risk that the birds and the mice will eat it.

(l) The distinction between *tukuy* "all" (expressing totality) and *llapa* "all" (expressing exhaustiveness) tends to be abandoned in favor of the former term for both senses. The Huarochirí manuscript and the Cotahuasi letters record only *tukuy*. Ávila's *Tratado* also prefers this form to express both totality and exhaustiveness, although it does keep a parallel use of *llapa* in some cases. The form *lliw*, used to express totality in modern Cuzco Quechua—Ávila's native dialect—does not appear in the *Tratado*. Everything points to the interpretation that this usage of *tukuy*, and the disappearance from the *lengua general* of the original distinction between totality and exhaustiveness, reflect simplifying influences from Spanish.[39]

1.3 Syntax

(m) Quotations are *introduced* by the word *ñispa* "saying." In Quechua dialects of the continuous zone the gerund *ñispa* (or its dialectal variants) usually *closes* the citation of the direct speech, to separate it off from other words. In the *lengua general* the reverse order is often observed, calqued on Spanish.

> *Kaykunaqa riman* **ñispa** *"unanchanchik ichach ari chay."*[40]
> These speak **saying** "we think it may be so."
> *Qayllaykumuptinri tapurqan* **ñispa**: *imallaktam munanki.*[41]
> And when he arrived he asked [**saying**]: What is it you want?

With the exception of the case of *tukuy*, all of the innovations listed above are to do with discourse structure and cohesion, that is, the system by which clauses are linked to each other within an utterance, and utterances to each other within the discourse. One might add the use of expressions like *huk mita* "one time" or *huk punchaw* "one day," which appear repeatedly in texts in the *lengua general*, in particular in the Huarochirí manuscript, to introduce some particular event after first setting out a general situation. This procedure is not usual in the speech of monolinguals today and also represents a calque from Spanish.

In my view, the above observations necessarily imply that the documents from which the examples have been drawn reflect one and the same linguistic tradition, and that this consisted not only of a written language—for the more erudite and purist a text is, the less these forms and structures appear—but also a spoken one. The changes that characterize it arose as nonnative phenomena in the history of Quechua. The indigenous author of the Huarochirí manuscript, for example, learnt as a second (or third) language a form of Quechua already profoundly restructured by Spanish. Traces of this phenomenon are numerous indeed in the manuscript, where the numeral *huk* "one" is often used as an indefinite article, on the model of Spanish (also as in English *a/an*).

> *Chaysi huk rasu pachakta yayanqa qumurqan.*[42]
> So his father gave him **a** coat of snow.

It follows from the above that *huk* combined with the contrastive suffix *-taq* is what the manuscript employs to express the concept of "other," which native Quechua does not in principle distinguish semantically from "one":

> *Chaypis huk urqutaq rasusapa, mana lluqaypaq,* huamayaco *sutiyuq urqu.*[43]
> There is **another** mountain covered in snows, that cannot be climbed and is called Huamayaco.

2. Historical Circumstances in Which the *Lengua General* Arose

Under what social circumstances do innovations of the type that we have just observed tend to arise? That Quechua suffixes were reinterpreted on the basis of the structure of Spanish, and Quechua terms created as equivalents to Spanish *o, ya, de nuevo, a veces, pero,* and *cuando* (respectively "or," "already," "again," "sometimes," "but," and "when"), implies that the *lengua general* formed or was transformed in interaction between Indians and Spaniards. More precisely, these innovations imply a significant relaxation of the Quechua norm, and considerable input from Spaniards in the emergence of a new one. Historical sources offer a glimpse of a sociolinguistic situation that makes for a plausible context in which a language like that characterized above could have arisen.

2.1 The Colonial City: Cradle Where the
Lengua General Arose

Around 1550, Domingo de Santo Tomás pointed out, in the prologue
to his *Lexicón*, that the *lengua general* had never before been so "generally used almost by everyone" as "nowadays," "because with all the
communication, deals and trade that some have with others, and as
people come together in the Christians' towns and their markets, both
for their own dealings and in service of the Spaniards, in order that
those of different provinces might understand each other, they use this
general language."[44] Indeed thanks particularly to research by Steven
Stern, we know that the Indians very soon opened up to the new commercial economy: no small number of them became artisans or traders,
while others hired out their labor in the new towns or the mines for
wages, so as to gain access to the money economy, and not only to pay
tribute.[45] In the sixteenth and seventeenth centuries, the best way for
an Indian to become wealthy was precisely to engage with the Spanish
economy. This dynamic seems to have been the main driver behind
the spread of the *lengua general*. Some 30 years after Domingo de
Santo Tomás, the Jesuit, Blas Valera, described the same phenomenon
in more detail, signaling the prestige that the *lengua general* enjoyed
among the Indians:

> We see that the common Indian folk who come to Lima or to Cuzco
> or to the Cuidad de la Plata or the mines of Potosí, and who need to
> earn their food and clothing by the work of their own hands, merely
> by constant custom and familiarity in dealing with the other Indians,
> without being given rules or opportunity to speak it, in just a few
> months come to speak the language of Cuzco with great facility, and
> when they return home to their own lands, with this new and nobler
> language that they have learnt they pass for more noble, more sophis-
> ticated and more capable in their understandings; and what they
> most value is that the other Indians of their villages honour them
> and regard them more highly, for this royal language that they have
> learnt.[46]

Also witness to these temporary migrations was Balthasar Ramírez, who
observed that in Cuzco there were "many yanaconas many hatunlunas
who go there on their business, and in service as if in *repartimiento* to the
town."[47] Knowledge of Spanish was of course quite widespread among the
Indians settled in the towns. In Cuzco, for example, seventeenth century
archival documents mention many Indians "able to speak the Spanish language." In the towns, the role of the clergy in spreading Spanish should not
be underestimated, for in principle they were expected to teach it to children. In 1588 Bartolomé Álvarez, the parish priest in Charcas, noted that

he was a contemporary of the first "curacas and sons of curacas who were raised in the priests' home and had learnt Spanish there."[48] Knowledge of Spanish often went hand in hand with some degree of literacy and instruction in Spanish culture, as Álvarez relates with some concern.[49] In the last third of the sixteenth century, many primers in Spanish were circulating among the Indians in Cuzco,[50] suggesting that they were attempting to acquire literacy in that language. It would appear that knowledge of Spanish conferred a position of strength in relationships of social communication.

Furthermore, we know that Quechua was spoken by all or almost all the Spaniards born in Peru itself. In 1653, the Jesuit Bernabé Cobo observed for instance that "in the main those who were born and brought up in this land know the language of the Indians like a mother tongue."[51] Historical testimonies to this effect are innumerable both for central Peru and for Cuzco, Charcas, and Tucumán. Colonial towns were characterized, then, by a tendency toward bilingualism in the *lengua general* and Spanish, certainly highly favorable to language interference of the form described above.

Studies in dialectology and urban linguistics show that dialects that develop in towns, given that they involve much inter-dialect and inter-language communication, are receptive to rapid changes and susceptible of evolving toward simpler morphological and phonological systems, just as their speakers are more attuned to external norms. Indians whose native tongues were different languages within the Quechua, Aymara, or other families appear to have learnt the *lengua general* within a new environment, the town, where the Spaniards stood at the center of the communication network. It was the latter who were thus able to confer their own normative system on the *lengua general*, while its new Indian speakers accommodated to the Spaniards' ways of speaking. The *lengua general* seems to have spread through the semi-urban colonial network (the *reducciones*). At the beginning of the seventeenth century, the Huarochirí manuscript stands as the richest illustration of how Indians appropriated this new variety of Quechua for themselves.

2.2   The Place of the Lengua General within the Family Tree of Quechua Dialects

The *lengua general* was no homogeneous reality. It must have had regional varieties whose specificities probably continued to accentuate as it increasingly gained in popular currency. Moreover, it underwent, under the clergy's pen, various degrees of standardization, which is not my task to address here. Despite this, the *lengua general* did not cease to represent a single linguistic tradition whose dialectal roots should be an object of research. Was it an offshoot of the lingua franca of

Tawantinsuyu? Did it descend from some other pre-Hispanic vernacular variety? Did it arise entirely within the colonial period, out of various sources? Did it derive from Cuzco Quechua? I shall limit myself to one observation on these points.

There is one indication that the *lengua general* did not derive from Cuzco Quechua, even if that dialect may have exerted some influence upon it. A text like the Huarochirí manuscript uses the verb suffix -*pu*- "toward another participant" exclusively to orient the action toward some participant other than the grammatical object, such that a sense of beneficiary can arise:

> *Llamaykiktam nakapunki.*[52]
> You will slaughter one of your llamas **for him** [Pariacaca].

This corresponds to the use of the same suffix in Quechua dialects of central Peru and in modern Ayacucho Quechua. Cuzco Quechua, however, has extended the use of -*pu*- to other functions, very often to indicate also a change to a new state, as a consequence of -*pu*- having taken on the meaning of the completive verb suffix -*xa*- in Aymara, an important substrate of Cuzco Quechua. The use of -*pu*- to indicate a change in state is common in Cuzco texts of the seventeenth century, such as the "auto sacramental" (allegorical religious play) *El robo de Proserpina* by Juan de Espinosa Medrano. In the *Tratado* by Ávila, who had left Cuzco for the archbishopric of Lima in 1592 at the age of 18, -*pu*- behaves as in the Huarochirí manuscript. Only in a handful of fixed expressions such as *ripu*- "leave" or *kawsarimpu*- "resurrect" does it express a change of state. These observations suggest that the colonial *lengua general* originated in a dialect other than that of Cuzco, and one less influenced by Aymara. It remains for future philological inquiry to look into this puzzle.

2.3 Traces of the Lengua General in Modern Varieties of Southern Quechua II

A further question that remains to be researched is the impact of the *lengua general* on local dialects, or its diversification into modern dialects. Again I shall limit myself to a few observations. North of the old Lima-Potosí axis, in the center and central-north of Peru, where there were no Spanish towns or large mining centers in the sixteenth and seventeenth centuries, pre-Hispanic language diversity survived. This is the area where Quechua I dialects are currently spoken. Further south, in the regions of Huamanga, Cuzco, Collao, Charcas, and Tucumán, various traces of the innovations described above are still to be found.

2.3.1 *Ayacucho Quechua*

The so-called "Ayacucho Quechua" today occupies the space that in colonial times was organized around Huamanga. From the sixteenth century on, this town held jurisdiction from the confluence of the Mantaro and Huarpa rivers, to the north, as far as the southern *punas* of Lucanas and the Andahuaylas area. Within this region a trading circuit was established through which production from each zone was brought together in the urban centers, particularly the two main ones of Huamanga and Huancavelica.[53] In the period immediately before Spanish rule, the population of the future *repartimientos* dependent on Huamanga was concentrated in the *puna* zones that extended continuously from Huancavelica to Parinacochas (the provinces of Angaraes, Chocorbos, Lucanas and Soras). The lower-lying valley or *quebrada* zones were populated by *mitmas*, particularly the valley of the Pampas river, wherein stood the Inca administrative center of Vilcas. The Huarpa valley, where Huamanga would be founded, seems to have been little populated in the period immediately preceding the Spanish Conquest, with the majority there also *mitma*,[54] while the town of Huamanga was populated by *yanaconas*.[55] At the beginning of the sixteenth century there does not seem to have been a Quechua-speaking population of local origin in this valley, for in 1542 the *cabildo* of Huamanga indicates that "all the Indians of this province [are] *mitimaes*."[56] The town of Huamanga was thus created as a multi-ethnic settlement with Indians from Chachapoyas and Cañaris, and *yanaconas* from Lurinhuanca, Lurinchilques, Angaraes, Huanacondores and probably other origins too.[57] Still at the end of the sixteenth century, Aymara dominated in the more heavily populated parts of the region, that is, along the western cordillera, in particular in the provinces of the Lucanas and the Soras, even if, according to the *Relaciones Geográficas de Indias*, in some places in both provinces there survived "most ancient and particular" languages.[58]

The data currently available suggest that at the time of Spanish Conquest the presence of Quechua in the area that would later become the ambit of Ayacucho Quechua represented a recent implantation of *mitmas* mostly from further north or from Cuzco. At the present state of our historical knowledge, data on the presence of non-*mitma* Quechua-speakers in the area now occupied by Ayacucho Quechua are very scarce or ambiguous. It remains for future research to ascertain whether a "Proto-Ayacucho Quechua" existed before the colonial period in some part of the area now occupied by Ayacucho Quechua (in the Huarpa valley, or the Andahuaylas region?) or whether this dialect emerged from a coming together of the Quechua speech of the *mitmas* brought by the Incas, the lingua franca of pre-Hispanic times and/or the colonial *lengua general* (to which one must add the Aymara of the high-altitude zones). In any case, Ayacucho Quechua is characterized by having been penetrated, more deeply than Cuzco Quechua, by the structures of Spanish, in ways that recall the phenomena observed here for the *lengua general*. As one example, I might mention the existence of true relative pronouns formed by adding the assertive suffix *-m(i)* to the original interrogative pronouns. (Compare how Spanish and English relatives, such as *como* and *how*, parallel their equivalent question-words *¿cómo?* and *how?*) This creates constructions that do not exist in other Quechua dialects, where the use of the assertive suffix *within* a phrase would run counter to the very structure of the language:

> *Llaqtanchikkunapi yachanchik llapallan llaqtakunapi **imaynam*** preveni*kuyta u **imaynam** kawsayninchikkuna* cuida*kuyta*.[59]
> In our villages we know, like they do in all villages, **how** to guard against it [hail] or **how** to look after the crops we've sown.

Ayacucho Quechua also makes frequent use of the time conjunction *maypacha* "when," which as we have seen is a creation of the *lengua general*, innovation (k) above. This conjunction is so integrated into the local dialect that it can even appear *within* a phrase nominalized by the gerund:

> *Hinaspa **maypacha** lliw chayarikamuspaña riki qaparirun*.[60]
> And **when** the whole show turns up, then they [the thunderbolts] really start howling.

On the level of word structure ("morphology"), Ayacucho Quechua is characterized by a phenomenon almost unknown in Cuzco Quechua: borrowings of Spanish derivational suffixes. The verb suffix *-tya-/-tiya-* "intermittent action" derives from Spanish *-tear*, and the augmentative *-su* from Spanish *-azo*. The impact of the *lengua general* can also be detected in how in the Huamanga area *tukuy* "all, everything" is used largely in expressions whose origins lie in calques from Spanish: *tukuy tuta* from *toda la noche* ("all night"), instead of *tutantin as maintained in other dialects; *tukuy rikchaq* from *toda clase* ("all sorts of"); *tukuy sunqunwan* from *con todo el corazón* ("with all his/her heart"); and so on. Other than in these expressions, Ayacucho Quechua too does maintain the distinction between *llapa* to express exhaustiveness, and *lliw* to express totality.

2.3.2   Cuzco Quechua

The Quechua specialists of the Third Lima Council are most explicit in pointing out that around 1580 Cuzco and its surrounding area were undergoing rapid language change, when they refer to the exceptionally curious way in which **some people** of Cuzco and the lands about it make use of words and expressions so exquisite and obscure as to **step beyond the limits of the language that one would call Quichua proper**, introducing words that by chance were **used in olden times**, and now are no longer, or making use of words **once spoken by the Incas** and lords, or taking them from other nations with whom they have dealings.[61] (Third Lima Council, emphasis added)

As can be seen here, the Council's team excluded from the language of their translation those traits that were most specifically Inca, and this for two reasons. The first was standardization: they banished forms that were too localized, preferring instead alternatives that enjoyed a wider geographical distribution, to ensure that their texts would be understood by the largest possible number of speakers. The second was that these more widespread forms represented a variant of Cuzco Quechua that was undergoing change and was thus distinct from that used "in olden days" by the Incas and continued to some degree by "some people." This new norm was most probably the one that was establishing itself among the urban population of Cuzco, constantly renewed by the input of migrants who hailed from various provinces within the bishopric.[62] In justifying its choice to translate into this type of Quechua, the Council team seems to be alluding to a *questione della Lingua* that was perhaps a matter of some debate at the time. Indeed the lexicographical and grammatical work of Diego González Holguín, produced at the same time as the Third Lima Council's work, represents the opposite choice: his *Gramatica* describes a morphological system much more complex than the one that appears in the texts of the Third Council; and it was the latter's system that would impose itself in Cuzco Quechua over the course of the seventeenth century.[63] As one example, González Holguín describes 24 verb suffixes of which only 15 have survived into modern Cuzco Quechua. The phenomena of simplification and sensitivity to an external norm, already mentioned above, seem to have asserted themselves to the full on the Quechua spoken in the city of Cuzco at the end of the sixteenth century.

That was no doubt what also caused, over the course of the seventeenth century: the replacement of the particle *i* "yes" by the more general form *arí*, its own use calqued on that of Spanish *sí*; the abandonment of the three-way opposition between the gerunds *-sti-*, *-spa*, and *-pti-*, in favor of the simple *-spa/-pti-* contrast; the obsolescence of the *-naq* "-less, without" suffix in favor of a combination of the *-yuq* "with, having" suffix together with the negative particle *mana*; the reversal of some sound changes such as *haqi-* "leave" replaced by the more conservative form *saqi-*; and the abandonment of the vocabulary of limited geographical range that can still be seen in abundant use in the works of Diego González Holguín[64] and Juan Pérez Bocanegra.[65] It is nonetheless interesting to note that these phenomena are not as deep structurally as those that affected the Quechua of Ayacucho and, more powerfully still, of Collao and Charcas.

2.3.3   The Dialects of Collao and Charcas

Sources such as the *Copia de curatos* analyzed by Alfredo Torero show that at the beginning of the colonial period, speakers of Quechua in Collao and Charcas were *mitmas* and *yanaconas* settled in small groups among populations who natively spoke Aymara, Puquina, and Uruquilla.[66] The implantation of *mitmas* in these regions goes back to the Inca period and concerned principally the *quebrada* zones. The Pocona valley, for example, was populated by *mitmas* originally from the Jauja valley. Growing numbers of *yanaconas* was a colonial-era phenomenon bound up with the appearance of haciendas, also in the *quebrada* zones. During colonial times these zones took on great economic significance as suppliers of grain to the towns founded by the Spaniards, in particular Potosí which by the beginning of the seventeenth century had risen to a population of 150,000. It is probably this that explains why Quechua, not Aymara, came to predominate in these towns, and at length spread, at the expense of local languages, into the rural areas that progressively articulated themselves around the towns. Charcas Quechua reached southward as far as Tucumán, Santiago, and Córdoba, cities and regions whose production was also oriented toward Potosí. The timing of this spread of Quechua through Collao, Charcas, and Tucumán remains to be clarified.

The Quechua that spread through these regions split into two branches: that of the northern Titicaca basin, including the north of the present-day department of La Paz, which I shall term "Collao Quechua"; and that of central and southern Bolivia, which I shall term "Charcas Quechua," and which extended as far as Tucumán. The two are sharply distinguished from each other by how they adopted different substrates in different ways. In these areas, Quechua presence in pre-Hispanic times seems to have been even weaker than in the region today covered by Ayacucho Quechua. In Collao and Charcas Quechua we once more encounter some of the innovations identified above in the *lengua general*.

(a) Of all Quechua dialects, that of Charcas alone uses the question topic suffix *-ri* also as a non-question suffix: *Chay señorari nisqa...* "And that woman said..."[67]

(b) Collao and Charcas Quechua use the *-rayku* suffix to mark any type of cause, on the model of the use of *porque* ("because") in Spanish.

(c) In the Collao Quechua of the north of the La Paz department, vowel dissimilation is unknown: *waykurikupunku* "they went back in."

(d) To express totality, the Quechuas of the north of the La Paz and Cochabamba use *tukuy* in all contexts, as in the *lengua general*, and *llihu* or *lliwk*, respectively, in the sense of "extremely." The word *llapa* seems to be unknown in both dialects.

We might also note that Collao Quechua shares with the *lengua general* the use of the *-paq* form of the genitive following a consonant, where Ayacucho and Cuzco Quechua show *-pa*.[68] From all appearances, the Collao and Charcas dialects are directly related to the *lengua general* reflected in Peruvian documents of the seventeenth century.

3. Conclusion

Studies of Quechua historical linguistics and dialectology have failed to take sufficiently into account the complexity of the phenomena entailed by a language spoken for several centuries in a sharply differentiated, multi-ethnic and relatively urbanized society. The *lengua general* seems to have been forged or recomposed in colonial towns, both primary and secondary, through the interrelationship between Spaniards and Indian labor. The former asserted a norm for this language, which the latter then reproduced. With its abundant use of adverbs and the impoverishment of Quechua's verb morphology, the *lengua general* was verging on a significant break with the language's typology. Nonetheless, as it spread to the regions around each colonial town, the *lengua general* became a vernacular and, under the influence of the local substrates of Quechua (autochthonous or *mitma*), of Aymara or of other languages, it seems to have reverted to a more native model, more agglutinating and less analytical. In any case, modern Southern Quechua dialects all entail the mediation of the *lengua general*, as witnessed by the written documents of the sixteenth and seventeenth centuries. Quite what reach the *lengua general* had, in its role as a lingua franca, remains to be studied in detail: for the moment we remain unsure of how far it served as a means of communication between or just within regions, that is, within the bounds determined by the administrative and economic spaces that formed around the colonial towns.

Notes

1. Alfredo Torero, *El quechua y la historia social andina* (Lima: Universidad Ricardo Palma, 1974), pp. 194–95.
2. Rodolfo Cerrón-Palomino, "Unidad y diferenciación lingüística en el mundo andino," *Lexis: Revista de lingüística y literatura* 11:1 (1987), 71–104, see 83.
3. Ibid., 87. *ayllus*

4. César Itier, "Lengua general y quechua cuzqueño en los siglos XVI y XVII," in Luis Millones, Hiroyasu Tomoeda, and Tatsuhiko Fujii (eds.), *Desde afuera y desde adentro. Ensayos de etnografía e historia del Cuzco y Apurímac* (Osaka: National Museum of Ethnology, 2000), pp. 47–59; César Itier, "La propagation de la langue générale dans le sud du Pérou," in Bernard Lavallé (ed.) *Le savoir, pouvoir des élites dans l'empire espagnol d'Amérique* (Paris: Université de la Sorbonne Nouvelle Paris III, 2001), pp. 63–74.

5. "Standard Colonial Quechua was essentially a written medium that was manifested orally through text-based performances. It is not at all clear that it ever spread as a true spoken language, independently of pastoral writing"; Alan Durston, *Pastoral Quechua: The History of Christian Translation in Colonial Peru, 1550–1650* (Notre Dame, IN: University of Notre Dame Press, 2007), pp. 109–10.

6. Willem F. H. Adelaar and Jorge Trigoso Pérez, "Un documento colonial quechua de Cajamarca," in S. Dedenbach-Salazar Sáenz, C. Arellano Hoffmann, E. König, and H. Prümers (eds.), *50 Years of Americanist Studies at the University of Bonn. New Contributions to the Archaeology, Ethnohistory, Ethnolinguistics and Ethnography of the Americas* vol. 2 (Bonn: Bonner Amerikanistische Studien, 1998), pp. 641–51; Alan Durston, "La escritura del quechua por indígenas en el siglo XVII. Nuevas evidencias en el Archivo Arzobispal de Lima (estudio preliminar y edición de textos)," *Revista Andina* 37 (2003), 207–36; Durston, "Native Language Literacy in Colonial Peru: The Question of Mundane Quechua Writing Revisited," *Hispanic American Historical Review* 88:1 (Feb. 2008), 41–70; César Itier, "Lengua general y comunicación escrita: Cinco cartas en quechua de Cotahuasi—1616," *Revista Andina*, 17 (1991), 65–107; Itier, "Un nuevo documento colonial escrito por indígenas en quechua general: La petición de los caciques de Uyupacha al obispo de Huamanga (hacia 1670)," *Lexis: revista de lingüística y literatura* 16:1 (1992), 1–21; Itier, "Las cartas en quechua de Cotahuasi. El pensamiento político de un cacique de inicios del siglo XVII," in Bernard Lavallé (ed.), *Máscaras, tretas y rodeos del discurso colonial en los Andes* (Lima: Instituto Francés de Estudios Andinos / Instituto Riva-Agüero, 2005), pp. 41–71; Gerald Taylor, "Un documento quechua de Huarochirí—1607," *Revista Andina* 5 (1985): 157–85; Gerald Taylor, "Dos mapas del pueblo de Cocha-Laraos (1595, 1597)," *Amerindia* 19–20 (1995), 151–62.

7. The term *koine* is applied to a common language superimposed on a set of dialects or speech varieties in a given geographical area.

8. Huanca Quechua, for example, distinguishes *siqi-* "hang (execute)" from *šiqi-* "strip a leaf from a branch, or the fibre from an agave plant by sliding it off the stem" (Cerrón-Palomino 1976). The traditional spelling <Cuzco> reflects the same contrast between /s/ and

/š/ (ipa /s/ and /ʃ/ respectively) in the Quechua spoken by the Incas, which formerly distinguished the sibilant in *Qusqu* from that in *pišqu* "small bird."

9. The dialects of central Peru retain a contrast in affricates which northern dialects (Ecuador) and southern dialects (southern Peru, Bolivia, and Argentina) have lost, and which reflects a probable contrast in Proto-Quechua between non-retroflex */č/ and retroflex */ĉ/ (ipa /tʃ/ and /ʈʂ/ respectively). Huanca Quechua, for example, distinguishes *čaki* "dry" from *ĉaki* "foot."

10. For simplicity I transcribe examples here only in current orthography, followed by a translation into English by Paul Heggarty, on the basis of both the original Quechua, and the Spanish translation I provided. The latter in some cases was my own translation, in others that given by the editor of the text cited (e.g., by Ávila himself, for all examples taken from his *Tratado de los Evangelios*).

11. The *-ri* suffix in the Huarochirí manuscript and other texts in the "general language" is not directly related to the emphatic *-ri* suffix present in Ferreñafe and Cajamarca Quechua, where it represents a grammaticalisation of the particle *ari* "then." Its use is better explained as a reinterpretation of the Cuzco Quechua *-ri* question suffix on the model of the Spanish conjunction *y* ("and") and its own topic function. Cuzco *-ri* perhaps also developed from *ari*, but its use has been calqued on the model of the Aymara question topic suffix *-sti*. The following example, in modern Cuzco Quechua, clearly illustrates the possibility, for a Spanish-speaker, of establishing a parallel between *-ri* and Spanish *y*: *Wasiykipiri maypitaq puñunki?* "And at home, where do you sleep?"

12. Gerald Taylor (ed.), *Ritos y tradiciones de Huarochirí*, second revised ed. (Lima: Instituto Francés de Estudios Andinos / Banco Central de Reserva del Perú / Universidad Particular Ricardo Palma, 1999), IV: 6. In this and all following references to this same edition of the Huarochirí manuscript, the number in roman numerals identifies the chapter, while that in arabic numerals identifies the number assigned to that utterance in Taylor's edition.

13. Itier, "Las cartas en quechua de Cotahuasi," p. 62.

14. Francisco de Avila, *Tratado de los evangelios, que nuestra madre la iglesia propone en todo el año…* (Lima: Jorge López de Herrera, 1646), p. 8.

15. Taylor (ed.), *Ritos y tradiciones de Huarochirí*, V: 15.

16. Taylor (ed.), *Ritos y tradiciones de Huarochirí*, XVI: 28.

17. Itier, "Las cartas en quechua de Cotahuasi," p. 56.

18. Avila, *Tratado de los evangelios*, p. 9.

19. Francisco de Avila, *Segundo tomo de los sermones de todo el año, en lengva indica, y Castellana, para la enseñanza de los Indios, y extirpacion de sus Idolatrias* (Lima: Jorge López de Herrera, 1648), p. 112.

20. Taylor (ed.), *Ritos y tradiciones de Huarochirí*, XIII: 27.

21. Willem Adelaar has already observed that combinations of verb suffixes are rare in the Huarochirí manuscript, compared to the central and southern dialects (1994: 143).
22. Taylor (ed.), *Ritos y tradiciones de Huarochirí*, XXI: 16.
23. Avila, *Tratado de los evangelios*, p. 29.
24. Taylor (ed.), *Ritos y tradiciones de Huarochirí*, X: 32.
25. Itier, "Las cartas en quechua de Cotahuasi," p. 66.
26. Taylor (ed.), *Ritos y tradiciones de Huarochirí*, IX: 37.
27. Avila, *Tratado de los evangelios*, p. 433.
28. Juan de Espinosa Medrano (César Itier, crit. ed.), *El robo de Proserpina y sueño de Endimión. Auto sacramental en Quechua* (Lima: Instituto Riva-Agüero, 2010), vv. 644–45.
29. Taylor (ed.), *Ritos y tradiciones de Huarochirí*, VII: 14.
30. Itier, "Un nuevo documento colonial," 16 (utterance number).
31. Although Antonio Cusihuamán (1976: 96) records "*ñataq-ñataq.* adv. m. Frecuentemente, una y otra vez." ("Frequently, time and again"), I have not observed any use of this expression in the speech of rural communities in the Cuzco region, but only in texts written by speakers for whom Spanish is their dominant language.
32. Taylor (ed.), *Ritos y tradiciones de Huarochirí*, VI: 33.
33. Petición de Antabamba, in Durston, "La escritura del quechua por indígenas en el siglo XVII," p. 226.
34. Taylor (ed.), *Ritos y tradiciones de Huarochirí*, V: 55.
35. Avila, *Tratado de los evangelios*, p. 107.
36. Taylor (ed.), *Ritos y tradiciones de Huarochirí*, IX: 82–83.
37. Taylor (ed.), *Ritos y tradiciones de Huarochirí*, XVI: 10.
38. Avila, *Segundo tomo de los sermones*, p. 16.
39. Willem Adelaar maintained that there was a close relationship between the Quechua of the Huarochirí manuscript and the dialects of northern Peru. One of the main arguments in favor of this thesis would be the exclusive use of *tukuy*, in the manuscript, to express the concept of wholeness, where both QI and southern QII dialects would use mostly *llapa*, save for Ayacucho Quechua with its contrastive use of *tukuy* and *llapa*. As in the Huarochirí manuscript, in the northern dialects "*llapa-* is unknown as a lexical root, and all of its functions are performed by *tukuy*" (1994: 148). In fact, as we shall see, exclusive use of *tukuy* is not confined to the dialects of northern Peru, for it is found also in the dialect of the north of La Paz department in Bolivia, an offshoot of the *lengua general*.
40. Taylor (ed.), *Ritos y tradiciones de Huarochirí*, IV: 8.
41. Avila, *Tratado de los evangelios*, p. 160.
42. Taylor (ed.), *Ritos y tradiciones de Huarochirí*, V: 85.
43. Taylor (ed.), *Ritos y tradiciones de Huarochirí*, XVII: 7.
44. Domingo de Santo Tomás, *Lexicon, o Vocabulario de la lengua general del Perv*, facs. ed. (1560; Madrid: Ediciones de Cultura

Hispánica—Agencia Española de Cooperación Internacional, 1994). Paul Heggarty's translations of the original texts: "generalmente usada quasi de todos"…"el día de hoy"…"Porque con la communicacion, tracto, y grangerias que al presente tienen unos con otros, y concurso en los pueblos de los christianos, y mercados dellos, assi para sus contractaciones, como para el servicio de los españoles, para entenderse entre si los de diversas provincias, usan desta general."

45. Steve J. Stern, *Los pueblos indígenas del Perú y el desafío de la conquista española* (Madrid: Alianza Editorial, 1986).

46. In "El Inca" Garcilaso de la Vega, (Aurelio Miró Quesada, ed.), *Comentarios Reales de los Incas* (1609; Caracas: Biblioteca Ayacucho, 1976), book VII, chapter II. Blas Valera indicates also that in other provinces the "courtly language" introduced by the Incas had been lost, and "not without great harm to the preaching of the Gospels" (Garcilaso, book VII, chapter I). It is probable that reference was being made here to what is today central Peru, which did not see any spread of the *lengua general*, since it remained untouched by the establishment of large Spanish towns and important mining centres.Original text: "…vemos que los indios vulgares, que vienen a la Ciudad de los Reyes o al Cuzco o a la Ciudad de la Plata o las minas de Potocchi, que tienen necesidad de ganar la comida, y el vestido por sus manos y trabajo, con sola la continuación, costumbre y familiaridad de tratar con los demás indios, sin que les den reglas ni manera de hablar, en pocos meses hablan muy despiertamente la lengua del Cuzco, y cuando se vuelven a sus tierras, con el nuevo y más noble lenguaje que aprendieron, parecen más nobles, más adornados y más capaces en sus entendimientos; y lo que más estiman es que los demás indios de su pueblo los honran y tienen en más, por esta lengua real que aprendieron."

47. *Yanaconas* were Indians who had abandoned their "originary communities" and were the personal servants of Spaniards; *repartimiento* was a grant of Indian labor made to Spaniards by the Crown, levied among the members of originary communities.

48. Bartolomé Alvarez (María del Carmen Martín Rubio, Juan J. R. Villarías Robles, and Fermín del Pino Díaz, eds.), *De las costumbres y conversión de los indios del Perú. Memorial a Felipe II* (1588; Madrid: Ediciones Polifemo, 1998), p. 267.

49. Ibid., pp. 267–70.

50. Juan Carlos Estenssoro Fuchs, *Del paganismo a la santidad. La incorporación de los indios del Perú al catolicismo, 1532–1750* (Lima: Instituto Francés de Estudios Andinos / Pontificia Universidad Católica del Perú / Instituto Riva-Agüero, 2003), pp. 119–20.

51. Bernabé Cobo, *Historia del Nuevo Mundo* (1653; Madrid: Atlas, 1964), p. 403.

52. Taylor (ed.), *Ritos y tradiciones de Huarochirí*, XIII: 56.

53. Jaime Urrutia, *Huamanga: Región e historia, 1536–1770* (Huamanga: Universidad Nacional de San Cristóbal, 1985).

54. Ibid., pp. 23–25.

55. Ibid., p. 46.

56. Raúl Rivera Serna (ed.), *Libro del Cabildo de la Ciudad de San Juan de la Frontera de Huamanga—1539–1547...* (Lima: Casa de la Cultura del Perú, 1966), p. 100.

57. Lorenzo Huertas Vallejo, "Poblaciones indígenas en Huamanga colonial," in Amalia Castelli, Marcia Koth de Paredes, and Mariana Mould de Pease (eds.), *Etnohistoria y antropología andina* (Lima: Museo Nacional de Historia, 1981), pp. 131–44, see p. 138.

58. Alfredo Torero, "Lingüística e historia de la sociedad andina," in *Lingüística e indigenismo moderno de América* (Trabajos presentados al XXXIX Congreso Internacional de Americanistas), vol. 5. (Lima: Instituto de Estudios Peruanos, 1975), pp. 221–59. The name of the province of Chocorbos very probably derives from *chuqi urpu* "golden jar" in Aymara, from which we can also presume that this too was an Aymara-speaking province. The expression *chuqi urpu* likewise appears in the Huarochirí manuscript to designate a ritual object: Taylor (ed.), *Ritos y tradiciones de Huarochirí*, p. 287. Original text: "particulares antiquísimas."

59. Radio Quispillacta, "Llaqtanchikpa sunqun" program, March 18, 2003.

60. Radio Quispillacta, "Llaqtanchikpa sunqun" program, March 18, 2003.

61. Tercer Concilio de Lima, *Doctrina Christiana, y catecismo para instrvccion de los Indios...* (Lima: Antonio Ricardo, 1584), p. 74. Paul Heggarty's translation of the original text: "la demasiada curiosidad, con que algunos del Cuzco, y su comarca vsan de vocablos, y modos de dezir tan exquisitos, y obscuros, que salen de los limites del lenguaje, que propriamente se llama Quichua, introduziendo vocablos que por ve(n)tura se vsauan antiguamente, y agora nò, o aprouechandose de los que usauan los Ingas, y señores, o tomandolos de otras naciones con quien tratan."

62. For the period 1559–1597, Gabriela Ramos observes, on the basis of wills made by Indians as registered in Cuzco, that roughly half of those making their wills came from places other than Cuzco itself, more than half of them from settlements within the bishopric. For the following period, there is a rise in the proportions of those making their wills who were either from Cuzco or from other localities within the bishopric: Gabriela Ramos, "Muerte, conversión e identidad en los Andes peruanos. Lima y Cuzco, 1532–1670," unpublished Ph.D. dissertation, University of Pennsylvania, 2001, pp. 197–98; see also Ann Wightman, *Indigenous Migration and*

Social Change: The Forasteros of Cuzco, 1570–1720 (Durham, NC: Duke University Press, 1990).

63. Diego González Holguín, *Gramatica y arte nveva de la lengva general de todo el Peru, llamada lengua Qquichua, o lengua del Inca* (Lima: Francisco del Canto, 1607).

64. González Holguín, *Gramatica*; González Holguín, *Vocabvlario de la lengva general de todo el Perv llamada Qquichua, o del Inca* (Lima: Francisco del Canto, 1608).

65. Juan Pérez Bocanegra, *Ritval formvlario e institvcion de cvras* (Lima: Geronymo de Contreras, 1631).

66. Alfredo Torero, "Lenguas y pueblos altiplánicos en torno al siglo XVI," *Revista Andina* 10 (1987): 329–405.

67. Yolanda Lastra, *Cochabamba Quechua Syntax* (The Hague: Mouton, 1968), p. 41.

68. The *-paq* genitive appears, albeit not systematically, in the Huarochirí manuscript, the Cotahuasi letters, and the Chipao petition.

Chapter 4

"Mining the Data" on the Huancayo-Huancavelica Quechua Frontier

Adrian J. Pearce and Paul Heggarty

The traditional view of the linguistic prehistory of the Quechua family is founded on the assumption of a fundamental split between two deep branches, Quechua I and II. The validity of this classification is increasingly disputed, however, with critics arguing that the Quechua "Continuous Zone" shows not a split pattern but a dialect continuum, with the "missing link" to be found between the Central (QI) and Southern (QIIc) poles. Nonetheless, the region between Huancayo (southernmost QI) and Huancavelica (northernmost QIIc) provides the strongest evidence for a sharp QI~QII split, in the form of a relatively distinct linguistic frontier (or "isogloss bundle").

This chapter first briefly surveys the linguistic arguments for the transition being rather more gradual than is usually imagined. It then considers how, in practice, an originally more continuous dialect transition in this region could later have been disturbed, so as to leave the more sharply defined linguistic frontier observed today. One scenario that could explain such an effect would be a late and significant demographic movement into the region just south of the frontier, of populations drawn from regions further to the south-east. What historical reality might fit with such a scenario? We here recall and develop an original insight of César Itier, that the colonial *mit'a* for the mercury mines at Huancavelica, just to the south of this frontier, may provide the key.

To investigate our hypothesis in detail we examine colonial draft and census records to assess two key questions. Just how significant was the demographic impact of the drafts, and over which periods within the colonial era? And which regions contributed the highest proportions of draftees to the Quechua-speaking population mix of the Huancavelica area? The result is a case study in just how much both history and linguistics stand to gain from a fuller understanding of the very different data sources that constitute the other discipline's independent "window on the past." By converging these separate perspectives we frame a more complete and holistic vision of the Andean past, a cross-disciplinary whole greater than the sum of its parts.

1. Quechua's Internal Frontier

The Quechua scattered through the Andes, in an arc from southern Colombia to north-west Argentina, is far from a homogenous language. Rather, it is a diverse family of languages and "dialects," many intelligible only partially and with difficulty, or scarcely at all, to speakers of the others. The distribution of these languages is shown in Figure 0.1 in the introductory chapter to this volume.

Across this great expanse, Quechua is generally grouped into four main separate territorial units. From north to south these are: *Northern* (mostly Ecuadoran), *North Peruvian*, *Central*, and *Southern* Quechua. With one exception, each of these units is geographically isolated from each of the others. This isolation of itself offers a first and most immediate explanation for the distinctiveness of each region's Quechua vis-à-vis the others', even if this masks details of their relationships and origins which are in truth considerably more complex.

The exception is to be found within the so-called Continuous Zone of Quechua-speaking territory. This runs for some 1500km, from the northern limits of Ancash, in the north-central highlands of Peru, all the way south to the Lake Titicaca region and the border with Bolivia, where it abuts on the other main indigenous language family that survives in the Andes, Aymara. Roughly in the middle of this Continuous Zone lies a discontinuity, however, an internal "linguistic frontier" where the southernmost forms of Central Quechua, as spoken in the Huancayo region, meet the northernmost forms of Southern Quechua, spoken around Huancavelica. The frontier seems even clearer in the traditional alternative nomenclature, in whose terms this borderline is where the "QI" subgroup abruptly ends, and "QIIc" begins. The nature of this frontier, and how it came to be, are the subject of this chapter.

2. The Distribution and Classification of Quechua: Family Tree or Continuum?

The traditional vision of Quechua follows a "family tree" model of language classification. This is widely recognized to be an idealization of a usually more complex reality in how languages diverge, but in many cases a valid and useful one. In terms of a family's history, implicit in it is an assumed primary, deep-time bifurcation into two main branches, setting the Quechua of central Peru, alias QI, against that of all other regions, QII. The contrast is also sometimes seen as one of Central versus North-South Quechua respectively.

Figure 4.1 reproduces Cerrón-Palomino's[1] presentation of this traditional "family tree," which shows the detail of how North-South Quechua subdivides: roughly, into North Peruvian (part of QIIa), Ecuadoran (QIIb) and Southern (QIIc) Quechua. Note how the well-known Cuzco variety forms just one sub-part of Southern Quechua, alongside the Quechua of the Huancavelica and Ayacucho regions, and that of Puno, Bolivia, and north-west Argentina.

The basis for the primary QI~QII division lies in contrasts on a number of linguistic criteria, elevated to the status of key features "diagnostic" of whether any particular Quechua dialect should be classified as QI or QII (we return later to the circular logic this betrays). Those most commonly taken to define the groups are listed in Table 4.1.

In the decades since it was first proposed, however, the traditional "branching tree" model has increasingly come under fire from many quarters. A series of regional forms of Quechua have been reported on, none of which fit well into the original QI~QII tree. Either the same dialect falls on different sides of the QI~QII fence, from one of the defining criteria to the next; or neighboring varieties, very little different to each other on all other criteria, end up scattered either side of the "ancient" split. Those highlighted in the boxes (with solid edges) in Figure 4.1, for instance, all hail from nearby villages within just a single province of the Lima department: Yauyos.

Taylor's research on the North Peruvian Quechua outposts, traditionally the northern sub-branch of QIIa (the box in dotted outline in Figure 4.1), questioned whether they could really be described as QII at all; he considers them "mixed" QI/QII varieties instead.[2] Meanwhile, work on fast-vanishing Quechua varieties all along the westernmost edge of the middle section of the Continuous Zone, the highlands of the Lima department, revealed many more infelicities in the traditional classification. Features of Pacaraos Quechua set it apart from its "QI sisters."[3] And in Yauyos, Taylor uncovered a veritable "dialectal microcosm" of the wider Quechua family, a sub-continuum that represents nothing less than a "missing link" between the Central (QI) and Southern (QIIc) poles.[4]

Landerman concluded that the QI~QII distinction effectively boils down to a single criterion, of which the first three in Table 4.1 are really just sub-parts.[5] In principle, no one criterion has any greater intrinsic validity than any of the dozens on which regional Quechuas differ from each other, and which would give quite different "classifications."

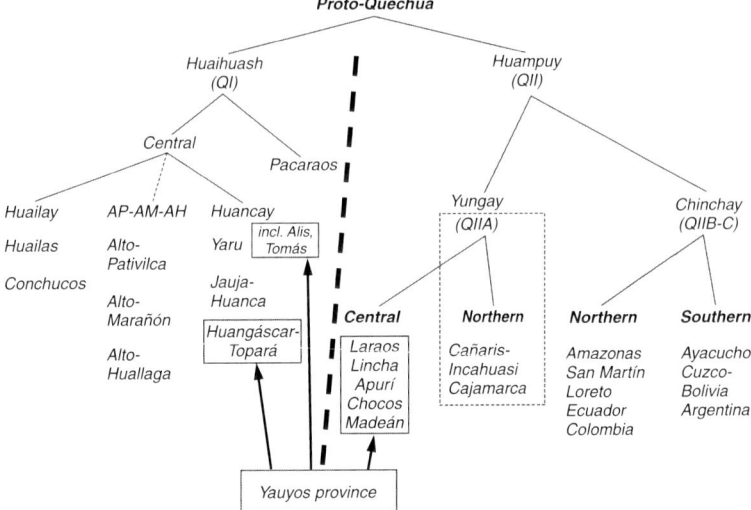

Figure 4.1   The Quechua "family tree"—as per the *traditional* classification (adapted from Rodolfo Cerrón-Palomino, *Lingüística quechua* (Cuzco: Centro de Estudios Regionales Andinos "Bartolomé de las Casas," 1987; reprinted 2003), p. 247.

Table 4.1   Traditional linguistic criteria for the QI–QII "split"

	Criterion	QI (Central) core	QIIC (Southern) core
1.	Long vowels present?	YES	NO
2.	1st person possessor on nouns	–: (long vowel)	–y
3.	1st person subject on verbs	–: (long vowel)	–ni
4.	1st person object on verbs	–ma–	–wa–
5.	Locative suffix	–čaw	–pi
6.	"Ablative" suffix(es)	–piq(-ta)	–man-ta
7.	Progressive suffix	–yka–	–čka–
8.	Same subject subordinator suffix	–r	–spa
9.	Retroflex ĉ merged with č?	NO	YES

Yet for all their criticisms, neither Taylor nor Landerman took his own logic to its ultimate conclusion. Taylor suggests a basic *three*-way, not two-way split for Quechua, while Landerman despairs that there is simply no way to choose between three possible configurations of binary branching tree. The stumbling block is that both their visions remain wedded to the tree idealization. Yet linguistics knows only too well an alternative mechanism by which languages may naturally diverge: the "wave" model, resulting in a geographical pattern of a *dialect continuum*.

To explain this briefly, consider three contiguous regions A, B and C, as depicted in Figure 4.2 below. In the process by which a dialect continuum emerges, a first language change, our "innovation 1", spreads by wave to cover areas A and B, but not area C. Innovation 2, meanwhile, spreads in such a way that it ends up shared by areas B and C, but not A. And a true multidimensional continuum is completed when innovation 3 covers areas A and C, but not B. The three dialect relationships A~B, A~C, and B~C cannot fit *any* tree structure, because the criteria—or on a map, the "isogloss" lines of the three innovations—cross-cut each other. Over time, hundreds of such changes arise and overlap in different waves to leave a fully–fledged progressive continuum. A helpful way to visualise the nature of the continuum is in terms of a color spectrum, or indeed a two–dimensional incremental color palette, such as the traditional "red–yellow–blue" schema for mixing paints, or the "red–blue–green" (RBG) palettes typically used for selecting particular hues in computing. It is a simple matter to tell apart distant points within the palette that are prototypically red, yellow or blue; but not to identify any particular cut–off point or "frontier" between them, across the gamut from "prototypical" yellow through countless incremental hues to green and ultimately to prototypical blue. Likewise, while it is simple to distinguish a prototypical Ancash variety of QI from the variety of QIIc spoken in distant Cuzco, the forms of Quechua spoken in Yauyos are very much intermediate, and fall neatly into neither QI nor QII.

Across a dialect continuum, what accounts for the degrees of closeness between the speech of the various sub-regions within it is not how long ago a binary "split" happened, because there never was any such event, but how coherent the speaker communities across that continuum remained through time. Simple geographical distance typically serves as a rough proxy for this, such that more distant regions end up more different from each other in their speech, closer ones less different.

3. Why Does It Matter for Archaeologists or Historians?

For the readership of this book, the question is why a debate internal to linguistics about classification models should matter to those outside the discipline. For (pre)historians, the value lies in how the classification of a language family is tantamount to a record of past forces—demographic, social, and cultural—that acted upon the populations that spoke it; with good reason the sub-discipline is known as "comparative-historical" linguistics, for these two components go inseparably together. Opposing models of Quechua classification correspond in principle to different visions of the prehistory of the entire Continuous Zone (and

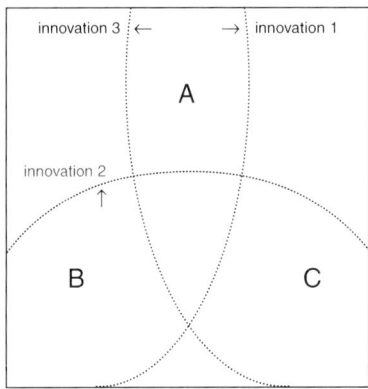

Figure 4.2   Schematic representation of how a dialect continuum arises through *cross-cutting* language changes ('innovations') spreading in waves to overlap differently with each other. Even after just three changes, the actual relationships between dialects A, B and C cannot validly be represented by any branching tree.

the Quechua pockets of northern Peru), and to different explanations for how the frontier between Huancayo and Huancavelica came into existence.

Indeed, aside from the linguistic data per se, a quite separate dissatisfaction with the traditional classification lies in the many infelicities that it seems to have forced upon Torero's model for setting Quechua (and Aymara) prehistory into the real-world contexts in which their speakers lived. His primary QI~QII branch requires that the original Proto-Quechua-speaking population split relatively early into two groups, who migrated apart from each other into geographically distinct secondary homelands: more northerly for Proto-QI, more southerly for Proto-QII[6]; see also the map by Cerrón-Palomino.[7] These two branches then developed in isolation, acquiring their own distinct variant forms on each of the key criteria listed in Table 4.1. Eventually, one or both of these speaker populations expanded further, until the two eventually met at a line between Huancayo and Huancavelica.

Certainly, this scenario would neatly account for a fault-line between already differentiated QI and QII forms of Quechua. It does not, however, explain the Yauyos continuum, nor the Quechua outposts of northern Peru. Above all, the proposed links with polities in the archaeological chronology are beset with contradictions and mismatches of scale, on each of the levels of geography, chronology, and causation. To account for the series of branching events in his tree, Torero has to imagine an intricate sequence of migrations that force him to extend his initial chronology for Quechua, and associate major language expansions with relatively small-scale polities such as Cajamarquilla (QII), or not clearly with any at all (QI). The one most powerful polity, meanwhile, unquestionably in the right place at the right time, is the Wari Middle Horizon, but Torero assumes it was *Aymara*-speaking, contradicting widespread recognition that across much of the Continuous Zone Quechua has spread over an Aymara *sub*strate, not the reverse.[8]

Together, these objections have led Beresford-Jones and Heggarty[9] to advocate a radical new departure for both the classification and external history of Quechua. They argue that the time has come to bite the bullet, and definitively abandon the branching tree model for Quechua, and the now 45-year-old terms and concepts of QI and QII. Instead they propose a single expansion and a dialect continuum model for the entire Continuous Zone, with merely some *later* bundling of isoglosses between Huancayo and Huancavelica.

This prompts and paves the way for a complete revision also of the prehistory of the major language dispersals of the Andes, and how they correlate with the material culture record. Above all, Beresford-Jones and Heggarty associate the Wari Middle Horizon with Quechua, suggesting that Aymara had been spread *earlier*, perhaps by the Chavín Early Horizon. Quechua did *not* divide into two separate Proto-QI and Proto-QII units; rather, Wari alone dispersed its Proto-Quechua in just a single and largely contemporaneous expansion, across the extent of its direct control, which moreover makes for an uncannily close match with the Quechua Continuous Zone. Over the centuries since, regional divergence would have gradually increased across this continuous Quechua-speaking territory, as per the standard dialect continuum model. The significant difference between the distant prototypical Central and Southern poles thus reflects not separate migrations and chronologies, but the usual process by which degree of coherence and interaction between speaker communities is largely a function of the sheer geographical distance between them. The Yauyos "sub-continuum" fits perfectly into this framework, which also offers a new explanation for the "mixed" character of North Peruvian Quechua varieties—or rather, their failure to fit well into either QI or QII. They would derive from outposts of Wari control in the far north, such as Cajamarca, isolated beyond the Continuous Zone and which thus developed more idiosyncratically.

Obviously, this radical break with existing thinking calls for a thorough and detailed justification of many issues in both linguistics and archaeology, for which we direct readers to the longer account in Beresford-Jones and Heggarty.[10] Here we focus on just one key issue, the pattern that a dialect continuum model seems to leave unexplained: the relatively sharp linguistic discontinuity at the Huancayo-Huancavelica "frontier." For this is where the interest for historians lies, since it is historical records that may hold the answer to the conundrum.

4. Central versus Southern Quechua: Frontier or Transition?

A first question to clarify is just how sharp this supposed "frontier" actually is. The core criteria listed in Table 4.1 certainly establish a clear contrast between Central and Southern *poles* of the Continuous Zone, and do usefully define the *prototypical* configurations of each. Other than for these few criteria, however, neither of the two sub-zones can be considered remotely homogenous on countless other important linguistic criteria.

On the contrary, each sub-zone is itself a dialect continuum. Cerrón-Palomino could hardly be more categorical on this for the entire span from Ancash through Huánuco and Pasco to Junín, including Huancayo: "the cross-cutting of isoglosses that characterizes [all Central Quechua bar Pacaraos] makes it impossible to use the tree model, even schematically."[11] Southern Quechua is often so described too, not least as regards the transition in the importance of aspirated and ejective consonants absent in Huancavelica and Ayacucho, but found progressively more significantly through Apurímac and into Cuzco, and strongest of all in the far south.

In all these respects, then, the Continuous Zone does indeed resemble a prototypical dialect continuum. The only objection concerns the nature of the pattern in the areas *between* the Central and Southern zones: a sharp frontier, or a gradual transition? If one plots on a map the dividing lines in the use of the variant forms on each of the criteria in Table 4.1, do these various "isoglosses" coincide in all changing at once and together along the same geographical fault line? Or do they change one by one across an extensive area?

The answer, it turns out, is a bit of both. Certainly, on the eastern side of the QI~QII "crossover zone," between the cities of Huancayo and Huancavelica, the frontier is relatively sharp: most of the traditional diagnostic criteria do form an "isogloss bundle." Following our color analogy, Central Quechua yellow to the north runs up sharply against Southern Quechua blue to the south. Immediately to the west, however, in the highland interior of the southern half of the Lima department, lies none other than the Yauyos province. Here is where Taylor and Landerman stress that the traditional diagnostic criteria form anything but a bundle, but on the contrary map as a sequence of spaced out isoglosses. "Central" fades only gradually and imperceptibly into "Southern" Quechua, with nowhere that one could unequivocally pinpoint as where the "border" between them lies. Here, our Central yellow fades but gradually into Southern blue, through progressive shades of

"Intermediate Quechua" green. Yauyos (and neighboring parts of Junín and Ica) present a string of dialects recalcitrant to an unequivocal classification as either QI or QII.

The overall pattern, then, is of an isogloss *bundle* to the east, which as one moves west toward Yauyos unravels into a continuous *fan*-shape, a typical configuration in dialectology. The Quechua pattern is directly reminiscent of the famous "Rhenish Fan" that defines the extended transition from Low, through Central, to High German: again, a sharper bundle to the east, but a smooth continuum to the west. Similarly, the contrast across France between northern *oïl* and southern *oc* dialects is a bundle to the west, but splinters into the Franco-Provençal fan to the east. In Iberia too, an archetypal continuum across the north, from Galicia to Catalonia, resolves progressively as one proceeds southward, into bundles that delineate more sharply Portuguese, Castilian, and Catalan.

In each of these cases where the underlying history *is* known, the fan pattern does *not* go back to two groups separating, developing apart and then later coming "back" together at a frontier. On the contrary, both France and Iberia were settled largely contemporaneously by speakers of the same ancestral Latin, without significant division. Only later, as the centuries went by, did this gradually diversify into a dialect continuum, within which isoglosses came to cross-cut, fan, or bundle. These various patterns are generally assumed to develop in line with whatever local geographical and political configurations determined the exact degrees of interaction and coherence between speech communities across the continuum. Isoglosses typically bundle where language changes spreading across a continuous territory come up against some "fault line," across which the degree of contact between neighboring populations is relatively limited: a geographical obstacle, or an ethnic, cultural, or political dividing line.

In France, though, despite several proposals, it remains unclear quite what underlies the *oïl~oc* isogloss bundle; nor should it be overstated how sharp a linguistic frontier it really represents.[12] In Iberia, correspondence with political factors is clearer, though population movements doubtless played a role too. As the *Reconquista* fought gradually southward, its *three* northern poles of Galicia, Burgos (then Toledo/Madrid), and Catalonia led to an increasingly clear *three-way* bundling of isoglosses between Portuguese, Castilian, and Catalan. The Rhenish Fan, likewise, is not taken as continental West Germanic splitting into a deep Low versus High German branching tree, but a dialect continuum through Central German, which sharpened only to the east with the progressive expansion of the early Mediaeval *Ostsiedlung*.

In the light of these known precedents, the Yauyos fan and the dialect continuum nature of all of the rest of the Continuous Zone are of themselves all but enough to give the lie to the idea of a deep QI~QII split.

Admittedly, in theory it might be possible for intense contact to turn an originally sharp linguistic frontier into a more gradual transition. Perhaps a detailed survey of *Fronterizo* speech of the Uruguay-Brazil borderlands might reveal traces of such a pattern, for instance. Nonetheless, by far the more usual real-world explanation is that even a bundling of isoglosses does *not* normally reflect a frontier where originally separate languages met, but an *initial continuum* upon which only *later* developments in the external context gave rise to a linguistic "fault line." This may reflect a geographical, cultural, or political determiner of a discontinuity in the degree of local-level interaction between speakers on either side, and/or *later* population movements that disturb the original smooth continuum.

The second half of this chapter will seek to uncover what such contexts might have been that could explain the case of the Huancayo-Huancavelica isogloss bundle. But before that come two basic questions. Just how sharp actually is the supposed linguistic frontier? And how much of it has anything to do with the putative QI~QII contrast in any case? A full treatment of those questions requires consideration of linguistic details beyond the space available in this chapter. Readers may consult also section 3 of the paper by Beresford-Jones and Heggarty,[13] and to the references contained therein; here we must limit ourselves to the main principles.

4.1 Idiosyncrasies of Huanca Quechua

Even to the extent that there is a clear linguistic difference between Huancayo and Huancavelica, one should beware jumping to the conclusion that it is necessarily to be attributed only, indeed even primarily, to the supposed QI~QII contrast. Much of what makes for the "frontier" has nothing to do with the QI~QII criteria at all. Rather, many of the most distinctive traits behind perceptions of the "frontier" go back to a series of idiosyncratic changes limited almost exclusively to Huanca Quechua (or indeed, just sub-regions of it), shared neither to north nor south. Huanca Quechua replaces /r/ with /l/, for example, and /q/ with glottal stop /ʔ/, vowel length, or complete absence. Long vowels end up much more common than in other Quechua regions, and occur in places quite unexpected, and with entirely different meanings. The central "Waycha Huanca" zone also changes <ch> to retroflex <tr> (i.e., /tʃ/→/tʂ/); while <ch> resurfaces in different words, in place of original <ll> (i.e., /ʎ/→/tʃ/). Grammatically, Huanca Quechua is unique in having developed a definite article, in forms now unrecognizable to Quechua-speakers from other regions. Even the basic word *I* (and *me*, *we*, *us*, etc.) is in much of the Huanca region derived from the root */jaqa/ rather than normal */ɲuqa/.

Such changes happen to be exceptionally salient ones that impact unusually heavily (as much, if not more so, than most of the "diagnostic"

QI~QII criteria) on intelligibility for speakers of other Quechua dialects. Precisely this is why Wölck can report that "some Ayacucho Quechua ["QII"] speakers seem to consider the Quechua of Huánuco ["QI," and much further north] more intelligible than that of Huancayo ["QI"]."[14] Yet in the other direction, "The Huancayo-Quechua speaker can understand the Huancavelica variety without particular problems."[15] Much of the supposed frontier, then, lies not in any QI~QII contrast; it is just that Huanca Quechua is "out on a limb."

4.2   The Huanca Region as a Sub-Continuum Linking Central to Southern Quechua

Even if one sets aside the established criticisms of the supposedly "diagnostic" criteria in Table 4.1 that place Huanca Quechua with QI,[16] counterbalancing them are others that, on the contrary, place the *entire region* squarely with QII. Cerrón-Palomino identifies at least three such significant suffixes.[17]

Most revealing of all is criterion 7, however: for Huanca Quechua has *both* the typical "QI" and "QII" forms, in slightly different meanings.[18] Far from supporting a QI affiliation of Huanca Quechua, this criterion by itself would seem to deny the realism of any stark QI~QII split, and instead characterize Huanca explicitly as a *transitional* central band within a wider overall dialect continuum right through the Continuous Zone.

Indeed, no end of further criteria paint a picture of the Huanca region as just such a sub-continuum. Firstly, Huanca Quechua itself is defined as a unit by just a single criterion: the presence of the definite article. (Again, one might well ask: Why this rather than any other?) The /r/ → /l/ change is also distinctive, but not exclusive. And neither has anything to do with the putative QI~QII contrast.

Otherwise, every single supposedly "Huanca" trait discussed by Cerrón-Palomino falls into one of two types.[19] Either they are unique to just *sub-zones* of Huanca Quechua, contributing to its distinctiveness and impressions of a sharp frontier with Huancavelica, but irrelevant to the QI~QII issue. Or, more telling still, they are shared with neighboring dialects: southern parts of the Huanca region share characteristics with Southern "QIIc" Quechua; northern parts with Central "QI" Quechua.[20] Among such criteria are the use of -*yki* versus -*nki* as second–person subject marker in the past tense; the presence versus absence of the -*yši* transitivising suffix; the use of -*ta* versus -*kta* to mark direct object; the use of -*man* versus -*kta*~-*ta* to mark the *in*direct object; diminutive -*ča*; even the use of "Huanca" [ŝ], which spreads into northern Huancavelica.[21] Similarly in vocabulary, Huanca patterns with its neighbors both north and south in ways quintessential of a dialect continuum.[22]

Such criteria are of very similar grammatical ilk to the supposedly "diagnostic" QI~QII ones, and in principle just as valid for classificatory purposes. All these isoglosses patently do *not* bundle at the Huancayo-Huancavelica frontier, but fan progressively through the larger Huanca region, precisely as the dialect continuum scenario would predict. Within the traditional classification, such characteristics have had to be "explained away," and are *assumed* to be due to later "contacts" across the QI~QII frontier. But the data per se by no means necessarily support that interpretation, rather than the alternative that they go back to an original dialect continuum which has *only in part* resolved to a bundle of a few isoglosses between Huancayo and Huancavelica.

5. If Not QI~QII, Then How Did the Huancayo-Huancavelica Frontier Arise?

So on closer inspection, the linguistic evidence in fact seem to favor a picture of an *underlying* dialect continuum. But for all that, we hardly wish to deny the evident fact that upon that continuum, a not inconsiderable number of isoglosses—most of the criteria in Table 4.1—have indeed come to bundle at the Huancayo-Huancavelica frontier. Even once one strips away the illusion of the striking Huanca idiosyncrasies, irrelevant to the QI~QII question, this bundling of isoglosses remains, and still cries out to be accounted for. So, if not by already distinct QI and QII varieties expanding to meet each other, then how else, within a dialect continuum arisen after Quechua had spread over the entire Continuous Zone in just a single expansion?

Claims are hardly lacking as to some form of ethnic distinctiveness of the "Huancas," carried over also to the sociocultural and "political" levels. Could these have been significant enough to impart a linguistic impact, and not just in the noted idiosyncrasies of Huanca Quechua? The fact that isoglosses do bundle here, but do not outside the Huanca ethnic area in Yauyos, certainly fits with some form of specifically "Huanca" distinctiveness. It could conceivably even go back to a preexisting linguistic frontier, such that when Quechua first spread here it was learned by speakers of different languages either side of the boundary, whose native tongues imparted different "substrate" impacts to it right from the start. Other than suggestions that the region might formerly have spoken Aymara,[23] however, we have little to go on but speculation.

A "Huanca" distinctiveness may well turn out to be part of the explanation. Archaeological and ethnohistorical sources (as discussed briefly by Cerrón-Palomino)[24] might in due course shed greater light on such questions. For the remainder of this chapter, however, we look to an alternative possible explanation, one that could account for the isogloss bundle as a *post*-Columbian creation, on which historical sources offer an answer.

This switches the focus, moreover, to the other side of the frontier, the Huancavelica rather than the Huancayo region. And it invokes not in situ "distinctiveness" but a quite different mechanism to account for the disruption to the smooth transitions of an archetypical dialect continuum: the physical movement of populations from one part of the continuum to another. To return to our color palette analogy: how might some such movement explain the now unusually sharp change from Central Quechua yellow to Southern Quechua blue at the Huancayo-Huancavelica boundary, losing the subtle transition through shades of green in Yauyos to the west? One scenario that could have produced this would be a relatively *late* population movement, once the continuum had already arisen: speakers from more southerly areas with by now clearly defined Southern Quechua "blue," transplanted northward into the Huancavelica area, in such numbers as to swamp the local intermediate "green" Quechua, reinforcing the southern characteristics of Huancavelica speech, and sharpening the transition to the "yellow" of Huancayo to the north. It is as if the artist of the Quechua dialect map had dragged more blue across his palette onto the green, mixing them to a deeper shade now much closer to southern blue than to northern yellow.

Let it be clear that the initial idea here was not our own, but a suggestion by César Itier as to what historical reality might explain the Huancayo-Huancavelica frontier. This does not, however, implicate Itier in the "Wari as Quechua" proposal, on which his maintains his own independent views (see Itier this volume).

6. The Colonial *Mita*: Cause of the Huancayo-Huancavelica Quechua Frontier?

César Itier's insight rests upon the single most striking feature of Huancavelica throughout the period of Spanish rule from the sixteenth century onward: the presence of the greatest mercury mine in the Americas, and among the richest sources of mercury anywhere in the world. Mercury was of central importance to the colonial economy of the Andes, because it was the key element in the refining of silver, produced in vast quantities at mines such as those at Potosí in modern Bolivia. Mercury was the main catalyst in the process by which silver was separated from its ores, and it was this that lent the Huancavelica mines their crucial significance. The colonial state threw itself behind production at Huancavelica, where (in contrast to the silver-mining sector) it never relinquished ownership of the deposits, which were leased for exploitation by private mining entrepreneurs. And within a decade of their discovery in the early 1560s, the state mobilized its considerable energies to guarantee the mines an abundant and reliable workforce, through a great draft of forced labor levied on the native population of the surrounding provinces. Called *mita* after the system of communal labor for state projects and public works under the Incas (Quechua *mit'a*, or "turn"), this draft demanded that a fixed proportion of the male tributary population of the obligated provinces (typically a seventh) should work at the mines each year. Like the directly comparable draft established for the Potosí mines, the Huancavelica *mita* was created by the most influential of the early colonial viceroys of Peru, Francisco de Toledo, in the early 1570s. It then survived throughout the colonial period, until a catastrophic collapse in 1786 effectively ended large-scale production at the mines. Throughout this period, so many Indian workers died from mercury poisoning and other hazards that the mine has been called *la mina de la muerte*, or "the mine of death."[25]

The suggestion developed in these pages, then, is that the colonial *mita* might have prompted a movement of population into the Huancavelica region sufficiently powerful as to permanently affect the Quechua spoken there, "artificially" enhancing its southern attributes and so disrupting the pre-Columbian dialect continuum. But, if the Huancavelica *mita* is indeed to contribute to our understanding of the linguistic scenario on the Huancayo-Huancavelica divide, then two key issues require consideration: (1) How many Quechua speakers did the labor draft bring in to the region, and were they sufficiently numerous as to have brought about a lasting change to the linguistic panorama there?; and (2) Which regions were these people drawn from, and were they the "right" regions, in linguistic terms, to have brought about the pattern we see today?

Answering these questions is by no means straightforward, given complexities in both the *mita* as a historical phenomenon and the sources that describe it. Let us take first the question of numbers. We shall see hereafter that, in fact, more than just a single *mita* brought native laborers into Huancavelica and its environs. Nevertheless, the most significant and enduring draft was unquestionably that which serviced the quicksilver mines. The *official* mining draft (as distinct from the *real* draft, discussed in the following paragraph) was set by Toledo at its inception at a little more than 3,000 laborers (or *mitayos*) per year: a very high figure. It is unlikely that so many Indians ever actually made the annual journey to the mines, and the subsequent history of the official draft is of an almost immediate drop to around 2,300 laborers, followed by a further reduction to 1,400 workers in the early 1620s, and finally, stability from 1645 at less than half the latter figure. Official quotas for the *mita* were fixed in periodic contracts (*asientos*) signed between the Crown and the mining guild (*gremio de mineros*), and the trend can be traced quite clearly through the figures established in these contracts: in 1590, 2,274 *mitayos* were assigned to the draft; in 1598–1604, 1,600 (reflecting a deliberate reduction enforced by over-production at the mines); in 1608, 2,300; in 1618, 2,200; in 1623, 1,400; in 1630, 1,400 once more; and in 1645, 620 Indians.[26]

The official draft remained unchanged at 620 laborers per year from the *asiento* of 1645 until the end of the colonial era. But long before then, the *real* number of Indians serving bore little resemblance to the official quota. The real draft was subject to rapid decline for a number of reasons, not least drastic depopulation of the obligated provinces due to successive waves of epidemic disease and the reluctance of *mitayos* to serve in the notoriously dangerous mines. A substantial shortfall in the real draft was first noted as early as the 1610s, and was attested to repeatedly in colonial documentation thereafter. By 1629, only about half the official draft actually served (about 700 Indians), while a year later a figure of fewer than 1,000 Indians was given. From around 1650, there was a further sharp drop, to fewer than 500 Indians, and in the 1680s from 300 to 400 natives actually served their "turn." There was some recovery in the early eighteenth century, to from 450 to 550 Indians in the 1720s and 1730s. But by the early 1750s, the real draft had declined once more, to fewer than 400 Indians per year, and in the late 1770s a figure of just 175 was given.[27]

The decline in the official *mita* to little more than 600 Indians per year before 1650, and more importantly the evidence that only part of the official figure actually served the draft, might place in doubt the long-term impact of *mitayos* on the population of Huancavelica and its district. In fact, however, a range of additional factors need to be taken into account when calculating the impact of the draft. One basic point is that many, if not most, *mitayos* brought their wives and children with them when they came to serve their turn; in short, the migration prompted by the *mita* was much larger than the number of *mitayos* alone. A further and perhaps still more important phenomenon is the emergence at Huancavelica from an early date of a *free-wage* labor force, which might be supposed to have derived from broadly the same population as the *mita*, and which very considerably reinforced its effects. Free-wage labor at Huancavelica seems to have been far more important than has generally been recognized. As early as 1613, some 1,500 laborers were available for hire in the town, or about two-thirds the number of draft workers, while in the late 1650s wage labor was said to outnumber the draft.[28] So far as the Crown and the mining entrepreneurs were concerned, indeed, the free sector compensated for the decline in the official and real drafts in procuring a stable labor force for the mines.

For reasons which will become clear in the concluding paragraphs to this section, the relevance of free labor to our theme depends on free laborers having arrived from the same regions that sent *mitayos* to the mines. Although it is far more difficult to establish the origin of free laborers than it is that of *mitayos*, there are grounds to suppose not only that most free labor came from the *mita*-yielding provinces, but that it came approximately in proportion to the inflow of workers from each province. Of course, for the *mita* to have had any significant long-term impact on linguistic patterns in the Huancavelica region would presumably require *mitayos* settling in the region permanently, rather than returning to their home provinces at the year's end as the nature of the *mita* would suggest. And sure enough, from the beginning of the seventeenth century, it was noted that Indians remained in Huancavelica after the end of their turn, hiring themselves out as free-wage laborers; the 1,500 laborers available for hire in 1613, for example, were "individuals who had finished their mita."[29] It seems probable that the majority of free laborers first arrived in Huancavelica as *mitayos*, or learned of the supposed benefits of working there from *mitayos* returning to provinces which were, moreover, by definition among the nearest to the mines. This is a controversial topic, since it would appear to belie the more lurid claims made for very high native-worker mortality at the mines: if Huancavelica really was the *mina de la muerte*, then why would workers voluntarily remain there, even for wages?[30] Nevertheless, the phenomenon of *mitayos* remaining in Huancavelica was understood, at least by some, to have contributed powerfully to the depopulation of the obligated provinces, in contrast to the prevailing view that depopulation was caused by mortality at the mines (or by the flight of Indians precisely so as to avoid the draft).[31]

There are, in fact, further grounds to emphasize the potential of the mines to attract a large and lasting immigrant population. One has already been hinted at: there was not, in fact, a single "Huancavelica mita." Indians in Huancavelica and neighboring Huamanga (the modern Ayacucho) might be subject to a number of drafts, for the service of officials of state or church or for a variety of public works.[32] Most of these were purely local *mitas*, drawing on the population of the town or the surrounding province, but some drew from much further afield: the key instance for our purposes was the 100 Indians from the province of Chumbivilcas, far to the south-east, assigned to work in monasteries, convents, and the hospital in Huancavelica. The latter draft (established in the seventeenth century parallel to the mining draft) proved unusually resilient, and may have been the only *mita* still bringing significant numbers to the town after 1800.[33]

Still more importantly, we should emphasize that Huancavelica itself was an artificial settlement, founded solely to host the workers and mining entrepreneurs, and the civil and ecclesiastical establishment that ministered to them. The population of the city was probably around 5,000 from the late sixteenth to the late seventeenth century, and may have reached 8,000 or even 10,000 by around 1800.[34] Cities typically set the linguistic tone and play the driving role for their hinterlands, as "centers of innovation" to which the surrounding areas gradually accommodate. The establishment and rapid growth of Huancavelica thus could not fail to ensure that it would be this incoming population that would necessarily set the dominant linguistic pattern, and largely supplant the form of Quechua natively spoken in this sparsely populated region.

In summary, we shall never have a completely clear picture of the number of Quechua-speakers the Huancavelica mines brought into the region. The disparity between official and real numbers of Indians serving the *mita*, and the difficulty of tracing accurately the size and provenance of the free-wage sector, among other factors, conspire against any absolute measurement. All that can be said with confidence is that during their relatively brief heyday from the 1570s to the 1610s, the mines attracted thousands of people into the region every year: a major influx. What proportion of these people remained in Huancavelica is difficult to calculate, but there are grounds to suppose that, on the one hand fueling, on the other bolstered by, the free-wage sector, it was considerable. It is also to be emphasized that the "new town" status of the city, and its constant renewal by fresh immigration, meant that its population remained resolutely based on outsiders, as would the form of Quechua spoken there. From the 1610s onward a decline in the *mita* was apparent, which became much more marked from the 1640s. Nevertheless, it continued to bring significant numbers of migrants into the region for another century and a half, until the eve of independence after 1800.

To return to our starting point, then: in our view, immigration on this scale and over this time frame could indeed, as César Itier proposed, have permanently altered the linguistic complexion of the Huancavelica region. It should be emphasized that the population of this region, already devastated by disease, was not large: the early seventeenth-century chronicler, Francisco López de Caravantes, indicates that the tributary population of the *entire region* subject to the *mita* was just 69,000 at its establishment in the 1570s, and had fallen to 25,000 by the late 1620s.[35] The influx of thousands of people into Huancavelica and its province, Angaraes, during the 40 years or so after the establishment of the *mita*, reinforced more modestly but consistently for a further century and a half, was surely sufficient to bring about lasting change to the linguistic panorama there. The many thousands of current and former *mitayos* and their families, among so small a total population, would have made up such a high *proportion* that they could hardly fail to have a major linguistic impact.

This conclusion, though important, leaves unresolved our second major question: Which region did the workers and their families come from, and could immigration from this region have created the *particular* linguistic pattern we see today? Describing the region subject to the Huancavelica *mita* brings its own complications, not least because official sources are often surprisingly vague regarding the provinces included. These provinces also changed quite frequently over time, principally to reflect demographic changes within and among them. Toledo originally established the *mita* at some 40 leagues around the town, and some sources indicate that 13 provinces were at first included, although in its mature form this number fell to 9. On occasion, the provinces of Aymaraes, Azángaro, Omasuyos, Parinacochas, and Yauyos, in addition to Chumbivilcas, feature in official lists. The inclusion of Azángaro and Omasuyos is particularly surprising, since these provinces lie many hundreds of miles to the south-east, in the case of Omasuyos on the eastern shore of Lake Titicaca. Both provinces appear to have contributed only during the earliest period: Omasuyos features only in *asientos* to 1618, while Azángaro features only up to 1629. Similarly, the inclusion of small numbers of *mitayos* from Aymaraes, Parinacochas, and Yauyos seems to have been a late-colonial innovation, these provinces featuring mainly in a report dated 1726.[36] The nine main provinces constituted a more compact grouping: Andahuaylas, Angaraes, Chocorbos (corresponding to part of the province of Castrovirreyna), Cotabambas, Huanta, Jauja, Lucanas, Tarma, and Vilcashuamán.[37] It is often thought that the *mita* coincided with the bishopric of Huamanga, but this is only partly true; thus, Cotabambas and Chumbivilcas were in the bishopric of Cuzco, while Tarma and Jauja belonged to the archbishopric of Lima.

A glance at Figure 4.3 immediately suggests a striking pattern for the nine main provinces obligated to the Huancavelica draft: they were strongly skewed toward the regions to the south and east of the town. Only two provinces lay to the north of Angaraes itself: Tarma and Jauja. The remaining provinces lay in a contiguous bloc due south or southeast, with Cotabambas an outlier close to the borders of Cuzco. Here, then, lies clear indication that Itier's hunch was indeed correct, for this is precisely the region capable of supplying the "right" kind of Quechua speakers, those who would artificially sharpen the linguistic frontier at Huancavelica by making the speech of Angaraes more "southern". And we can add still further weight to the argument, since in terms of the *mita*, not all provinces were equal; on the contrary, some supplied far more *mitayos* than others. Under the *asiento* of 1629, Cotabambas alone supplied 409 workers out of an official draft of some 1,400, while Andahuaylas supplied a further 250, signifying that the two most southeasterly provinces supplied almost half of the total draft (46 percent).[38] Tarma and Jauja, the provinces to the north, supplied 23 percent of the draft in the same contract; but under the asiento of 1645, Cotabambas and Andahuaylas again supplied by far the largest contingent (285 out of 620 *mitayos*, or again 46 percent), while Tarma and Jauja contributed a negligible 35 workers.[39] Meanwhile, we have seen that during the early years of the Huancavelica *mita*, still more southerly provinces such as Azángaro were also included, while in later times a significant contingent came from Chumbivilcas, due south of Cotabambas. In short, the evidence seems conclusive that most migrants drawn to Huancavelica by the colonial mining industry were speakers not just of Southern ("QIIc") Quechua, but of varieties of it considerably more southerly than the region's own original native speech.

7. Conclusion

The first part of this essay discusses a key but controversial feature of the linguistic panorama of the Andes: the existence of an apparent divide between the varieties of Quechua spoken in Huancayo and Huancavelica in central Peru. A fresh look at the criteria on which such a divide is premised tends to question its substance, since there are grounds at least as strong (indeed in our view stronger) for regarding the Quechua language family as forming a dialect continuum throughout the "Continuous Zone," from northern Ancash to the Lake Titicaca region. We also challenge the relevance of such a divide to long-standing interpretations of the deep history of the Quechua family, based on an ancient split into two branches which then (re-)encountered each other in this central region. Nevertheless, it remains clear that a considerable number of isoglosses, including most of those on which such a deep split is usually based, have indeed come to bundle at the Huancayo-Huancavelica frontier. This constitutes at the very least an anomaly—a discontinuity in the continuum—and demands an explanation.

The second part of the essay suggests that, far from some ancestral sub-division, followed by expansion and divergence and a re-encounter in the Central Andes, the linguistic complexion of Huancavelica and the differences with the Quechua spoken to the north can be explained in a very different way. The divide came about, in our view, through a much later, post-Columbian process: massive immigration by Quechua speakers from more southerly provinces, drafted by the colonial state to work in the Huancavelica mercury mines. The scale and persistence of this immigration was sufficient to alter the Quechua spoken in Huancavelica and its province permanently, making it more southern and artificially sharpening the linguistic boundary with the region immediately to the north.

This essay thus stands as an example of how linguistics and history can complement each other directly and fruitfully, applying their separate data

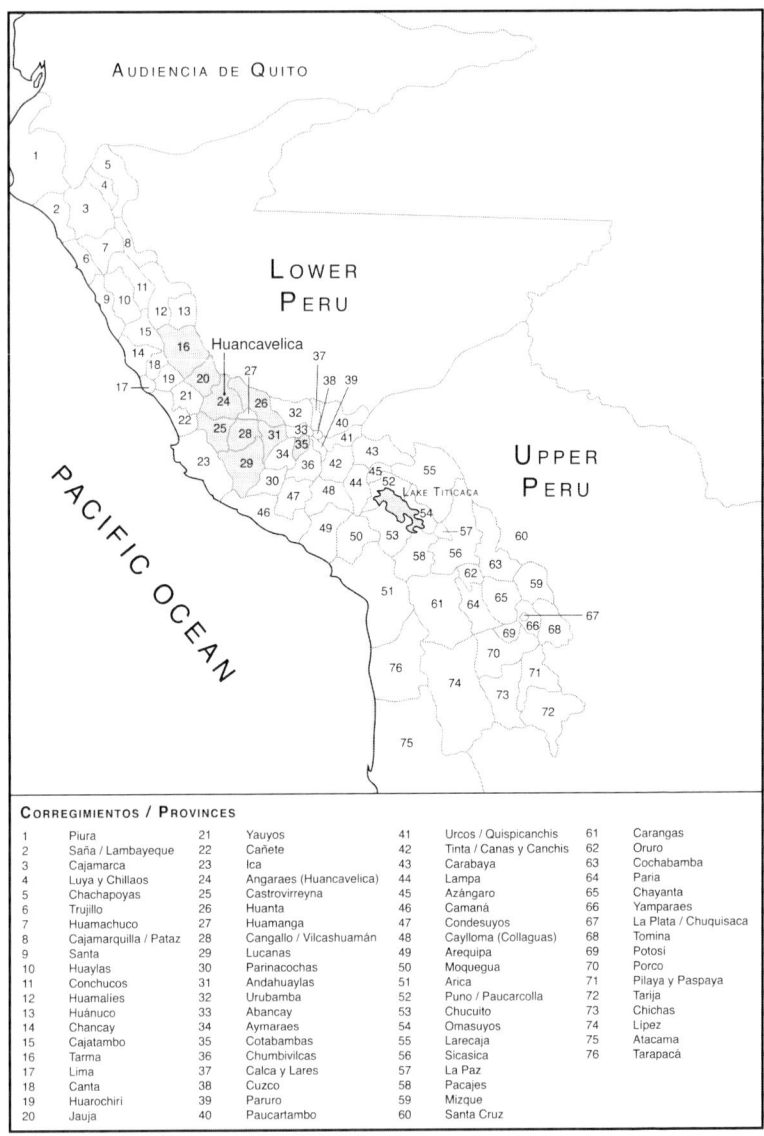

Figure 4.3 The nine main provinces obligated to the Huancavelica draft—shown shaded.

sets and techniques to resolve major questions of interest and importance to both. For, by providing an explanation for the Huancayo-Huancavelica divide which is divorced from traditional deep histories of the Quechua family, the work contributes to the wholesale reclassification of that family and rewriting of its ancient history which is currently underway (Heggarty and Beresford-Jones, forthcoming). And for historians, that the colonial *mita* should have permanently altered the language spoken in Huancavelica and its environs deepens our understanding of the impact of the colonial state, and of its scope to affect fundamental aspects of the lives of native Andeans.

Notes

1. Rodolfo Cerrón-Palomino, *Lingüística quechua* (Cuzco: Centro de Estudios Regionales Andinos "Bartolomé de las Casas," 1987; reprinted 2003), pp. 33–93.
2. Gerald Taylor, *Estudios de dialectología quechua (Chachapoyas, Ferreñafe, Yauyos)* (Lima: Universidad Nacional de Educación Enrique Guzmán y Valle, 1994).
3. Willem F. H. Adelaar, *Morfología del Quechua de Pacaraos* (Lima: Universidad Nacional Mayor de San Marcos, 1987).
4. Gerald Taylor, "Yauyos, un microcosmo dialectal quechua," *Revista Andina* 3 (1984), pp. 121–46; Gerald Taylor, "Algunos datos nuevos sobre el quechua de Yauyos (Vitis y Huancaya)," *Revista Andina* 9 (1987), pp. 253–65.
5. Peter N. Landerman, "Quechua Dialects and their Classification," unpublished Ph.D. dissertation, University of California at Los Angeles, 1991.
6. Alfredo Torero, "Lingüística e historia de la sociedad andina," in A. Escobar (ed.), *El reto del multilingüismo en el Perú* (Lima: Instituto de Estudios Peruanos, 1972), pp. 51–106; Torero, "El comercio lejano y la difusión del quechua. El caso del Ecuador," *Revista Andina* 4 (1984), pp. 367–89; and Torero, *Idiomas de los Andes. Lingüística e historia* (Lima: Instituto Francés de Estudios Andinos / Horizonte, 2002), p. 125.
7. Rodolfo Cerrón-Palomino, *Lingüística Aimara* (Lima: Centro de Estudios Regionales Andinos "Bartolomé de las Casas," 2000), p. 378.
8. Cerrón-Palomino, *Lingüística Aimara*, p. 378.
9. David G. Beresford-Jones and Paul Heggarty, "Broadening our Horizons: Towards an Interdisciplinary Prehistory of the Andes", in Paul Heggarty and David G. Beresford-Jones (eds.), *Archaeology and Language in the Andes* (London and Oxford: British Academy / Oxford University Press, forthcoming).
10. Beresford–Jones and Heggarty, "Broadening our Horizons."
11. Rodolfo Cerrón-Palomino, *Lingüística quechua*, p. 230.
12. R. Anthony Lodge, *French: From Dialect to Standard* (London: Routledge, 1993), pp. 71–84.
13. Beresford-Jones and Heggarty, "Broadening our Horizons."

14. Wolfgang Wölck, "Las lenguas mayores del Perú y sus hablantes," in A. Escobar (ed.), *El Reto del Multilingüismo en el Perú* (Lima: Instituto de Estudios Peruanos, 1972), pp.189–216.

15. Rodolfo Cerrón-Palomino, "Lengua y sociedad en el Valle del Mantaro: Primera parte: Quechua fronterizo," *Amerindia* 12 (1987), §4.24.

16. For example, Landerman, "Quechua Dialects and their Classification."

17. Cerrón-Palomino, "Lengua y sociedad en el Valle del Mantaro," §5.

18. Cerrón-Palomino, "Lengua y sociedad en el Valle del Mantaro," §5.

19. Cerrón-Palomino, "Lengua y sociedad en el Valle del Mantaro."

20. Cerrón-Palomino, "Lengua y sociedad en el Valle del Mantaro," §5.

21. Cerrón-Palomino, "Lengua y sociedad en el Valle del Mantaro", p. 163.

22. Cerrón-Palomino, "Lengua y sociedad en el Valle del Mantaro", §5.

23. Cerrón-Palomino, "Lengua y sociedad en el Valle del Mantaro," §2.23.1.

24. Cerrón-Palomino, "Lengua y sociedad en el Valle del Mantaro," §3.

25. The standard history of the mines up to 1700 is Guillermo Lohmann Villena's, *Las minas de Huancavelica en los siglos XVI y XVII* (Seville: Escuela de Estudios Hispano-Americanos, 1949). Relatively little is available in English, but see Arthur Preston Whitaker, *The Huancavelica Mercury Mine: A Contribution to the History of the Bourbon Renaissance in the Spanish Empire* (Cambridge, MA: Harvard University Press, 1941), and Adrian J. Pearce, "Huancavelica 1700–1759: Administrative Reform of the Mercury Industry in Early Bourbon Peru," *Hispanic American Historical Review* 79:4 (Nov. 1999), 669–702.

26. Figures for successive *asientos* in Lohmann Villena, *Las minas de Huancavelica*, pp. 97, 145, 161, 178, 222, 253, 265–66, 284–85, 331.

27. Lohmann Villena, *Las minas de Huancavelica*, pp. 238, 270, 288, 290, 354, 360, 397, and 404 (for the figure for 1685); Adrian J. Pearce, "The Peruvian Population Census of 1725–1740," *Latin American Research Review* 36:3 (Oct. 2001), 69–104, see 94–95; Luis J. Basto Girón, "Las mitas de Huamanga y Huancavelica," *Publicaciones del Instituto de Etnología*, 8 (Lima, 1954), 9.

28. An important contribution on this subject is Barbara Bradby, "The 'Black Legend' of Huancavelica: The Mita Debates and Opposition to Wage-Labour in the Colonial Mercury Mine," in Julio Sánchez Gómez and Guillermo Mira Delli-Zotti (eds.), *Hombres, Técnica, Plata. Minería y Sociedad en Europa y América, Siglos XVI–XIX* (Seville: Aconcagua, 2000), pp. 227–57; see also Lohmann Villena, *Las minas de Huancavelica*, pp. 210–11, 238, 357–58.

29. Lohmann Villena, *Las minas de Huancavelica*, 224, 238.

30. Kendall W. Brown, "Workers' Health and Colonial Mercury Mining at Huancavelica, Peru," *The Americas* 57:4 (Apr. 2001), 467–96, very much supports the "Black Legend" of the lethal nature of labor at the mines.

31. Lohmann Villena, *Las minas de Huancavelica*, pp. 224–5.

32. Basto Girón, "Las mitas de Huamanga y Huancavelica," pp. 5–7, 9–24.

33. Carlos Contreras, *La ciudad del mercurio: Huancavelica, 1570–1700* (Lima: Instituto de Estudios Peruanos, 1982), p.49; Basto Girón, "Las mitas de Huamanga y Huancavelica," p. 9.

34. Contreras, *La ciudad del mercurio*, pp. 42–45.

35. Francisco López de Caravantes (Guillermo Lohmann Villena & Marie Helmer, eds.), *Noticia General del Perú* 6 vols. (1630; Madrid, 1985–89), vol. 4, p. 207.

36. Marqués de Casa Concha, "Relación del estado que…tiene, la Real Mina de Guancavelica," 1726, Archivo General de Indias, Seville, Audiencia de Lima, copies in legajos. 469, 479.

37. Summaries of provinces included in successive asientos in Lohmann Villena, *Las minas de Huancavelica*, pp. 252, 274, 331, 414. Viceroy Melchor de Liñán y Cisneros, "Relación de gobierno," 1681, in Lewis Hanke (ed.), *Los virreyes españoles en América durante el gobierno de la casa de Austria: Perú* 7 vols. (Madrid: Ediciones Atlas, 1978–80), vol. 5, pp. 180–273, discusses the long-lived *asiento* of 1645 and refers specifically to these nine provinces; see pp. 226–27.

38. López de Caravantes, *Noticia General del Perú*, vol. 4, pp. 207–9, gives a detailed breakdown of the asiento of 1629.

39. Lohmann Villena, *Las minas de Huancavelica*, p. 331.

Part II

Reform, Independence, and the Early Republic

Chapter 5

The Bourbon Reforms, Independence, and the Spread of Quechua and Aymara

Kenneth J. Andrien

The extant historical evidence provides little indication that policies enacted by the colonial state had any dramatic effect on the use of Quechua and Aymara in the Andes during the eighteenth century and the independence era. By the eighteenth century, colonial officials had become more tolerant of the two major vernacular language families, Quechua and Aymara, particularly with the spread of popular piety among the Andean peoples. Even the political and religious turmoil surrounding the move to replace the religious orders with secular priests in Amerindian parishes (beginning in 1749), the expulsion of the Jesuits in 1767, attempts by the Crown to require that Andeans learn Castilian in the four years following the Great Andean Rebellions from 1781 to 1783, the rise of Liberal reform with the Constitution of 1812, and the rise of national states that limited indigenous participation in politics, apparently had no profound impact on language spread and use in the Andes. Instead, historians most often point to the process of ethnogenesis taking place over a long period in the Andes, which can be traced in the documentary evidence from the eighteenth century. Linguists, anthropologists, and historians can find a great deal of information about ethnogenesis and its impact on language use and spread by examining documentation surrounding a number of topics, such as migration, forced labor drafts (*mita*), the spread of epidemic diseases, urbanization, religious evangelization, church-state conflicts, education in rural schools, hispanicized Indians (*indios ladinos*), and colonial repression of Andean cultural and religious practices.

* * *

Historians of the Andes have seldom focused directly on the spread and use of the two major language families of the region, Quechua and

Aymara. In general, historians tend to rely on an examination of writ-ten documents—published materials or a variety of different types of written sources drawn from libraries or archival repositories. As a result, the absence of any clear evidence that Andean civilizations used alpha-betic writing to communicate concrete or abstract ideas hinders histori-cal scholarship on pre-Columbian civilizations.[1] Even after the arrival of the Spanish invaders in 1532, European alphabetic symbols proved alien mechanisms for recording the sounds and words of Andean languages, and very few indigenous language documents written in European script exist for the colonial era.[2] By contrast, in Mesoamerica the indigenous peoples had developed advanced forms of pictorial and phonetic writ-ing, so writing down their languages in European alphabetic script came relatively quickly and easily. Within the first generation of contact, indig-enous scribes produced texts in their native languages and in Castilian, a practice that continued throughout the colonial era, leaving a wide array of mundane administrative records written in indigenous lan-guages. Indeed, this extensive body of indigenous language documents in Mesoamerica has spawned the "New Philology," a school of historians (associated with James Lockhart) who attempt to use this documenta-tion as a window into the "interior of colonial indigenous society in ways fundamental to any understanding of culture."[3] The lack of similar types of indigenous language sources for the Andes has forced historians of the region to rely on Castilian language documents, which provide no direct data on language change, classification and the distribution of the Quechua and Aymara language families.[4] Nonetheless, historians of the Andean world do address important factors that led to the production of documentation, which holds the promise of yielding much information about the spread and use of Quechua and Aymara in the Andes by the eighteenth and early nineteenth centuries.

1. Introduction: Early Debates about Language Policies in the Andes

The sixteenth-century expansion of Spain into the Andes coincided with the crusading zeal of the late *Reconquista,* leading to the Christian con-quest of the Iberian Peninsula's last Muslim kingdom of Granada in 1492. At the same time late medieval and early Renaissance scholars began codifying Castilian grammar, vocabulary, and orthography, and privileging the use of alphabetic writing over oral traditions. During this period Castilian began to replace Latin as the language of govern-ment in the kingdoms of Spain and later in its empire. As Ferdinand and Isabella conquered Granada, and Spain entered its period of overseas expansion by 1492, the humanist Elio Antonio de Nebrija published his grammar of Castilian, followed in 1517 by his orthography, which both linked the invention of the alphabet and language with the consolidation of a Christian empire ruling over less "civilized" peoples. The ideas of scholars, such as Nebrija, provided the rationale for teaching Castilian to indigenous peoples, laying the foundation for colonizers to use the Latin alphabet and Castilian grammar to write down Andean languages.[5]

The only analogue to European writing in the Andes was the *quipu* (or to be correct in modern Quechua orthography, *khipu*), a system of colored, knotted cords arranged to convey meaning, but over time Spanish authorities found the *quipu* too esoteric and unintelligible, so they disparaged and later prohibited the use of these devices in legal cases.[6] Spaniards simply could not invest the power of record keeping solely to native leaders and skilled interpreters of the knotted cords (*quipucamayocs*), and they judged the *quipu* inferior to European alphabetic writing. After the Third Lima Church Council in 1582, colonial authorities began systematically destroying *quipu* and ignoring the evidence presented by *quipucamayocs*.[7] By the early seventeenth century, this important form of Andean communication had given way to alphabetic writing in Castilian, and to a limited extent, in Quechua.

The Spanish Crown and the church pursued two distinct language policies for the Andean peoples simultaneously—political separation and conversion by using vernacular languages, particularly Quechua and Aymara, and at other moments pushing for more cultural incorporation by having religious and political interactions in Castilian. These contradictory strategies often worked at cross-purposes. The Crown usually encouraged education in Castilian, but at various times it also supported efforts by clerics, particularly the Jesuits, to use Quechua and Aymara in evangelizing. Such activities facilitated the establishment of written norms for these languages, a process greatly advanced by the publication of grammars and vocabularies, such as those of the Jesuit linguists, Diego González Holguín (for Quechua) in 1607–1608 and Ludovico Bertonio (for Aymara) in 1612.[8] The use of Quechua and Aymara, however, also prompted considerable criticism. The Council of the Indies recommended that the Crown ban any official use of both languages in 1596, as it had outlawed Arabic in the Iberian Peninsula a generation earlier.[9] King Philip II refused to do so, but his successors grew increasingly skeptical about religious instruction in indigenous languages, giving an added impulse to teaching Andeans Castilian.[10]

Even policies of the Third Lima Council (1581–1583) demonstrated vividly these contradictory tendencies. Following the dictates of the Council of Trent (1545–1563) the Council sponsored translating church manuals used in conversion into the two major vernacular languages, Quechua and Aymara. In the case of Quechua, authorities employed Southern Peruvian Quechua as the standard for translations (which they thought represented the *lengua general* of the Incas), resulting in translations of the *Doctrina Christiana y catecismo para la instruccion de indios; Confesionario para los curas de indios;* and *Tercer catecismo y exposicion de la doctrina Christiana por sermones.*[11] At the same time, the Council outlawed the use of Andean *quipu* and authorized civil and church authorities to destroy them. These abrupt shifts in colonial language policy continued throughout the colonial period, as authorities periodically feared that preserving Andean languages ensured the continuation of native religious heresies and even fomented periodic rebellions.[12] Nevertheless, the use of Quechua and Aymara in evangelization never led to the creation of any large-scale production of routine administrative documents written in these languages by indigenous officials during the colonial period, as in New Spain. Instead, indigenous scribes commonly wrote in Castilian.

2. Late-Colonial Policies and Andean Language Use

As Christianity continued making slow and steady inroads within Andean communities during the second half of the century, a greater tolerance among many clergymen for the use of the vernacular languages, Quechua and Aymara, developed. Andeans regularly attended local religious festivals, which became larger and more ostentatious ceremonial occasions. The familiar festivals, saints' holidays, and devotional objects associated with Catholic worship gave indigenous communities the opportunity to celebrate, to evoke the divine, and to share a sense of common purpose and mutual obligation. In addition, church leaders moved away from forcible extirpation of "pagan" Andean religious practices, and they began emphasizing Christian concepts of love and charity, which along with popular rituals, appealed to Andeans.[13] This greater religious toleration encouraged the use of Quechua and Aymara (as the most commonly spoken indigenous languages) in church ceremonies. Occasional extirpation trials persisted, but over time priests and the church hierarchy generally ignored or downplayed evidence of recurring indigenous religious practices or any subterranean ties between vernacular languages and traditional Andean rituals and Christian festivals. The miracles associated with popular religious icons, such as the Virgin of Copacabana in the Lake Titicaca region, for example, apparently were associated by Andeans with the pre-Columbian deity, Viracocha, the Andean creator god.[14] By the eighteenth century, however, most churchmen exploited these connections, preaching in Quechua, Aymara, and other indigenous tongues to increase popular expressions of faith, instead of viewing them with such intense suspicion. Indeed, indigenous languages became an important vehicle for propagating the faith.[15] Popular piety in its many different forms served to lure Andeans to churches, despite the indigenous tendency to continue mixing Catholicism with enduring traditional religious beliefs. During this period, Castilian and Andean vernacular languages existed in a more easygoing coexistence (*convivencia*). The Marqués of Valle Umbroso, for example, claimed to be a descendant of the Incas, wore Inca-style clothing, and spoke Quechua.[16] Indeed, one scholar even refers to the period as an Inca language renaissance, as plays, art, cultural events, and religious fiestas evoked a romanticized indigenous past, even a renewal of interest in the works of the mestizo intellectual, El Inca Garcilaso de la Vega.[17]

Some scholars have argued that this *convivencia* between Castilian and indigenous vernacular languages suffered a serious reversal during the reign of Ferdinand VI (1746–1759) as reformers in Spain attacked the powers of the church, particularly the religious orders.[18] Such moves against the power of regular clergy altered significantly the traditional partnership between church and state in the Spanish Atlantic Empire. Habsburg Spain and its overseas empire had formed a "composite monarchy," comprised of distinct provinces or kingdoms, united only by a common monarch.[19] The most influential of these early Bourbon clerical reforms began on October 4, 1749, when the Crown issued royal edicts (*cédulas*) ordering that all indigenous parishes (*doctrinas de indios*) administered by religious orders in the Archdioceses of Lima, Mexico City, and Santa Fé de Bogotá be transferred to the secular clergy.[20] After determining that the process was proceeding without any strong popular protests in support of the orders retaining their parishes, the Crown issued a further edict on February 1, 1753, extending the process of secularization to *doctrinas* in all dioceses of Spanish America.[21] With these landmark edicts, the Bourbon dynasty began stripping the religious orders of parishes that they had administered since the sixteenth century. The edicts of 1749 and 1753 signaled an important step in advancing the power of the renewed Bourbon state over the Catholic Church, reflecting the advance of "regalism" over the composite monarchy ruled by the Habsburgs. Given that the regular orders had long supported evangelization in indigenous languages, the secularization decrees supposedly led to the spread of Castilian, as secular priests less schooled in Quechua and Aymara forced local parishioners to worship in that language, rather than indigenous vernaculars.[22]

The edicts of secularization provoked strong opposition from the regular orders in the Viceroyalty of Peru, who made the issue of language training a central component in their argument for retaining their rural parishes. The provincial of the Franciscans took a leading role in opposing the edicts, arguing that his order had received these parishes not because of any shortage of secular priests, but because of "defects" among the secular clergy. He argued that the mendicants simply did a better job of converting and ministering to indigenous peoples, and replacing friars with mere secular priests would compromise the spiritual welfare of neophytes in the parishes. Moreover, he argued there were not enough qualified secular clergy to serve in the *doctrinas de indios*, since so few priests had adequate language training. Without advanced training in vernacular languages, the provincial contended that secular clergymen could not minister effectively to their indigenous charges, undermining the whole evangelization effort in the Andes.[23]

The archbishop of Lima, Pedro Antonio de Barroeta y Ángel, took the lead in contesting this Franciscan attack on the language capabilities of secular priests. Barroeta contended that all secular priests assigned to rural *doctrinas de indios* had to pass public examinations (*oposiciones)* proving their qualifications for available parish positions, especially their ability in the vernacular language of the parish. According to the bishop, there were large numbers of secular clergy born in the viceroyalty, who grew up speaking both indigenous languages and Castilian, so finding priests competent in local vernaculars for the *doctrinas de indios* was not difficult. Moreover, since the vice regency of Francisco de Toledo (1569– 1581) the University of San Marcos in Lima had a Chair in Quechua, who was to test linguistic capabilities of prospective parish priests ministering to the Andean peoples.[24] These tests were public, unlike the examinations conducted by the regular clergymen.[25] In order to emphasize his support for appointing priests capable of preaching in native languages, Archbishop Barroeta issued a decree on August 1, 1754, requiring that all secular clergymen seeking appointments in indigenous parishes demonstrate public proficiency in the vernacular language of their parishioners, most often Quechua or Aymara.[26]

The arguments advanced by the Franciscans about language competency among available secular clergymen for the *doctrinas de indios* apparently had little impact on King Ferdinand or his chief minister, the Marqués de la Ensenada. As Ensenada made clear to the viceroy: "The express and absolute resolution of the King is the complete divestment of the regulars from the parishes."[27] In consequence, the secularization of the rural parishes proceeded apace. As a report of the bishops of the Viceroyalty of Peru indicated, by 1760 most of rural parishes of the regular orders had been filled by secular priests. All of the church leaders attested that only priests with demonstrated linguistic ability received appointments in the *doctrinas de indios.*[28] While the bishops may have exaggerated the qualifications of secular priests appointed to replace the orders in rural parishes, there is no hard evidence that the quality of language preparation of the secular clergy differed significantly from their predecessors from the regular orders. Complaints about the incompetency of parish priests in indigenous languages persisted, but accounts of such abuses had existed before the edicts of secularization, including those lodged against members of the regular orders.

Some scholars also have averred that the expulsion of the Jesuits in 1767 removed a religious order that had sponsored using indigenous languages in evangelization, particularly Quechua and Aymara. Two members of the Society of Jesus, Diego González Holguín and Ludovico Bertonio, had even written important Quechua and Aymara dictionaries and grammars. Moreover, the Jesuits remained committed to cultural syncretism in evangelization, using paintings of Inca emperors in their schools for the children of indigenous ethnic leaders (*caciques*) to connect Andean and Christian traditions for their students. The Jesuits also maintained an ongoing commitment to education by running the schools for the children of *caciques* in Lima (Colegio del Príncipe, founded in 1616) and Cuzco (Colegio de San Francisco de Borja, founded in 1621).[29] Finally, the Society of Jesus supported an extensive network of missions in the Amazon region, Paraguay, and on the frontiers of Misque and La Paz.

During the reign of King Charles III (1759–1788) political and religious leaders, called regalists, favored expanding royal control within Spain and the empire, at the expense of papal jurisdiction and the powers wielded by religious orders, particularly the influential Society of Jesus. Ongoing squabbles between the Crown and the Jesuits over the Society's intransigence about paying the tithe on proceeds from their extensive New World estates proved a particularly contentious issue that contributed to deteriorating relations. Leaders of the Society claimed that King Philip II had exempted the order from the tithe in a royal edict of January 17, 1572, as a reward for their evangelization efforts in the Indies, and that this concession had been confirmed several times by the papacy. Controversy over the payment of the tithes flared up during the reign of Ferdinand VI, whose two chief ministers, José de Carvajal y Lancaster and the Marqués de la Ensenada formed a pro-Jesuit faction at court, along with the king's influential Jesuit confessor, Francisco de Rávago. Under the influence of these advisors, Ferdinand VI agreed to a compromise with the Jesuits on the tithe. Henceforth the order would owe a 3.3 percent tithe of the produce on its New World estates, not the normal 10 percent.[30] During the reign of Charles III, however, Crown authorities successfully convinced the King to demand the full 10 percent tithe. In fact, the matter was not resolved until December 4, 1766, when the Crown ordered the Jesuits to pay the full tithe.[31] After the alleged complicity of the Jesuits in the popular riots in Madrid in 1766, regalists and their allies among clerics hostile to the Society in Spain gained enough power to convince King Charles to issue an edict on March 27, 1767, ordering the expulsion of the Jesuits from Spain and its empire.[32]

Although expelling the Jesuits had serious consequences for education, intellectual life in the empire, and for frontier missionary work, the extant documentation indicates that it apparently had little impact on preaching in indigenous languages at the parish level. Apart from their missionary activities along the frontiers of the viceroyalty, the Jesuits had little day-to-day involvement in ministering to Andeans in the *docrinas de indios*, where the indigenous peoples lived and worked. A study of rural parishes conducted by the viceroy in charge of overseeing the seculariza-tion process in Peru, José Manso de Velasco, indicated that the Society controlled only 13 of the 564 indigenous parishes in the viceroyalty—one in Lima, eight in Misque, and four in La Paz. The 12 parishes in Misque and La Paz were tied to frontier missions, where the Jesuits undoubtedly preached in indigenous languages. On the other hand, the small parish in Lima was Santiago del Cercado (the city's indigenous quarter), and it supported their school for the children of *caciques,* the Colegio del Príncipe.[33] Since instruction in this school was conducted exclusively in Castilian, that relatively modest enterprise had little impact on the use of Quechua, Aymara, and other indigenous languages throughout the Viceroyalty of Peru. Despite their support for preaching in indigenous languages and their sensitivity to preserving indigenous cultural heri-tages, the Society had little influence over the language of evangelization in the vast majority of the *doctrinas de indios.*

The evidence indicates that the Crown's attempts to eradicate Quechua and Aymara as spoken languages following the revolts of Tupac Amaru (in the Cuzco region), Thupa Katari (in the La Paz district), and Tomás Katari (in Chayanta) had only a limited long-term impact on the daily use of indigenous tongues. The *visitador general* of Peru, José Antonio Areche, ordered all Quechua speakers to speak Castilian within four years, and he abolished the Chair in Quechua at the University of San Marcos, which had been filled since the vice regency of Francisco de Toledo (1569–1581).[34] Areche further declared that the indigenous peoples "are to dress in our Spanish clothing and speak the Castilian language. The use of schools will be introduced with more vigour than up to now under the most rigor-ous penalties for those who do not attend."[35] The bishop of Cuzco, Juan Manuel Moscoso, also demanded that descendents of the Inca cease wear-ing indigenous ceremonial dress, performing Andean dances, and using Quechua in church ceremonies. Moreover, Areche, and his chief advisor, Benito de Mata Linares, also attempted to stamp out any signs of Inca revivalism. They ordered the destruction of all paintings that invoked images of Tawantinsuyu, including those displayed in the Jesuit school of San Francisco de Borja in Cuzco. They also banned the circulation of Garcilaso de la Vega's *Comentarios reales.* Both men then tried unsuccess-fully to have the Crown abolish the traditional office of *cacique,* fearing that these indigenous leaders might foment new revolts. Finally, Crown authori-ties imposed the intendancy system in 1784, with one of its expressed goals being the "extirpation of the Indian languages."[36]

Despite such efforts to stamp out the speaking of Quechua and Aymara, many contemporary accounts pointed out the difficulties of forcing Andeans to replace indigenous languages with Castilian. Members of the Inca nobility continued to use Quechua names, and by 1791 royal officials in Cuzco even referred to members of the local indigenous *cabildo* (town council) as "*electores Yngas*" rather than "*electores indios.*"[37] The intendant of Arequipa, Antonio Alvarez y Jiménez, attempted to "extirpate" Andean languages by establishing schools to teach Castilian in his district, but he admitted that the "total elimination of [indigenous languages] is not easy."[38] Even Bishop Moscoso, remarked in frustration:

> I understand that the presses are wearing out from printing ordinances and laws to take the Indians' language away from them, and that in keeping with the royal edicts about this matter, earnest prelates order it with grave asperity during inspections of their diocese, prescribing that the young be taught Castilian. What good does this do, when the Indians continue to speak their own languages, and so tenaciously, that they speak three languages as completely different as Quechua, Aymara, and Puquina?[39]

The Crown also proposed that each community should set aside agricultural or grazing lands, with the proceeds going to support local schools, but this proposal too proved unworkable in most regions.[40] A dramatic expansion of the parish school system needed to teach young Andeans Castilian was simply beyond the financial resources of both the Crown and the church in the aftermath of the Great Rebellions. According to historian David Garrett: "Literacy and Spanish made inroads in rural society in the last decades of the viceroyalty, but a serious assault on Quechua and Aymara would have been utterly impossible...."[41]

Nonetheless, in some areas the Bourbon Reforms did promote the founding of schools to educate indigenous children in Castilian. In Trujillo, for example, Baltazar Jaime Martínez Campañón, who served as bishop from 1779 to 1791, introduced publicly supported primary schools for indigenous boys and girls in Castilian that emphasized religion and practical skills—reading, writing, and basic arithmetic. The bishop ordered all students within half a league from any town or village to attend a school. He claimed to have established 54 primary schools, including boarding schools in Trujillo and Cajamarca in his diocese. While little is known about the fate of these schools after Martínez Campañón left Trujillo for Bogotá in 1791, the Crown ordered the newly established intendants in Peru to found similar public schools to teach indigenous children in Castilian.[42] The purpose of this support for public education in Castilian was to eradicate the sedition that had led to Andean insurrections in the 1780s. Nonetheless, historians know very little about how extensive or successful public and even private efforts were to educate indigenous children in Castilian during the late eighteenth century. It is clear, however, that as late as 1820 the colonial government was still trying, without any notable success, to establish local schools in every indigenous parish.

Even the rise of Spanish Liberalism and the promulgation of the Constitution of 1812 apparently had only a limited impact on replacing indigenous languages with Castilian throughout the realm. In the confusion following Napoleon Bonaparte's invasion of Spain in 1807, a Liberal government formed in Cádiz and framed a new constitution in 1812, which proposed wide-ranging reforms within the empire. Among the most controversial of the Constitution's provisions was awarding full citizenship to Amerindians, abolishing indigenous tribute levies, and giving indigenous people the right to vote in local municipal elections throughout the empire. Ending the legal status of "Indian" and encouraging Andean participation in politics undoubtedly would have required the indigenous peoples to learn Castilian, the language of the state.

Andean communities differed in their responses to these innovations. The reforms effectively ended the corporate status of indigenous communities, ending tribute and forced labor levies, but also making them subject to losing communal lands and to paying new colonial taxes, such as the sales tax (*alcabala*). In those provinces more isolated from market forces, on balance, the abolition of the head tax appeared a boon, because meeting the new burdens would not have amounted to the sums paid in tribute. For communities that participated actively in market exchanges, however, the prospect of paying the full array of sales taxes, tithes, and other duties carried a much stiffer price tag and threatened future economic prospects. Even more importantly for colonial authorities, ending Amerindian tribute also imperilled the nearly bankrupt royal treasury. In the end, the Viceroy of Peru, José Fernando de Abascal, simply refused to abide by this abolition order.[43] Finally, the return to Spain of King Ferdinand VII in 1814 ended all Liberal experiments in representative government and social reform, as the Crown tried to reestablish the old absolutist colonial order. As a result, the short phase of Spanish Liberal reforms and the widespread failure to implement them meant that such innovations probably had little long-term impact on the spread of Castilian at the expense of indigenous languages in most regions of the Andes. Many of the policies of Spanish Liberals were ultimately carried out under the republican regimes in the Andes during the nineteenth century, but Quechua and Aymara continued as commonly spoken languages in most Andean communities, despite campaigns that seemingly tried to undermine their everyday use.

Quite apart from the natural resistance of Andeans to give up their native languages in favor of Castilian, powerful colonial interest groups had no particular desire to advance literacy in Castilian among the indigenous peoples. Many peninsular and creole elites understood well the power of language in maintaining the subordination of indigenous peoples. Castilian was the language of the state and its court system, and as long as Andeans did not speak it, they could be more easily manipulated and prohibited from attaining greater social mobility. Landowners, bureaucrats, and judges understood that their domination of literacy in Castilian was a powerful tool in controlling the indigenous peoples, particularly in the wake of the rebellions of the 1780s. Rural priests also may have been reluctant to advance literacy, which would undermine much of their role as mediators between indigenous parishioners and the outside world. Even bilingual Andeans (called *indios ladinos*) serving as local caciques or scribes derived considerable power within indigenous communities by their knowledge of Castilian and Andean languages. It is no small wonder that the Crown and later the governments of the Andean republics never mustered the resources to instruct all indigenous communities in Castilian and to eradicate the use of the principal indigenous languages. Language and subordination were closely linked. Indeed, Quechua and Aymara persist to the present day as living, spoken languages in indigenous highland communities of the Andes.

3. Ethnogenesis and Documentary Evidence on Indigenous Languages

While none of the historical events of the eighteenth and early nineteenth centuries appear fundamental turning points in the spread or contraction of indigenous languages, they did generate abundant documentary evidence about the use of Andean vernacular languages. Although the voices of Quechua and Aymara speakers in these documents may be faint, evidence about indigenous languages does appear in a wide range of primary sources. By the eighteenth century the Andean peoples had formulated survival strategies that promoted ethnogenesis—a process whereby Andean ethnic groups formed a shared cultural system and a social order that transformed them into new identifiable culture groups, who saw themselves as different from the wider social landscape. [44] This effort to create a new, shared sense of identity emerged within a history of violent changes—demographic collapse, forced relocations, new work regimens, forced and voluntary migrations, and religious change, which had begun following the conquest and were well advanced by the eighteenth century.[45] Language, as one among the many markers of ethnicity in the Andes, was an integral part of this process of ethnic reformulation and regeneration, as different kin groups came into contact with each other and invented or changed elements of their ethnic identity. While Andean ethnic groups spoke a wide range of languages when the Spaniards arrived in 1532—such as Quechua, Aymara, Puquina, Moche (Yunga), and Uru—by the eighteenth century the most prominent, commonly spoken languages or *lenguas generales* were Quechua and Aymara.[46] By the seventeenth and certainly by the eighteenth century, extant documentary sources provide abundant evidence of changes affecting language use and ethnicity in the Andes. Taken together with linguistic data, archaeological materials, ethnographic evidence, and work in cultural studies, historians and scholars from other disciplines can find and interpret new evidence in the documentary record about indigenous languages in the late colonial Andes.

The resettlement policy of Viceroy Toledo and forced or voluntary migrations of indigenous peoples undoubtedly had an influence over time on indigenous languages, and these population movements produced rich archival documentation stretching from the sixteenth to the early nineteenth centuries. Toledo, for example, ordered the resettlement of Andean communities into large, Spanish style towns, called *reducciones*.[47] This forced resettlement plan affected over 1.5 million Andeans, bringing together dispersed extended kinship groups (*ayllu*) or even larger ethnic groups.[48] In addition, Toledo's massive program of the *mita* for Potosí forced over 13,500 male tributaries each year (most often accompanied by their families) to work as mine workers in that remote highland mining city, whose population swelled to 120,000 inhabitants by 1620. Cities such as Lima, Cuzco, Quito, or La Paz also attracted migrants, who changed cultural practices in new urban environments. As indigenous men and women of modest social origins gained some measure of prosperity in urban market economies of the Andes, they frequently adopted clothing styles that the Inca had restricted to Andean elites. Others wore European-style fashions.[49] Indeed, one prominent linguist, César Itier, has argued that forced and voluntary migration to Spanish mining towns and cities promoted the process of koinéization or linguistic unification, leading to the spread of Southern (or Cuzco) Quechua long before the eighteenth century in the Andes. Itier argues that a class of urban indigenous residents of cities such as Potosí, Lima, and Cuzco promoted a process of linguistic convergence and homogenization, leading to the spread of Southern Quechua. Abundant documentation in Spanish and Andean archives exists that may help to support or challenge Itier's bold, controversial argument about language use.[50]

Epidemic diseases led to cultural changes as whole communities became transformed when waves of European epidemics (influenza, smallpox, measles, plague and other infectious diseases) caused the pre-invasion population of what is now modern-day Peru to fall from approximately nine million to just under one million by the arrival of Toledo in 1569. Densely populated lowland areas suffered the greatest losses, where over 95 percent of the population perished, while more scattered mountain valleys experienced less severe mortality rates.[51] Nonetheless, the indigenous population of the Andes did not stabilize until the 1650s, and then only to suffer another setback when new epidemics hit the north Andes in the 1690s and the Central and Southern Andes between 1719 and 1730.[52] Whole communities disappeared in the wake of these epidemics, leading groups of Andeans to congregate with other ethnic groups, forming new ethnic configurations, which undoubtedly had some impact on the spread or contraction of different indigenous language families.

The devastating losses from epidemic diseases, heavy tribute and *mita* obligations, Spanish usurpations of community lands, and even the lure of market participation led many Andeans to leave their *ayllu* permanently. Few areas in the Andes experienced more out migration than those provinces of Perú and Alto Perú subject to the Potosí *mita*. As epidemics thinned the population in these regions, the burdens of corvée labor became onerous in many *ayllu*, encouraging traditional residents of indigenous communities (*originarios*) to migrate to other regions. Once ensconced in another community, the Andeans could claim the status of *forasteros*, who were outsiders with no claim on community lands. This also allowed the *forasteros* to claim a lower tribute rate and an exemption from the *mita*. By 1646 over 36 percent of the population in these provinces was officially listed as *forasteros*; by the census of the Duque de la Palata in 1683 that number had risen to 54 percent.[53] Severing ties with their *ayllu* promoted the reformulation of traditional lifestyles, social practices, and cultural identities in new communities. In rural zones many *forasteros* acquired land among other ethnic groups through sharecropping, rental, or outright purchase, sometimes being absorbed into the communities where they had come to reside. In other cases, groups of migrants constituted a separate *ayllu* of *forasteros* in rural areas, representing a mix of different ethnic groups.[54] Over time, these *forasteros* intermarried and took on a blend of cultural values, which undoubtedly had an impact on the particular forms of Quechua and Aymara spoken.

Abundant documentation about the Roman Catholic Church, particularly concerning evangelization, extirpation trials, and church-state conflicts, has the potential to reveal a great deal about language use by the late colonial period. Recent work on Quechua translations of sacred Christian literature has revealed divisions within the church over language policy and the difficulties of imposing a single standard form of Quechua or Aymara by churchmen seeking to convert Andeans to Catholicism. As Alan Durston has remarked: "Translation itself can be understood as a way of establishing relations—often hierarchical ones—between languages, and thus between cultures and groups of people."[55] Understanding shifts in language policy in evangelization provides important information on shifting ideologies within the church over converting indigenous peoples. It also underscores the responses of indigenous people to these conversion efforts. Such responses are seen most clearly in the documentation relating to seventeenth-century efforts by churchmen to extirpate ongoing Andean religious practices in the Archdiocese of Lima, such as the worship of Andean shrines (*huacas*), lineage deities *(chancas)*, or the mummified remains of ancestors (*malquis*). Extirpation trials have produced abundant documentation on Andean religious practices, and the need to translate the testimony of Andean witnesses demonstrates the pervasiveness of indigenous languages. The trials also document ongoing difficulties in translating Christian doctrine into indigenous languages. Likewise, confessional manuals written in Andean languages to aid priests in interrogating penitents are an important source of information on language. These materials exemplify the difficulty of cultural exchange between Europeans and Andeans, indigenous resistance to Catholic teachings, and differing views about sin, morality, and sexuality.[56] Finally, eighteenth-century conflicts over clerical fees, the secularization of the *doctrinas de indios,* and preaching in vernacular Andean languages all reveal a great deal about the persistence or disappearance of different indigenous languages.

Another important topic capable of yielding important information about language in the Andes is the role of bilingual (and often bicultural) Andeans. Andeans who knew Spanish customs and language, most often called *indios ladinos* in colonial documentation, could bridge European and indigenous cultures, revealing the complexities of colonial society. While the most famous of these *indios ladinos* was Felipe Guaman Poma de Ayala, many others followed, serving as assistants to priests in evangelization or extirpators of idolatry, as messianic leaders, litigants in colonial courts, or even as writers of petitions or memorials.[57] A number of documents, written in Castilian, to protest against colonial abuses and propose concrete reforms to the Crown remain in various archival repositories, including the memorials of the north Andean *curaca* Vicente Morachimo (1732) and the mestizo Franciscan lay brother, Fray Calixto de San José Tupac Inka (1749), in the eighteenth century.[58] The memorial of Fray Calixto even harkened back to earlier writings by Domingo de Santo Tomás and Guaman Poma, calling for a series of reforms, including indigenous self-governance and free entry into the secular clergy and the religious orders for Andean ethnic leaders.[59] Studying such Andean *indios ladinos* and also mestizo petitioners, who could navigate in both Hispanic and Andean cultural traditions, have the potential to yield a great deal of information about languages and cultural change in the Andes.

Crown efforts to suppress Quechua and Aymara within four years after the defeat of the revolts of the 1780s apparently failed to replace indigenous languages with Castilian, but the whole endeavor did generate archival documentation about indigenous languages in the Andes. As Crown officials strove to stamp out any remaining vestiges of Inca revivalism, they wrote about the need to teach Andean peoples Castilian. Royal officials believed that Quechua, Aymara, and any other indigenous languages were vestiges of a backward past that at best impeded progress and at worst served to foment rebellion and the violent overthrow of the Spanish colonial order. To help eradicate the use of these indigenous languages, the Crown issued laws banning their use, and Crown officials were commanded to found schools to instruct indigenous children in Castilian. Historians know little about how extensive or successful public and even private efforts were to educate indigenous children in Castilian during the late eighteenth and early nineteenth centuries. Nonetheless, a detailed examination of these efforts to establish widespread network of public schools to teach Andeans Castilian could yield much information about the persistence or contraction of indigenous language use in the eighteenth and early nineteenth centuries.

4. Conclusion

Scholarly interest in the evolution of Andean colonial society during the eighteenth and early nineteenth centuries has led to an impressive output in interdisciplinary publications over the last 30 years. At the same time, historians have made few contributions to the study of language use in the Andes, even though the extant primary sources exist for them to make significant future advances, particularly in collaboration with scholars from other disciplines interested in language spread and use, such as anthropologists or linguists. The lack of alphabetic writing in pre-Columbian Andean societies and the paucity of colonial documents written in indigenous languages also have impeded the development of a "New Philology for the Andes," following the approach pioneered by James Lockhart and his students of Mexico. Nonetheless, a wide variety of published and manuscript sources exist for the Andes, which have the potential to yield much about the spread and use of major indigenous language families. Controversies over evangelization, forced and voluntary migrants, the spread of epidemic diseases, educational policies, and interpreters or bicultural *indios ladinos,* and the Great Age of Andean insurrections have all generated official documents that promise to contain much information on indigenous languages in the late colonial period. A reexamination of these sources may well lead to substantial breakthroughs in scholarly knowledge about Andean languages, particularly the most widely spoken language families, Quechua and Aymara.

The promise of such scholarly advances can only be enhanced by collaborations among scholars from different disciplines. The challenge of interpreting the past lends itself to a variety of disciplinary and interdisciplinary methods. This is particularly true for issues of great complexity, such as language use in the multiethnic indigenous communities of the Andes. Linguists, anthropologists, and archaeologists have made substantial progress in studying the use and spread or contraction of language families. Historians and scholars from these disciplines, who are willing to undertake collaborations that stretch across disciplinary boundaries, have the potential to make substantive and methodological advances in studying indigenous languages.

Such collaborations even have the potential to inform contemporary political debates. For too long, language and literacy in the Andes have been associated with political subordination. Quechua and Aymara speakers have faced discrimination, first in colonial society, and later in the independent nation states formed in the Andes. From the writings of Nebrija in 1492 to the present day, Castilian has been the language of domination. Interest in the past is frequently oriented by issues formulated in the present. Understanding the use, spread, and contraction of indigenous languages in the colonial era is also relevant to concerns in the present, and both are pertinent to the future.

Notes

1. The case for narrative *quipu* is made in the recently published work of Laura Laurencich Minelli (ed.), *"Exsul Immeritus Blas Valera Populo Suo" e "Historia et Rudimenta Linguae Piruanorum": Indios, gesuiti, e spagnoli in due documenti segreti sul Perú del XVII secolo* (Bologna: CLUEB, 2007), and in Carlo Animato, Paolo A. Rossi, and Clara Miccinelli (eds.), *Quipu: Il nodo parlante dei misteriosi Incas* (Genoa: Edizioni Culturali Internazionali, 1989). The existence of narrative *quipu* remains a very controversial issue among specialists. Frank Salomon approaches the possibility of narrative *quipu* with some skepticism; see Frank Salomon, *The Cordkeepers: Khipus and Cultural Life in a Peruvian Village* (Durham, NC: Duke University Press, 2004). Other specialists, such as Jeffrey Quilter and Gary Urton, speculate that *quipus* could encode narratives; see Jeffrey Quilter and Gary Urton (eds.), *Narrative Threads: Accounting and Recounting in Andean Khipu* (Austin: University of Texas Press, 2002), pp. 3–21.
2. George Urioste has uncovered some mundane documents written in Quechua, but nothing on the order of what scholars have uncovered for Mexico; James Lockhart, "Trunk Lines and Feeder Lines: The Spanish Reaction to American Resources," in Kenneth J. Andrien and Rolena Adorno (eds.), *Transatlantic Encounters: Europeans and Andeans in the Sixteenth Century* (Berkeley and Los Angeles: University of California Press, 1991), pp. 90–120, see p. 120. See also Alan Durston, "Native Language Literacy in Colonial Peru: The Question of Mundane Quechua Writing Revisited," *Hispanic American Historical Review* 88:1 (Feb. 2008), 41–70.

3. Eric Van Young, "The New Cultural History Comes to Old Mexico," *Hispanic American Historical Review* 79:2 (May 1999), 211–47, see 234.

4. An overview of the New Philology and its contributions to scholarship may be found in an article by one of its practitioners. See Matthew Restall, "A History of the New Philology and the New Philology in History," *Latin American Research Review* 38:1 (Feb. 2003), 113–34.

5. Kenneth J. Andrien, *Andean Worlds: Indigenous History, Culture, and Consciousness under Spanish Rule, 1532–1825* (Albuquerque: University of New Mexico Press, 2001), p. 108.

6. On the Third Lima Council, see Alan Durston, *Pastoral Quechua: The History of Christian Translation in Colonial Peru, 1550–1650* (Notre Dame, IN: University of Notre Dame Press, 2007), pp. 86–104; Bruce Mannheim, *The Language of the Inka since the European Invasion* (Austin: University of Texas Press, 1991), pp. 66–67.

7. See Gary Urton, *Signs of the Inka Khipu: Binary Coding in the Andean Knotted String Records* (Austin: University of Texas Press, 2003), p. 22; and Urton, "From Knots to Narratives: Reconstructing the Art of Historical Record Keeping in the Andes from Spanish Transcriptions of Inka *Khipus*," *Ethnohistory* 45:3 (Summer 1998), 409–38.

8. Diego González Holguín (intr. Ramiro Matos Mendieta and prol. Raúl Porras Barrenechea), *Vocabulario de la lengua general de todo el Perú llamada lengua quichua o del Inca* (1608; Lima: Universidad Nacional de San Marcos, 1989); González Holguín, *Gramática y arte nueva de la lengua general de todo el Perú, llamada lengua Quichua, o lengua del Inca* (1607; Heppenheim: Frany Wolf, 1975); Ludovico Bertonio, *Arte de la lengua Aymara* (1612; Leipzig: B. G. Teubner, 1879); Bertonio, *Vocabulario de la lengua Aymara* (1612; La Paz: Radio San Gabriel, 1993).

9. The seventeenth-century jurist, Juan de Solórzano y Pereyra, argued that indigenous languages in the Indies could be banned by royal decree, just as the Crown had prohibited the use of Arabic. See Juan de Solórzano y Pereyra, *Política Indiana* (1647; reprinted Madrid and Buenos Aires: Compañía Ibero-Americana, 1930), vol. 1, p. 402, vol. 2, xxxvi, p. 36; cited in Mannheim, *The Language of the Inka*, p. 68.

10. Ibid., p. 70.

11. Durston, *Pastoral Quechua*, pp. 86–96; Mannheim, *The Language of the Inka*, pp. 66–67.

12. Mannheim, *The Language of the Inka*, pp. 68–71.

13. For three major studies of the extirpation trials, see Kenneth Mills, *Idolatry and Its Enemies: Colonial Andean Religion and Extirpation, 1640–1750* (Princeton: Princeton University Press, 1997); Nicholas

Griffiths, *The Cross and the Serpent: Religious Repression and Resurgence in Colonial Peru* (Norman: University of Oklahoma Press, 1996); and Juan Carlos Estenssoro Fuchs, *Del paganismo a la santidad. La incorporación de los indios del Perú al catolicismo, 1532–1750* (Lima: Instituto Francés de Estudios Andinos / Pontificia Universidad Católica del Perú / Instituto Riva-Agüero, 2003).

14. The cult of the virgin has also been traced to Kotakawana, the Andean god of fertility. Rodolfo Cerrón-Palomino finds the association with Copacabana a false etymology in a personal note to the editors. Veronica Salles-Reese, *From Viracocha to the Virgin of Copacabana: Representation of the Sacred at Lake Titicaca* (Austin: University of Texas Press, 1997).

15. Mannheim, *The Language of the Inka*, pp. 65–68.

16. Ibid., p. 71, citing Bernard Lavallé, *Le marquis et le marchand: Les luttes de pouvoir au Cuzco (1700–1730)* (Paris: CNRS, 1987).

17. Mannheim, *The Language of the Inka*, pp. 71–74.

18. Sajid Alfredo Herrera, "Primary Education in Bourbon San Salvador and Sonsonate, 1750–1808," in Jordana Dym and Christophe Belaubre (eds.), *Politics, Economy, and Society in Bourbon Central America, 1759–1821* (Boulder: University of Colorado Press, 2007), pp. 17–45, see pp. 21–23.

19. John H. Elliott, "A Europe of Composite Monarchies," *Past and Present* 137 (Nov. 1992), 48–71, see 51.

20. Archivo General de Indias (hereinafter AGI), Lima, 1596, Cédula real to Virrey del Perú, Buen Retiro, 4 octubre de 1749, and a second edict sent to the Archbishop of Lima, AGI, Lima, 1596, Cédula real to Arzobispo de Lima, Buen Retiro, 4 octubre de 1749.

21. Kenneth J. Andrien, "The Coming of Enlightened Reform in Bourbon Peru: Secularization of the *Doctrinas de Indios*, 1746–1773," in Gabriel Pacquette (ed.), *Enlightened Reform in Southern Europe and its Atlantic Colonies, ca. 1750–1830* (Farnham: Ashgate, 2009), pp. 183–202, see pp. 183–84.

22. The process of secularization in New Spain has been studied by David A. Brading, *Church and State in Bourbon Mexico: The Diocese of Michoacán, 1749–1818* (Cambridge: Cambridge University Press, 1994), pp. 62–81; David A. Brading, "Tridentine Catholicism and Enlightened Despotism in Bourbon Mexico," *Journal of Latin American Studies* 15:1 (May 1983), 1–22; William B. Taylor, *Magistrates of the Sacred: Priests and Parishioners in Eighteenth-Century Mexico* (Stanford: Stanford University Press, 1996), pp. 83–6, 506–10; Dorothy Tanck de Estrada, *Pueblos de Indios y educación en el México colonial, 1750–1821* (México: El Colegio de México, 1999), pp. 161–69; Brian Belanger, "Secularization and the Laity in Colonial Mexico: Querétaro, 1598–1821," unpublished Ph.D. dissertation, Tulane University, 1990; Francisco Morales Valerio, "Secularización

de doctrinas: Fin de un modelo evangelizador en la Nueva España?" *Archivo Ibero-Americano: Revista Franciscana e Estudios Históricos* 52:205–208 (1992), 465–96; Ernest Sánchez Santiró, "El nuevo orden parroquial de la ciudad de México: Población, etnia, y territorio (1768–1777)," *Estudios de Historia Novohispana* 30 (Jan.–June 2004), 63–92; and Virve Piho, *La secularización de las parroquias en la Nueva España y su repercusión en San Andrés Calpan* (México: Instituto Nacional de Antropología e Historia, 1981).

23. Archivo San Francisco de Lima (hereinafter ASF), Registro II, No. 2:24, folios 441–43.
24. Durston, *Pastoral Quechua*, p. 79.
25. ASF, II, No. 2:24, ff., 445–45 verso.
26. AGI, Lima, 1596, Decreto de Pedro Antonio de Baroeta y Angel, Lima, 1 agosto, 1754.
27. AGI Lima, 1596, Marqués de la Ensenada to Conde de Superunda, Madrid, 1 febrero 1753.
28. AGI, Lima, 1596, Lima, Pedro Antonio Arzobispo de Lima to crown, Lima, 2 enero de 1760. AGI, Lima, 1596, Jacinto Obispo de Arequipa to crown, Arequipa, 13 marzo de 1759; AGI, Lima, 1596, Phelipe Obispo de Guamanga to crown, Guamanga, 14 marzo de 1759. AGI, Lima, 1596, Francisco Xavier Obispo de Trujillo to crown, Trujillo, 5 diciembre de 1759. AGI, Lima, 1596, Juan Obispo de Cuzco to crown, Cuzco, 16 febrero de 1760; Cayetano Obispo de La Plata to crown, La Plata, 15 febrero de 1760.
29. Monique Alaperrine-Bouyer, *La educación de las elites indígenas en el Perú colonial* (Lima: Instituto Francés de Estudios Andinos, 2007); Mannheim, *The Language of the Inka*, p. 65.
30. AGI, Indiferente General, 2085A, Buen Retiro, 24 febrero de 1750.
31. AGI, Indiferente General, 3085A, Madrid, Real Cédula, 4 diciembre de 1766.
32. John Lynch, *Bourbon Spain, 1700–1808* (Oxford: Basil Blackwell, 1989), pp. 280–90; AGI, Indiferente General, 3087, el Pardo, 27 marzo de 1767.
33. AGI Lima, 1596, Conde de Superunda to crown, Lima, 20 noviembre de 1751.
34. It was beyond the capacity of this Chair in Quechua to examine all candidates for parish work, even in the *Audiencia* of Lima, and in most dioceses skilled members of the cathedral chapter examined candidates for competency in Quechua and other indigenous languages. Durston, *Pastoral Quechua*, pp. 115–23.
35. Mannheim, *The Language of the Inka*, p. 74.
36. Ibid.
37. David T. Garrett, *Shadows of Empire: The Indian Nobility of Cusco, 1750–1825* (Cambridge and New York: Cambridge University Press, 2005), p. 216.

38. Mannheim, *The Language of the Inka*, pp. 74–75

39. Ibid.

40. There is no study of education in the Andes comparable to the work done on New Spain. See Tanck de Estrada, *Pueblos de indios y educación en el México Colonial.*

41. Garrett, *Shadows of Empire*, p. 216.

42. An important recent article exploring this important topic is Susan E. Ramírez, "To Serve God and King: The Origins of Public Schools for Native Children in Eighteenth-century Peru," *Colonial Latin American Review*, 17:1 (June 2008), 73–99.

43. On the impact of the Constitution of 1812 see, Jaime E. Rodríguez O., *The Independence of Spanish America* (Cambridge and New York: Cambridge University Press, 1998).

44. Christopher C. Fennell, *Crossroads and Cosmologies: Diasporas and Ethnogenesis in the New World* (Gainesville: University Press of Florida, 2007), pp. 1–2.

45. Jonathan D. Hill (ed.), *History, Power, and Identity: Ethnogenesis in the Americas, 1492–1992* (Iowa City: University of Iowa Press, 1996), p. 1.

46. On the languages spoken in the former Inca Empire, see Willem F. H. Adelaar with Pieter C. Muysken, *The Languages of the Andes* (Cambridge and New York: Cambridge University Press, 2004), pp. 165–410; Rodolfo Cerrón-Palomino, *Lingüística Aimara* (Lima: Centro de Estudios Regionales Andinos "Bartolomé de las Casas," 2000); Alfredo Torero, *Idiomas de los Andes. Lingüística e historia* (Lima: Instituto Francés de Estudios Andinos / Horizonte, 2002).

47. The most recent study of the Toledan *reducciones* is a dissertation: Jeremy Ravi Mumford, "Vertical Empire: The Struggle for Andean Space in the Sixteenth Century," unpublished Ph.D. dissertation, Yale University, 2005.

48. John Hemming, *The Conquest of the Incas* (New York: Harcourt, Brace & Company, 1970), p. 395.

49. Karen B. Graubart, *With Our Labor and Sweat: Indigenous Women and the Formation of Colonial Society in Peru, 1550–1700* (Stanford: Stanford University Press, 2007), pp. 121–57; and Ana María Presta, "Undressing the *Coya* and Dressing the Indian Woman: Market Economy, Clothing, and Identities in the Colonial Andes, La Plata (Charcas), Late Sixteenth and Early Seventeenth Centuries," *Hispanic American Historical Review* 90:1 (2010), 41–74.

50. Alan Durston finds Itier's argument unconvincing, for example. See Durston, *Pastoral Quechua*, p. 47; César Itier, "Lengua general y quechua cuzqueño en los siglos XVI y XVII," in Luis Millones, Hiroyasu Tomoeda, and Tatsuhiko Fujii (eds.), *Desde afuera y desde adentro. Ensayos de etnografía e historia del Cuzco y Apurímac* (Osaka: National Museum of Ethnology, 2000), pp. 47–59; Itier,

"La propagation de la langue générale dans le sud du Pérou," in *Le savoir, pouvoir des élites dans l'empire espagnol d'Amérique* (Paris: Université de la Sorbonne Nouvelle Paris III, 2001), pp. 63–74.

51. Jeffrey A. Cole, "An Abolitionism Born of Frustration: The Conde de Lemos and the Potosí Mita, 1667–1673," *Hispanic American Historical Review* 63:2 (May 1983), 307–33.

52. Suzanne Austin Alchon, *Native Society and Disease in Colonial Ecuador* (Cambridge and New York: Cambridge University Press, 1991), pp. 89–99; Karen Vieira Powers, *Andean Journeys: Migration, Ethnogenesis and the State in Colonial Quito* (Albuquerque: University of New Mexico Press, 1995), pp. 45–80; Ann Wightman, *Indigenous Migration and Social Change: The Forasteros of Cuzco, 1570–1720* (Durham, NC: Duke University Press, 1990), pp. 150–54.

53. Andrien, *Andean Worlds,* p. 90.

54. Wightman, *Indigenous Migration and Social Change*, pp. 63, 74, 89–92, 224–25.

55. Durston, *Pastoral Quechua*, p. 1.

56. Regina Harrison, *"True" Confessions: Quechua and Spanish Cultural Encounters in the Viceroyalty of Peru* (College Park: University of Maryland, Latin American Studies Centre, 1992) pp. 1–44.

57. The pioneering work in this area is Rolena Adorno, "Images of *Indios Ladinos* in Early Colonial Peru," in Kenneth J. Andrien and Rolena Adorno (eds.), *Transatlantic Encounters: Europeans and Andeans in the Sixteenth Century* (Berkeley and Los Angeles: University of California Press, 1991), pp. 232–70. An excellent unpublished study is: John Duffy Charles, "Indios Ladinos: Colonial Andean Testimony and Ecclesiastical Institutions, 1583–1650," unpublished Ph.D. dissertation, Yale University, 2003.

58. AGI Lima, 442, "Manifiesto de los agravios, vexaciones, y molestias que padecen los indios del reyno del Perú," Madrid, 3 septiembre de 1732; Francisco A. Loayza (ed.), *Fray Calixto Túpak Inka: documentos originales y, en su mayoría, totalmente desconocidos, auténticos, de este apóstol indio, valiente defensor de su raza, desde el año 1746 a 1760* (Lima: Pequeños grandes libros de historia de América, 1948).

59. Kenneth J. Andrien, "The *Noticias Secretas de América* and the Construction of a Governing Ideology for the Spanish American Empire," *Colonial Latin American Review* 7:2 (1998), 175–79.

Chapter 6

Reindigenization and Native Languages in Peru's Long Nineteenth Century (1795–1940)

Adrian J. Pearce

An important question in the language history of the Andes concerns the roots of the modern decline of Quechua—the dominant native language of Peru, and still today the largest indigenous language family of the Americas. Noting the excellent prospects for Quechua even under Spanish colonialism from the sixteenth to the late eighteenth centuries, distinguished linguists have posed the key question of when the change occurred that "brought about the cultural and social decline of Quechua, thus producing its inevitable marginalisation."[1] César Itier, in a view endorsed by Willem Adelaar, has placed the crucial shift some time between 1750 and 1850. This period is seen as key, since it witnessed major changes in the social status of Quechua, brought about in part by repressive measures following the Great Rebellion of Túpaq Amaru II in the early 1780s. In discussing the case of Cuzco, Itier notes the disappearance around independence of the upper stratum of native society, "either by impoverishment, or by incorporation into the creole stratum."[2] Adelaar points to the "deliberate attack on the prestige and use of Quechua" of the post-Túpaq Amaru decrees as undermining the language.[3] In summary, "the social, cultural and ideological context…during the last Bourbon decades and the beginning of the Republic had turned radically adverse to Quechua as an instrument of communication."[4] Although still spoken by a great many native peasants, Quechua was doomed in the long run by the loss of its native elite and the turning away from the language of provincial creoles.

In contrast to this view, the present essay argues that the roots of the decline of Quechua lay not in the independence or early republican eras, but subsequently, in the late nineteenth and early twentieth centuries. This fresh interpretation draws upon a striking current in recent historical writing on early republican Peru, that which explores the phenomenon of "reindigenization," which affected much of the Andes during this period, and very probably reinforced the use of Quechua there. Reindigenization (or "reindianization") was first detected by historians in the 1950s, primarily on the basis of census records and in demographic terms. More recently, it has been extended to embrace a broader phenomenon of resurgence experienced by native Andeans following independence in the 1820s. The evidence suggests that this resurgence took place in the context of the collapse of the national states, particularly in Peru and Bolivia and above all in the highland provinces, as a result of severe dislocations occasioned by independence itself and the lengthy period of political turmoil and economic stagnation that followed. This collapse, or at least the weakening of the heavy hand of the state in the Andes, permitted a reflorescence of native populations oppressed since the Conquest. But while the demographic, economic, and political dimensions of reindianization have been explored in some depth, its cultural aspects have barely been addressed—including its implications for the survival or decline of native tongues.

Neglect of the topic to date notwithstanding, reindigenization can make a major contribution to our understanding of the histories of native languages in the Andes. In a seminal contribution to the literature of this question, the historian Paul Gootenberg suggested that early republican reindianization "is the root cause of contemporary Peru's extraordinary indigenous presence"—a remark presumably applicable to native language use.[5] And sure enough, as we shall see, the vitality of native languages in Peru (and Bolivia) was almost certainly bolstered by reindigenization, beginning before 1830 and perhaps much earlier, and continuing until as late as the 1940s in some regions. What is more, in concrete terms, indigenization—rooted in the *specific* political and economic circumstances of the early republic—may help to explain the *specific* linguistic patterns that emerged by the end of this period. In these pages, the latter point is developed primarily with regard to a further important question, that of the decline of the native languages of the northern highlands and coast of Peru (which with the exception of Quechua died out during the decades either side of 1900). In the first exploration of the relation between reindigenization and native languages, then, this work sets out first to detail (at some length) the main arguments of the intriguing historical literature of the subject (focusing mainly on Peru, but where appropriate, also on Bolivia). It then advances some conclusions as to its significance for the history of native languages during the century following independence.

Reindigenization: The Demographic Case

Until relatively recently, the early republican period was understood to have been peculiarly traumatic for native peoples in the Andes. On the one hand, the colonial burden of native tribute was restored after independence, albeit under a revised republican terminology, along with forced labor regimes. On the other hand, a triumphant liberal ideology launched an assault on the very basis of the Indian community, its communal landholdings. Regarding traditional communities as inefficient anachronisms, and seeking to convert natives into independent Republican smallholders, in 1824 Simón Bolívar decreed the transfer to Indians of full property rights to their lands, including the parceling out of all community lands.[6] No restrictions were placed on subsequent sale of these lands, however; and combined with the freeing from royal restraint of regional elites in the sierra, there occurred a rapid erosion of the traditional native world. In an influential article dated 1970, Jean Piel wrote that "in their credulity, passivity and ignorance, the peasants of the communities were in a weak defensive position when it came to the redistribution of land."[7] Frederick Pike remarked that "Indian communities after independence were subjected to the systematic assault of white and *mestizo* landowners...Indians soon lost their land to creoles and *mestizos* of the sierra and also to opportunistic adventurers from the coast. As a result many native communities disappeared."[8] The overall result, in this tradition of scholarship, was perhaps surprising but nonetheless beyond dispute: during the decades following independence, "the Indian was worse off than he had ever been under the Spanish rule."[9]

An early inkling that native peoples' experience of the republic might have been rather less bitter than this vision implied came as long ago as 1952, but in work whose implications were long neglected. In the latter year, George Kubler published a slim study titled *The Indian Caste of Peru, 1795–1940*, based on extensive research in Peruvian historical demography. Some 40 years later, in 1991, Paul Gootenberg published his own outstanding analysis, "Population and Ethnicity in Early Republican Peru: Some Revisions," based upon a careful review of Kubler's figures, supplemented by newly discovered census materials. The findings of these studies were surprising. Kubler concluded that the native population of Peru grew strongly during the first three-quarters of the nineteenth century, even rising slightly as a proportion of the total. From making up fractionally less than 58 percent of the population in 1795, Indians came to constitute more than 59 percent by the mid-1850s, and showed little retreat as late as the first modern census in 1876.[10] Gootenberg's findings differed from Kubler's in important details, but confirmed them in essence: Gootenberg suggests that Indians numbered some 759,000 in 1795, when they made up 61.3 percent of the total population. By 1827, this proportion had risen slightly, to 61.6 percent, and by 1876 it had fallen only slightly, to just under 58 percent. Only by 1940 (the date of the second republican census) did Indians for the first time cease to be a majority in the country, numbering 2,856,000 and making up 46 percent of the population of Peru.[11]

These studies concluded, then, that Peru's indigenous population remained broadly stable in proportional terms, even increasing slightly, between the 1790s and the late 1820s, and showed only modest decline until as late as the 1870s. Indeed, Gootenberg emphasizes that "speaking hypothetically," the Indian population would have held firm at 62 percent in 1876 had it not been for the loss of perhaps 300,000 Indians in epidemics in the 1850s and the boosting of the nonnative population by the immigration of some 90,000 Chinese coolies. These findings were remarkable because they suggested that the early republican period was unique as one in which Peru's native population held its own, and even recovered somewhat, against the slow but seemingly inexorable tide of *mestizaje*. The half-century or more following the 1790s thus stood as the only period since the Spanish Conquest in the 1530s during which Peru's population experienced some measure of *reindigenization*, since after the 1870s, what Gootenberg calls "modern mestizaje" again took hold.[12] Of course, population growth might have occurred in circumstances that were adverse to native peoples; but in fact, as we shall see, this same period seems to have been unusually favorable in terms of the broader conditions affecting Indians. For Bolivia, meanwhile, a comparable study found that the native population actually fell by some 17 percent between 1838 and 1877, primarily due to epidemics, drought, and famine. Nevertheless, this study also identified an important reinforcement of Indian communities in Bolivia during this period, as discussed below.[13]

Kubler and Gootenberg's striking conclusions hold true for the population of Peru as a whole; but they also discuss population trends at the level of individual provinces and regions of the country, and here too their work yielded surprising results. On the one hand, as we shall see, in particular provinces or regions, the indigenization trend was far more marked than the aggregate national figures imply. On the other hand, the resilience of the native population was far from uniform across the country; rather, by 1876, the provinces with Indian majorities were concentrated mainly in the highlands, and above all in the center and south. By 1940, the trend was even more marked: Indian majorities prevailed virtually throughout the highlands, from Huaylas in the center to Puno in the south. Mestizo majorities, by contrast, existed almost throughout the northern highlands and along most of the coast. Kubler thus concluded that what became the twentieth-century truism of Peru as a country with an indigenous highlands and a mestizo littoral in fact became "a political reality only in the [60 or so] years before 1940."[14]

Since Gootenberg's article, the most striking research on the demography of this topic concerns the period 1876 to 1940, and the phenomenon of "late indigenization": that which occurred largely subsequent to 1876. This phenomenon has been discussed above all by Mark Thurner, in work focused primarily on Huaylas-Ancash. Thurner observes that from the 1790s to the 1850s, the population of this region was split virtually evenly between Indians and non-Indians, with natives constituting about 51 percent. But an "important Indianization trend" then occurred between 1850 and 1940, "with the largest leap occurring some time after 1876." By 1940, 62 percent of the population of Ancash was indigenous, and 38 percent white or *mestizo*; "in other words, between 1791 and 1940 the indigenous / non-indigenous ratio had shifted dramatically from nearly 1:1 to almost 2:1."[15] Thurner says little about the causes of this late indigenization, and indeed the phenomenon remains poorly understood. It runs contrary to the general trend after the 1870s, after all, which we have seen was toward growing *mestizaje* and proportional native decline. Thurner points out, however, that the case of Ancash was far from unique, since to judge from Kubler's data, "eleven highland provinces exhibited this late indigenisation trend." These provinces were concentrated in two "ethnogeographical islands," one in the north around the Callejón de Huaylas, the other in the south from Huancayo to Puno; the 11 provinces were Abancay, Andahuaylas, Aimaraes, Conchucos, Huamalíes, Huari, Huaylas, Jauja, Paruro, Tayacaja, and La Unión.[16] And there were others: Nils Jacobsen demonstrates that population growth in the province of Azángaro actually slowed down between the 1790s and the mid-1820s, and "underwent only minimal growth" from the latter period until 1876. But between 1876 and 1940, it again "became sufficiently robust to overcome the effects of epidemics, emigration, and military recruitment." In the 1790s, Azángaro's native population already made up almost 90 percent of the total for the province; throughout the period 1850 to 1940, this figure stood at nearly 96 percent.[17]

Peruvian demographic history prior to the late twentieth century presents exceptional challenges. Gootenberg began his 1991 study with the bracing remark, "all numbers on the makeup of Peru's republican population are wrong, the one point on which historians can agree." Kubler wrestled at length with data for Indian and non-Indian (*casta*) populations drawn in many cases from tax records, and which represented *fiscal* categories. In discussing reindigenization, Olivia Harris pondered "how far such 'fiscal Indians' accepted their new identification in cultural and social terms," suggesting for example that mestizos assumed native status so as to gain title to the lands they occupied.[18] Other scholars, too, have pointed to ways that growth in Indian populations might have been boosted "artificially."[19] Nevertheless, Gootenberg defends the practical utility of the data he analyzes;[20] and these data have not been subject to serious challenge by historians. In concluding this section, I would emphasize the significance claimed for reindigenization by its leading scholars. Kubler noted that the phenomenon held back the proportional decline of the native population by six or seven decades, in that "the colonial rate of caste-change, had it prevailed after 1795 unchanged to the present, would have reached the caste percentages of 1940 in 1876." By the same token, "the Indian population of Peru would today be less than 30 per cent of the total, instead of nearly 42 per cent."[21] And as we have already seen, Gootenberg makes a still more ambitious claim: that "this phenomenon is the root cause of contemporary Peru's extraordinary indigenous presence."

Explaining Reindigenization: State Collapse and Economic Crisis

What was the root cause of reindigenization? What permitted native populations to recover, it would appear, not only in demographic terms, but (as we shall see) economically and politically as well? During the period that runs from independence in the 1820s until at least the 1850s, and in most senses still later (until the 1870s or even the War of the Pacific of 1879–1883), historians look to two kinds of explanation. The first lies in the chronic political instability that marked the early republic. This instability is readily traced in statistical form: between 1821 and 1845, Peru experienced on average one change of regime per year, and the Constitution was rewritten six times over.[22] The caudillo Agustín Gamarra faced seventeen rebellions and conspiracies during his four-year presidency alone (1829–1833),[23] and the later 1830s were marked by the violent episode of the Peru-Bolivia Confederation (1836–1839). Partly reflecting and partly fueling political instability was the chronic fiscal crisis, for until the late 1840s, budget deficits typically ran at 30 percent.[24] All of this translated into military weakness, too, since historians agree that early republican armed forces were insufficient for the autonomous defence of the state.[25] For Gootenberg, then, "the early nineteenth century represents a period when dominant white society was weakened by the stresses of economic decay, political chaos, and institutional uncertainties of the colonial transition."[26] For Charles Walker, "beset by constant weakness…the regional and national states could not lead the effort to increase the exploitation of the peasants or decrease their political autonomy."[27] The result may be conceived in terms of a partial collapse or withdrawal of the state, evident above all in the highlands, the region of densest native settlement. Not even the onset of the "Guano Age" from the late 1840s, with its higher revenues and more stable creole state, altered this basic equation, since such development as guano generated remained tied to the coast, where it held the attention of statesmen through to the 1870s.[28]

The second general explanation for the apparent buoyancy of the native world is economic, and lies in the crisis of the creole economy: both domestic and export-oriented. This crisis began with the long and devastating wars of independence, with disruption to production, destruction of haciendas and mining infrastructure, and loss of life. Peru's greatest twentieth-century historian, Jorge Basadre, wrote that "Independence in Peru, in the immediate aftermath, was more of a disaster for the national economy than for that of other countries."[29] During the ensuing decades, the economy continued to be undermined by the political instability already discussed and by poor links with the burgeoning economies of the north Atlantic world. Jacobsen states that crisis in textile workshops, early stagnation in mining output, rising transportation and credit costs, and depressed commodity and land prices, all affected landholding and commercial elites far more than they did peasants.[30] Gootenberg presents a regional survey that emphasizes the contraction of creole economies and the rise of native ones; in the Colca Valley in the south, for example, "the colonial elite misti society of hacendados and miners practically vanished with independence," and "Indians took to hawking their alpaca wool directly to Arequipan merchants." Further north, "Ayacucho suffered the long-term collapse of white commercial activities, save for coca production, with its obvious dependence on the peasant economy," while in the Mantaro Valley, "the flourishing Indian trade center of Huancayo contrasted markedly with the decaying colonial Hispanic town of Jauja." Even in Cerro de Pasco, where silver production again surpassed colonial levels by the 1840s, "the mining industry itself had to adjust production schedules to the needs of agrarian rhythms."[31]

Particularly significant to our purposes here, the hacienda—the major competitor to and predator on native landholdings—shared fully in this early republican crisis. Isolated from profitable export markets, incapable of attracting sufficient native labor, and lacking strong backing from the state, haciendas now not only ceased to encroach on native lands, as they had during the colonial period, but actively contracted in several regions. In a section of his book on Azángaro titled "The Languishing Estates", Jacobsen found little evidence of hacienda expansion onto Indian lands before the 1850s.[32] In the Cuzco region, the number of haciendas actually fell by almost half, from 647 in 1785 to 360 in 1845.[33] Some of the clearest evidence for this process relates to Bolivia: in Cliza, in Cochabamba, the proportion of haciendas lying vacant rose from just 0.6 percent in 1838, to 63 percent in 1877. In Mizque, "the total number of haciendas declined from 129 (with no vacancies) in 1838 to 78 (with 45 vacancies) in 1877)." Erwin Grieshaber demonstrates that throughout Bolivia as a whole, from 1838 to 1877, the proportion of Indian tributaries living in traditional communities grew from 70 to 75 percent, population decline notwithstanding, while the proportion living on haciendas declined from 29 to 24 percent. The result was very high proportions of Indians still living in communities; in provinces of La Paz, even in 1838, Omasuyos had 58 percent communal tributaries, Sicasica 70 percent, and Pacajes 81 percent.[34] In Peru, in Azángaro more than three-quarters of Indians lived outside livestock estates as late as the 1870s, while in the mid-1840s, 84 percent of Indians in rural Cuzco lived in communities.[35]

Gootenberg summarizes the results of all these processes by observing that

> naturally isolated and sheltered by the breakdown in national politics, communications, and markets during the caudillo era, indigenous communities were left mainly to themselves. No army of local officials entered their hamlets, and the local hacendado was reduced to first among equals. Thus Indians were freed from the traditional (or increasingly intrusive) oppressions of the colonial regime, and enjoyed, if by default, a penurious respite from the market pressures of emerging capitalism.[36]

Florencia Mallon, in work on the central highlands, presents a documented example of a regional elite bereft of the "backing of a centralized and effective state" and incapable of imposing itself on its native peasantry.[37] It was these factors, then, that permitted the recovery of indigenous populations and lifeways.

Revisiting Reindigenization: The Native Economy

Paul Gootenberg was perhaps the first scholar to carry the study of reindianization beyond the demographic aspect, and to begin to explore its "compelling historical and anthropological implications." In doing so, he was clear as to the hazards he faced, noting that this part of his research was "not just preliminary but speculative as well."[38] Some 20 years later, research in this area remains relatively limited. But it is abundant enough for us to "speculate" on rather firmer grounds than were available to Gootenberg.

To begin with, it now appears that Indians in early republican Peru experienced not only demographic recovery, but an economic resurgence as well. Erick Langer argues, indeed, that "the early nineteenth century represents a period of the dominance of the Andean ethnic economies not witnessed since the middle of the sixteenth century." This was so because "both the internal and export economies of Bolivia and highland Peru…were highly dependent upon what might be termed the 'ethnic economies' of the Indian communities."[39] Thus, not only did Indians fare relatively well in economic terms, but the national economy—especially the mining and wool sectors—was sustained by them:

> Indian trade was crucial to the economies of the Andean region. Mining activities depended heavily on goods and pack animals the Indians provided. Fairs thrived only where the Indian hinterland provided sufficient producers and consumers…To a large extent, the rhythms of agricultural and transhumance cycles during the early nineteenth century determined how and when trade with non-Indians took place…Urban markets during this period were very small…and trade outside the urban centers, dominated by Indian community members, provided the underpinning of the Andean economies.[40]

In economic terms, it is possible that Indians enjoyed certain inherent advantages during the early republic. The ability to draw on community resources may have permitted a speedier recovery after the independence wars, for example, while the relative weight of tribute declined over time, as native populations rose more swiftly than the tax.[41] But the basis of native wealth was unquestionably the more fundamental factor of ongoing native control of land, in most cases throughout the period to at least the 1870s. It is now clear that the liberal decrees of the 1820s "privatising" Indian lands had relatively little impact, and that by and large, Indian communities retained control of their lands well into the second half of the century. In a context of low land values, a depressed rural economy, and crisis in the hacienda sector, native landholdings were preserved, and in some cases may even have expanded.[42] And as we have seen, not only did communities retain control of their lands, but many were reinforced over this period, and still accounted for strong majorities of native populations in key highland regions.

Native influence over the principal productive industries ultimately derived from control of land and from vigorous engagement in trade. Indians supplied the major mining centers with vital necessities, such as llamas, fuel, and salt; more importantly, they seem to have done so very much on their own terms.[43] In trade, in the best-known and most striking case, native communities in southern Peru now exploited strong British industrial demand for wool from their vast flocks of camelids. Across several decades, they maintained substantial control of this trade by selling their wool directly in Arequipa or at the great trade fairs that sprang up across the Andes from the 1830s.[44] Among these fairs, none was greater than that held at Vilque, near Puno, each year at Pentecost, to which traders came not only from a wide Peruvian hinterland, but from Bolivia and as far away as Argentina. The major stock of the fair was wool, and Indians bought an extraordinary range of imported goods in return. An astonished French traveller in the mid-1840s witnessed the finest merchandise, including French cloth and jewels and Swiss clocks, exhibited alongside sacks of coca and coarse Cuzco garments.[45] The volume of business at Vilque may have reached 2,000,000 pesos by the 1840s, and "'Indians' share of wool exports remained substantial as late as 1876."[46] And although this topic has been little studied, native engagement in trade elsewhere seems to have mirrored the case of the wool industry: Indian communities in Oruro studied by Langer, for example, became "very active in commerce with the world outside Bolivia, as importers and exporters, transporters of most trade goods, and smugglers." Trading in silver and goods such as cotton, they operated from southern Peru to northern Argentina, and their activities across these regions were far greater than prior to independence.[47]

Indeed, scholars suggest that rising prosperity within some communities may have precipitated social change, as disparities in wealth accentuated intercommunity tensions, and wealthier individuals sought to evade responsibilities such as those of the *cargo* system of community offices.[48] Interethnic relations may have intensified, too, as wealthy Indians lent money outside their communities, "making them feel more equal, or perhaps even superior" to non-Indians,[49] and perhaps becoming more Hispanized in the process. But we must be careful not to overstate our case: most Indians remained extremely poor during these years. Walker notes that "well-being" is a separate issue from autonomy and control of resources, while Gootenberg includes poverty among the factors swelling the native population during the early republic—reflecting the retreat into communal self-sufficiency in a depressed economy.[50] Even at the Andean fairs, Langer reminds us that exploitation of Indians by non-Indians was "rampant." Nevertheless, he also concludes of both silver mining and the wool industry that "one gets the sense that the Indians controlled the rhythm of trade" during this period. He argues that not only were fairs such as Vilque subject entirely to the Andean agricultural calendar, but the business undertaken there was subject (at least in part) to Andean moral precepts regarding trade—including an emphasis on personal ties.[51] Certainly, in reflecting on native wealth and economic agency, the comments of our wide-eyed French traveller to Vilque are striking:

> This elite among the Indians of the sierra counts among its principal riches the numerous flocks that wander the altiplano of the Collao. It is this elite that cultivates the scarce valleys between the mountains. It is this elite that supplies the merchants of the coast with the

majority of the products of the country that they export directly to Europe. It is among this elite, in the end, that may perhaps be found one of the most fertile seeds of the vital forces called upon to flourish one day in Peru.[52]

Revisiting Reindigenization: Indians and Political Life

And not only did native economic activity revive during the post-independence decades: it appears that Indians gained strength in political terms also. An influential model for this question was established in the early 1980s by Tristan Platt, based mainly on research on northern Potosí in Bolivia. Platt argued that the early republican state in Bolivia was so weak, and so utterly dependent for its revenues on income from Indian tribute, that native communities acquired considerable political bargaining power. They used this power primarily to defend their lands and community structures; indeed, Indians came to understand their relationship with the state in Bolivia in the terms of a "reciprocal pact," in which payment of tribute or forced labor services guaranteed the state's respect for community land-holdings. Platt cites cases of communities in the early 1880s that actively resisted abolition of these obligations precisely because of their perception of an implicit pact with the state. He notes that moves against community lands in the 1860s and again from the 1880s were violently resisted because in the eyes of the *ayllus*, they provoked a "*loss of legitimacy* by the creole state."[53] The result was that "the state's fiscal needs and the fear of a caste war in a militarily weak state made any meaningful reform [of Indian communities] impossible until the second half of the nineteenth century."[54] And, while there is now recognition that northern Potosí was not necessarily representative of Bolivia as a whole, neither was this region unique. Tribute provided around 40 percent of state revenues in Peru before the guano age; in Cuzco, it provided between 40 percent and 70 percent (rarely less than 50 percent) between 1826 and 1845. Here, too, then, "structural conditions...favoured negotiations over heavy-handed despotism in relations between authorities and the Indians."[55]

Christine Hühnefeldt was the first scholar seriously to study peasant interaction with national politics during the era of independence.[56] For the period that followed, perhaps the major study of recent years is Cecilia Méndez' *The Plebeian Republic*, which is based upon the Huanta rebellion of 1825–1828—the only large native revolt of the post-independence years. The details of this revolt need not concern us here, but Méndez exploits the Huanta case to make the broader argument that "native Andean peasant leaders played an active role in the play of politics of the early republican state." This was so because of the weakness of the state, and above all the need of feuding caudillos in the period to the 1840s to garner troops, supplies, and other support among the native communities. Méndez titled her book *The Plebeian Republic*—a term she limits to the period 1820–1850—in large part so as to reflect this degree of peasant engagement with, and influence over, national politics. Thus, Huanta's

> dense ayllu population actively engaged with the state, not in "patri-monial" or "ancient-regime" terms, as the ayllus of northern Potosí, studied by Platt, did (that is, seeking to maintain "corporate privi-leges"), but rather in the unruly terms ushered in by the early caudi-llo politics and the language of possibilities that…liberal politicians opened up in their desperate quest for constituents.

To attract rural followers, caudillos were obliged to resort to "the lan-guage of citizenship"; and as a result, the caudillo era may have consti-tuted a rare moment when "citizenship…was carried out in the rural areas."[57] Other scholars, noting the lesser engagement of peasants with national politics in Peru as opposed to Mexico or elsewhere, have pointed precisely to the instability of the caudillo era, which could make the choice of political alliance a hazardous one.[58] But one can only be impressed by the extraordinary contrast between the fate of the Huanta rebels and the savage retribution meted upon Indian rebels in the late colony. The leader of the revolt, Antonio Huachaca, neither surrendered nor was captured, and later met one Peruvian president and reportedly received a general's uniform from another. Méndez writes, "the early republi-can state, faced with its first and only peasant rebellion in forty years of republican rule…condoned, forgave, and granted pardons. Later on, it rallied around peasants, begged, implored, and called them 'citizens' and 'saviors of the nation'. In a word, it negotiated." And more broadly, Méndez argues that the death penalty in Peru was now rarely applied for crimes against property, but served strictly political ends, suggesting that "social differentiation and class confrontation…were not nearly as sharp in the early caudillo period as they were to become decades later."[59] The fiscal and military weakness of the early republic, then, "helps to explain why nineteenth century rebellions were small and localized in comparison to the great insurrections of the late eighteenth century."[60] There would be no further significant native revolts in Peru until the late 1860s, and afterward until the mid-1880s.

The Tide Turns: Ideology and Economy from the 1870s to the 1920s

If conditions remained broadly favorable for native communities from independence to the 1870s, most historians agree that they turned sharply adverse for them over the half-century that followed. We have already noted that liberal reforms of the 1820s were long thought to have had a dramatic negative impact on Peru's native communities. This view is now discredited; but a new assault on Indians took place in the second half of the nineteenth and early twentieth centuries, and there is little doubt as to its impact. In a major essay on this topic, Jacobsen describes the quarter-century to the mid-1870s as the high watermark for liberalism in Peru, as for other countries. Some key legislation was promulgated as early as the 1850s: the Civil Code in 1852, and abolition of tribute in 1854.[61] By defining Indians as individuals, and removing their rights to communal existence, these measures "marked the beginning of the republic's sustained assault on Indian communities."[62] The first real signs of change in the political, economic, and social systems inherited from the colony followed, in the 1860s and 1870s.[63] Nevertheless, in the central highlands, until the 1870s elite hegemony "remained relatively weak and circumscribed."[64] More broadly, Gootenberg argues that "by all recent accounts, the climax of pressures on Indian and rural communities had to wait until after the wrenching disruptions of the War of the Pacific."[65] Indeed, the chief impact on native communities, including wholesale loss of land, may date from later still—the 1890s and 1900s.

It should be stressed that the deterioration in conditions for Indians derived from far more than government policy or ideology alone; it was rooted in wider pressures, economic and even demographic. Strong native population growth throughout the century in many regions finally translated into excess population, leading to forced migration from native communities to haciendas, mining camps, or cities.[66] More importantly, by the 1870s, and strongly from the 1880s, market pressures in the highlands increased greatly, as Peru became better integrated into international free-trade circuits.[67] The expansion of rail transport both accompanied and reinforced this process, with lines between Arequipa and Puno completed in the 1870s and between Lima-Callao and La Oroya in the 1890s. Throughout the country, traditional elites or entrepreneurial outsiders responded to new opportunities by renewing their interest in land and its commercial development, from haciendas to mining. In the central highlands, hacendados increased the production of wool, meat, and butter for the metropolitan market, while also investing in mining and subtropical agriculture in the Chanchamayo and nearby valleys.[68] And between 1875 and 1900, the great wool industry of the southern highlands was prised from native hands and passed to those of hacendados and British merchants, whose capitalized business reached "right to the thickest herds tucked away in the high sierra."[69] The 1870s thus marked the decline of the wool fairs, including that at Vilque, which by the early twentieth century was "abandoned," with Vilque itself described as "a sad little town on the desolate *puna*."[70] For the structure of rural land-holding, meanwhile, the results were unambiguous: the late nineteenth century witnessed an end to the crisis of the hacienda, which now embarked on a period of rapid expansion. These years witnessed "the vigorous expansion of the hacienda at the expense of the Indian communities throughout the Andean region". Indeed, "the years around World War I may be considered the high point of the Peruvian hacienda in its long trajectory since the sixteenth century."[71]

The result of these broad shifts, then, was drastic disenfranchisement of native communities in both economic and political terms. This process is seen most clearly in widespread losses of native lands to creole and mestizo landowners and merchants or wealthy peasant families. Jacobsen notes that in one province of the altiplano, from the mid-1880s, Indian communities "lost between one-third and one-half of the lands they still held during the 1850s." He goes on, "during the first decade of the twentieth century...communities in many regions were losing more land than in any preceding decade."[72] Jacobsen discusses the native communities of Piura on the north coast, for example, especially Catacaos—a stronghold of the Tallán language. In Catacaos, the republican era seems to have witnessed a weakening of traditional communal structures, with exacerbation of "internal economic differentiation as well as the development of a more fluid notion of community." Vigorous and strategically intelligent resistance to hacienda and entrepreneur encroachment failed to prevent the loss of almost 80 percent of irrigated lands in this district by 1914—even if some leading Indian families themselves became hacendados.[73] In Bolivia, the assault on native lands began earlier, under the regime of Mariano Melgarejo (1864–1871), whose legislation declaring all community land as state property and attempting to auction it off "left the Indian communities reeling." Langer offers a moving depiction of the formerly prosperous communities of Oruro, who kept their lands but were "pauperized" and "reduced to working mainly as agriculturalists on very poor fields." He goes on: "Their world had shrunk, from encompassing a vast area from southern Peru to northern Argentina, to comprising only their hamlets, and perhaps also the silver and tin mines to which they migrated now not as merchants but as lowly mine workers."[74] And Langer and others have emphasized that disenfranchisement was political, too, influenced in part by new and "scientific" forms of racism imported from Europe. In short, "Andean Indians were rejected as full citizens in Peru and Bolivia at the same time they were marginalized economically."[75] Small wonder, then, that the relative social peace of the early republic was now broken, with major Indian rebellions occurring in Puno in 1867 and Huaylas in 1885.[76]

Reindigenization and Native Languages

To return to the question with which we opened, then: What are the implications of reindigenization for our understanding of the histories of languages in the Andes, particularly the decline of native languages? For Quechua—my main concern here—the evidence suggests that reindigenization increased both the absolute number of speakers, and the proportion of the population that spoke the language. In the context of rising native populations, reasonable degrees of access to land and prosperity, and the diminished presence of the creole state and its representatives, the default assumption is that the Andes became not only more "indigenous," but more indigenous-speaking. And indeed, there are few signs of any decline of Quechua before the twentieth century. The claim in the 1870s that "two-thirds of all Peruvians were *indígenas* who spoke only Quechua" was clearly exaggerated, with the census of 1876 indicating that less than 58 percent of the population was indigenous.[77] But we have seen that in some provinces—Huaylas and Azángaro are outstanding examples—the proportion of Quechua speakers was likely to be much higher, at much later periods. Thurner addresses the linguistic consequences of (late) indigenization in Huaylas-Ancash explicitly, noting that by the census of 1940, "most people in Huaylas were monolingual Quechua speakers, while 95 percent of the total population could speak Quechua." With 38 percent of the same population white or mestizo, the former figure naturally "suggests a high degree of bilingualism," making Quechua inevitably "the primary medium of social exchange" in the region.[78]

Any review of the rich travel literature of the nineteenth and early twentieth-century Andes confirms the impression of native language dominance, generally in the absence of Spanish bilingualism, everywhere outside the very centers of the towns and cities. Some brief samples of this literature will underscore the point. In the central highlands, in 1836, the British traveller W. Smyth undertook a journey from Lima to Huánuco and thence down the river Huallaga. In the settlement of Obragillo, about a league north of Canta inland from Lima, he still found a population that spoke "both the Quichua (the old language of the Incas) and Castilian." But in Culluay, a further day's ride on, Smyth recorded that "most of the natives speak only the Indian language." In Cerro de Pasco he wrote that "the Quichua language is generally spoken by the miners and lower orders, few of whom know Spanish." In Huánuco, Smyth noted that "the Quichua language is that generally spoken by the lower orders, and is understood by most of the upper classes," while in a nearby village few of the inhabitants understood Spanish.[79] W. M. Lewis Herndon, tracing part of the same route in the early 1850s, found of the inhabitants of La Oroya that "very

few of them spoke Spanish."[80] Further to the north, in the Callejón
de Huaylas, E. W. Middendorf (who lived in Peru for three periods
between the 1850s and 1880s) recorded that though almost all the
inhabitants of the town of Caraz spoke Spanish, and all understood it,
"the natives of the small villages of the valley speak among themselves
solely in Quechua." Similarly, in Chavín de Huantar, in the Callejón de
Conchucos to the east, Middendorf reported that "the Indian population and also part of the mestizos, use Quechua."[81]

Unsurprisingly, the high incidence of Quechua monolingualism
described in many of these accounts was replicated outside the central Peruvian Andes. In the south, in Lampa province in the department of Puno, Heinrich Witt noted in 1826 that "the population is
composed almost exclusively of Indians...These Indians understand
very little Spanish, unless they understand none at all; their language is
'Quichua,' the original language of Peru."[82] In Cuzco, the celebrated
traveller Ephraim Squier noted in the early 1860s that "seven-eighths
of the population...are pure Indians; and a knowledge of Quichua
is almost absolutely necessary for open intercourse with the mass of
its inhabitants."[83] Some 40 years later, Geraldine Guinness estimated
that only about a quarter of Cuzco's population (5,000 out of 19,000)
could "understand any Spanish; the rest are Kechua-speaking, brown-
skinned people."[84] And as late as the mid-1920s, A. F. Tschiffely strug-
gled to find a Spanish-speaking guide as he rode through the region
north of the Apurímac.[85] Finally, in northern Peru, Middendorf noted
of Cajamarca that "the Indians of the surrounding region speak the
ancient language of the country, and many have no knowledge whatever of Castilian" (though in the city itself "only the inferior classes of
the population understand Quechua"). Of the town of Chachapoyas,
across the valley of the Marañón, Middendorf recorded that "most of
the population speaks only Spanish, but all understand Quechua." By
contrast, of "the Indians and mestizos of the province" he wrote that
"though they understand Spanish and make use of it in the affairs of
daily life, nevertheless in their private life (*trato íntimo*), the ancient
general language still predominates."[86]

Quechua, then (and surely Aymara also, in its own strongholds),
remained the dominant language in the regions where it was spoken
throughout the nineteenth century. It may be, indeed, that Quechua
actually spread during this period, into regions where it was not previously current. This intriguing topic lies beyond the scope of this essay,
though there are tantalising suggestions that poorer whites in particularly remote corners of the sierra themselves became "Indianized" during
this period, perhaps even in linguistic terms.[87]

The health and long-term survival of languages, nevertheless, depend
on more than the number of speakers alone; social and political status

also play determining roles. We have seen that César Itier and Willem Adelaar have argued that the period between 1750 and 1850 proved crucial to the long-term decline of Quechua, partly due to the decline of the native Quechua-speaking elite around the time of independence, and partly to repressive measures implemented in the aftermath of the Túpaq Amaru Rebellion of the early 1780s. It is true that independence brought key changes, provoked above all by the political division of the region in which Quechua was spoken and the decline in its use as a lingua franca.[88] But although the evidence is limited, there are few signs of any shift in practice in elite attitudes against Quechua until decades after 1850. It may be worth emphasizing, for instance, that the post-Túpaq Amaru decrees are unlikely to have had much real effect. Historians have learnt to be skeptical regarding the practical implementation of royal laws in the Indies. I join Kenneth Andrien (in this volume) in citing David Garrett's study of the Indian nobility of Cuzco, which concludes that "a serious assault on Quechua and Aymara would have been utterly impossible"—a sentiment that surely also holds true so far as the social prestige of the language was concerned. "As always in the colonial Andes," Garrett further remarks, "execution fell far short of the intent and language of the laws."[89]

In fact, evidence from travel narratives, though somewhat anecdotal, appears to suggest unambiguously that bilingualism in Quechua and Spanish remained the norm among provincial whites, with Quechua used privately as well as in public dealings with Indians. Moreover, Quechua appears to have lost none of its prestige among these provincial elites. Clements Markham, the distinguished British traveller and later president of the Royal Geographical Society, travelled in Peru in the early 1850s, and invested considerable effort in learning Quechua. His remarks on the latter and its relation with provincial creoles are particularly striking:

At the present day, the Quichua...is spoken as generally and with almost as much purity as in the time of the Incas; not only by the poor Indians, but by the descendants of Spaniards of every rank of society in the sierra. As their nurses are always Indian girls, Quichua is the first language they speak, while Spanish is learnt afterwards, and studied at school. At certain intervals a sermon is preached in Quichua, in the churches of the larger towns; and in the villages the priests use no other language. The Indian bards, too, attend at the dinner and evening parties in the farms of their masters, and chant Quichuan melodies as accompaniments to the dance: and all classes seem attached to the old language of the Incas...It is agreeable to find that the beautiful language of the Incas has been zealously cultivated by the descendants of their conquerors.[90]

Markham's own experiences seem to bear out this view of attachment to Quechua among provincial elites. He spent a month in Ayacucho in the south-central highlands with the aim of "mastering colloquial Quechua," and was taught there by the sisters of the Prefect, Manuel Tello. One of the sisters collected Quechua songs, and Markham noted that "songs in alternate lines of Spanish and Quechua are also in vogue at Ayacucho and at Cuzco." He further claimed that these songs were "now very common," and saw them as a product of the "attachment of the upper classes in the Sierra to the Indian tongue."[91] In Yanaoca, the capital of Canas province south of Cuzco, Markham joined the daughter of the subprefect, Victoria Novoa, and one Dr Taforo, from Chile, on a morning trip, during which "Dr Taforo and Victoria enlivened the way by singing, the one Chilean, the other Quechua songs."[92] Neither was Markham alone in remarking on use of Quechua by provincial elites; in Ayacucho some quarter of a century earlier, Heinrich Witt fell victim to the practical joke of a young woman of one of the local Spanish families who "taught me some words in Quechua, and when I managed to pronounce them adequately, I was told that their meaning was different from that which she had had me believe."[93]

It will be noted that in these passages, it is creole women who feature most prominently as Quechua speakers, a feature noted also for earlier periods.[94] But the public use of Quechua by male officials and landowners was also remarked upon frequently. In 1826, Heinrich Witt watched as an "intendant or subprefect" and landowner in Lampa "addressed a long speech in the Quichua language" to the Indians on his estate.[95] In Huanta in the early 1900s, Reginald Enock witnessed lengthy pleas made by natives to the town's governor, entirely in Quechua, to which "the gobernador listens patiently and judicially, and then announces his decision."[96] In Bolivia, in the 1920s A. F. Tschiffely was aided in understanding a native fiesta because "luckily the local government official who accompanied me spoke both Quichua and Spanish and interpreted some of the things they were telling to their saint."[97] Even in Moyobamba, in the north in modern San Martín, it was said around 1830 that among a population "composed mostly of whites and mestizos…Quechua is the tongue preferred even by those who are not of indigenous race."[98] The use of native languages by priests, too, appears to have been very widespread, as accounts from Lampa in the 1820s, Yurimaguas and Uchiza (in Maynas) ca. 1830, or Cuzco in the early 1900s make clear.[99] In a work published in 1860, S. S. Hill even describes meeting an Englishman in Puno, Mr Morris, a long-term resident of La Paz, who deployed "their native tongue" in an abortive attempt to make fun of the market women.[100]

As Alan Durston has remarked elsewhere in this volume, from the 1850s, Quechua began to be invoked in "scholarly projects of national self-awareness," and in the 1870s there occurred "a significant Quechuist boom." At this time, Quechua was referred to by members of the elite as the "national language" or "the Peruvian language," and efforts were made to aid its acquisition, that Durston suggests were taken seriously. It must be stressed that Durston, like Marisol de la Cadena for the period of the 1920s, is careful to emphasize the highly problematic nature of these elites' relationship with Quechua. This relationship was often based on racist disdain for the Quechua-speaking peasantry and even for con-temporary Quechua, amid romantic eulogizing of the Inca past and the construction of an "elite Quechua" ("Capac Simi").[101] Zoila Mendoza has recently argued for more fluid exchanges and interactions between artists and intellectuals, of different social sectors of rural and urban Cuzco, than De la Cadena would suggest.[102] But in more recent times, there is little doubt that the divorce between the Quechua-speaking elite and the great majority of peasant speakers did great damage to the lan-guage (and continues to do so).[103]

Nevertheless, it is difficult to regard elite attitudes as "radically adverse to Quechua as an instrument of communication" much before the twen-tieth century. Reindigenization, broadly understood, suggests strongly that the deepest roots of the modern decline of Quechua lay not before 1850, but precisely in the period from the 1870s to the 1920s—the decades discussed earlier as marking a sharp deterioration in conditions for Peru's indigenous peoples. In this period, and not before, Indians experienced wholesale loss of land, enforced withdrawal from trade, and widespread pauperization, in addition to active exclusion from the body politic. They now slipped into marginalization and poverty, assuming a character in Peruvian national life *only* "largely accurate from the early twentieth century onward."[104] In short, with the assault on native lands and economies of the late nineteenth and early twentieth centuries, Indians were regarded less ambiguously as objects of disdain, includ-ing in the regions where Quechua was spoken. Ongoing demographic indigenization in a minority of provinces notwithstanding, it was these sweeping social and economic changes that began to sap the social pres-tige of Quechua—rather than late-colonial decrees, or even the decline of the native nobility around the time of independence.

It should be emphasized here that the decline of Quechua was not consummated during this period, or indeed until some decades later. Regional creole elites in Peru continued to speak the language well into the twentieth century, in Cuzco even using it to produce Quechua-language literature.[105] Quechua remained dominant in Cuzco and other provincial cities, in fact, where high levels of popular monolingualism were accompanied by routine creole bilingualism. Only *after* the 1920s did non-Indians and urban populations begin to shun the language, as "a sign of stigma, of inferiority."[106] This shift occurred with increasing urbanization and urban prosperity, the growth of the state, migration from rural areas, and penetration of formal education into the country-side; in short, the hallmarks of mid-twentieth century global develop-ment. If conditions for native peoples in Peru deteriorated significantly from the 1870s, then, conditions for the Quechua language seem to have remained little altered for a further half-century. But in the broadest view, Quechua's modern decline can be seen as the product of globalis-ing processes, with origins in the late nineteenth-century export boom, and consummation ongoing since at least the 1940s.

Finally, as suggested earlier, reindigenization may have the capacity to contribute to explaining the *specific* linguistic pattern obtaining in the Andes by the early twentieth century. This topic remains almost entirely to be explored, and I shall give a single, necessarily tentative, example here. Among the seeming enigmas in the linguistic history of Peru is the disappearance from the northern highlands and coast of all native lan-guages, except for a few isolated inland pockets of Quechua. This region was once home to numerous tongues, including Quingnam, Mochica, Culli, and the languages of the coast of Piura, including Tallán—of which Catacaos was among the last redoubts. Quingnam probably disap-peared during the late colonial period; but the others endured far longer, and appear to have finally succumbed within the same few decades at the end of the nineteenth and beginning of the twentieth centuries. The Piuran languages are last attested firmly in the late nineteenth century, for example, while the last known speakers of Mochica were recorded in the 1920s and those of Culli in the 1930s.

The reasons for the demise of these northern languages remain obscure; as Adelaar remarks, "we know almost nothing of the manner in which these languages disappeared."[107] Their decline should surely be attributed in part to vulnerability due to restricted geographies and low numbers of speakers,[108] and had probably been in process for some time (as the early death of Quingnam would indicate). The suggestion here, however, is that the process of reindigenization that appears to have bol-stered Quechua in the center and south of Peru may have operated differ-ently, or indeed have failed to operate at all, in the north—and that this might form part of the explanation for the final demise of the northern tongues. This process can be seen as operating in a number of ways; for example, Adelaar has questioned the putative role of the hacienda in the decline of northern native languages, since "in other parts of Peru the *hacienda* system did not noticeably harm the survival of Quechua."[109] But the hacienda suffered different fates in different regions of the Andes, and may have remained stronger in the north than it did in the south of Peru or in Bolivia.

For the most telling evidence, however, we must return to our starting point, and the demographic work of George Kubler and Paul

Gootenberg. As we have seen, Kubler's study suggested that already by the 1850s, the Peruvian provinces displaying non-Indian majorities were concentrated in the north of the country, both on the coast and in highlands. These provinces included Jaén, Chota, Trujillo, Huamachuco, and Pataz provinces, corresponding to the modern regions of central and northern Cajamarca and all of La Libertad.[110] Gootenberg's fresh census data yielded similar results, with just 9 of 57 provinces nationally showing non-Indian majorities in 1827, including the northern block of Jaén, Trujillo, Huamachuco, and Pataz.[111] Between the 1790s and the 1850s, in the north there was growth in the Indian population in the provinces of Piura and Chachapoyas. In both Piura and Jaén, this growth continued until as late as the census of 1876. But by the latter date, "the block of northern provinces, composed of Conchucos, Trujillo, Cajamarca, Chota, and Chachapoyas, became more markedly mestizo." As a result, by the 1870s, already "Piura and Chachapoyas were separated by a great mestizo block." And over the following period, up to 1940, even in Piura "the great Indian increases during the preceding period rapidly abated." Although Piura and several of its sub-regions still showed Indian majorities in 1940, since 1876 the region had gained non-Indian population, Piura itself "at the rate of more than 31 per cent in 64 years."[112]

In summary, explanation for the final extinction of the native languages of the north may lie in the absence of any strong process of reindigenization as occurred in the central and southern highlands. More correctly, it lay in an opposing process of *mestizaje*, apparent in this region from unusually early date, with mestizo majorities in most provinces firmly consolidated by the 1870s—including in the heartlands of the Culli and Mochica languages. Indians continued to inhabit these regions, but they formed a dwindling minority within a population that spoke not native languages, but Spanish. And this process would only continue: of the six provinces most characterized by Culli toponymy, in Huamachuco (Sánchez Carrión), described as "the main historical centre of the Culli-speaking people,"[113] non-Indians already accounted for almost 57 percent of the population in 1876, and this figure rose above two-thirds by 1940. In Cajabamba, the shift was dramatic, from 54.4 percent non-Indians in 1876, to 88.8 percent in 1940. Only in Pallasca (in northern Ancash) did the non-Indian majority retreat slightly by 1940, from 54.5 percent to 52.6 percent;[114] it may be no coincidence, then, that the last known speakers of Culli were to be found in Pallasca.[115] Meanwhile, we have seen that from the 1870s, native communities throughout Peru experienced loss of lands, impoverishment, loss of population to haciendas, mining camps, and towns, and growing discrimination. It was surely in this context, then, that the remaining native languages of the north died out over approximately the following human lifespan.

Conclusion

Reindigenization remains a little-known topic. It was little known during its heyday: recent studies of elite attitudes to Peru's native population during the early republic find little if any awareness of the newfound
vitality of the native world.[116] Since Gootenberg's seminal 1991 article,
few scholars have addressed the topic directly, while this essay is the first
to consider its linguistic implications. The principal history of Quechua
since the Conquest, for example, also published in 1991, barely discusses
the nineteenth century.[117] Nevertheless, sufficient major studies now exist
to have set reindigenization as a demographic, economic, and political
phenomenon on firm grounds. This essay draws two major conclusions
for the native language history of Peru. First, the deepest roots of the
modern decline of Quechua lie not during the decades either side of independence, but almost a century later, between the 1870s and the 1920s.
Second, indigenization holds an important key to the final demise of the
native languages of the northern coast and highlands (bar Quechua),
because its absence led to mestizo majorities in this region by the 1870s
or earlier. Broad processes of erosion of native lifeways then sealed the fate
of the northern tongues by the early twentieth century. Finally, I would
emphasize that in reaching these conclusions, I have done little more than
apply data mostly already known to historians to major problems debated
by linguists. And in that sense, this essay also aspires to illustrate the value
of the broader exercise attempted in this volume.

Notes

1. Willem F. H. Adelaar, "Comentario a las ponencias de J. C. Godenzzi
   y C. Itier," in César Itier (ed.), *Del siglo de oro al siglo de las luces.
   Lenguaje y sociedad en los Andes del siglo XVIII* (Cuzco: Centro
   de Estudios Rurales Andinos "Bartolomé de las Casas," 1995),
   pp. 113–16, see p. 115.
2. César Itier, "Quechua y cultura en el Cuzco del siglo XVIII: De la
   'lengua general' al 'idioma del imperio de los incas'," in César Itier
   (ed.), *Del siglo de oro al siglo de las luces. Lenguaje y sociedad en los
   Andes del siglo XVIII* (Cuzco: Centro de Estudios Regionales Andinos
   "Bartolomé de Las Casas," 1995), pp. 89–111, see p. 105.
3. Adelaar, "Comentario a las ponencias," pp. 115–6; reiterated in
   Willem F. H. Adelaar with Pieter C. Muysken, *The Languages of
   the Andes* (Cambridge and New York: Cambridge University Press,
   2004), p. 183.
4. Itier, "Quechua y cultura," p. 106.
5. Paul Gootenberg, "Population and Ethnicity in Early Republican
   Peru: Some Revisions," *Latin American Research Review* 26:3
   (1991), 109–57, see 135.

6. Nils Jacobsen, "Liberalism and Indian Communities in Peru, 1821–1920," in Robert H. Jackson (ed.), *Liberals, the Church, and Indian Peasants: Corporate Lands and the Challenge of Reform in Nineteenth-Century Spanish America* (Albuquerque: University of New Mexico Press, 1997), pp. 123–70, see pp. 128–29.

7. Jean Piel, "The Place of the Peasantry in the National Life of Peru in the Nineteenth Century," *Past & Present* 46 (Feb. 1970), 108–33, see 118–19.

8. Frederick B. Pike, *The Modern History of Peru* (New York: Frederick A. Praeger, 1967), pp. 66–67.

9. Thomas Mockett Davies, "Indian Integration in Peru: A Half Century of Experience, 1900–1948," unpublished Ph.D. dissertation, University of New Mexico, 1970, pp. 33–34. This version has proven surprisingly enduring: it was reproduced in its purest form by as distinguished a scholar as Henri Favre in work of the mid-1990s: *El indigenismo* (1996; Mexico City: Fondo de Cultura Económica, 1998), pp. 33–34.

10. George Kubler, *The Indian Caste of Peru, 1795–1940: A Population Study based upon Tax Records and Census Reports* (Washington, DC: Smithsonian Institution, 1952).

11. Gootenberg, "Population and Ethnicity," pp. 139–40.

12. Ibid., pp. 139–41.

13. Erwin P. Grieshaber, "Survival of Indian Communities in Nineteenth-Century Bolivia: A Regional Comparison," *Journal of Latin American Studies* 12:2 (Nov. 1980), 223–69, see 252–53.

14. Kubler, *The Indian Caste of Peru*, p. 43; map 6, p. 45; and map 8, p. 50.

15. Mark Thurner, *From Two Republics to One Divided: Contradictions of Post-colonial Nationmaking in Andean Peru* (Durham, NC: Duke University Press, 1997), pp. 129–30, 190–91.

16. Ibid., p. 130.

17. Nils Jacobsen, *Mirages of Transition: The Peruvian Altiplano, 1780–1930* (Berkeley: University of California Press 1993), pp. 22, 27–28.

18. Olivia Harris, "Ethnic Identity and Market Relations: Indians and Mestizos in the Andes," in Brooke Larson and Olivia Harris (eds.), *Ethnicity, Markets, and Migration in the Andes: At the Crossroads of History and Anthropology* (Durham, NC: Duke University Press, 1995), pp. 351–90, see pp. 360–61.

19. See e.g., Gootenberg, "Population and Ethnicity," pp. 148–49; Grieshaber, "Survival of Indian Communities," pp. 254–55, 257.

20. Gootenberg, "Population and Ethnicity," p. 118.

21. Kubler, *The Indian Caste of Peru*, p. 65 and Figure 1.

22. Peter F. Klarén, *Peru: Society and Nationhood in the Andes* (New York: Oxford University Press, 2000), p. 137.

23. Cecilia Méndez, *The Plebeian Republic. The Huanta Rebellion and the Making of the Peruvian State, 1820-1850* (Durham, NC: Duke University Press, 2005), pp. 48, 192.
24. Klarén, *Peru*, p. 144.
25. Méndez, *The Plebeian Republic*, pp. 51, 242; Charles Walker, "Los indios en la transición de colonia a republica: ¿Base social de la modernización política?," in Henrique Urbano (ed.), *Tradición y modernidad en los Andes* 2nd ed. (Cuzco: Centro de Estudios Regionales Andinos "Bartolomé de las Casas," 1997), pp. 1–14, see p. 11.
26. Gootenberg, "Population and Ethnicity," p. 135.
27. Charles F. Walker, *Smoldering Ashes. Cuzco and the Creation of Republican Peru, 1780-1840* (Durham, NC: Duke University Press, 1999), pp. 201–2.
28. Brooke Larson, "Andean Highland Peasants and the Trials of Nation-Making during the Nineteenth Century," in Frank Salomon and Stuart Schwartz (eds.), *The Cambridge History of the Native Peoples of the Americas*, vol. 3 *South America* (Cambridge: Cambridge University Press, 2000), part 2, pp. 558–703, see p. 626; Gootenberg, "Population and Ethnicity," p. 150.
29. Cited in Méndez, *The Plebeian Republic*, p. 70.
30. Jacobsen, *Mirages of Transition*, p. 75.
31. Gootenberg, "Population and Ethnicity," pp. 146–48; for Cerro de Pasco, José Deustua, "Routes, Roads, and Silver Trade in Cerro de Pasco, 1820–1860: The Internal Market in Nineteenth-Century Peru," *Hispanic American Historical Review* 74:1 (Feb. 1994), 1–31, see pp. 4–5.
32. Jacobsen, *Mirages of Transition*, pp. 108–27.
33. Walker, *Smoldering Ashes*, pp. 205–6.
34. Grieshaber, "Survival of Indian Communities," pp. 225, 236, 242–43, 246.
35. Jacobsen, *Mirages of Transition*, p. 141; Walker, *Smoldering Ashes*, pp. 205–6.
36. Gootenberg, "Population and Ethnicity," pp. 145–46; see also Larson, "Andean Highland Peasants," p. 626.
37. Florencia Mallon, *The Defence of Community in Peru's Central Highlands: Peasant Struggle and Capitalist Transition, 1860-1940* (Princeton: Princeton University Press, 1983), pp. 54–57.
38. Gootenberg, "Population and Ethnicity," pp. 110, 141.
39. Erick D. Langer, "Indian Trade and Ethnic Economies in the Andes, 1780–1880," *Estudios Interdisciplinarios de América Latina y el Caribe* 15:1 (Jan.–June 2004), 9–33, see 10.
40. Ibid., 21.
41. Erick D. Langer, "Bringing the Economic Back In: Andean Indians and the Construction of the Nation-State in Nineteenth-Century Bolivia," *Journal of Latin American Studies* 41:3 (Aug. 2009),

527–51, see 549; Langer, "Indian Trade and Ethnic Economies," p. 18; Walker, *Smoldering Ashes*, p. 201.

42. Walker, *Smoldering Ashes*, pp. 205–6; Larson, "Andean Highland Peasants," pp. 621–22.

43. Langer, "Indian Trade and Ethnic Economies," p. 18–19; Langer, "Bringing the Economic Back In," pp. 534–36; Mallon, *The Defence of Community*, pp. 55–56.

44. Walker, *Smoldering Ashes*, p. 205; Langer, "Indian Trade and Ethnic Economies," pp. 19–20.

45. Adolfo de Botmiliau, "La feria de Vilque en el Collao, 1846," in Estuardo Núñez (ed.), *El Perú visto por viajeros* 2 vols. (Lima: Ediciones Peisa, 1974–75), vol. 2, pp. 69–76, see pp. 73–74.

46. Michael J. Gonzales, "Neo-Colonialism and Indian Unrest in Southern Peru, 1867–1898," *Bulletin of Latin American Research* 6:1 (1987), 1–26, see 5–6; Klarén, *Peru*, pp. 142–43.

47. Langer, "Bringing the Economic Back In," pp. 533–37.

48. Langer, "Bringing the Economic Back In," pp. 544–47; Jacobsen, "Liberalism and Indian Communities," pp. 147–48, 155.

49. Langer, "Bringing the Economic Back In," p. 546.

50. Walker, "Los indios en la transición," p. 10; Gootenberg, "Population and Ethnicity," p. 146.

51. Langer, "Indian Trade and Ethnic Economies," pp. 20–21, 23.

52. Botmiliau, "La feria de Vilque," p. 71. Botmiliau appears mistakenly to have believed that these were semi-Hispanised Indians from towns and haciendas.

53. Tristan Platt, *Estado boliviano y ayllu andino: Tierra y tributo en el norte de Potosí* (Lima: Instituto de Estudios Peruanos, 1982), pp. 94–104.

54. Erick D. Langer and Robert H. Jackson, "Liberalism and the Land Question in Bolivia, 1825–1920," in Robert H. Jackson (ed.), *Liberals, the Church, and Indian Peasants: Corporate Lands and the Challenge of Reform in Nineteenth-Century Spanish America* (Albuquerque: University of New Mexico Press, 1997), pp. 171–92, see p. 181.

55. Walker, *Smoldering Ashes*, pp. 188–89, 203–4; but see also Walker, "Los indios en la transición," p. 11.

56. Christine Hühnefeldt, *Lucha por la tierra y protesta indígena: Las comunidades indígenas entre colonia y república, 1800–1830* (Bonn: University of Bonn, 1982).

57. Méndez, *The Plebeian Republic*, pp. 22, 237–38.

58. Walker, "Los indios en la transición," p. 11.

59. Méndez, *The Plebeian Republic*, pp. 199–200, 217, 236, 241–42.

60. Gonzales, "Neo-Colonialism and Indian Unrest," p. 3.

61. Jacobsen, "Liberalism and Indian Communities," pp. 139–42.

62. Larson, "Andean Highland Peasants," p. 623.

63. Gootenberg, "Population and Ethnicity," p. 151.
64. Mallon, *The Defence of Community*, pp. 42–43.
65. Gootenberg, "Population and Ethnicity," p. 151.
66. Jacobsen, "Liberalism and Indian Communities," p. 158.
67. Major accounts of this period include, but are not limited to, Alberto Flores Galindo, *Arequipa y el sur andino: Ensayo de historia regional (siglos XVIII–XX)* (Lima: Editorial Horizonte, 1977); Mallon, *The Defence of Community*; and Nelson Manrique, *Yawar mayu: Sociedades terratenientes serranas, 1879–1910* (Lima: Instituto Francés de Estudios Andinos, 1988).
68. Mallon, *The Defence of Community*, p. 57.
69. Larson, "Andean Highland Peasants," pp. 631–33.
70. G. M. Wrigley, "Fairs of the Central Andes," *Geographical Review* 7:2 (Feb. 1919), 65–80, see 78; also Langer, "Indian Trade and Ethnic Economies," p. 25.
71. Jacobsen, "Liberalism and Indian Communities," p. 153.
72. Ibid., p. 156.
73. Ibid., pp. 149–52, 155–56.
74. Langer, "Bringing the Economic Back In," pp. 547–48.
75. Langer, "Indian Trade and Ethnic Economies," p. 26; on scientific racism, see also Jacobsen, "Liberalism and Indian Communities," p. 157.
76. Gonzales, "Neo-Colonialism and Indian Unrest," offers a useful survey for the South.
77. Cited by Durston, this volume.
78. Thurner, *From Two Republics to One Divided*, pp. 129–30, 190–1.
79. W. Smyth, *Narrative of a Journey from Lima to Para...* (London: John Murray, 1836), pp. 23, 26, 43, 67, 71.
80. W. M. Lewis Herndon, *Exploration of the Valley of the Amazon* (Washington: Taylor & Maury, 1854), p. 69.
81. E. W. Middendorf, *Perú: Observaciones y estudios del país y sus habitantes durante una permanencia de 25 años* 3 vols. (1893–1895; Lima: Universidad Nacional Mayor de San Marcos, 1973), vol. 3, pp. 25, 82.
82. Heinrich Witt, *Diario 1824–1890: Un testamento personal sobre el Perú del siglo XIX* 2 vols. (Lima: Banco Mercantil, 1992), vol. 1, pp. 95–96.
83. Ephraim George Squier, *Peru. Incidents of Travel and Exploration in the Land of the Incas* (1877; New York: AMS, 1973), p. 455.
84. Geraldine Guinness, *Peru: Its Story, People, and Religion...* (London: Morgan & Scott, 1909), p. 128.
85. Aimé Félix Tschiffely, *Tschiffely's Ride* (1933; London: 1952), p. 108.
86. Middendorf, *Perú*, vol. 3, pp. 129–30, 178.
87. Henri Favre, "Relaciones sociales y procesos culturales: Los fenómenos de indianización en Huancavelica durante los siglos

XIX y XX," in J. P. Deler and Y. Saint-Geours (eds.), *Estados y naciones en los Andes: Hacia una historia comparativa: Bolivia—Colombia—Ecuador—Perú* 2 vols. (Lima: Instituto de Estudios Peruanos, Instituto Francés de Estudios Andinos, 1986), vol. 1, pp. 323–24; Luis Miguel Glave, personal communication, Seville, Oct. 2010.

88. César Itier, "Quechua, Aymara and Other Andean Languages: Historical, Linguistic and Socio-Linguistic Aspects," paper presented at the Maison de l'Amérique Latine, Paris, January 16, 2002.

89. David T. Garrett, *Shadows of Empire: The Indian Nobility of Cusco, 1750–1825* (Cambridge and New York: Cambridge University Press, 2005), p. 216.

90. Clements R. Markham, *Cuzco: A Journey to the Ancient Capital of Peru* (London: Chapman and Hall, 1856), pp. 197, 200.

91. Clements R. Markham (Peter Blanchard, ed.), *Markham in Peru: The Travels of Clements R. Markham, 1852–1853* (Austin: University of Texas Press, 1991), pp. 62–63, 67; Markham, *Cuzco*, pp. 197–99, gives a short sample of one of these Spanish-Quechua songs.

92. Markham (Peter Blanchard, ed.), *Markham in Peru*, pp. 89, 97–98, 118–19.

93. Witt, *Diario*, vol. 1, p. 239.

94. Itier, "Quechua y cultura," pp. 98–99.

95. Witt, *Diario*, vol. 1, p. 109.

96. Reginald Enock, *The Andes and the Amazon: Life and Travel in Peru* (London: T. Fisher Unwin, 1907), p. 73.

97. Tschiffely, *Tschiffely's Ride*, p. 53.

98. Eduardo Poeppig, *Viaje al Perú y al Río Amazonas, 1827–1832* (Iquitos: CETA, 2003), p. 337.

99. Witt, *Diario*, vol. 1, pp. 98, 256; Poeppig, *Viaje al Perú*, p. 344; Guinness, *Peru*, p. 150.

100. S. S. Hill, *Travels in Peru and Mexico* 2 vols. (London: Longman, Green, Longman, & Roberts, 1860), vol. 2, pp. 2–3, 7–9, 11.

101. Marisol De la Cadena, *Indigenous Mestizos. The Politics of Race and Culture in Cuzco, Peru, 1919–1991* (Durham, NC: Duke University Press, 2000), pp. 76–77.

102. Zoila S. Mendoza, *Creating Our Own: Folklore, Performance, and Identity in Cuzco, Peru* (Durham, NC: Duke University Press, 2008), especially the Introduction and Chapter 5.

103. Tim Marr, "Neither the State nor the Grass Roots: Language Maintenance and the Discourse of the Academia Mayor de la Lengua Quechua," *International Journal of Bilingual Education and Bilingualism* 2:3 (1999), 181–97.

104. Langer, "Indian Trade and Ethnic Economies," p. 9.

105. César Itier, *El teatro quechua en el Cuzco*, vol. 1 (Lima: Instituto Francés de Estudios Andinos / Centro de Estudios Regionales Andinos "Bartolomé de Las Casas," 1995); vol. 2 (Lima: Instituto

Francés de Estudios Andinos / Centro de Estudios Regionales Andinos "Bartolomé de Las Casas," 2000).

106. Itier, "Quechua, Aymara and Other Andean Languages," p. 160.

107. Adelaar, "Comentario," p. 116; also Willem F. H. Adelaar, "Unprotected Languages: The Silent Death of the Languages of Northern Peru," in Anita Herzfeld and Yolanda Lastra (eds.), *Las causas sociales de la desaparición y del mantenimiento de las lenguas en las naciones de América* (Hermosillo: Universidad de Sonora, 1999), pp. 205–22, see pp. 215–17.

108. This factor might also help explain the equally enigmatic survival of pockets of Quechua in the northern highlands, even today, as outliers or remnants of a much larger and more robust language community.

109. Adelaar, "Unprotected Languages," p. 217.

110. Kubler, *The Indian Caste of Peru*, maps 3–4, pp. 41–42. Unfortunately, the equivalent data for Lambayeque is lacking.

111. Gootenberg, "Population and Ethnicity," Table 8, pp. 137–38. Chota is here subsumed within the province of Cajamarca. The urban districts (*Cercados*) of Lima, Cuzco, and Arequipa also showed non-Indian majorities.

112. Kubler, *The Indian Caste of Peru*, pp. 43, 47, 59. It may be worth emphasizing here that a close identification between native language use and indigenous status is primarily a modern trait. Census takers during the colonial and early republican periods made little link between the two phenomena. It is highly unlikely that people who ceased to speak native languages ceased to be counted as "Indian" as a direct result; if they had been, they would immediately have ceased to pay tribute—hardly a desirable outcome for the census taker! It is thus also highly unlikely, in my view, that data suggesting a mestization trend in the northern highlands and coast are simply a record of indigenous speakers switching to Spanish, thus adding to the "mestizo" count while subtracting from the "Indian" one.

113. Adelaar with Muysken, *The Languages of the Andes*, p. 401.

114. Kubler, *The Indian Caste of Peru*, Table 2.

115. Disaggregated data for the other provinces (Julcán, Otuzco and Santiago de Chuco) are unavailable. For Mochica, according to Kubler, Trujillo province showed 67.4 percent non-Indians by 1876, and 90.1 percent by 1940. Data for the key province, Lambayeque, are deficient, though we may note that Lambayeque's native population was on a downwards trajectory: it fell from 63.5 percent of the total in the 1790s, to perhaps 51.7 percent by as early as the late 1820s (Kubler, *The Indian Caste of Peru*, Table 2; Gootenberg, "Population and Ethnicity," Table 8).

116. Manuel Andrés García, *De peruanos e Indios: La figura del indígena en la intelectualidad y política criollas (Perú: siglos XVIII–XIX)*

(Huelva: Universidad Internacional de Andalucía, 2007), pp. 118–39; Rebecca Earle, *The Return of the Native: Indians and Myth-Making in Spanish America, 1810–1930* (Durham, NC: Duke University Press, 2007).

117. Bruce Mannheim, *The Language of the Inka since the European Invasion* (Austin: University of Texas Press, 1991).

Chapter 7

Quechua Political Literature in Early Republican Peru (1810–1876)

Alan Durston

This chapter will examine how Quechua was recruited into Peruvian national politics from the independence wars (1810s and 1820s) to Peru's crushing defeat in the War of the Pacific (1879–1883), which was followed by a long period of stabilization and reconstruction. It focuses on the use of Quechua in political propaganda and legislation while also examining discourses and policies concerning Quechua's place in the incipient nation-state.

The nineteenth century is easily the most neglected in the post-Conquest history of the Quechua languages. The early republican Quechua literature can seem lacklustre compared to what the colonial period has left us: while Paul Rivet and Georges de Créqui-Montfort's bibliography of the Quechua and Aymara languages lists dozens of nineteenth-century items in Quechua, few seem representative of oral or popular language and culture, and even the Christian missionary literature is often derivative.[1] One could also point to a decline in quality, in that nineteenth-century writers and scholars of Quechua sometimes come across as dilettantes or even seem to lack basic competence in the language. With the exception of César Itier, Quechuists have largely ignored the period. The booming historiography on the nineteenth-century Andes, on the other hand, has barely touched upon indigenous language sources.

The nineteenth-century Quechua literature from Peru does, however, offer something that the colonial period lacks entirely: a series of explicitly political texts stretching from the wars of independence (ca. 1810–1825) to the Manuel Pardo government (1872–1876), on the eve of War of the Pacific (1879–1883). Three very different groups of texts can be distinguished: (1) political manifestos and calls to arms from the Independence Wars; (2) panegyric texts dedicated to caudillos from the first, conflict-ridden generation of republican life (especially the 1830s); and (3) translations of important laws affecting the indigenous population from the 1860s and 1870s, a period when liberal reform movements attempted to extend their influence to the "interior."

That national elites should have paid *some* attention to Quechua may seem unsurprising, given that it was spoken by most Peruvians and may even have been gaining ground during precisely this period.[2] No statistics on language seem to be available for the nineteenth century, but in the 1870s proponents of Quechua instruction for the elite claimed that two-thirds of all Peruvians were *indígenas* who spoke only Quechua.[3] In the 1876 national census around 58 percent of a total population of 2.7 million were considered *indígenas*.[4] In reality, of course, not all *indígenas* were monolingual Quechua speakers—many people classed as such also (or only) spoke Spanish, and there was a substantial Aymara presence in the altiplano. On the other hand, Peruvian writers tended to gloss over the fact that Quechua was spoken by everyone, whites included, in much of the highlands, something that foreign travelers were more likely to observe.[5] Itier estimates that in the early twentieth century between half and three-fourths of the *urban* population of Cuzco spoke only Quechua, and that Spanish monolingualism was practically nonexistent.[6] However, Quechua had little or no presence in Lima and elsewhere on the coast, or in Peru's second largest city, Arequipa. According to a Frenchman who lived in Peru in the 1840s, "[i]t would not be possible to find five persons either at Lima, Arequipa or any other city of the coast, moving in *good society*, able to understand, much less speak Quichua, unless they were originally from the Sierra . . . ."[7] The divide between coast and highlands would only widen during the succeeding decades.

Wartime Propaganda

The unique circumstances of the independence wars provoked the florescence of an unprecedented political literature in Quechua that was deployed in printed flyers and pamphlets by royalist as well as pro-independence forces. The first such texts were issued by the leaders of the Rio de la Plata independence movement and were directed at what is now highland Bolivia, which had been part of the viceroyalty based in Buenos Aires. Between 1810 and 1816 the *Rioplatense* patriots issued Quechua, Aymara, and Guaraní translations of important decrees, including a proclamation of independence, as well as manifestos aimed at recruiting the inhabitants of what would become the republic of Bolivia to their cause.[8]

The first Quechua text I know of expressing the new liberal doctrines in what would soon become the Republic of Peru is not a pro-independence document. In 1813 the archbishop of Lima arranged for the translation and printing of a *Proclama a los habitantes de ultramar* issued by the Cadiz Regency in the wake of the *cortes* (parliament) and Constitution of 1812.[9] The lengthy text explained the political situation in Spain (which was mostly under French control, with Ferdinand VII a prisoner of Napoleon), the holding of the Cadiz *cortes*, and the ideals concerning rights, freedoms, and political representation enshrined in the Constitution.

In 1819, some years after the liberal experiment in Spain had been crushed with the return of Ferdinand VII to the throne, two pro-independence Quechua proclamations addressing the indigenous population of Peru were printed in Chile, recently liberated by José de San Martín as the first phase of his plan to attack royalist forces in Peru. One was issued in San Martín's name, and the other, in Chilean general Bernardo O'Higgins's, both urging support for the expedition that would soon set out for the Peruvian coast.[10] Similarities in dialectology, orthography, and style between the two Quechua texts strongly suggest that they are the work of the same person. A third proclamation was issued in Peru by San Martín in 1821, perhaps after the occupation of Lima.[11]

A veritable propaganda war in Quechua ensued between pro-independence forces based in Lima and royalists in the highlands under the command of general José Canterac from his base in Jauja. Rivet and Créqui-Montfort reproduce two Quechua proclamations issued by Canterac on August 1, 1822.[12] One addresses the inhabitants of Huánuco, Conchucos, Huamalíes, and Huaylas, while the other speaks to the *puna* (high plateau) folk of Cerro de Pasco and Lake Junín. A guerrilla war was going on in these areas between royalist forces and local *montoneros* (guerrilla fighters) who supported San Martín, and the leaflets offer an amnesty to *montoneros* who switched sides. The second text refers to an intensive propaganda campaign by San Martín, much of which was presumably in Quechua.[13] I have come across one example of a pro-San Martín Quechua flyer aimed specifically at this part of the Andes: a bilingual proclamation printed in Lima in 1822 (probably before the Canterac flyers) and directed at the province of Jauja.[14]

On October 10, 1822, after San Martín had relinquished command of independent Peru, the country's first Congress issued a bilingual proclamation *a los indios de las provincias interiores* in which they announced an "army of liberation" that was being sent into the sierra (in reality, the Peruvian government was in disarray and would soon lose Lima itself to royalist forces).[15] A final document that deserves mention here is a manuscript titled *Las yndias de la vecindad de Lima a los soldados americanos del exercito real*, which urges soldiers fighting in Canterac's army to join the patriot cause.[16] Little contextual information is available for this document, but a reference to José de la Riva Agüero as president of Peru dates it to early 1823. The "letter" is signed *las peruanas* and addresses the soldiers as brothers. It seems likely that it employs a sisterly voice for rhetorical effect (rather than actually being written by or on behalf of Quechua-speaking indigenous women from Lima), in line with the tendency to find female embodiments for the nation. This is the most recent example of independence-era Quechua propaganda in Peru that I am aware of. Late in 1823 Simón Bolívar took over the independence struggle and soon defeated the royalist forces. Quechua manifestos issued by Bolívar may yet surface, but their apparent absence seems indicative of a change in strategy. Bolívar brought with him a more effective army than San Martín, and was thus less reliant on local support. Coming from present-day Venezuela, Bolívar may also have been less aware of the importance of indigenous languages in the Andes. San Martín, on the other hand, was born in a Guarani-speaking area (the province of Corrientes), and had also been exposed to the *Rioplatense* patriots' early use of indigenous languages in print as a political tool.

The Quechua texts aimed at Peru fall neatly into two groups from both dialectological and stylistic perspectives. The first group includes the Cadiz *Proclama* and the proclamations of San Martín, O'Higgins, and the Peruvian Congress. These texts share a markedly literary tone and a number of dialectal features that were specific to Cuzco Quechua. The second group consists of texts aimed specifically at the central highlands: the two Canterac proclamations, the Jauja leaflet, and the 1823 "letter" purportedly written by the Indian women of Lima. These four documents have a singular importance as the oldest known self-standing texts in Central Quechua. While they were aimed at different areas of the central highlands that lay to the north of the royalist base in the Mantaro valley, the two Canterac texts are very similar in dialectological terms. They seem closest to the modern Huánuco/Huallaga varieties, both lexically and phonologically (especially the voicing of /q/). The other two documents in this group, both pro-independence ones, are good examples of "Huanca" (Mantaro Valley) Quechua.[17] It makes perfect sense that the patriot propaganda machine would have been focused on this area, as it was the royalist base, while royalists directed their efforts at neighboring areas that were not under their control.

I will focus briefly on the language of the first group of (Cuzqueño) texts. Itier observes that the vocabulary of the Cadiz *Proclama* is reminiscent of the late colonial plays from Cuzco, and suggests that this vocabulary derives from a literary tradition rather than the contemporary spoken language.[18] The other texts in this group also bear the imprint of what could be called "literary Cuzqueño"—an ornate, archaizing register that developed in the eighteenth century and whose archetype is the play *Ollantay*.[19] This register is closely associated with the key ideological phenomenon of

Incaism (the urge to recover or claim a lost Inca heritage) that was especially strong among the creole elite and indigenous nobility of Cuzco.[20]
Itier notes a tendency to avoid Spanish loans where possible, by replacing
them with Quechua neologisms or archaisms, and regards this as a characteristic of nineteenth-century Quechua texts, noting that the tendency
is already present in the late colonial plays, which are set in Inca or early
colonial times.[21] Bernardo O'Higgins's proclamation, for instance, uses
quipucamayoc (/kipukamayuq/[22] "*quipu* specialist") for "notary," *mama-
cochapi pahuac guasicuna* (/mamaquchapi pawaq wasikuna/ "houses that
race on the sea") for "ships," and *hillapa* ("lightning") for "gun"—*hillapa*
or *hillappa* also appears in other documents of this group, especially the
Cadiz *Proclama*.[23]

The contrast with the Central Quechua texts could not be greater.
Aside from the fact that they employ other varieties of Quechua, the texts
aimed at the central highlands are far less ornate and do not shy away
from Spanish loanwords. There can be little doubt that the texts of the
first group would have been less widely intelligible, in particular because
of their tendency to use archaisms and neologisms instead of what must
have been widely understood loans. Why was "literary Cuzqueño" used
in these texts? Without knowing the identity of any of the translators I
can only speculate here, but a number of explanations come to mind.
First of all, these texts were not directed at a specific geographical area
within Peru, so Cuzco Quechua was in a sense the default variety. It
is also likely that this register was thought to give the translations the
dignity and elevated style appropriate to the Peruvian Congress, the *lib-
ertadores*, or the Cadiz Regency.

Most importantly, lexical purism and archaism was consistent with the
Incaist content of the first group of texts, especially because many of the
terms used to replace Hispanicisms were associated with Inca culture.
Incaism was a key rhetorical strategy for independence leaders, serving to
express the break with Spain and summon a separate history for the new
nations.[24] These texts are full of invocations of the Incas: their addressees are defined as the descendants of the Incas or as the inhabitants of
Tahuantinsuyu, and (the Cadiz *Proclama* aside) indigenous figures from
Manco Capac to Tupac Amaru II and Pumacahua are called upon as
precursors of the independence struggle.[25] The language of the proclamations served to "Incanise" their creole authors, who were assuming the mantle of the Incas by speaking like them—the proclamation of
the Peruvian Congress explicitly claimed for itself the authority of "our
beloved Incas."[26]

Lexical purism is often associated with linguistic nationalism.
Following this logic, avoiding Hispanicisms could have served as an
implicit linguistic declaration of independence from Spain. This may not
seem applicable to the texts in question, which were issued on behalf of

political classes that mostly did not know Quechua, but Itier suggests that these texts contain the first inklings of an imagining of Quechua as the language of a Peruvian nation that included non-Indians.[27] In fact, the proclamation of the Peruvian Congress referred to Quechua as a common language that the members shared with their indigenous addressees.[28] At the same time, however, Quechua was being identified with a "nation" in the more traditional sense of an ethnic group—in other words, an indigenous nation. Itier notes that the term *quechuas* is used, perhaps for the first time, as an ethnonym for the inhabitants of the Inca empire in a letter of the archbishop of Lima concerning the Quechua translation of the Cadiz *Proclama*.[29] The title of the O'Higgins manifesto defines its audience as the Quechua, Aymara, and Puquina "nations" (*llaccta* /llaqta/—the term is discussed below), in other words, three distinct peoples defined on a linguistic basis (the inclusion of a Puquina *llaccta* is surprising given that the Puquina language could not have been very widely spoken at this date).[30] Any identification of Quechua with a multiracial Peruvian "nation" was as yet an inchoate one.[31]

The question of how liberal concepts were translated into Quechua in these texts calls for a full study in its own right. Even seemingly basic concepts like "freedom" and "independence" presented translation problems. The complexity of the task was enhanced by the fact that liberal concepts were new in Spanish, too, and key terms like *nación* and *patria* were undergoing radical transformations in the process of acquiring their full modern sense.[32]

Some terms were introduced as loans even in the most purist translations. They were generally accompanied by brief glosses—for instance, the 1823 proclamation of the Peruvian Congress renders "constitution" as *camachicuy Constitucion sutiocc* (/kamachikuy "Constitución" sutiyuq/ "the command called 'Constitution'").[33] There may have been more than an effort to enhance intelligibility behind this style of glossing—it also served a purist agenda by putting the Spanish term in sanitary quotes, thus preserving the boundaries of the language. In many cases no gloss is provided, but the word *ñiscca* (/ñisqa/, "called" or "known as") is added to the loan, simply indicating that it is not a regular Quechua term.[34] Interestingly, the far more demotic "letter" from the Indian women of Lima makes no effort to explain or sanitize terms like *república*, *nación*, and *presidente*, using them as if they had already been incorporated into the language.[35] Yet another option was to simply avoid translating difficult terms or to use extended paraphrases, and in fact many of these translations are loose ones to say the least.

At least one existing Quechua term assumed great prominence in translating liberal language: *llaccta* (/llaqta/, /marka/ or /malka/ in Central Quechua). While the colonial dictionaries gloss /llaqta/

as "town," and this continues to be its most common use, it is better defined as a community of people. In the Huarochirí Manuscript /llaqta/ could even refer to the *huaca* or founding ancestor of a supra-*ayllu* group, and there are colonial texts where it is used with a meaning approximate to "country."[36] In the texts of the independence wars and beyond it was used consistently to translate concepts like republic, nation, and fatherland. Two additional key terms were derived from /llaqta/: *llaccta masi* (/llaqta masi/ "compatriot," literally "someone who shares a /llaqta/ with someone else") and *llacctayocc* (/llaqt-ayuq/ "citizen," literally "someone who has a /llaqta/").[37] Of course, when a writer invoked his or her *llaccta masi* the expression could be misinterpreted as referring only to fellow natives of a town rather than all Peruvians, but the same could happen with a Spanish term like *patria*.

Finally, the language of these texts can be examined for what it tells us about their intended audience. With the exception of the Cadiz *Proclama* the texts in the first (Cuzqueño) group are explicitly addressed to Indians, while the Central Quechua texts define their audience in regional terms with no mention of ethnicity. In principle, they were all aimed at monolinguals (and hence Indians), as anyone else would have been directly exposed to a barrage of Spanish-language propaganda. The texts may have important implications for Quechua literacy levels among monolinguals, although the expectation was probably that they would reach large audiences by being orally transmitted by priests and the remnants of the *curaca* class. On the other hand, it is clear that language choice (of Quechua, and of a special kind of Quechua) in the first group of texts had important symbolic functions. This suggests that their intended audience was not strictly, or even primarily, monolingual. The Quechua-speaking creole elite of the highlands, especially priests, may also have been targeted. Even if they were also being exposed to propaganda in Spanish, Quechua would have been an especially effective medium for transmitting the kinds of nativist messages that were so important in patriot ideology. On the other hand, the appeal of Incaist symbolism among the indigenous population, particularly the remnants of the *curaca* (noble) class, only a few decades after the Tupac Amaru Rebellion should not be underestimated. Either way, these texts probably required some form of elite mediation (beyond the simple act of reading aloud) to explain archaisms like *quipucamayoc* to a broader audience. We also need to consider the role of simple disconnect between intended audiences and the sometimes fantastic notions that the authors and translators held about them, as when O'Higgins addressed his manifesto to a Puquina "nation" as well as a Quechua and an Aymara one.

In Praise of Caudillos

In its 1822 proclamation the first Peruvian Congress promised to provide the country's Constitution and other important documents in
Quechua.[38] However, the period stretching from Simón Bolívar's dictatorship (1824–1826) to Ramón Castilla's *pax andina* (1845–1862)
seems to have produced neither translations of legislation nor explicit
political manifestos. What we have instead is a small group of panegyric texts *addressed to* some of the most important political leaders of the time. More programmatic political statements may yet be
uncovered from this period, but the fact that what has surfaced so far
consists mostly of personal praise seems consistent with the nature of
caudillo power.

Early republican Cuzco had a tradition of welcoming visiting political leaders with elaborate fiestas emphasizing the city's Inca heritage, in
which laudatory poems or speeches were performed by actors playing
the role of Inca emperors.[39] It appears that these texts were often in
Quechua—I am aware of three examples of the genre. The oldest is an
1834 verse text dedicated to President Luis José de Orbegoso and reproduced by E.W. Middendorf, who provides no attribution or provenance.
Middendorf includes what sounds like a stage direction: "The Inca
[emperor] of Peru rises from his grave and speaks." The resurrected Inca
humbly welcomes Orbegoso to Cuzco as God's chosen one.[40] In 1839 a
Quechua welcome, also in verse, was addressed by a young man dressed
as an Inca emperor to Orbegoso's archrival, Agustín Gamarra, upon his
triumphal entry to Cuzco after the defeat of Andrés de Santa Cruz and
the Peru-Bolivian Confederation. The text, which was distributed as a
printed flyer, hails Gamarra for having liberated Cuzco (or perhaps Peru)
from the Confederation, celebrates his victory at the crucial battle of
Yungay, and depicts him as an heir of the Incas.[41] A third example of this
genre dates from 1851 and is a bilingual printed farewell to the prefect of
the department of Cuzco, general José Miguel Medina, lavishly praising
his accomplishments and contributions to the city, which included its
first library and museum.[42] It is signed "todos los Incas hijos de Mancco,
y Mama Occllo." The text asks Medina to forgive his local detractors
(which the Quechua version refers to as "Jews" and "dogs"), suggesting
that it had a polemical background. While I have not seen the Quechua
original of the Gamarra text, the other two fall clearly into the "literary
Cuzqueño" tradition.[43] The preoccupation with avoiding Spanish loans
is especially apparent in the Medina text, which refuses to incorporate
terms like "museum" and "library," using extended paraphrases instead.

A final example of political literature from this period is a poem or song
titled *Auka yana kocha* ("hostile black lake") reproduced by Middendorf,
again without attribution.[44] In this brief text the speaker refers to a black

lake as a place of death, and asks a condor to convey the news of his demise there to his parents. Middendorf notes that the "black lake" is in fact the Lake Yanacocha where Gamarra was defeated in a major battle against the Peru-Bolivian Confederation in 1835. While the text has no explicit political content, it is a lamentation of Gamarra's defeat and of the deaths of many of his followers and could thus be considered an anti-Confederation manifesto. It lacks Incaist vocabulary and rhetoric, and is strongly reminiscent of present-day folk songs in its use of parallelism and the prominence given to natural entities.

The panegyrics to Orbegoso, Gamarra, and Medina reflect the Cuzqueño elite's efforts to portray themselves as successors to the Incas while also ingratiating themselves with powerful political figures. At the same time, these texts were propaganda on behalf of the addressees and may have been engineered by them. This is suggested by the fact that the Gamarra and Medina texts, at least, were printed, and that they are explicitly polemical, containing attacks on their political opponents. Caudillos may have sought to legitimize themselves both locally (in Cuzco) and nationally through these apparently spontaneous expressions of allegiance by the Cuzco elite. It appears that Quechua political propaganda could also take more vernacular forms, as is suggested by the composition *Auka yana kocha*. This indicates the existence of two different registers of political discourse—a highbrow, Incaist one probably intended for the elite, and a more popular one.

Beyond what can be inferred from this small corpus, the first generation of Peru's independent life seems an especially promising period for studying the place of Quechua in national politics, which at this time were dominated by caudillos of highland origin whose precarious hold on power often relied on their ability to forge alliances with sectors of the peasantry.[45] This was a formative period of conflict between opposing political, social, and economic models—in particular the struggle between highlands-based free-trade liberals who favored an alliance with Bolivia, on the one hand, and coast-based, protectionist conservatives who were more friendly with Chile, on the other.[46] Was either band particularly "pro-Quechua"?

Conservative interests in this period might be portrayed as having an anti-Quechua leaning. Cecilia Méndez notes that the (then conservative) Limeño elite's opposition to Santa Cruz's Peru-Bolivian Confederation was partly motivated by racial fears of a new state in which indigenous and highland elements would predominate to an even greater degree, and by their contempt for the mestizo Santa Cruz.[47] One of the rather cruel satirical poems of the conservative Limeño aristocrat and writer Felipe Pardo y Aliaga has Santa Cruz's Indian mother address him plaintively in broken, Quechua-inflected Spanish, calling him *huahuachay* (/wawacháy/ "my darling child") and *Andrescha* ("little Andrés").[48]

As Méndez points out, however, this contempt for the modern Indian
did not exclude the deployment of Incaist rhetoric, which in general
seems to have been used more consistently by conservatives than liberals.[49] Agustín Gamarra, the dominant leader on the conservative side,
was ridiculed for his indigenous heritage by liberals just as much as his
rival Santa Cruz was by conservatives.[50] Pardo y Aliaga praised Gamarra
precisely for his rhetorical abilities in Quechua: "with one word...he
could make 12,000 Indians suddenly kneel down."[51] Quechua was not
ridiculous when it was deployed in favor of one's political interests. If
I am correct in thinking that the welcome/farewell speeches were at
least partly engineered by their recipients, then we have conservatives
(Gamarra) as well as liberals (Orbegoso and Medina) making use of
written Quechua propaganda.

Liberating the Indians with the Language of the Incas

During the 1840s and 1850s the guano boom enabled the development of a much stronger and more stable national state based in Lima.
As a result of both the expansion of the state and of the commercial
bonanza, a liberal bourgeoisie developed in Lima that would soon
demand a larger role in national politics. This demand translated into a
political party, the Partido Civil, which came to power in 1872 with the
election of Manuel Pardo (1872–1876). The *Civilista* program included
broader political participation, economic modernization, and universal education. The elite involved in the *Civilista* project had also been
developing a sensitivity toward the plight of the Indian masses of the
"interior," particularly during the 1860s. Indians had to be relieved of
the oppression and exploitation they suffered at the hands of local elites
and, most importantly, educated so that they could understand their
rights and become active citizens, economic free agents, and (eventually) full members of the republic.[52]

Interest in Quechua seems to have paralleled the rise of *Civilismo*,
culminating in the 1870s, when there was a significant Quechuist
boom.[53] Quechua first began to be invoked in the scholarly projects of
national self-awareness of the 1850s. Mariano Rivero and Johann Jakob
von Tschudi's 1851 treatise on Peruvian antiquities included an extensive chapter on Quechua by the Swiss von Tschudi, and issued a call for
"some erudite and truly patriotic Peruvian" to dedicate himself to the
study of Quechua and to establishing the foundations for a Quechua
literature.[54] Mateo and Mariano Felipe Paz Soldán's *Geografía del Perú*,
a foundational description of the national territory whose publication in
1862 was financed by President Ramón Castilla, also paid attention to
Quechua, especially as a source for place-name etymologies.[55]

Under the Manuel Pardo government Quechua came to be perceived, at least by an influential group within the elite, as a medium of national unity. In 1874 it was being taught at the elite national school of Nuestra Señora de Guadalupe in Lima, where Pardo had studied. The instructor was Leonardo Villar, a medical doctor from Cuzco and an accomplished Quechuist.[56] In 1873 and 1874 José Fernández Nodal and José Dionisio Anchorena (respectively) published Quechua grammars, in Anchorena's case with full backing from the Pardo government.[57] These were the first significant works on Quechua by Peruvians since independence, and they were intended primarily to foment the study of the language among the national elite.

Both writers claimed that two-thirds of all Peruvians were *indígenas* who spoke only Quechua. Since it was they who supported the state financially, and since Quechua was the autochthonous language of Peru, the burden lay with the Spanish speakers to bridge the linguistic divide and educate their fellow citizens in their mother tongue.[58] Anchorena argued that whites (*los blancos*) had to learn Quechua (which he claimed could be done in two or three months with the use of his grammar and a dictionary that he hoped to publish) in order to overcome the bad feelings that separated them from *los indígenas*.[59] Fernández Nodal went further, referring to Quechua as the "national language" or "Peruvian language" and stating that it was a national embarrassment that it was not being taught in Peru's schools and universities.[60]

The notion that Quechua was the "Peruvian language" was not uncommon among elite thinkers of the second half of the nineteenth century.[61] As much as the fact that Quechua was a majority language, this discourse followed on the logic of the isomorphism of language and nation, which required that Peru have a distinctive and autochthonous national language—it was precisely around this time that linguistic nationalism was truly coming into its own in Europe itself.[62] In particular, it was believed that for a true national literature to develop in Peru it would have to be in Quechua—Itier argues that Fernández Nodal's grammar was largely directed at providing models and instruments for the development of a Quechua literature based on European canons.[63] The same can be said of Anchorena's work, which includes a lengthy appendix on versification where he provided Quechua translations of Spanish verse compositions, including the Peruvian national anthem and a poem about the battle of Junín.[64]

In spite of these forward-looking objectives, both Anchorena and Fernández Nodal saw Quechua fundamentally as the language of the Incas, which is how they identified it in the titles of their grammars. The first motive that Anchorena gives for studying Quechua is a philological one: it was only through Quechua that the achievements of the

Incas could be unveiled.[65] Fernández Nodal spoke of the task of restoring Quechua to its imperial splendor through the study and cultivation of the remaining fragments, which had been preserved in the work of colonial missionaries like Domingo de Santo Tomás and Diego González Holguín.[66] Even though the most prominent of their proclaimed objectives was to facilitate communication with *indígenas*, Anchorena's and Fernández Nodal's work is strikingly bookish in nature and shows little knowledge of, or even interest in, contemporary spoken forms of Quechua.[67]

The publication of Anchorena's grammar in 1874 was financed by the government that first had it peer-reviewed by Leonardo Villar and another prominent Quechuist, the polymath José Sebastián Barranca. Pardo signed a decree ordering the state press to print one thousand copies, a fifth of which were to be given to the Ministry of Public Instruction.[68] The Pardo government seems to have viewed Anchorena's work primarily as an instrument for spreading Spanish among Quechua speakers, or at least justified its sponsorship by claiming (very implausibly) that it would have this effect. However, Anchorena's proclaimed objective of aiding the acquisition of Quechua by the elite was also mentioned, and the fact that it was being taught at the Colegio de Nuestra Señora de Guadalupe suggests that this objective was taken seriously.[69]

Anchorena had already served the *civilista* government as a sort of official Quechuist the previous year (1873), when the state press published a booklet containing his Quechua version of new legislation concerning municipal councils.[70] But this was not the first piece of Peruvian legislation to be translated into Quechua: that distinction seems to belong to an 1867 decree by President Mariano Ignacio Prado, a liberal general. Its translation is associated with the work of the Sociedad Amiga de los Indios (1867–1871), an organization that lobbied for the interests of the indigenous population and was in some respects a precursor to the Partido Civil.[71] In addition to swaying public (elite) opinion, the society sought to promote knowledge of legal rights among the indigenous population. It was led by Juan Bustamante, a businessman and politician from Puno. The newspaper *El Comercio* ran a column on Indian affairs in which members of the society published letters and reports, many of which were compiled in a book titled *Los indios del Perú* by Bustamante and published in 1867. Shortly afterward a conservative rebellion overthrew Prado, and Bustamante was killed in an effort to mobilize an indigenous peasant army in support of Prado.[72]

It is in *Los indios del Perú* that we find a Quechua translation of an 1867 presidential decree implementing Simón Bolívar's 1825 ban on forcing Indians to provide labor for public works or private interests.[73] The Quechua text is relatively free of archaisms and literary language, and is closer to the Ayacucho varieties than to Cuzco Quechua.[74] Spanish loanwords are accompanied by glosses in the style of the independence-period texts—for example, *subprefecto niscca camachicucc* (*/subprefecto nisqa kamachikuq/* "the official [literally, 'person who gives orders'] called 'subprefect'").[75] The category *llaccta* retains its key role in translating republican concepts—for example, *llacctayocc* (citizen) and *hatun-llaccta* (republic or state, literally "big *llaccta*").[76] Aside from a tendency to try to reproduce the sentence structure of the Spanish original (a common pitfall among inexperienced translators) the Quechua text is about as intelligible as could be expected.

The efforts of the Sociedad Amiga de los Indios must have served as a precedent for the Pardo government's decision to make new legislation concerning municipal councils available in Quechua. The extensive Ley Orgánica de Municipalidades of 1873 ordered the creation of locally elected councils at the departmental, provincial and district levels to oversee public infrastructure, services, and schooling. Immediately after it was passed in Congress, Pardo ordered that the portion of the law concerning district-level councils be translated into Quechua by Anchorena, anticipating that many prospective members would not know Spanish (clearly it was believed that the same did not apply to councils in the provincial and departmental capitals). The translation was to be distributed to local authorities and read on feast days after mass.[77]

The resulting booklet was published the same year, and contains an appendix with quotes from important legislation concerning Indians and an *arancel eclesiástico* with the approved fees to be charged for sacraments.[78] Anchorena's translations are idiosyncratic, to say the least. Itier doubts that they would have been widely intelligible because of Anchorena's frequent use of neologisms and archaisms.[79] Indeed, anyone attempting to decipher the translations would have had to constantly refer to a lengthy glossary provided at the end of the booklet, which according to Anchorena consisted of Quechua terms that had fallen out of use in some areas.[80] His Quechua is in fact a unique personal creation and not at all in the "literary Cuzqueño" or any other tradition.

Anchorena prologued his translation by stating that Peru had had its own municipal legislation since the eleventh century thanks to Manco Capac and his successors. If his translation used Spanish terms for public offices and institutions, it was not, claimed Anchorena, because Quechua lacked such terms, but because they had been forgotten as a result of the Spanish Conquest.[81] Most of the archaisms and neologisms were used to translate semitechnical terms like "to administer" or "to resolve" that did have rough equivalents in spoken varieties or would have been easily paraphrased. Anchorena was aiming for an exact word-for-word correspondence (so far as this was possible with Quechua morphology) and in order to achieve it he dredged up terms from colonial dictionaries (sometimes changing their meaning), borrowed them from Aymara, or (most frequently) invented them from scratch. The term "neologism" seems inadequate for such creations, because neologisms are usually compounds made from elements that already exist in the language.[82]

Anchorena's translation probably did little to accomplish the Pardo government's objective of making the new municipal legislation more widely available. The fact that such an odd translation could have been written, let alone sponsored by the Peruvian state for such an important purpose, is surprising, but also indicative of a broader tendency of the time to "reinvent" Quechua. Fernández Nodal took similar liberties, especially in the version of *Ollantay* he included in an appendix to his grammar. He claimed to be presenting a corrected version of the original text, but what he actually did was rewrite it to regularize the rhyme scheme, rendering much of it nonsensical and even ungrammatical.[83]

It is worth noting that Anchorena's and Fernández Nodal's claims to Quechua expertise did not go unchallenged at the time. In a scathing critique of Fernández Nodal's work, Gavino Pacheco Zegarra mentioned that he had found him incapable even of basic conversation in Quechua and attacked his "corrected" version of the *Ollantay*.[84] I have not come across critiques of Anchorena's translation of the Ley Orgánica de Municipalidades or information on why he was chosen as translator,[85] but he did face difficulties publishing his grammar the following year. Leonardo Villar reviewed two different versions at the behest of President Pardo and finally recommended publication on the grounds that Anchorena had made a commendable effort in a much neglected field, but not without noting that his work was still deeply flawed.[86] Both Pacheco Zegarra and Villar were Cuzqueños who had some familiarity with the city's literary traditions and were doubtless native speakers of Quechua.

Epilogue and Conclusions

The Chilean occupation and the upheavals that followed it do not seem to have generated any Quechua texts. Beginning in the 1890s there was a florescence of Quechua theatre in Cuzco that peaked in the 1910s, garnering national attention in a time of intensifying interest in Peru's indigenous past. Itier's research has shown that the authors of these historical plays sought to resurrect "Inca Quechua" by drawing on Cuzco's colonial literary traditions, but also that they used Inca drama as a medium of thinly veiled political commentary, including criticism of the oligarchic *Civilista* governments.[87] Important developments in Quechua letters were taking place in other parts of Peru as well. During the first decade of the twentieth century a resident and one-time mayor of the town of Tarma (in the central highlands) named Adolfo Vienrich made an important break with Quechuist traditions. Vienrich, who was the son of a German immigrant with an elite *Tarmeña*, produced novel studies of Quechua folklore based in part on direct observation of the Quechua oral culture of the area. Most surprisingly, he published a short-lived bilingual periodical using the local variety of Quechua. In its first editorial he urged Indians to confront racial scorn by becoming literate and taking pride in their language.[88] When reformist president Guillermo Billinghurst sent Teodomiro Gutiérrez Cuevas to investigate peasant grievances in the Puno in 1913, the latter publicized his mission with a Quechua flyer.[89] This flyer, possibly the first such document to appear since the independence wars, anticipated the frequent use of Quechua propaganda under Augusto B. Leguía's dictatorship (1919–1930), a topic which is yet to be investigated.[90] Generally speaking, the first two decades of the twentieth century inaugurated a period when elites and middle sectors from different highland towns studied and wrote Quechua—including locally spoken varieties—as a means of advancing a wide variety of *indigenista*, regionalist, nationalist, and social reformist projects.[91]

When we view the nineteenth-century literature in its totality, it is hard to avoid the conclusion that elite interest in Quechua was sporadic and marginal to nation-building efforts that were increasingly centered on the coast. It is clear nonetheless that concerns specific to the early republican context resulted in new forms of written Quechua, and that these forms varied in revealing ways from independence to the War of the Pacific. The political literature of the independence wars constitutes a unique corpus resulting from unique circumstances. It is also a very diverse corpus, with a stark contrast between the Central Quechua texts, which were clearly meant to sway ordinary people directly involved in the fighting, and the highbrow Cuzqueño texts. The latter's bookish and archaizing language suggests that the medium was an important part of the message, and thus that their intended audience was not necessarily monolingual or even indigenous. Above all, it reflects how their authors wanted to be perceived, in particular their desire to assume the mantle of the Incas and the legitimacy they felt came with it. Something similar is apparent in the panegyric texts dedicated to national leaders in the years following independence, which allowed both speakers and addressees to "play Inca" (sometimes literally). At the same time, these early republican texts reflect a very different form of polemic, one in which the persona of the caudillo played a central role.

The Lima-based *Civilista* project of the 1860s and 1870s promoted Quechua as an instrument to uplift the downtrodden Indian and as a medium of national unity, but the rhetorical nationalization of Quechua was a double-edged sword. On the one hand, it meant that in spite of the profound divisions between coast and highlands, and the increasing marginalization of the latter, some members of the national elite developed an intense interest in Quechua.[92] But it also meant that certain requirements and expectations—contradictory ones—were imposed on Quechua. Anchorena and Fernández Nodal wanted to endow Quechua with the literary and conceptual resources of a European language while also viewing it as an heirloom from the Inca Empire. In the absence of linguistic and philological training (neither Anchorena nor Fernández Nodal were schooled in the Cuzqueño literary tradition) such projects could degenerate into pure fantasy. Anchorena's idiosyncratic (not to say unintelligible) translations speak to the contradictions of treating Quechua as the "national language," the "language of the Incas" and an instrument for communicating with *indígenas* all at the same time. They also suggest a gaping divide between the state and the Quechua-speaking majority and an apparent failure on the part of national elites to develop a republican political and legal language in Quechua. However, we should not be too hasty in considering Anchorena's work representative of the elite Quechuist enterprise of the period. In particular, the Quechua text in Bustamante's *Los indios del Perú* could not be more different from Anchorena's writings, and shows continuities in terminological solutions with independence-era documents that could be construed as a tradition that further examples may help uncover.

Acknowledgements

I thank Paul Heggarty, César Itier, and Adrian Pearce for their keen observations on drafts of this chapter, and Cecilia Méndez for sharing important documents. I am also grateful to David Beresford-Jones, Paul Heggarty, and Adrian Pearce for organizing the unique colloquium in which I first presented some of the ideas developed here.

Notes

1. Paul Rivet and Georges de Créqui-Montfort, *Bibliographie des langues aymará et kichua*, 4 vols. (Paris: Institut d'Ethnologie, 1951–56).
2. See Paul Gootenberg, "Population and Ethnicity in Early Republican Peru: Some Revisions," *Latin American Research Review* 26:3 (1991), 109–57, and Adrian Pearce's chapter in this volume.
3. José Fernández Nodal, *Elementos de gramática quichua ó idioma de los yncas* (Aylesbury and London: Watson and Hazell, [1873]), vi–vii; José Dionisio Anchorena, *Gramática quechua ó del idioma del imperio de los incas* (Lima: Imprenta del Estado, 1874), v.
4. Gootenberg, "Population and Ethnicity," pp. 140, 142.
5. Clements R. Markham, *Cuzco: A Journey to the Ancient Capital of Peru* (London: Chapman and Hall, 1856), p. 197.

6. César Itier, *El teatro quechua en el Cuzco*, vol. 1 (Lima: Instituto Francés de Estudios Andinos / Centro de Estudios Regionales Andinos "Bartolomé de Las Casas," 1995), pp. 27–29.

7. Paul Marcoy, *Travels in South America. From the Pacific Ocean to the Atlantic Ocean*, vol. 1 (New York: Scribner, Armstrong, & Co, 1875), p. 59, n. 1 (emphasis in original).

8. Rivet and Créqui-Montfort, *Bibliographie*, vol. 1, pp. 231–34, 235–42, 244–46, 263–73. See also the texts in Quechua, Aymara, and Guarani in Ministerio del Interior, *Comisión Honoraria de Reducciones de Indios, Publicación N⁰. 1. La situación actual de los indios argentinos frente a los decretos…* (Buenos Aires: 1935); I thank César Itier for sharing this publication with me. A discussion of the *Rioplatense* literature, long overdue, is beyond the scope of this study.

9. Rivet and Créqui-Montfort, *Bibliographie*, vol. 1, pp. 247–60. The *Proclama* was translated into several indigenous languages—for an extensive study of the Tzotzil Maya version, see Robert M. Laughlin, *Beware the Great Horned Serpent! Chiapas Under the Threat of Napoleon* (Albany, NY: Institute for Mesoamerican Studies, 2003).

10. Rivet and Créqui-Montfort, *Bibliographie*, vol. 1, pp. 497–99, 275–77.

11. Ibid., pp. 281–82.

12. Ibid., pp. 282–84.

13. Ibid., p. 284.

14. Vicente Gago, "Proclama del Dr. Vicente Gago, capellan del hospital militar de Santa Ana, a sus paisanos los habitantes de la provincia de Jauja, en su lengua nativa y peculiar" (Lima: Imprenta de Rio, 1822)—a two-page imprint at the John Carter Brown Library.

15. Rivet and Créqui-Montfort, *Bibliographie*, vol. 1, pp. 285-87.

16. Anonymous, "Las yndias de la vecindad de Lima a los soldados americanos del exercito real"—two-page manuscript at the Museo Nacional de Historia, Lima, Peru. I thank Cecilia Méndez for giving me a photograph of this very interesting document.

17. Rodolfo Cerrón-Palomino, personal communication.

18. César Itier, "Quechua y cultura en el Cuzco del siglo XVIII: De la 'lengua general' al 'idioma del imperio de los incas'," in César Itier (ed.), *Del siglo de oro al siglo de las luces. Lenguaje y sociedad en los Andes del siglo XVIII* (Cuzco: Centro de Estudios Regionales Andinos "Bartolomé de Las Casas," 1995), pp. 89–111, see pp. 102–3, n. 8.

19. See Itier, "Quechua y cultura"; and Bruce Mannheim, *The Language of the Inka since the European Invasion* (Austin: University of Texas Press, 1991), pp. 71–73.

20. Mannheim, *The Language of the Inka*, pp. 71–73; see Natalia Majluf, "De la rebelión al museo: Genealogías y retratos de los incas, 1781–1900," in Thomas B. F. Cummins (ed.), *Los incas, reyes del Perú* (Lima: Banco de Crédito, 2005), pp. 253–319.

21. Itier, "Quechua y cultura," pp. 103–4, n. 9.
22. Here and elsewhere I quote Quechua words and phrases in the original spelling, followed by a transcription in the modern phonological alphabet between forward slashes if there is a significant difference. I do not represent modified stops when they are not distinguished in the original spelling.
23. Rivet and Créqui-Montfort, *Bibliographie*, vol. 1, pp. 249, 276.
24. Rebecca Earle, *The Return of the Native: Indians and Myth-Making in Spanish America, 1810–1930* (Durham, NC: Duke University Press, 2007); cf. Majluf, "De la rebelión al museo," pp. 260–75.
25. Rivet and Créqui-Montfort, *Bibliographie*, vol. 1, pp. 249, 277, 498.
26. Rivet and Créqui-Montfort, *Bibliographie*, vol. 1, pp. 287–88.
27. Itier, "Quechua y cultura," p. 104.
28. Rivet and Créqui-Montfort, *Bibliographie*, vol. 1, pp. 287–88; cf. Itier, "Quechua y cultura," p. 104, n. 11.
29. Itier, "Quechua y cultura," p. 104.
30. Rivet and Créqui-Montfort, *Bibliographie*, vol. 1, p. 276.
31. One might argue that an Incaist, nativist, or protonationalist "meta-message" could not have been intended for the Cadiz *Proclama*, as it was not a pro-independence text. Here the choice of "literary Cuzqueño" may have responded to purely stylistic considerations (achieving an august tone), or the translator, working at a considerable remove from the authors, may have had his own designs. It could also be suggested that there was an effort on the part of the Spanish authorities to preemptively appeal to nativist sentiments both among creoles and Indians, as is suggested by the decision to have the *Proclama* translated into indigenous languages in the first place.
32. See Eric J. Hobsbawm, *Nations and Nationalism since 1780: Programme, Myth, Reality* (Cambridge: Cambridge University Press, 1990), pp. 14–16.
33. Rivet and Créqui-Montfort, *Bibliographie*, vol. 1, p. 286.
34. Ibid., pp. 253, 498.
35. Anonymous, "Las yndias."
36. Gerald Taylor, "Introducción a la edición de 1987," in Gerald Taylor (ed.), *Ritos y tradiciones de Huarochirí*, second revised ed. (Lima: Instituto Francés de Estudios Andinos / Banco Central de Reserva del Perú / Universidad Particular Ricardo Palma, 1999), xxvii–xxviii; César Itier, personal communication.
37. Rivet and Créqui-Montfort, *Bibliographie*, vol. 1, pp. 276, 277, 498.
38. Ibid., p. 286.
39. Majluf, "De la rebelión al museo," p. 238; Charles F. Walker, *Smoldering Ashes. Cuzco and the Creation of Republican Peru, 1780–1840* (Durham, NC: Duke University Press, 1999), pp. 164–72.

40. E. W. Middendorf, *Dramatische und lyrische dichtungen der keshua-sprache* (Leipzig: F. A. Brockhaus, 1891), pp. 258–60.
41. Luis Miguel Glave, *La república instalada. Formación nacional y prensa en el Cuzco, 1825–1839* (Lima: Instituto de Estudios Peruanos, 2004), pp. 227–29; Walker, *Smoldering Ashes*, pp. 168–69.
42. Rivet and Créqui-Montfort, *Bibliographie*, vol. 1, pp. 343–45. Medina cannot be characterized as a caudillo, but this text shares key characteristics with the speeches to Orbegoso and Gamarra.
43. Itier, "Quechua y cultura," p. 102.
44. Middendorf, *Dramatische und lyrische dichtungen*, p. 263.
45. Cecilia Méndez, *The Plebeian Republic. The Huanta Rebellion and the Making of the Peruvian State, 1820–1850* (Durham, NC: Duke University Press, 2005), pp. 241–43.
46. Paul Gootenberg, *Between Silver and Guano: Commercial Policy and the State in Postindependence Peru* (Princeton, NJ: Princeton University Press, 1989).
47. Cecilia Méndez, "Incas Si, Indios No: Notes on Peruvian Creole Nationalism and Its Contemporary Crisis," *Journal of Latin American Studies* 28:1 (1996), 197–225.
48. Méndez, "Incas Si, Indios No," p. 208. Santa Cruz's mother was more likely to have been an Aymara speaker.
49. Ibid., p. 213, n. 36; Walker, *Smoldering Ashes*, pp. 170–1.
50. Walker, *Smoldering Ashes*, pp. 177–78. Gamarra was from Cuzco and his mother was thought to have been an Indian, at least by his detractors (ibid.).
51. Ibid., p. 123.
52. Ulrich Muecke, *Political Culture in Nineteenth-Century Peru: The Rise of the Partido Civil* (Pittsburgh: Univerity of Pittsburgh Press, 2004).
53. César Itier, *El teatro quechua en el Cuzco* vol. 2 (Lima: Instituto Francés de Estudios Andinos / Centro de Estudios Regionales Andinos "Bartolomé de Las Casas," 2000), pp. 17–21.
54. Ibid., p. 17.
55. Mateo Paz Soldán and Mariano Felipe Paz Soldán, *Geografía del Perú* (Paris: Fermin Didot, 1862).
56. Anonymous, *Memoria que el Ministro de Estado en el Despacho de Instrucción, Culto, Justicia y Beneficencia presenta al Congreso Nacional de 1874* (Lima: Imprenta del Universo, 1874), p. 9; Raul Porras Barrenechea, *Fuentes históricas peruanas (apuntes de un curso universitario)* (Lima: Instituto Raul Porras Barrenechea, 1963), p. 41.
57. Fernández Nodal was from Arequipa and spent much of his life abroad: Gavino Pacheco Zegarra, *Ollantai. Drame en vers quechua du temps des incas* (Paris: Maisonneuve, 1878), p. 128. The title page of his grammar gives Cuzco as its place of publication, but no date.

It was in fact printed in London, and the date of publication seems to have been 1873 (Rivet and Créqui-Montfort, *Bibliographie*, vol. 1, p. 462). I have not been able to find any biographical information about Anchorena other than what little he reveals in his two publications. He was both a lawyer and a military man (with the rank of lieutenant colonel). He was clearly well connected with the *civilista* elite.

58. Anchorena, *Gramática quechua*, v; Fernández Nodal, *Elementos de gramática quichua*, vii–viii. Anchorena and Fernández Nodal seem to be referring to the indigenous tribute when they state that *indígenas* supported the state, but this tax was not in effect at their time of writing.
59. Anchorena, *Gramática quechua*, v–vi, vii.
60. Fernández Nodal, *Elementos de gramática quichua*, vii–viii.
61. Itier, *El teatro quechua en el Cuzco*, vol. 2, pp. 17–22.
62. Ibid., p. 20; see Hobsbawm, *Nations and Nationalism*, pp. 101–30.
63. Itier, *El teatro quechua en el Cuzco*, vol. 2, p. 20.
64. Anchorena, *Gramática quechua*, pp. 118–41.
65. Anchorena, *Gramática quechua*, v.
66. Fernández Nodal, *Elementos de gramática quichua*, viii–xii.
67. Itier, "Quechua y cultura," p. 103; Itier, *El teatro quechua en el Cuzco*, vol. 2, p. 20.
68. Anchorena, *Gramática quechua*, viii.
69. Anonymous, *Memoria*, xlviii–xlix.
70. José Dionisio Anchorena, *Traducción al quechua de la ley orgánica de municipalidades en lo relativo a los concejos de distrito* (Lima: Imprenta del Estado, 1873).
71. Muecke, *Political Culture*, p. 59.
72. See Nils Jacobsen, "Civilization and its Barbarism: The Inevitability of Juan Bustamante's Failure," in Judith Ewell and William H. Beezley (eds.), *The Human Tradition in Latin America: The Nineteenth Century* (Wilmington, DE.: SR Books, 1989), pp. 82–101.
73. Juan Bustamante, *Los indios del Perú. Compilación hecha por Juan Bustamante* (Lima: J. M. Monterola, 1867), pp. 138–43. I thank Cecilia Méndez for making these pages available to me. Interestingly, both of the copies of this rare book that I was able to consult in Lima (at the Biblioteca Nacional and the Instituto Riva-Agüero) lack the appendix containing legislation of interest to Indians. Rather than an act of censorship, the mutilation probably reflects popular demand for these texts. I have not found any information on who translated the Prado decree or on whether it had first been published elsewhere. Martín Monsalve states that the Sociedad Amiga de los Indios "published copies of the decrees by San Martín, Bolívar, and Castilla in favour of the indigenous population in Spanish, Quechua, and Aymara" and distributed the copies to indigenous communities, but I am uncertain as to the source

for this statement: Martín Monsalve, "Civil(ized) Society and the Public Sphere in Multiethnic Societies: Struggles over Citizenship in Lima, Peru (1850–1880)," unpublished Ph.D. dissertation, State University of New York, Stony Brook, 2005, p. 203.

74. For example, the use of the demonstrative pronoun *huac* /wak/ (Bustamante, *Los indios del Perú*, p. 140), the verb *ccaya-* (/qaya-/ "to call," ibid., p. 141); and the subordinator *–stin* (ibid.).

75. Bustamante, *Los indios del Perú*, p. 138.

76. Ibid., pp. 140–41.

77. Government of Peru, *Ley Orgánica de Municipalidades* (Lima: Imprenta del Estado, 1873), pp. 55–57.

78. Anchorena, *Traducción al quechua*, pp. 28–46.

79. Itier, *El teatro quechua en el Cuzco*, vol. 2, p. 19.

80. Anchorena, *Traducción al quechua*, v, pp. 48–53.

81. Anchorena, *Traducción al quechua*, iii–v.

82. Some of the terms in Anchorena's glossary are recorded in Diego González Holguín's exceptionally detailed dictionary of Cuzco Quechua published in 1608, but rarely appear anywhere else—*yuptura-* "to assemble" (recorded by González Holguín as "to count people") and *hayrata* "penalty" are examples: Diego González Holguín (intr. Ramiro Matos Mendieta and prol. Raúl Porras Barrenechea), *Vocabulario de la lengua general de todo el Perú llamada lengua quichua o del Inca* (1608; Lima: Universidad Nacional de San Marcos, 1989), pp. 158, 372. Others seem to be Aymaraisms: for instance, *marcca* "territory of a district" seems to come from /marka/ "town" (in Central Quechua as well as Aymara), and *millkuy* "resolution" is reminiscent of a verb recorded by Ludovico Bertonio as *pronunciar bien, o mal las palabras*: Ludovico Bertonio, *Vocabulario de la lengua Aymara* (1612; Cochabamba: Centro de Estudios de la Realidad Económica y Social, 1984), p. 221. However, there seems to be no precedent at all for a long list of terms that Anchorena used constantly, such as *mairu-* "to administer," *hiyuta-* "to approve," *racpa-* "to resolve," *pircu* "complaint," and *pake* "ordinary, common." While Anchorena's grammar does contain a number of neologisms it is nowhere near as lexically inventive.

83. Fernández Nodal, *Elementos de gramática quichua*, pp. 417, 421–41.

84. Pacheco Zegarra, *Ollantai*, p. 128.

85. The law was passed on April 7, 1873, and the decrees ordering the Quechua translation and giving the task to Anchorena are both dated April 12 (Government of Peru, *Ley Orgánica de Municipalidades*, pp. 53, 55–57). This may suggest that there was not much of a debate or selection process.

86. Leonardo Villar, "Informe del Dr. Leonardo Villar, sobre la Gramática Quechua del Dr. José D. Anchorena," *Boletín de la*

Sociedad Geográfica de Lima 11:11 (1901), pp. 175–83. Villar points primarily to errors and inconsistencies in Anchorena's orthography, but also to some grammatical issues.

87. Itier, *El teatro quechua en el Cuzco*, vol. 2, pp. 25–26, 42–47.

88. For a recent re-edition of Vienrich's studies of Quechua folklore (originally published in 1905 and 1906) see *Azucenas quechuas / Fábulas quechuas* (1905–1906; Lima: Ediciones Lux, 1999). Vienrich's periodical was titled *La Aurora / Pacha huarai* and the first issue was published in January 1904. A facsimile edition of the first two issues was published by Gonzalo Espino Relucé in *Guaca* 1/1 (2004), pp. 92–108. Espino Relucé has also written a monograph on Vienrich: *Adolfo Vienrich. La inclusión andina y la literatura quechua* (Lima: Universidad Ricardo Palma, 2004).

89. A facsimile of the flyer can be found in Jorge Basadre, *Introducción a las bases documentales para la historia de la república del Perú con algunas reflexiones*, vol. 2 (Lima: Ediciones P. L. Villanueva, 1971), p. 669. In 1915 Gutiérrez Cuevas assumed the name Rumi Maqui (Quechua for "hand of stone") and led an indigenous rebellion in the Puno area; see Nils Jacobsen, *Mirages of Transition: The Peruvian Altiplano, 1780–1930* (Berkeley: University of California Press 1993), pp. 339–43. His career parallels that of Juan Bustamante in many regards.

90. See Rivet and Créqui-Montfort, *Bibliographie*, vol. 3, pp. 314, 328–29, 396, 412.

91. See Rivet and Créqui-Montfort, *Bibliographie*, vols. 3–4.

92. It seems significant in this regard that at least two leading figures of the Quechuist boom of the 1870s, Fernández Nodal and Barranca, were not native speakers (Barranca was from Acarí, on the coast of Arequipa—Porras Barrenechea, *Fuentes históricas peruanas*, p. 39). Anchorena, Barranca, Fernández Nodal, Villar and others found time for their Quechuist enterprises while working as lawyers, doctors, and university professors.

Part III

Towards Present and Future

Chapter 8

The Quechua Language in the Andes Today: Between Statistics, the State, and Daily Life

Rosaleen Howard

This chapter offers a comparative examination of the situation of the Quechua language in Ecuador, Peru, and Bolivia in the present day, taking into account the historical processes that have led to the similarities and differences to be observed. It is divided into three main sections: (i) a discussion of the statistics on numbers and distribution of speakers; (ii) a review of language policy in the three States, with particular reference to issues of language related identity politics and language rights; and (iii) an illustration of the ways in which processes of language contact have impacted upon the forms of the language as used in daily life, by means of a brief case study from each country. I then close with some critical reflection on the relationship between these three levels of analysis.

Introduction

The many variant forms of the Quechua language[1] are spoken across the Andean region of South America, from southern Colombia, through highland and lowland Ecuador, parts of northern, central and southern Peru, highland Bolivia, and parts of northwest Argentina.[2] In relations of mutual influence with both Spanish and the other main Andean language, Aymara, Quechua gives shape to a heterogeneous range of sociolinguistic fields that defies generalized description. Marleen Haboud for Ecuador,[3] Andrés Chirinos Rivera for Peru,[4] and Xavier Albó for Bolivia,[5] have gone far in describing this sociolinguistic variability based on a blend of quantitative and qualitative research findings, including the outcomes of censuses and surveys. Hornberger and Coronel-Molina offer a broad and detailed overview of the status of the languages from the perspective of the sociology of language,[6] while Howard analyzes qualitative (interview) data from the three core Quechua-speaking countries of Ecuador, Peru, and Bolivia.[7] More recently, Andrade Ciudad provides an overview of the situation of the indigenous languages in Peru, including Quechua, in light of the 2007 census in that country;[8] while Plaza Martínez offers a grammatical sketch of the Quechua of Chuquisaca and Northern Potosí (Bolivia), based on hitherto unpublished field data.[9] The variety and complexity of the sociolinguistic scenarios in which Quechua is spoken is due to grammatical and lexical variability, the range of language contact features that arise, and the diversity of social contexts in which it is found.

In this chapter, I shall discuss the present-day sociolinguistic situation of Quechua with particular reference to highland Peru, Bolivia, and Ecuador.[10] While Spanish predominates among the upper and middle classes, in urban settings, and in coastal regions, and Quechua is more prevalent among rural agriculturalists, as far as highland zones are concerned there is not always a clear-cut class-based rural-urban dichotomy between Spanish and Quechua-speaking populations. In the highlands, the relative social and geographical distribution of the two languages grew ever more complex from the colonial period onward. Due to the formerly feudal land tenure system and associated labor structure, as well as eventual trade and intermarriage, relations between Spanish and Quechua-speaking sectors became increasingly intertwined over the centuries. While Quechua monolingualism persisted in the countryside, Spanish-Quechua bilingualism among the landowning and provincial urban classes was a growing phenomenon, at least up to the Agrarian Reform period of the mid-twentieth century. Since then, with the acceleration of rural to urban migration, Quechua speakers have increasingly shifted to Spanish, or relatively stable Quechua-Spanish bilingualism has evolved. Thus, broadly speaking, Quechua today spans various social classes and is spoken in both rural and urban settings.

At one end of the scale, Quechua monolingualism prevails in some areas of Peru and Bolivia among indigenous campesino sectors. By contrast, in Ecuador, where Quechua is called "Quichua," the indigenous class is characterized by Quichua-Spanish bilingualism. Mestizos in Ecuador, despite living in close proximity to Quichua-speaking populations, are primarily Spanish monolingual. In Peru and Bolivia, on the other hand, various permutations in use of the two languages constitute a range of class identities. In the department of Cuzco, for example, while Quechua monolingualism prevails in highland provinces such as Paruro and Chumbivilcas (as the statistics will show), in provincial capitals such as Ocongate bilingualism is a component of mestizo identity,[11] in a way similar to the town of San Pedro de Buenavista (central Bolivia) as studied by Howard-Malverde.[12]

Cuzco city offers another permutation, as this is the home of the High Academy of the Quechua Language of Cuzco (Academia Mayor de la Lengua Quechua del Qosqo, AMLQQ), founded in the early 1950s. The Academy's members are bilingual, urban dwelling, and culturally mestizo. In many cases, their families descend from the landowning classes of the hacienda era. Self-styled "cultivators" of the Quechua language (they use the term "cultor"),[13] the "Académicos" promote the language by producing literary works, dictionaries, and grammars in Quechua, and teaching classes in the university. Many of them hold strong views on linguistic correctness, cultivating a puristic form of Quechua that tolerates none of the Spanish lexical and syntactic influences to be found in the spontaneous speech of the rural Quechua speaker. This purism informs a historically rooted ideology of "Incanism" bound up with a concern to affirm regional cultural authority as guardians of the language, protecting it both from the "barbarisms" of the rural speaker (the term is theirs)[14] and the scientific opinions of university trained linguists from Lima.[15]

In Cochabamba city, the range of urban identities is marked by the use of Spanish, Quechua, or a combination of the two. On the one hand, the mixed Spanish-Quechua speech (so-called *quechuañol*) can be heard among the traders of the city's extensive street market and in peripheral residential areas.[16] On the other hand, a more self-conscious academic Quechua is spoken by the Spanish-Quechua bilingual members of Cochabamba's Quechua Language Academy (affiliated to Cuzco's AMLQQ), who, again, tend to descend from families who had their base in the Quechua-speaking provinces in previous generations, and some of whom teach the language in secondary and higher education.[17]

The Quechua Language in Current Statistics

Censuses are only an approximate indication of actual numbers and distribution of speakers for a number of reasons, for example, the fact that stigma attaches to the speaking of an indigenous language in some contexts, and the fact that the ability to speak the language is not put to the test by census takers. As Albó has remarked, census responses may well reflect the attitudes of speakers rather than actual linguistic competencies.[18] Table 8.1 gives figures for numbers of Quechua speakers by country based on the latest censuses. With the exception of Bolivia in 1992 and 2001, as we shall see later (Tables 8.5 and 8.6), censuses have not been designed to reveal the proportion of indigenous language monolinguals to speakers bilingual with Spanish, although, using survey data from other sources, it is possible to extrapolate estimated figures on bilingualism, as Haboud has done for Ecuador.[19]

Table 8.2 shows that for Peru, going by the 2007 census, around 13 percent of the population over five years of age learned Quechua as a

Table 8.1 Quechua speaking populations by country based on latest available census data

Country	Colombia	Ecuador	Bolivia	Perú	Argentina
Census date	1993	2001	2001	2007	1999
Total population	33,109,840	11,919,399	8,274,325	28,220,764	36,600,000
Quechua speakers	20,000	499,392	2,124,040	3,360,578	300,000

(Adapted from Hornberger and Coronel-Molina, "Quechua Language Shift": 20; Peruvian figs. from Andrade Ciudad, "Las lenguas indígenas")

Table 8.2 Peru: Population over 5 years of age according to language learned in childhood. [Source: *Perfil Sociodemográfico del Perú, Censos Nacionales 2007: XI de Población y VI de Vivienda.* 2nd ed. (Lima: Instituto de Estadística e Informática, 2008)]

Language	1993 census	%	2007 census	%	% variation
Total	19 190 624	100	24 687 537	100	
Spanish	15 405 014	80.3	20 718 227	83.9	3.6
Quechua	3 177 938	16.6	3 261 750	13.2	−3.3
Aymara	440 380	2.3	434 370	1.8	−0.5
Other native language	132 174	0.7	223 194	0.9	0.2
Foreign language	35 118	0.2	21 097	0.1	−0.1
Speaking impaired	–	–	28 899	0.1	–

mother tongue, a drop of about 3 percent since 1993. However, in terms of absolute numbers there was a rise of nearly 100,000 speakers over the intercensus period.

Andrés Chirinos Rivera's analysis of the 1993 Peruvian census gave a breakdown of numbers of speakers of Quechua and Aymara by department for Peru. Percentages of Quechua speakers ranged from 0.2 percent in Piura to 76.6 percent in Apurímac. Working from the 2007 census, Andrade Ciudad notes that Apurímac remains the department with the highest proportion of speakers, although this has dropped to 60 percent. The department of Cuzco leads in terms of absolute numbers (566,585) amounting to 46 percent. While the department of Lima has a low number of Quechua speakers in percentage terms (5.5 percent) it is worth noting that in terms of absolute numbers it is second only to Cuzco (477,014 speakers).[20]

Table 8.3 gives an example of the high rates of Quechua mother-tongue speakers to be found in some highland provinces, here the case of Chumbivilcas (department of Cuzco) according to the 1993 census. The failure of the census to measure bilingualism means that we cannot read rates of Quechua monolingualism from the table alone; my own

Table 8.3 Department of Cuzco, Peru. Numbers of speakers by language above 5 years of age. [Source: *IX Censo de Población y IV de Vivienda, 1993.* (http://www .inei.gob.pe, 1 de mayo de 2004)]

Census population	pop. > 5 years	Spanish mother tongue	%	Quechua mother tongue	%
Cuzco department	913.635	307.920	33.7	560.101	61.3
Cuzco province	247.626	166.774	67.35	71.384	28.83
Chumbivilcas province	59.855	2.587	4.32	53.991	90.28
Llusco district	4.929	156	3.18	4.568	93.22
Quiñota district	3.144	84	2.7	2.925	94.35

observations in the field allow me to suggest that this was extensive, however.[21]

To take another example, field research in Tantamayo (Huamalíes province, department of Huánuco) (Table 8.4) going back to the early 1980s enables me to compare language distribution and use in that period with the present, based on firsthand observation. Residents of the town were everywhere Spanish-Quechua bilingual, 25 years ago, while bilingualism in the countryside was rare and Quechua monolingualism common. By the time of the 1993 census, the level of Quechua use had fallen away due to massive out migration provoked by *Sendero Luminoso* (Shining Path) and army presence in the valley in the intervening period. Bilinguals came increasingly to suppress their use of the language, and not to transmit it to the younger generations.[22] Despite this trend, Table 8.4 indicates a 50:50 balance between Spanish and Quechua mother-tongue speakers in Tantamayo. Again, as the Peruvian census lacks data on bilingualism, the figures on numbers of Quechua speakers are certainly conservative.

Of the countries under discussion, Bolivia has excelled in its last three censuses in the relative usefulness of questions posed about languages spoken. In particular, in 1992 and 2001 resulting data sets give us breakdowns on monolingualism and bilingualism, and 2001 results give insight into variables of gender, place of residence and identity self-ascription. Tables 8.5 and 8.6 are adapted from Molina and Albó's analysis of the 2001 census results.[23] Table 8.5 gives a differentiated breakdown of the figures for Spanish, Quechua, Aymara, Guaraní, and "other native languages," and "foreign languages."

Here, the total percentages per language add up to over 100 percent due to the fact that any individual may speak more than one language. In many parts of the country bilingualism between Spanish and an indigenous language is common; trilingualism is also a feature, for example in

Table 8.4 Department of Huánuco, Peru.Numbers of speakers by language above 5 years of age. [Source: IX Censo de Población y IV de Vivienda, 1993. (http://www.inei.gob.pe, 1 de mayo de 2004)]

Census population	Population > 5 years	Spanish mother tongue	%	Quechua mother tongue	%
Huánuco department	575,395	374,630	65.11	171,052	29.73
Huamalíes province	48,263	17,555	36.42	27,999	58.08
Tantamayo District	2,387	1,134	49.3	1,130	49.13

Table 8.5. Evolution of Bolivian population by languages spoken, 1976–2001 (Adapted from Molina B. & Albó, *Gama étnica y lingüística*, Table 5.3)

Year of Census	1976		1992	(> 6 years)	2001	(> 6 years)
Language	1000's	%	1000's	%	1000's	%
Spanish	3,210.0	78.8	4,594.1	87.4	6,097.1	87.7
Quechua	1,594.0	39.7	1,085.8	34.3	2,124.0	30.6
Aymara	1.156	29.8	1,237.7	23	1,462.3	21.0
Guaraní and other native languages	56.0	1.1	129.6	2.5	101.2	1.5
Foreign languages			118.2	2.2	241.4	3.4
Bolivia total population	4,613.4	100.0			8,261.2	100.0
Total > 6 years			5,256.3	100.0	6,948.6	100.0

the north of Potosí department and in Oruro department, where many people speak Quechua, Aymara, and Spanish.[24] Table 8.6 gives the figures on monolingualism and bilingualism respectively.

This table makes clear that in 2001 the country was divided 50:50 between Spanish monolinguals and those who spoke an indigenous language with or without Spanish in addition. From 1976 to 1992 the trend was toward increased bilingualism with Spanish and a concomitant dip in native language monolingualism; from 1992 to 2001 there was a drop of almost 10 percent in bilingualism with corresponding rise in Spanish monolingualism. Nonetheless, over the latter period native language monolingualism remained steady in percentage terms. This may be partly due to rise in population numbers and increased geographical reach in census taking. However, it is interesting to note that the 1992 to 2001 period in Bolivia coincided with the years (1994–2003) when education policy for indigenous children in rural areas focused on Bilingual Intercultural Education (Educación Intercultural Bilingüe, EIB) under

Table 8.6. Linguistic evolution by type of language spoken, Bolivia, 1976–2001. (Adapted from Molina B. & Albó, *Gama étnica y lingüística*, Table 5.1)

Type of language spoken	Year of Census		
	1976	1992	2001
		6 yrs or above	5 yrs or above
Native language only	20.4	11.5	11.8
Native language and Spanish	43.3	46.8	37.5
Spanish only and/or foreign language	36.3	41.7	50.5
Total (%)	100.0	100.0	100.0
Total in thousands	4,613.4	5,256.3	7,174.7

the terms of the 1994 Education Reform. EIB fostered the use of indigenous languages in the classroom, both as languages of instruction and as a subject to be studied alongside Spanish. It could be that the EIB era helped to stabilize native language use among primary school children in rural areas, while other social and economic factors (especially rural to urban migration) encouraged shift to Spanish among the middle age bands (i.e., the most economically active and mobile sectors of the population). The figures also need to be set in the context of the urban-rural distribution of the indigenous languages in Bolivia, which has evolved in a surprising way over the same period, as shall now be seen.

The usefulness of the 2001 Bolivian census also lies in the fact that it asked questions about ethnic identity. The question, asked only of people over 15 years of age, "Do you consider yourself to belong to one of the following originary peoples?" ("¿Se considera perteneciente a alguno de los siguientes pueblos originarios?") gave a choice of answer between Quechua, Aymara, Guaraní, Chiquitano, Mojeño, Other, None. The response threw up a total of 62 percent self-identifying as indigenous. If we take this figure in conjunction with the 49.3 percent of the population over the age of five who claim to speak an indigenous language (Table 8.6), it becomes clear how self-ascribed ethnic identity and linguistic repertoire are not in direct correlation. To consider oneself indigenous in Bolivia does not necessarily mean that one speaks an Amerindian language. Conversely, many of the middle class (i.e., "non-originary") Spanish-Quechua bilinguals found in Bolivian towns and cities do not consider themselves indigenous in the sense of "Indian,"[25] as is also the case in Peru.[26] In Ecuador the case is different again, in so far as those who self-ascribe as indigenous are predominantly Quichua-Spanish bilingual,[27] while, as already noted, criollo and mestizo sectors are predominantly Spanish monolingual.

Another important finding of Molina and Albó has to do with the geographical distribution between rural and urban areas of those who consider themselves indigenous in Bolivia. Since the Agrarian Reform in the mid-twentieth century there was an accelerated move by the non-indigenous minority from their reduced land bases to the cities; it is not therefore surprising that in 2001, 79.2 percent of this demographic group are found to live in urban areas. The surprise finding in 2001 was that the majority (55.6 percent) of those who consider themselves indigenous were also found to live in towns and cities.[28] The scale of this phenom-enon reaches its height in the city of La Paz, where 61.1 percent of the population considers itself to belong to a "pueblo originario."[29]

In Bolivia, the Andean languages are widely heard in urban settings. The marketplaces and peripheral residential areas of cities such as La Paz, Cochabamba, and Potosí provide vital spaces where they thrive. As Sichra observes: "The city of Cochabamba is marked by being tenaciously and persistently bilingual, despite the constant shift to Spanish that the indigenous languages suffer here as in the country in general."[30] This is in marked contrast to Lima where migration from the highlands triggers sweeping Quechua language loss.[31] Geography is obviously a factor here. Bolivian cities are in the heartland of the Quechua and Aymara-speaking areas; the need and opportunity to keep the languages alive is facilitated by proximity to the rural areas. I believe it also has to do with the fact that migration of Quechua speakers into Bolivian cities has accelerated since the beginning of the nineties, when the indigenous social move-ments were gathering momentum and the stigma attached to speak-ing the language was beginning to lessen. It is also the case that many Aymara-speaking people (for example in the city of El Alto) have double residence, straddling both urban and rural areas, a factor not taken into account in the census, possibly causing inflation of the figures.[32]

The numerical survival of the Andean languages up until and through the greater part of the twentieth century, as revealed by the statistics, may be explained by a series of factors: geographical isolation of the communities of speakers due to topography and poor communication infrastructure; poverty; lack of formal education in rural areas beyond the first few grades; illiteracy; and lack of opportunity for urban migra-tion. Furthermore, the interrelatedness of these factors is confirmed by a number of sources. In the case of Peru, for example, in the ten prov-inces with the highest poverty index and the lowest child development index, 83 percent of the population are speakers of an indigenous mother tongue.[33] Poverty seems to directly correlate with speaking the language; leaving the language behind is seen as a means to step out of poverty. As far as illiteracy is concerned, Godenzzi notes that "the departments with a higher number of Quechua speakers (...) have very high per-centages of illiteracy." Against a national illiteracy rate of 12.8 percent among the population over 14 years of age, in Apurimac and Ayacucho this reaches 36.9 percent and 32.7 percent respectively; in provinces such as Chumbivilcas where the percentage of Quechua mother-tongue speakers reaches over 90 percent (Table 8.3), illiteracy is around 44 percent.[34] It can also be noted that during Peru's internal war that ran for 15 years from the early 1980s to the mid-1990s the most badly affected departments were these same poverty-stricken regions with high indices of speakers of indigenous languages (departments of Ayacucho and Huánuco); 75 percent of those who were murdered or disappeared during the conflict were indigenous language speakers.[35]

At the same time, developments in the social, economic, and political spheres over the mid- to late-twentieth century gave impetus to change: agrarian reform, the universalization of education in rural areas, and increased migration being the principal among them, as Sichra observes:

> After agrarian reform, bilingualism in the Andean region is no longer an attribute of the landowners (*hacendados*) who, while being of mestizo origin, had settled in the countryside. It now becomes the result of the growth of migratory trends towards the city (…) as well as the outcome of the expansion of the education system and mass communications in the rural areas, which directly affect the indigenous population.[36]

The factors ensuring survival of the autochthonous language were increasingly viewed as obstacles to be overcome by parents aspiring for opportunities for their children beyond the rural sphere. While in the case of Cochabamba and some other highland towns bilingualism may have resulted from development, in other contexts full-scale shift from the indigenous mother tongue to Spanish became part of the transformative process.[37]

In sum, going by the censuses of the last two decades, despite the loss of Quechua speakers in overall terms,[38] in some areas the absolute numbers of speakers remain constant and have even risen due to population increase. Nonetheless, in percentage terms the community of speakers is clearly on the decline. In addition, the fact that the language's survival into the present has long been explained in terms of negative social indicators (poverty, illiteracy, poor infrastructure), with the corresponding negative impact on attitudes toward speaking it, has to be taken as a threat to its survival into the future. Since the 1990s, however, the state has stepped in more proactively to improve educational provision for indigenous children. This in turn has entailed language-planning initiatives aimed at raising the status of the indigenous languages in the minds of speakers and nonspeakers alike, with some degree of success.

The Role of the State in Guiding the Fate of the Quechua Language

Legal Instruments

In this section I shall review some developments in state language-planning policy from the turn of the 1990s. In that decade, the changing geopolitical landscape in Europe, democratization underway in Latin America, the 1989 International Labour Organisation (ILO) Convention 169 on the rights of "Indigenous and Tribal Peoples in Independent Countries," and the 1992 Columbus Quincentenary as a focus for the indigenous social movements, all made up the conjuncture for constitutional reform on the part of the Andean States, whereby, for the first time in post-Conquest history, political constitutions took account of the linguistic and cultural diversity of their subject populations. Thus, for example, the 1993 Peruvian Constitution declares that "all Peruvians have a right to their ethnic and cultural identity. The State recognizes and protects the ethnic and cultural plurality of the Nation. All Peruvians have the right to use their own language before any authority through the medium of an interpreter."[39] Bolivia and Ecuador followed suit with Constitutional Reforms in 1994 and 1998 respectively. It was only in the new millennium, however, that legislation began to appear that might support the idea of linguistic rights for speakers of indigenous languages in practice.

In Bolivia, Supreme Decree 25894 passed on September 11, 2000 recognized the majority of the nation's originary languages ("lenguas originarias") as "co-official."[40] However, a Decree does not carry the weight of a full-fledged law. By contrast, in 2003 the Peruvian Congress approved a Language Law ("Ley de Lenguas") that granted official status to the indigenous languages "in the zones where they predominate," thus falling short of unconditional officialization.[41] Further legislation came before the Congress in 2007, in the form of the draft "Law for the Preservation, Use and Diffusion of the Aboriginal Languages of Peru," which seeks to expand the territorially circumscribed "official" status of the indigenous languages to Peruvian territory as a whole. However, certain members of the Congress, as further discussed below, stridently objected to this proposal.

The new Constitution of Ecuador approved in September 2008 recognizes cultural and linguistic rights but is similarly timid about "official" status for any language other than Spanish:

> The State respects and promotes the development of all the languages of Ecuadoreans. Spanish is the official language. Quichua, Shuar and the other ancestral tongues are for official use by indigenous peoples under the terms of the law.[42]

Again, the principle of territorial circumscription is brought to bear on official status for indigenous languages. While a proposal for a law for the "applicability of ancestral languages" has been debated in the Congress,[43] no such law has yet been passed in Ecuador.

The new Bolivian State Political Constitution approved by popular referendum in January 2009 under the government of Evo Morales strengthens the terms of Supreme Decree 25894. The 2009 Constitution declares all 36 of the currently identified originary languages to be official in addition to Spanish and makes it a requirement for all state functionaries to speak the indigenous language of the regions to which they are posted, as well as Spanish.[44] However, the Language Law needed for implementation of these constitutional tenets still awaits ratification.

Education Policy

A key area in which governments are seeking to implement some of the precepts set out in their state constitutions is that of education for children who are mother-tongue speakers of indigenous languages. Prior to the 1990s, indigenous language education had been confined to pilot programs, often in the hands of missionary organizations, with transition to Spanish as a primary goal. A short-lived period of Peruvian state officialization of Quechua under the military government of Velasco Alvarado in 1975 (retracted under the 1979 Constitution)[45] gave rise to the path-breaking Experimental Bilingual Education Project (P-EEB), but this was nonetheless confined to the department of Puno.[46] A whole-hearted vision of bilingual education for indigenous children, as enabling maintenance of the vernacular mother tongue as well as acquisition of Spanish as a second language, had yet to evolve.[47]

The 1990 "World Congress on Education For All," held in Jomtien, Thailand, under UNESCO auspices, gave an important impetus to Andean state initiatives for linguistically and culturally appropriate education reforms. ILO Convention 169 further supported the new educational proposals worldwide. The combination of demands from the indigenous movements and increasing pressure of international development agencies and financial donors eventually led to the EIB model being adopted as national policy (in Ecuador in 1986; in Peru in 1991; in Bolivia in 1994). However, its implementation was more effective in those countries where there was more involvement of the indigenous organizations and less so where the initiative was top-down, driven by external financial incentives rather than political will from within. In this respect, some salient differences can be noted between the three countries.[48]

In the case of Ecuador, simultaneous recognition of the Confederation of the Indigenous Nationalities of Ecuador (CONAIE) and the launch of the Bilingual Intercultural Education Programme in 1986 were interrelated aspects of the state response to the demands of its indigenous movement. This was followed in 1989 by Ecuador setting up the National Directorate for Bilingual Intercultural Education (DINEIB), with autonomous ministerial status. This institutional mechanism gave Ecuador's indigenous people, with support until 2000 of the German Technical Development Agency (GTZ), a controlling hand in the administration of the designated EIB schools, teacher training through specially created EIB "Pedagogical Institutes," and a hand in recruitment.

However, the Ecuadorian model has not been without its problems. For example, the autonomy of the indigenous sector in education administration also led to sectarianism between the bilingual indigenous teachers and their Spanish monolingual colleagues.[49] The perception of the latter was that the criterion of bilingual competence (which, in the case of Ecuador, goes along with indigenous ethnicity) was taking priority over other credentials in the allocation of teachers to posts. Nonetheless, looked at from the point of view of improvements in social inclusion, Ecuador in the early 1990s was in the vanguard of indigenous professionalization, with indigenous men and women gaining university degrees and working as teacher trainers throughout the sector.[50]

In the case of Peru, the internal war that paralyzed the country from the early 1980s to the mid-1990s had much to do with why the momentum from the P-EEB in Puno was lost. Despite this, Constitutional Reform in 1993, a national census in the same year that updated official statistics on numbers of speakers, and the country's ratification of ILO Convention 169 in 1994, all paved the way for Peru eventually to act on its 1991 national policy. This it did in 1996, with the setting up of a National Unit for Intercultural Bilingual Education (UNEBI), upgraded to National Directorate (DINEBI) in 2000.[51] Under Alberto Fujimori's second term, which also witnessed the arrest and detainment of Sendero Luminoso leader Abimael Guzmán, the World Bank injected funds into Peru's education system, specifically for development of indigenous children's schooling. By comparison with Ecuador, however, due to the lack of indigenous political organization in the Peruvian highlands, these initiatives were taken by ministry employees in consultation with rural development NGOs in the departments, without the participation of indigenous organizations as such. Under Alan García's presidency since 2006, the momentum has again been lost. EIB has been subsumed within the National Directorate for Rural, Bilingual and Intercultural Education, its concerns subordinated to the wider educational needs of the rural population.

While Peru came to the fore in state-sponsored indigenous educational development in the 1970s, followed by Ecuador in the 1980s, at the start of the 1990s it was Bolivia that led the field. Here, EIB was rolled out under the 1994 Education Reform Act (Law 1565) across Aymara, Quechua, and Guaraní-speaking areas of the country, extending into Amazonia from 2000.[52] The Reform encountered strong political and attitudinal opposition from the left-wing teachers' unions and parents respectively. However, as the years went on, the pedagogical advantages of the EIB model seemed indisputable and the indigenous organizations became empowered by the system.

It was therefore ironic, and perhaps no accident, that the early years of the new millennium saw an ideological turnaround by the government. Under increasing pressure from the public to relax the thrust of the neoliberal reforms of the 1990s, government also began to rethink the terms of the 1994 Education Reform. With the election of Evo Morales in 2005, a new education team led by Aymara sociologist Félix Patzi drafted a new Education Reform bill that proposes radical curricular reform in favor of the indigenous population, and that intercultural and bilingual education be spread to all levels and contexts, urban and rural alike. However, the new Bill is unlikely to see passage through Parliament until after the December 2009 presidential elections. Meanwhile, many teachers, who had never been very convinced of its premises in the first place, no longer adhere to the 1994 Reform. Education for the indigenous majority finds itself in a legislative hiatus with pedagogical consequences as a result.[53]

Language Use and Language Ideologies: Between the State and Daily Life

In this section I shall illustrate how the Quechua language is lived in practice, by drawing on some of the interview data previously published in Howard.[54] Language is seen both as a vehicle for and an index of the way speakers socially position themselves and constitute their sense of cultural identity. This qualitative material lends substance to a sociolinguistic reality only glimpsed in skeletal form through the statistics presented in Current Statistics, in response to which latter the language planning initiatives discussed in The Role of the State were advanced.

The experience of Quechua monolingualism of the individuals whose lives go to make up the "93.22 percent" statistic provided for the district of Llusco (Chumbivilcas, Peru; Table 8.3) is here described by a man from that community, aged about 52 years (translated from Quechua):

ARC   Since the times of our ancestors we always learn Quechua, for in our village that is our language, that is how we must speak.

RH   And do you (singular) also know Spanish?

ARC   We know (exclusive plural) Spanish because they teach it to us
in school, and we go to the cities, and we learn it there, well a little.
Not always very well.[55]

Each time this speaker refers to the learning or knowing of a language
he uses the verb *yachay* ("to know"): Quechua is learned as part of the
everyday language acquisition process (*yachakuyku* "we learn"); Spanish
is taught in school (*yachachiwanku* "they teach us"); or it is learned by
going away to the cities (*yachamuyku* "we go away to learn"). The latter
phrase came up regularly in interviews with the Chumbivilcanos; migration to Arequipa and Cuzco is frequent, and Spanish language acquisition is an inherent, if not always very adequately achieved, part of that
experience.[56]

Julio Candia, dean of the University of Cañar (Ecuador), represents
the other end of the spectrum. Like other residents of Cañar city he
is Spanish monolingual, while living within a 15-minute walk of the
surrounding indigenous communities, where Quichua-Spanish bilingualism became widespread by the end of the twentieth century. In
sociolinguistic terms, the diglossia (distribution of languages in a multilingual society according to spatial and social criteria, and functions
of use) illustrated by this geographical, social and linguistic dichotomy
is of a particular type. To apply Fishman's framework, in Cañar we have
a case of "diglossia with bilingualism" from the rural Quichua-Spanish
speakers' perspective, alongside "diglossia without bilingualism" from
the perspective of Spanish-speaking town residents like Julio.[57] The pattern of language use combines with the criterion of ethnicity to feed
into people's sense of identity in significant ways, while also mapping
relations of power.

According to Don Julio's explanation, the dichotomy was not always
so stark.[58] Labor relations between the landed classes and the indigenous
communities in the days of the hacienda had necessitated regular communication across the social divide, and led both to indigenous people
acquiring Spanish, and white landowners learning Quichua.[59] But the
communicative need ebbed away, Don Julio says, after the Agrarian
Reform in the mid-1960s. Today, lack of social contact with the indigenous communities, combined with the fact of the latter's bilingualism,
has made it "unnecessary" for the Spanish speakers in town to learn
Quichua, to quote: "For us it is essential to learn Spanish, but learning
Quichua is not necessary, because we don't have the regular contact
that we should have to have," and he refers to indigenous people's bilingualism as a point in their favor: "They have all the merit for knowing
two languages."[60] In the course of this interview, the stark dichotomy
between Spanish monolinguals in town and indigenous bilinguals in
the countryside is expressed in the speaker's recurrent distancing use of
the pronoun "ellos" ("they") in referring to the other group.

By contrast with Ecuador, in Peru and Bolivia Quechua-Spanish bilingualism among the urban middle classes is more likely to have survived the effects of Agrarian Reform. Nevertheless such bilingualism was acquired in a context of ingrained racial prejudice, of which linguistic discrimination was an expression. People such as Julián Prado of Cuzco, a Quechua-Spanish bilingual member of the urban middle class, recalls learning Quechua while playing with the *campesino* children on trips with his parents to the countryside to see to the family cattle, in a decade we can calculate to have been around the 1940s, and in spite of his grandfather's attitude: "My grandfather used to punish me severely if he heard me speaking Quechua, 'that one's an Indian, only the Indians speak Quechua' [he would say]."

William Vega, also from Cuzco, of similar social background to Julián Prado but a generation younger, described how he learned Quechua as a second language in his teens due to spending long periods of time living in the countryside, his parents being schoolteachers assigned to the rural schools: "[My parents] were often in the countryside and because I wanted to communicate with the *campesino* children, and play with them, I began to learn Quechua, in the countryside."[61]

This scenario is one that commonly explains how people of mestizo origin in the Andes learnt, or reactivated use of, the indigenous tongue in the latter part of the twentieth century. Agrarian reform had removed the middle classes from the land, where, as previously mentioned, the opportunity for Quechua second language acquisition had naturally arisen. However, as rural schooling became generalized, descendents of the earlier displaced landowners were located to Quechua-speaking regions to take up posts as teachers, often taking their children with them.

As a Spanish mother-tongue speaker, William Vega represents his experience of acquiring Quechua through naturally occurring social contact as a positive one. From the other side of the fence, for the Quechua speaker having to acquire Spanish by socially situated means, without there being any formal pedagogical provision for the purpose, the experience is often portrayed as traumatic. Nicolás's account is typical of people of his generation (age 30 to 40 years), of rural origin (Chumbivilcas, Cuzco) and a Quechua monolingual until he reached his early teens:

As I can only speak "mote," I feel alone, sad, because I don't know how to speak Spanish. And other people move away from me. Once they know how to speak, they move away, and I am alone. And that's how it must be in the University, in Cuzco [. . .]. When we people from the countryside enter the University they don't talk to you, do they?[62]

The word "mote" is a popular term for the Spanish spoken by the mother-tongue Quechua speaker who has not fully approximated to Spanish

pronunciation, vocabulary, and syntax. Quechua influence particularly affects the Spanish vowel sounds, producing a stigmatized way of
speaking.[63]

A Quechua-Spanish urban bilingual teacher from Charcas province,
Bolivia, describes the "mote" phenomenon; the following is an extract
from a longer interview:

> They confuse the i with the e, and the o with u, right? Instead of
> saying "vida" they say "veda." Instead of saying "burro" they say
> "borro," right? And instead of saying "vista" they say "vesta." That's
> the problem with the vowel sounds. [. . .] But when they get here [to
> town], as there is television, video, and the teachers with them in the
> classroom, they start to correct themselves and they practically get rid
> of the blemish.[64]

The speaker's use of the word "blemish" (Spanish "tara") gives a hint of
his ideological stance. In the full transcript notions of linguistic "correctness," phenotypical "whitening," and bodily "cleanliness" are seen
to be associated with each other in the speaker's mind.[65]

The examples discussed so far exemplify some subjective experiences
of speakers in the Quechua-Spanish bilingual field, drawn from what we
might call the private sphere of daily social interaction. They also give
insight into the ways that perceptions of linguistic difference may inform
discriminatory discourses and practices, bound up with social fears,
concerns, and prejudices.[66] By contrast, I shall now turn to examples of
interactions drawn from the public sphere, that reveal some of the tensions around language policy and language use in formal settings.

Debates about language policy in the public sphere have weighty
consequences when aired through the press and mass media. I shall
present two recent and notorious cases, one from Bolivia and one from
Peru, in which the prejudices that sometimes operate at the highest
institutional level were exposed to public view. These emblematic epi-
sodes suggest that there is some way to go in order for language rights
to be translated from the letter of the law into greater social equality
in practice.

The first of these incidents occurred in the early days of the Bolivian
Constitutional Assembly session in Sucre, in August 2006. One of
the delegates of the MAS (government) benches, an indigenous leader
named Isabel Domínguez, raised an objection against the declaration of
an adjournment during a difficult moment in the debate. Her interven-
tion was unusual, for she spoke out in her native language, Quechua.
It was her use of this language that raised the hackles of a delegate on
the opposition (PODEMOS) bench, Beatriz Capobianco, who called
out furiously that "she should speak when she learns to speak Spanish."

Domínguez did not take lightly to this reaction, and the two had to be restrained from coming to blows.

The episode caused controversy in the press; sparked bloggers' debates on the Internet; and a spokesperson on behalf of the Assembly publicly condemned the discriminatory language. However, the issue of whether or not the indigenous languages were to be co-official with Spanish as languages of the Assembly was never really resolved. The irony of the situation was that the officialization of Bolivia's 36 indigenous languages was part of the very business of the Assembly, eventually to be written into the new Constitution.

In September 2007, the debate over the draft "Law for the Preservation, Use and Diffusion of the Aboriginal Languages of Peru" (mentioned above), which includes a proposal for the unconditional officialization of all Peruvian indigenous languages, caused a furore in the Peruvian Congress. Congresswoman Martha Hildebrandt, a linguist by training, took issue with it in scathing terms. In full view of journalists with digital video cameras, she made a personalized attack on the two indigenous Congresswomen (María Sumire and Hilaria Supe) who were proposing it, on grounds that they lacked appropriate professional credentials to debate matters linguistic at such a level. The incident created an outcry in the press; a video bearing witness to the belittling tones of Hildebrandt toward her indigenous colleagues went out on the video Internet site *YouTube*, giving rise to polemical discussion on blogs and TV programs for months following the incident.[67]

Concluding Remarks: Survival or Demise?

In this chapter I have adopted a hybrid methodology as a means to evaluate the current vitality and status of the Quechua language. Despite the well-known shortcomings of statistical data, the usefulness of a well-designed census such as Bolivia's of 2001 has been demonstrated. I have also attempted to put flesh on the bare bones of the statistics through verbal testimonies that reveal the lives behind the numerical tables. The language planning actions of the state, educational initiatives in particular, sit between the level of figures and the level of language use. At all these levels, ideologies are in play. Behind the drafting of any law on linguistic rights lies polemical debate in which indigenous leaders may struggle to make their voices heard in the face of Hispanocentrism and conservatism among their peers in government.

Social change in the Andes is now advancing so rapidly that indigenous language speakers get inexorably caught up in the desire to shift to Spanish, especially as the result of urban migration. As Xavier Albó observes, speaking of Bolivia, this happens even where the ideals of the speakers involved may lie elsewhere. Indigenous language maintenance is simply impractical within existing structures:

> I have seen many cases of indigenous leaders and even prominent lin-guists and presenters on Quechua and Aymara radio stations who, for reasons which are more practical than ideological, hardly use the origi-nary language with their younger children who were born in the city or arrived there at a young age, although they still use it with their older children.[68]

When language planning efforts go against the tide of societal language habits, attitudes and prejudices, as Marleen Haboud also argues: "The symbolic values of a language or even the strong emotional connection of speakers to it, cannot guarantee language maintenance."[69]

By the beginning of the new millennium, despite statistical evidence of a decline in numbers of speakers, social and educational conditions were evolving in some parts of the Andes that appeared to provide for language revitalization, not just as part of governmental education pol-icy, but as a social dynamic from the ground up. Evo Morales's landslide victory in Bolivia in 2005 raised expectations regarding the future of the indigenous languages; there was a surge of interest and Quechua appeared more widely than before in secondary school and university curricula;[70] and the new Language Law was drafted. But a political deadlock has divided the country along geographical and racial lines and sparked violent confrontations; there are now signs of disillusionment in the indigenous agenda that in turn threatens to compromise the teach-ing and learning of the language in institutional settings. The situation is evolving and merits the continued attention of researchers.[71]

In considering what the prospects are for the survival of Quechua and other indigenous languages in the future, I believe the relation-ship between language and identity is a crucial indicator. That a large majority of the people in Bolivia who self-ascribe as being of indigenous ethnicity now live in urban areas, yet do not necessarily speak the indig-enous languages, as revealed in the 2001 Bolivian census, is in my view a significant trend. My hypothesis here would be that the strength of indigenous identity, even where the vernacular language has fallen into disuse, may constitute the necessary condition for eventual language revitalization in subsequent generations. Recent Quechua revitalization among some sectors in the city of Cochabamba is evidence that this can potentially occur. Second generation migrants who reside in this city, descendants of provincial landowning families where bilingual-ism was prevalent among their parents' generation, having had their use of Quechua suppressed in childhood due to social prejudices of the day, allow it to flourish anew in adulthood as they carve out careers in language planning and education for which Quechua language skills are now requisite.[72]

Linguistic features of contact between Quechua and Spanish may be indicators of another sort as to the chances for survival of the Amerindian language. Kathryn Woolard argues convincingly that a flexible rather than a puristic attitude to language mixture on the part of speakers and language planners may increase the chances of language maintenance as opposed to language death.[73] While the phenomenon of Quechua-Spanish contact in the Andes has been well researched for Ecuador[74] and Peru,[75] and Sichra provides insights into the Cochabamba case,[76] Quechua-Spanish contact in Bolivia remains a relatively understudied topic. Further research would be needed to test the following hypotheses, which I derive from firsthand experience of the city over many years: Cochabamba Quechua is flexible in allowing Spanish lexical and syntactic influence without its integrity seemingly being threatened; Cochabamba popular Spanish is known and even valued for its Quechua inflections; the dogma of linguistic purism so prevalent in certain cuzqueño circles is not common here; the hybrid "quechuañol" way of speaking is intrinsic to the distinctive "cochala" identity, and the stigma of "mote" is to some extent allayed.

To go by cases of other languages around the world that have successfully gone through processes of revitalization, such as that of Welsh, an expansion of the functions of Quechua to spheres of activity associated with the modern and globalizing world would also seem highly desirable. The much-publicized launch of Google™ in Quechua (http://www.economist.com; August 17, 2006), Microsoft's development of a Quechua version of Word (http://www.newsvote.bbc.co.uk; August 25, 2006), and the introduction by the Peruvian mobile phone company Movistar of phone operators who offer their services in Quechua and Aymara (http://www.celularis.com; accessed November 8, 2009), are gestures in this direction. While they may be purely symbolic to start with, such gestures are vital in order to make a point, shift attitudes, and potentially to trigger changes in language practices.

As long as discriminatory social systems persist, along with the association between the indigenous language, technological simplicity, and poverty, people will aspire to Spanish. Where education programs can be put in place that effectively use both languages for the purpose of education, embed the teaching of Quechua in a culturally appropriate curriculum, are seen to assure the effective teaching of Spanish as a second language, are driven by the people themselves through their organizations, and involve society at large in the intercultural agenda, then there is a realistic chance that the indigenous language will grow in status and public attitudes may alter. Another important factor, which there is not the space to develop in the present study, will be the further development of Quechua as a written language, for spheres not limited to that of education.[77] If these conditions are not met then the evidence is that education can have the very opposite effect—parents react negatively for social reasons, and when the ideological climate changes, this can undermine an indigenous language's fortunes; education can be seen not necessarily to assure the survival of the indigenous language.

Acknowledgments

The author is grateful to Paul Heggarty for the opportunity to take part in the British Academy-sponsored meeting on "Language and History in the Andes" (Institute for the Study of the Americas (ISA), University of London, September 2008) at which a preliminary version of this chapter was presented. Thanks go also to the editors and the anonymous reviewer for critical comments on the earlier draft; also for their feedback, to the audience who heard a subsequent version at the ISA Research Seminar on November 4, 2009, chaired by Adrian Pearce; and to Luis Andrade Ciudad and Pedro Plaza for information and comments on the draft. All shortcomings remain the author's responsibility.

Notes

1. The Quechua language is better described as a "language family" due to the vast range of its variant forms, and the question of whether we should rather speak of the Quechua "languages" in this connection is a subject of debate among linguists. The variant forms of Quechua can also be referred to as "dialects," but I avoid the term here as it has acquired a pejorative connotation in the Andean countries, as a means to downgrade Quechua in relation to Spanish.
2. Alfredo Torero, "Los dialectos quechuas," *Anales Científicos de la Universidad Agraria* 2 (1964), 446–78; Torero, *El quechua y la historia social andina* (Lima: Universidad Ricardo Palma, 1974); Torero, *Idiomas de los Andes. Lingüística e historia* (Lima: Instituto Francés de Estudios Andinos / Horizonte, 2002); Rodolfo Cerrón-Palomino, *Lingüística quechua* (Cuzco: Centro de Estudios Regionales Andinos "Bartolomé de las Casas," 1987); Gerald Taylor, "Yauyos, un microcosmo dialectal quechua," *Revista Andina* 3 (1984), 121–46; Bruce Mannheim, *The Language of the Inka since the European Invasion* (Austin: University of Texas Press, 1991); Willem F. H. Adelaar with Pieter C. Muysken, *The Languages of the Andes* (Cambridge and New York: Cambridge University Press, 2004).
3. Marleen Haboud, *Quichua y castellano en los Andes ecuatorianos. Los efectos de un contacto prolongado* (Quito: Abya-Yala, 1998); "Quichua Language Vitality: An Ecuadorian Perspective," *International Journal of the Sociology of Language 167* (2004), 69–81.

4. Andrés Chirinos Rivera, "Las lenguas indígenas peruanas más allá del año 2000," *Revista Andina* 32:2 (1998), 453–79; Chirinos Rivera, *Atlas etnolingüístico del Perú* (Cuzco: Centro de Estudios Regionales Andinos "Bartolomé de las Casas," 2001).

5. Xavier Albó, *Bolivia plurilingüe. Guía para planificadores y educadores* (La Paz: UNICEF-CIPCA, 1995); Ramiro Molina B. and Xavier Albó, *Gama étnica y lingüística de la población boliviana* (La Paz: Programa de la Naciones Unidas para el Desarrollo, 2006).

6. Nancy H. Hornberger and Serafín M. Coronel-Molina, "Quechua Language Shift, Maintenance, and Revitalization in the Andes: The Case for Language Planning," *International Journal of the Sociology of Language* 167 (2004), 9–67.

7. Rosaleen Howard, *Por los linderos de la lengua. Ideologías lingüísticas en los Andes* (Lima: Instituto de Estudios Peruanos / Instituto Francés de Estudios Andinos / Pontificia Universidad Católica del Perú, 2007).

8. Luis Andrade Ciudad, "Las lenguas indígenas del presente," in Luis Andrade Ciudad and Jorge Iván Pérez Silva, *Las lenguas del Perú* (Lima: Pontificia Universidad Católica del Perú, 2009), pp. 36–79.

9. Pedro Plaza Martínez, "Quechua," in Mily Crevels and Pieter Muysken (eds.), *Lenguas de Bolivia*, vol. 1, *Ámbito andino* (La Paz: Plural Editores, 2009), pp. 215–84.

10. For information on Argentinean Quichua see Jorge R. Alderetes and Lelia Inés Albarracín, "El quechua en Argentina: El caso de Santiago del Estero," *International Journal of the Sociology of Language* 167 (2004), 83–93; for Colombian Ingano see Stephen H. Levinsohn, *The Inga Language* (The Hague and Paris: Mouton, 1976).

11. Penelope Harvey, "Women Who Won't Speak Spanish," in Pauline Burton, Ketaki Kushari Dyson, and Shirley Ardener (eds.), *Bilingual Women: Anthropological Approaches to Second Language Use* (Oxford: Berg, 1994), pp. 44–64.

12. Rosaleen Howard-Malverde, "'Pachamama is a Spanish word': Linguistic Tension between Aymara, Quechua and Spanish in Northern Potosí (Bolivia)," *Anthropological Linguistics* 37:2 (Summer 1995), 141–68.

13. Howard, *Por los linderos de la lengua*, p. 314.

14. Ibid., pp. 346–47.

15. Ibid., p. 326. The entrenched differences of opinion between members of the AMLQQ and linguists and education planners who are outsiders to Cuzco crystallize over whether the language should be represented in writing as having five vowels or three (Nancy Hornberger, "Five vowels or three? Linguistics and politics in Quechua language planning in Peru," in James Tollefson (ed.), *Power and Inequality in Language Education* (Cambridge: Cambridge University Press, 1995), pp. 187–205; Howard, *Por los linderos de la lengua*, pp. 323–27); what is apparently a linguistic debate in fact

expresses cultural, social and political rivalries between the Cuzco regionalists and the wider Peruvian State which go back at least to the period of the Tupac Amaru II uprising of the late eighteenth century (Mannheim, *The Language of the Inka*). The puristic Quechua promulgated by the Academy is a means for this group to distinguish itself from the rural Quechua speakers ("runa" or "Indians"), in terms of an elitist sense of their own historical identity; theirs is an exclusionary discourse in this respect. For further discussion see Mercedes Niño-Murcia, "Linguistic Purism in Cuzco, Peru: A Historical Perspective," *Language Problems and Language Planning* 21:2 (1997), pp. 134–61; Tim Marr, "Neither the State nor the Grass Roots: Language Maintenance and the Discourse of the Academia Mayor de la Lengua Quechua," *International Journal of Bilingual Education and Bilingualism* 2:3 (1999), 181–97; Marisol de la Cadena, *Indigenous Mestizos. The Politics of Race and Culture in Cuzco, Peru, 1919–1991* (Durham, NC: Duke University Press, 2000); Howard, *Por los linderos de la lengua*; Serafín M. Coronel-Molina, "Language Ideologies of the High Academy of the Quechua Language in Cuzco, Peru," *Latin American and Caribbean Ethnic Studies* 3:3 (Nov. 2008), 319–40.

16. Xavier Albó, *Los mil rostros del quechua. Sociolingüística de Cochabamba* (Lima: Instituto de Estudios Peruanos, 1974); Inge Sichra, *La vitalidad del quechua. Lengua y sociedad en dos provincias de Cochabamba* (La Paz: PROEIB Andes / Plural, 2003).
17. Howard, *Por los linderos de la lengua*, pp. 35–36.
18. Xavier Albó, "El futuro del quechua visto desde una perspectiva boliviana," *International Journal of the Sociology of Language* 167 (2004), 119–30, see p. 123; cf. Hornberger and Coronel-Molina, "Quechua Language Shift," p. 20.
19. Haboud, *Quichua y castellano*.
20. Andrade Ciudad, "Las lenguas indígenas del presente," p. 48.
21. Howard, *Por los linderos de la lengua*, pp. 31–32.
22. Howard, *Por los linderos de la lengua*, pp. 33–34.
23. Molina B. and Albó, *Gama étnica y lingüística*.
24. Howard-Malverde, "Pachamama is a Spanish word."
25. Howard, *Por los linderos de la lengua*.
26. De la Cadena, *Indigenous Mestizos*.
27. Haboud, *Quichua y castellano*; Howard, *Por los linderos de la lengua*.
28. Molina B. and Albó, *Gama étnica y lingüística*, p. 72.
29. Molina B. and Albó, *Gama étnica y lingüística*, p. 75, Figure 4.4.
30. Inge Sichra, "Trascendiendo o fortaleciendo el valor emblemático del quechua: Identidad de la lengua en la ciudad de Cochabamba," in Serafín M. Coronel-Molina and L. L. Grabner-Coronel (eds.), *Lenguas e identidades en los Andes. Perspectivas ideológicas y culturales* (Quito: Abya Yala, 2005), pp. 211–50, see p. 211.

31. Tim Marr, "The Language Left at Ticlio: Social and Cultural Perspectives on Quechua Language Loss in Lima, Peru," unpublished Ph.D. dissertation, University of Liverpool, 1998.
32. Molina B. and Albó, *Gama étnica y lingüística*, p. 74.
33. Chirinos Rivera, "Las lenguas indígenas peruanas," p. 455, citing UNICEF figures for Peru.
34. Godenzzi, Juan Carlos, "Literacy and modernization among the Quechua speaking population of Peru," in Nancy H. Hornberger *Indigenous Literacies in the Americas: Language Planning from the Bottom Up* (Berlin: Mouton de Gruyter, 1997), p. 239, cited by Serafín Coronel-Molina, "Functional Domains of the Quechua Language in Peru: Issues of Status Planning," *International Journal of Bilingual Education and Bilingualism* 2:3 (1999), 174.
35. Comisión de la Verdad y Reconciliación del Perú, *Informe Final* (2003); available at http://www.cverdad.org.pe. In Huánuco department, where I conducted fieldwork just before and just after the war, people made a clear association between the shift to Spanish and the experience of the "Sendero" years; this shift had been facilitated by migration to the cities away from the emergency zones; those who returned to the sierra after the danger had passed did not return to using Quechua on such a regular basis (Howard, *Por los linderos de la lengua*, p. 33).
36. Sichra, "Trascendiendo o fortaleciendo el valor emblemático del quechua," p. 214.
37. Howard, *Por los linderos de la lengua*, pp. 110–15; Marr, "The Language Left at Ticlio."
38. Chirinos Rivera, "Las lenguas indígenas peruanas."
39. Republic of Perú, *Constitución Política del Perú* (1993), Chapter. 1, art. 2, clause 19; Andrés Chirinos Rivera, *Perumanta hatun kamachina. Constitución Política del Perú 1993.* Traducción por A Chirinos. (Lima: Fondo Editorial del Congreso de la República Peruana, 1999).
40. Xavier Albó, *Educando en la diferencia: Hacia unas políticas interculturales y lingüísticas para el sistema educativo* (La Paz: Ministerio de Educación / UNICEF / CIPCA, 2002), p. 37.
41. Coordinadora Permanente de los Pueblos Indígenas del Perú (COPPIP), *Correo indígena*, 31 Oct. 2003.
42. "El Estado respeta y estimula el desarrollo de todas las lenguas de los ecuatorianos. El castellano es el idioma oficial. El quichua, el shuar y los demás idiomas ancestrales son de uso oficial para los pueblos indígenas, en los términos que fija la ley," *Constitución Política de la República del Ecuador, 2008*, Chapter 1, art. 1. http://www.ecuanex.net.ec/constitucion/indice.html.
43. www.aulaintercultural.org, July 2007.
44. Congreso Nacional (2008). Asamblea Constituyente de Bolivia. *Nueva Constitución Política del Estado.* Arts 5.I, 5.II.

45. Coronel-Molina, "Functional domains of the Quechua language," p. 169.
46. Nancy H. Hornberger, "Bilingual Education Success but Policy Failure," *Language in Society* 16:2 (1987), 205–26.
47. Utta Von Gleich, *Educación primaria bilingüe intercultural en América Latina* (Eschborn: Deutsche Gesellschaft für Zusamenarbeit, 1989); F. Chiodi (ed.), *La educación indígena en América Latina*, 2 vols. (Santiago and Quito: OREALC / GTZ / Abya Yala, 1990).
48. Hornberger and Coronel-Molina, "Quechua Language Shift," pp. 43–47; Howard, *Por los linderos de la lengua*, pp. 278–80.
49. Howard, *Por los linderos de la lengua*, pp. 280–88.
50. Nina Laurie, R. Andolina, and S. Radcliffe, "Indigenous Professionalization: Transnational Social Reproduction in the Andes," *Antipode* 35:3 (2003), pp. 463–90; Howard, *Por los linderos de la lengua*, p. 275.
51. Howard, *Por los linderos de la lengua*, p. 26.
52. Luis Enrique López-Hurtado Q., *De resquicios a boquerones. La educación intercultural bilingüe en Bolivia* (La Paz: PROEIB Andes / Plural, 2005).
53. Rosaleen Howard, "Education Reform, Indigenous Politics, and Decolonisation in the Bolivia of Evo Morales," *International Journal of Educational Development* 29:6 (2009), 583–93.
54. Howard, *Por los linderos de la lengua*.
55. Howard, *Por los linderos de la lengua*, pp. 89–90.
56. Ibid., pp. 90–1.
57. Joshua Fishman, "Bilingualism With and Without Diglossia; Diglossia With and Without Bilingualism," *Journal of Social Issues* 23:2 (Apr. 1967), 29–38.
58. Howard, *Por los linderos de la lengua*, pp. 122–23.
59. For example, Luis Cordero, prominent criollo landowner, university professor, and president of the Republic of Ecuador from 1892–1895, had extensive knowledge of the language as evidenced in his fine Spanish-Quichua dictionary compiled in 1892 (Luis Cordero, *Diccionario quichua-español español-quichua*. Cuenca: Universidad de Cuenca, 1967 [1892]). Cordero's work on Quichua is discussed in Rosaleen Howard, "'Why Do They Steal Our Phonemes?' Inventing the Survival of the Cañari Language (Ecuador)," in Eithne B. Carlin and Simon van de Kerke (eds.), *Linguistics and Archaeology in the Americas: The Historicization of Language and Society* (Leiden: Brill, 2010), Chapter 7.
60. Howard, *Por los linderos de la lengua*, p. 123.
61. Ibid., pp. 132–33.
62. Ibid., pp. 140–1.
63. Rodolfo Cerrón-Palomino, *Castellano andino. Aspectos sociolingüísticos, pedagógicos y gramaticales* (Lima: Pontificia Universidad Católica del Perú, 2003).

64. Howard, *Por los linderos de la lengua*, pp. 194–95.
65. For further discussion of this data see Rosaleen Howard, "Beyond the lexicon of difference: discursive performance of identity in the Andes," *Latin American Caribbean and Ethnic Studies* 4:1 (2009), 17–46.
66. Deborah Cameron, *Verbal Hygiene* (London: Routledge, 1995).
67. Enrique Ballón Aguirre, "La dentera multilingüe e intercultural en las sociedades andinas (conflictos de lengua, habla y escritura)," *Revista Andina* 49 (2009), 135–64.
68. Albó, "El futuro del quechua," p. 124.
69. Haboud, "Quichua language vitality," p. 81; related issues are discussed by Aurolyn Luykx "The Future of Quechua and the Quechua of the Future: Language Ideologies and Language Planning in Bolivia," *International Journal of the Sociology of Language* 167 (2004), 154–57.
70. Julieta Zurita, personal communication, Cochabamba, 2006.
71. Howard, "Education Reform, Indigenous Politics, and Decolonisation."
72. Howard, *Por los linderos de la lengua*, p. 112.
73. Kathryn A. Woolard, "Language Convergence and Language Death as Social Processes," in Nancy Dorian (ed.), *Investigating Obsolescence. Studies in Language Contraction and Death* (Cambridge: Cambridge University Press, 1989), pp. 355–67; see also Howard-Malverde, "Pachamama is a Spanish word," p. 144.
74. Pieter Muysken, "Media lengua," in Sarah G. Thomason (ed.), *Contact Languages: a Wider Perspective* (Amsterdam: John Benjamins, 1997), pp. 365–425; J. Gómez Rendón, *Typological and Social Constraints on Language Contact* (Amsterdam: Netherlands Graduate School of Linguistics, 2008).
75. Germán de Granda, *Estudios de lingüística andina* (Lima: Pontificia Universidad Católica del Perú, 2001).
76. Sichra, *La vitalidad del quechua*, pp. 112–16.
77. For advances in research on this area, see, for example, the contributions to Nancy H. Hornberger (ed.), *Indigenous Literacies in the Americas,* and Utta von Gleich "New Quechua literacies in Bolivia," *International Journal of the Sociology of Language* 167, 131–46.

Chapter 9

"Ya No Podemos Regresar al Quechua": Modernity, Identity, and Language Choice among Migrants in Urban Peru

Tim Marr

This chapter looks at the sociolinguistic behavior of Quechua-speaking migrants to urban areas of Peru, primarily Lima, and their descendants. It notes the marked reluctance of many to speak, pass on, or acquire Quechua in the capital. I describe the associations of Quechua with the past, history, old people, and geographical and social circumscription and suggest that, for many, Quechua is felt to be somehow incompatible with modernity and the desired self-image of the ambitious migrant. It is noted that this positioning of minority languages as "anti-modern" is in some ways a societal construct and a reflection of the power of the dominant language. However, I argue that to conceptualize language loss solely as a capitulation to dominant norms is to ignore or negate speakers' view of themselves as ambitious and forward-looking, and language shift to Spanish as a positive taking of power and a transformation of the self.

1. Introduction

Te juro madre mía/yo tengo que triunfar/he de viajar a Lima/lo tengo que lograr,/soy provinciano humilde/con ansias de luchar.

[*I swear to you, mother/I have to succeed in life/I have to go to Lima/I have to achieve it;/I'm a humble provincial/who has fighting spirit.*]
(From "*El Provinciano*" by Los Brillantes.)

Peru is home to the largest population of Quechua speakers in the Andean region; it is also a site of massive migration, and massive language shift. Since at least the 1950s, wave after wave of provincial migrants have poured into the capital and provincial centers, in the process transforming the urban space irrevocably, and creating a new and distinctive urban and peri-urban culture. Many of these migrants are, or have been, speakers of Quechua; but the language does not move with them.

Language shift from Quechua to Spanish typically begins with the first generation to arrive, who use the language increasingly infrequently, and pass it on to their children only in the rarest of circumstances. They may even deny all knowledge of it: in Lima, the Andean migrant who insists in his heavily accented Spanish that "*No, siñor, yo no hablo quichua*" is a recognizable comic "type"—a kind of South American Sam Weller. Hornberger and Coronel-Molina provide some helpful pointers as to why this might be so: they cite, for example, the necessity of Spanish in the employment market; linguistic shame (*vergüenza*—a commonly heard rationalization for language loss, and one which needs substantial teasing-out); fracturing of social networks; and cultural dislocation.[1] They touch on the idea of modernization constituting a risk to cultural maintenance, going on to note—with good reason, I think—that such modernization does not necessarily have to lead to cultural and linguistic loss;[2] referring in this regard to Fishman's appeal to, or rather for, "cultural democracy."[3]

In most of the cities of Peru, though, the evidence suggests that modernization, working with and through urbanization, *is* proving inimical to Quechua, and indeed, to the other indigenous languages. This is partly because "cultural democracy" has rarely been a salient characteristic of the Peruvian polity. However, it is also because the Peruvian national discourse, we might say national mindset, even among many Quechua speakers, and most obviously among migrants to the cities, tacitly (if regretfully) accepts it to be the case, or even actively wills it so. Modernization requires and reflects an individual and communal desire for "modernity." How modernity is conceived of is of course an extremely complex question, that involves ways of thinking about employment, housing, education, family relationships, and all the other things that go to make up a way of life: but here we are concerned with how the concept of modernity works upon language—and this does not favor Quechua.

I do not propose to discuss the situation of Quechua in Ecuador and Bolivia. These contexts deserve to be treated separately, given how different they are from Peru—if not so much historically and economically, very broadly speaking, then culturally and politically, especially of recent years. However, I would note that, in general, census information shows a steady, long-term decline overall in the use of indigenous languages in the Andean region, and particularly in urban areas (see Howard, this volume). There might be some recently urbanizing areas where the indigenous languages maintain a foothold, and it is without any doubt much more common to hear indigenous languages in La Paz or Potosí in Bolivia, or in some of the towns of Ecuador, than it is in almost any urban district of Peru. But the general principle that urbanization tends to lead to *castellanización* ("hispanization") holds remorselessly true.

Nor is it the intention here, to measure or describe in technical socio-linguistic terms the process of language shift among urban migrants. Rather, I attempt to provide some context and explanation for such shift from a social-cultural point of view, within which it is perfectly reasonable—indeed, it is indispensable—to consider the relations of power and inequality that give rise to language loss. However, it seems to me equally necessary to consider the possibility that speakers themselves, while very often regretting the loss of Quechua (in families and communities, and in themselves), may nonetheless and simultaneously regard language shift as a positive transformation of the self—an "act of identity" as Le Page and Tabouret-Keller put it.[4]

The quotes found at various points in the text from speakers of Quechua (and non-speakers and ex-speakers), are taken from recordings made by the author in the course of extended stays in Peru, mainly in Lima, and especially the shanty towns of the *cono sur* of Lima, between 1995 and 2005. The words are the speakers' own, and grammatical idiosyncrasies or inconsistencies have been left unmarked and uncorrected. The free translations are my own. The song lyrics are borrowed, with due thanks, from practitioners of that most quintessentially Peruvian of urbanized, migrant musical genres, *chicha*.

2. Spanish in the City: An Urban(-izing) Snapshot

History is not on the side of Quechua, or indeed of minority languages anywhere. In terms of historical processes, language shift looks very much like a one-way street; it correlates strongly with migration and urbanization, and is hence inescapable in rapidly urbanizing Latin America. Graddol is forthright on the global relationship between urbanization and language use:

> Urbanisation gives rise to shift to more-used languages, especially English, Spanish, Arabic, Chinese...[It] is one of the major contributors to linguistic change...Rapid social change brings with it linguistic change.[5]

This is indisputable. Graddol in fact goes on to claim (and this is more arguable) that "multilingualism is now easier to sustain"[6]—but while this might be true of some sociolinguistic contexts, it is emphatically not the case for Peruvian towns and cities, as will be shown in due course.

Nor is urbanization within states the only force acting upon language use: it goes hand in hand with global processes.

> Urbanisation, progressive aggregation of populations into larger identity groupings, especially nations and nation states, and the globalisation of economies and culture are making life difficult for the majority of spoken languages.[7]

The way of things almost everywhere. Some lesser-spoken European languages—for example, Irish, Welsh, Catalan, Basque—manage to more or less hold their own, for now, against the tide, often with heavy state and supra-state (especially EU) encouragement and financial subsidy; but there is little likelihood of such conditions obtaining for the present in Latin America. With regard to Peru, Hornberger and Coronel-Molina state that

> while Quechua migration has brought Quechua back into the city (R. Howard, personal communication, February 7, 2001), the language has not flourished; and Quechua does not appear to be making as strong a comeback in the large cities as one might expect considering the large number of Quechua immigrants.[8]

If we leave aside the suggestion that "one might expect" language maintenance in the large Peruvian cities, this is quite correct. It does at first sight seem surprising, if one compares Peru to other, superficially similar cases around the world—South Africa, say, or India or China—that the language spoken by so many migrants is so absent from urban areas. In the 1970s it was thought, or assumed, by some that the massive influx of Quechua speakers to Lima would result in wholesale change in the language usage of the capital.[9] And yet it did not happen, or at least not in the sense of Quechua becoming a familiar urban code. There is some evidence of Quechua having influenced mainly basilectal varieties of Spanish in Lima, to varying degrees, at the lexical, phonological, and syntactic levels, above all in the shanty towns.[10] But in the Lima-Callao conurbation, the focus of much of the migration of the last few decades, and home to what must presumably be some millions of Quechua speakers, the language is to be heard seldom in private domains and virtually never, except for symbolic or ironic purposes, in public ones. So ingrained is the notion that Lima constitutes a physical (psychological?) domain of Spanish that the ingenuous outsider's enquiry as to why, exactly, Quechua is not spoken there is likely to be met with a shrugged response along the lines of *"aquí se habla castellano, pues,"* ("well, here you speak Spanish") with no further explanation thought necessary.

If the focus of this chapter is Quechua loss among migrants to Lima, it is because this constitutes a particularly dramatic example of scale and speed in language shift. However, a similar, if perhaps sometimes less marked, process is observable in other Peruvian cities, and for that matter in other Andean countries. Rapid shift to Spanish was already close to universal among Quechua-speaking migrants to Arequipa, for example, in the 1980s;[11] and there are few grounds for thinking that this might have changed since. Even Cuzco, regarded by many Peruvians— not entirely accurately, of course—as the *cuna* ("cradle" or birthplace) and spiritual heartland of the language, is not immune. Manley reports with some optimism on the supposed "safe havens" for Quechua established in the city for domestic servants and market porters—the *Centro de Apoyo Integral a la Trabajadora del Hogar* and the *Asociación Civil "Gregorio Condori Mamani" Proyecto Casa del Cargador*, where residents are encouraged to maintain their mother tongue and take pride in it (at least some of the impetus for this coming from Europeans, it might be noted in passing).[12] While this is doubtless an admirable development in itself, the fact that it has been thought desirable or necessary testifies to the extent to which the urban environment disfavors Quechua language maintenance, even in the former capital of the Inca empire.

There is some anecdotal evidence that Quechua tends to be heard more in the streets of Huamanga (Ayacucho) than in other urban areas, but this has not yet been documented in any substantial way. In north Andean Cajamarca, in central cities such as Jauja and Huancayo, and in coastal towns with substantial migrant populations such as Trujillo, Pisco and Chimbote, Spanish is effectively the only game in town. Most smaller urbanized areas do not tend to differ significantly from this pattern, and there is little evidence that large-scale shift to Spanish is regarded by speakers themselves as a cause for great concern. Howard, for example, records that in Tantamayo, local journalists were keen to canvass her opinions as an "outsider" on the decay of some local archaeological remains, but were much less interested in her concern for the decay of local Quechua use. ("I was left with the impression that the topic would not have been discussed had I not introduced it.").[13]

Rapid and large-scale urban language shift in Peru is hence a given. The question, though, is why this should be the case. Do migrant (and other) speakers simply *choose* to abandon Quechua and shift to Spanish? Or is the use of Spanish effectively forced upon them in a context of social, cultural, and economic domination by the Spanish-speaking majority?

3. To What Extent is Language Shift a "Choice"?

In any given speech event, it might be thought, speakers are in principle free to speak in any language or variety which happens to form part of their linguistic repertoire. However, in the real world a speaker's code choice is of course constrained by a series of factors: the identity of the speaker's interlocutor and their relationship to one another; the ability of the interlocutor to understand the code chosen, or his/her willingness to accommodate; the norms with which the speech community tends to invest the setting or domain in which the speech event takes place; and so on. A speaker who failed to observe these underlying principles of code choice would risk being thought of as clumsy, uncooperative, confrontational, or ignorant.

Beyond this, too, of course, lies the wider question of societal power structures and the inequalities existing between speech communities. Bourdieu's characterization of certain codes and varieties as representing accumulations of "symbolic capital" in a linguistic marketplace has some elucidatory power, or at least offers a framework within which to think about how power is maintained or transmitted through sociolinguistic configurations.[14] Unlike real capital, though, language is not finite, and is not, once appropriated, easily kept to oneself. Heller notes that: "Bourdieu has insisted over and over again that it is precisely through appearing not to wield power that dominant groups wield it most effectively."[15] This might be true (though it is plainly an impossible argument either to prove or to refute, and is therefore of limited value). In any case, though, in the context of Lima, of Peru, it is perfectly obvious who wields power. And if Spanish represents symbolic capital, then obviously many Quechua speakers might wish to choose to grab some of it for themselves.

Again, in looking at code-switching, Heller points out that

> what emerges is the idea of people as agents, as actors of social life, who draw on complex sets of communicative resources which are unevenly distributed and unevenly valued. The systematicity appears to be at least as much a function of historically rooted ideologies (of nation and ethnicity) and of the ordering practices of social life as of language per se.[16]

Language resources are indeed "unevenly distributed and unevenly valued," and this must be counted a feature of societies, rather than a feature of language itself. It implies, though, for all that Heller elsewhere appears to accept the concept of linguistic hegemony, a fluidity, an individual linguistic potential ("people as agents...actors"), an acknowledgement of an element of *choice* in linguistic behavior that has not always been apparent in the literature.

By the 1980s, a number of commentators had developed an ideological critique of the entire notion of code choice in sociolinguistics, insisting that choice was in effect an illusion, and that societal power was always the ultimate determiner of language attitudes, and hence use. This position was presumably influenced at least in part by the work of Bourdieu, as referred to by Heller above (though this, it might be noted en passant, is often heavily French-oriented: it is not at all clear that Bourdieu's theses have the kind of universal applicability that is sometimes claimed). In London the Linguistic Minorities Project, setting out to defend the use of community languages (as they are often still, oddly, denominated), warned sternly against the "choice" view, with pointed use of inverted commas:

> The whole concept of language "choice" is in fact grounded in an individualistic notion of "free" choice as influenced by setting, audience, topic, etc…[A]ny discussion of the selection of appropriate language or alternation of varieties within a particular bilingual population has always to bear in mind the inequalities and conflicts that are faced by bilinguals in the processes of acquiring and using their different languages [17]

The astonishing linguistic diversity of twenty-first-century London perhaps suggests that an "individualistic" analysis could be a rather useful tool, after all: London speakers certainly do not seem to have bowed to the supposed hegemony of the *langue légitime*.[18] It is, though, difficult to disagree with the underlying suggestion that "language choice" is necessarily a rather relative, not to say slippery, concept. And yet, in seeking to understand the motivation of those migrants to Lima who to all intents and purposes become ex-speakers of Quechua in the first generation, it is important to acknowledge that they themselves often see language shift as being in some measure a positive and empowering process. It can be accepted without question that in Lima one has to speak Spanish (in this sense one has no choice); but motivation to shift springs also from a deeper level, one at which speaking Spanish represents not submission or accommodation, but aspiration, self-assertion, even resistance.

One aspect of this is purely materialist: it need hardly be remarked that in economic and social terms, the potential benefits of acquiring Spanish in Peru are substantial—and the potential consequences of not doing so rather serious. This is why Andean people have traditionally fought for the right to learn Spanish[19] and are often suspicious of the motivations of those—often outsiders, foreigners, or middle-class urban bilinguals—who would encourage them to maintain, and especially to have their children educated in, Quechua.[20] Resistance to language maintenance efforts, which is in effect what it amounts to, is understandably a difficult pill to swallow for many defenders of minority languages. While admitting that education-through-Quechua attempts are often "top-down" and that the paucity of Quechua maintenance projects that are truly locally based and locally initiated presents problems, Hornberger and King, in their wide-ranging and thorough discussion of these matters, finally stop short of noting that a good many Quechua speakers might actively wish or passively accept that their children should become monolingual Spanish speakers—and indeed might wish to think of *themselves* as having become Spanish speakers.[21] But this is surely one rational response, if admittedly not the only one, to the situation in modern-day Peru in which they find themselves. Most importantly for our present purposes, it is doubly true of migrants to the cities. As Hornberger and King themselves point out, starkly:

> Quechua continues to be strongly linked with the rural, uneducated and poor, while Spanish remains the primary language of national and international communication, literacy and education, and professional and economic success.[22]

This could hardly be clearer. And yet an ideologized discourse survived into the 1990s and beyond which suggested insistently that those who wished to respond to this unarguable reality by shifting to Spanish, or having their children educated in Spanish, were merely dupes of a hegemony which they were powerless to withstand or even comprehend. Weber, reviewing the successes and failures of bilingual education programs in Ayacucho at that time, states without further comment that

> in one of the Ayacucho programs an obstacle the organizers had not expected was the reaction of the parents against the use of Quechua in school […] The attitude was seen [by the organisers] as the result of the generations of subordination to the Spanish culture.[23]

It is perhaps defensible, though it is patronizing, to read the parents' opposition in terms of their "subordination to the Spanish culture." That this opposition was "not expected," though, by these organizers, is puzzling, to say the least. Apart from anything else, a cursory examination of the abundant literature already available at that time relating to mother tongue or bilingual education would have shown that such reactions are commonplace among minority language speakers, both migrant and settled, in many parts of the world, and are in no way peculiar to Peru.[24] The parents were, surely, responding pragmatically to the situation as they perceived it. More recent projects (e.g., the LEELA program—*Lecto-Escritura en Lengua Ancestral*—in Huánuco)[25] have recognized that any attempt to popularize mother-tongue education must address these concerns, in the case of LEELA by presenting the language as an aspect of cultural heritage in which one can and should take pride. This is a step forward, certainly, and appears to recognize at least that "resistant" parents are not merely lacking in self-knowledge; but it continues to assume that their perception of the sociolinguistic reality of their own country, and their own situation, is somehow mistaken or misguided.

The discourse that represents all preference for Spanish as, as it were, "false consciousness" (to use the Marxist term), is not only problematic for the reason that it is likely to have zero effect, or even a negative effect, on language maintenance efforts; though this is without doubt the case. Worse, if one is of the opinion that minority language speakers have been so oppressed for so long that they can no longer know what is best for themselves and their children, then it is easy to come to the conclusion that they need to be shielded from their own self-destructive instincts. Ludolfo Ojeda y Ojeda, a bilingual educationalist, writing about the *Región Inka* in southern Peru, reached what one hopes is the nadir of this kind of thinking by musing in the following terms on illiteracy among Quechua-speaking women:

> Creo, adelantando una opinión muy personal, que el llamado "analfabetismo femenino" es uno de los baluartes de la resistencia cultural indoperuana a la invasión cultural occidental; el haberla considerado sólo como una carencia a superar no hace justicia a la totalidad del problema.[26]

The inescapable implication here is that it is just as well that many Andean women remain uneducated and illiterate, whether this suits them and their children or not: in this way unsullied intergenerational transmission can be guaranteed, and the "authentic" language and culture will be saved. The cost of this saving to the individual and the community *as people* goes unremarked; it is the culture as an abstract entity that is regarded as all-important. César Itier, noting that this kind of worldview is, lamentably, far from uncommon among the self-appointed guardians of Andean culture, qualifies it accurately as "…una concepción spenceriana de las culturas como "organismos" que conservarían su integridad fuera de la historia y de la sociedad."[27] The corollary to this is that a substantial amount of discussion of language shift and loss takes place in a rarefied realm where the real interests, desires, and motivations of its subjects—or one might better say, agents—are unknown, ignored, or just disapproved of. (And this is worldwide, not just in Peru: one thinks of for example, the *ultras* of the Gaelic League who wished to ban or jam all foreign media in Ireland in their attempts to secure an Irish-only *Gaeltacht*).[28]

The conviction that individual "free choice" in language is something between being laughably naïve and a dangerous delusion underlies much of the most strident discussion of language maintenance. It was doubtless with this kind of discourse in mind that Joshua Fishman—a doughty and veteran campaigner for minority linguistic and cultural rights—felt he needed to go out of his way to state, explicitly, that language shift can be, for perfectly good reasons, a *choice*:

> Not all Xmen will seek […] protection for the cultivation of Xish language-in-culture and they should certainly be free to join the Yish mainstream entirely, or to consciously or unconsciously develop a "Yish-speaking Xish culture," as they prefer. In either of these latter instances, the material advantages associated with Yish culture will certainly be available to them, to help them build the kinds of life and the kinds of neighbourhoods that they prefer for themselves and their children.[29]

That those who wish to shift language "should certainly be free" to do so, and to "build the kinds of life and the kinds of neighbourhoods that they prefer"—should hardly need saying: but unfortunately it does.

Does this mean that linguists should merely observe the process of language shift and language loss, recording it dispassionately? Or, to put it another way, to what extent should the linguist be *engagé*? Dorian notes regretfully that many linguistic fieldworkers are in fact reluctant to become involved in language maintenance efforts in communities that are undergoing language shift (and are presumably relatively unworried about it). "[These fieldworkers] claim that scholars cannot dictate what should be important to the people they study."[30] But while Dorian is impatient of such seeming fatalism, with some reason, surely the fieldworkers have a point. At the very least, observers have a duty to consider, seriously and sympathetically, *why* speakers let their language fall into disuse, whether at the individual or societal level. To fail to do so, or to insist that shifting speakers are merely prey—as if they were sociolinguistic automata—to social forces beyond their control, is to risk robbing such speakers of their individuality and denying their capacity to make meaningful decisions about their own behavior. Better, perhaps, to take as a starting point the axiom that "social and cultural phenomena can be understood only if they are studied from the viewpoint of the participants, that is, as they appear to those who are actively involved in them."[31]

Much though Lima speakers (or often, former speakers) of Quechua tend to express regret for the loss of the language in their families and communities, they are generally in little doubt that they made a pragmatic and reasoned decision, even if this was by default, in the sense of not actively attempting to teach the children Quechua. One native speaker, from Huancabamba in the Central Andes, having brought up his children in Lima as monolingual Spanish speakers, simply saw no obvious, practical reason why they should have learned his own native language:

> Porque no hay necesidad de que los hijos puedan aprender ese idioma. El sentido práctico fundamentalmente de . . . del idioma ¿no? ¿Para qué o de qué les serviría a los hijos aprender este . . . el quechua? No.

> [Because there's no need for the children to learn that language. Basically, the practical aspect of the language, you know? Why, or in what way would it benefit the children to learn Quechua? No.]

As has already been indicated, this is not, of course, to pretend that language choice is always and entirely free, nothing more than an expression of individual will. Choice is necessarily constrained, particularly in postcolonial countries such as Peru, where, historically, power relations, cultural and racial prejudice, social inequality, harsh economic processes and "incorporative ideologies"[32] have tended unequivocally to help cast languages in shades of prestige and access to social mobility, or lack thereof. To elect to bring up one's family as Spanish-speaking in a Lima *pueblo joven* (shanty town) is not the same as to decide to add Spanish to one's repertoire, in a classroom setting, in a context—say, Europe or North America—where not doing so would have few, if any, negative consequences. It is not even the same as to decide to learn English, if one is a Spanish-speaking migrant to Florida or California.

Failure to consider this crucial distinction severely limits the usefulness of many "economistic" considerations of language learning and language choice, especially where these assume "X-as-a-foreign-language" environments. Ginsburgh et al., for example, discuss in some detail the relative weight of such factors in making the decision to learn another language as: numbers of speakers worldwide; the required investment in time and money; and ease or difficulty of learning (in terms of linguistic distance from one's mother tongue).[33] None of these factors, of course, would have much significance for a Quechua-speaking migrant to Lima, for the advantages of speaking Spanish, and the negative consequences of not speaking Spanish, as has already been suggested, are so obvious as to need no conscious thought at all.

It is a relatively small step from this to accepting tacitly that there is little point in maintaining the intergenerational transmission of Quechua in Lima, or even in continuing to speak it. To some extent this is a function of what Hornberger and King call "the loss of physical boundary domains,"[34] but in the mind of the (ex-) speaker it appears to be conceptualized and rationalized also as a bundle of received impressions about the role of the language in society and in the life of the speaker. Some of the key ones include (and these are characteristic of situations of this kind)[35]: the associations of Quechua with the past; with elderly people; with lack of socioeconomic utility; and so on.

Some of these factors are discussed in more detail below. There then follows a discussion of how a further important aspect of the Peruvian case makes itself felt among migrants: one that, related to self-image and psychological orientation, helps explain why Quechua tends not to be maintained in Lima to any great extent even as a second language alongside Spanish, which a materialist motivation to shift alone would not necessarily exclude. This is that Andean migrants to Lima, engaged in a personal and historical struggle to be accepted in the city and thereby in the nation at large, may see shift to Spanish as representing less a capitulation to than a kind of victory over the criollos, a defiant demand to be considered part of the mainstream. A crucial element in this is the association of Spanish with the kind of "self" the migrant wishes to be: modern, socially mobile, and forward-looking. Fundamentally, the psychological root of language shift in Peru, and the reason why a process of reversing language shift is for the present difficult to envisage, is that the migrant typically wishes to, as it were, choose modernity—and this necessarily implies language choice.

4. Some Factors Underlying Quechua Language Shift

Hornberger and King's discussion of the factors impelling language shift in the Andes is persuasive;[36] I try here, though, to illustrate how these factors play out in the context of migration and urbanization. My prognosis for the future of Quechua is a more pessimistic one than theirs; however, I do not believe that it departs greatly from the near-universal sense that the context of the twenty-first century is likely to be a uniquely difficult one for minority or lesser-spoken languages.

4.1 Associations with the Past

A glossy tourist guide to Peru, published in London, says of Cuzco that

> Indian vendors speak Spanish to tourists and Quechua to each other. Catholic nuns live in buildings once inhabited by Inca "chosen women" [...] Cuzco is a city where past and present collide in an uneasy mix.[37]

The Inca chosen women or *acllacuna* have long since passed into oblivion: Quechua continues to be the native tongue of millions. And yet the two are conflated and represented as symbols of the past, in uneasy "collision" with the present. In the same way, for many Peruvians—whether speakers of the language or not—Quechua is linked with the historical past, something "ancient." Nor is this necessarily meant dismissively. Told of my interest in the language, a young, middle-class office worker in Lima once exclaimed to me enthusiastically: "¿El quechua? Ay, ¡qué antiguo!" ("How ancient!"). The Academia Mayor de la Lengua Quechua and other Cuzco-centric (or Inca-centric) flag wavers must bear some responsibility for this.[38] The constant linking in public discourse of Quechua with the Incas, presumably in an attempt to establish historical legitimacy and authority for the language, has the unfortunate consequence of fixing it in the mind of the observer as associated inescapably with the past.[39]

Given this context, it is perhaps natural that Quechua, in the words of a teenager from a migrant family in the predominantly migrant Lima district of Villa El Salvador (and, unlike the office worker quoted above, the daughter of native Quechua speakers), "*suena más antiguo.*" ("Sounds older" or "sounds more old-fashioned"). But it is not only that much of the public discourse, whether aimed at Peruvians or foreigners, tends to cast the language in terms of history and the past: the brute mechanics of language shift across generations necessarily ensure that it becomes ineluctably and increasingly associated with old people.

4.2 Quechua and Elderly Speakers

A Lima-born woman in her mid-forties whose mother and grandmother are bilingual natives of Ayacucho recalls how she and her siblings used to think about the Quechua occasionally heard in the kitchen of their house in Lima, when they thought about it at all:

> Cuando escuchábamos a mi abuelita y mi mamá hablando quechua, no les hacíamos caso ... Ni siquiera nos parecía idioma; era cosa de viejitos, era para cuando los viejitos hablan sus cosas entre ellos.

> [When we used to hear my grandma and my mother speaking Quechua, we didn't take any notice of them. It didn't even seem like a language to us; it was an old people's thing, it was for when old people talk to each other about their own stuff.]

As a child, then, she perceived the language as being primarily a code of old age, rather than of geographical, or ethnic origin. Not even a language, really ("*ni siquiera nos parecía idioma*"). It was a generational marker: that is to say, before she became aware that her grandmother sometimes spoke differently because she came from Ayacucho, she assumed that she spoke this way *because she was old*. (The mother never spoke Quechua with anyone else in Lima, within the family or outside: the presence of the grandmother in the kitchen domain was the linguistic trigger, and the sole one.) Hence age may determine and be determined by language identity, in the mind of the listener if not of the speaker. A migrant of similar age now living in Villa El Salvador is similarly emphatic in remembering the generational distribution of Quechua in the village (near Jauja, in the Central Andes) where she grew up. Who would speak Quechua? The laughing answer:

> Ya tendría que ser una viejita, como te digo, las abuelitas […] Y los bien abuelitos, ¡no los que son abuelitos jóvenes!

> [It would have to be an old lady, like I told you, the old grandmas […] And I mean the really old ones, not the ones who have become grandparents while still young!]

Old people tend to speak Xish; younger people tend to speak Yish, to borrow Fishman's formulation. This pattern is an objective fact of code distribution in language environments in which intergenerational shift is taking place. And once such natural-seeming language attitudes become ingrained—take on the appearance of an obvious and absolute truth—then shift is likely to intensify even where there is an element of regret, even guilt, about the loss of the language. A teenage migrant from a remote Quechua-speaking district to the central city of Huancayo:

> El quechua muy poco los peruanos, o sea ahora, los de ahora, nosotros gente jóvenes, muy poco lo cultivamos, pues […] La gente andina lo debemos de practicar, pero no es así. O sea que la gente antigua nomás, pue. Porque ahora todos de nosotros, de nuestra … de la edad, casi nadie es quechua.

> [We Peruvians speak Quechua very little, that is, now, people now, young people like me, we don't keep it up much at all, really […] Andean people like me, we should speak it, but we don't. Well, only the old people. Because now all of us, of our … people of my age, almost nobody speaks Quechua.]

Where teenagers perceive the language to be the province of the elderly, the prospects for maintenance are grim indeed.

4.3   Lack of Social Mobility and Economic Opportunity

Soy muchacho provinciano/me levanto bien temprano/para ir con mis hermanos/ayayayay a trabajar./ No tengo padre, ni madre/Ni perro que a mí me ladre/sólo tengo la esperanza/ayayayay de progresar[40].
(From "*Soy Provinciano*" by La Nueva Crema)

"*Progresar*" is the key word here. And, the song suggests, Andean migrants are a hardy breed, unafraid of hard work, unencumbered by sentimental attachments, and keen to make their way in the world. This is self-mythologizing, doubtless, but the sentiment is a real one. A 30-something native Quechua-speaking migrant from the department of Huancavelica, now a journeyman builder living in Villa María del Triunfo (like Villa El Salvador, a former *pueblo joven*, now a legally established, still heavily migrant-populated *distrito* of Lima), told me of the place of his upbringing:

> ¡No hay nada! La chacra nomás. Allí no hay progreso. Por eso es que vienen todos a Lima, para progresar.

> [There's nothing! Just the fields. There's no progress there. That's why everyone comes to Lima, to get on in life.]

That "*allí no hay progreso*" is the archetypal lament of the "economic migrant" from wherever in the world. And for those who think of themselves as dynamic and energetic, the capital represents the antithesis of rural stagnation: that is to say, Lima (or, to a lesser extent, whichever provincial capital) is conceived of as being a place of progress and opportunity, or at least the possibility thereof, no matter what the hardships and difficulties may be, while the villages and towns of *el Perú profundo* are anything but.

When this view of the rural provinces is combined with the perceptions of Quechua outlined in the sections above, the resulting attitude to the language is a predictably damaging one. Quechua comes to be seen as the language of the isolated, the immobile: to be a Quechua speaker *both marks and compounds* one's marginalization from what progress there is to be had. As Hill and Hill noted of Tlaxcalan Nahuatl in the fast-urbanizing Mexico of the 1970s, the language had "…become defined as a 'village thing', which a forward-looking, ambitious person would do well to abandon."[41]

The felt connection between language shift and progress is picked up on by another speaker, born in 1960s Huancayo, who spoke Quechua as a child and who now works as a bus company clerk in central Lima. Having commented that there is little Quechua now to be heard in his native city, he explains why this is so:

> Ya están perdiendo ya…como se dice, ya se están civilizando…La civilización está llegando allí.

> [They're losing it now…as people say, they're becoming civilised now…Civilisation has reached there.]

He was laughing as he said it, and the cheerful brutality of this speaker's judgement on his native language and turf was doubtless in part meant to amuse, but the general attitude is undeniably consonant with that of many migrants to Lima, who feel themselves to have made tangible progress in their lives. The internalization of such attitudes by speakers like this one is the clearest possible sign that language shift is deeply embedded.

What of younger people? For one teenage girl, María, fretting impatiently at her provincial life in a village in Junín, it was English that represented excitement, adventure, and glamour: it is the language of tourists, the young, the mobile. Asked if she would like to learn Quechua, she replied:

> No, lo que a mí me gustaría es aprender a hablar inglés, pero quechua, no […] Qué bonito sería, o sea, con otra persona relacionarme y hablar los dos pues inglés […] Por eso me gustaría aprender, para así poderme comunicar con otras personas, también. Porque incluso a Huancayo van turistas, ya; y qué lindo sería que uno sepa el inglés y te pongas a conversar los dos ¿no? y ya pues, ahí lo entiendes.

> [No, what I would like is to learn English, but Quechua, no […] It would be so nice to get to know another person and for the two of us to speak English […] That's why I'd like to learn, so as to be able to communicate with other people. Because tourists go to Huancayo, too, these days; and it would be so lovely to be able to speak English and just start talking to one of them, wouldn't it? And that's it, you see what I mean.]

The reasons for María's lack of interest in learning Quechua can be guessed at without too much difficulty. If English is the key to the outside world, then Quechua is felt to be the language of those who are tied to the land, rooted and fixed, going nowhere.[42] Teenagers and adolescents tend to be peculiarly sensitive to the implications and associations of code choice, and feel these subtle nuances acutely.[43] María later left her village for Huancayo.

As for the very young: a middle-aged native Quechua-speaking woman in the *pueblo joven* of Tablada de Lurín, on the desert outskirts of Lima, a recent migrant herself, explained how she tried to comfort her primary-school-aged nephew when he was upset. A Quechua speaker recently arrived from the sierra, he had been teased remorselessly at school—mainly by fellow Quechua speakers (or self-styled ex-speakers), inevitably—because of his speech and background:

> A mi sobrinito lo fastidian, le dicen. Por ejemplo sobrenombre le ponen. Dicen los amigos, este … los amigos decir ¿no? papa seca. Ese molesta pues. Ese queja, me dice: tía, papa seca me dice. Y le digo: ¿pero si la papa seca es rica? Después le dicen papa huayro. Entonces le digo: ¿por qué tienes que … por qué te molestas porque si la papa huayro es rica con ajicito?[44]

[They tease my nephew, they say things to him. For example they give him nicknames, his friends, er…his friends call him, you know, papa seca. So he gets annoyed. He complains to me, he says: Auntie, they're calling me papa seca. And I say to him: So what, if papa seca is nice to eat? And then they call him papa huayro. So I say to him: why do you need to…why does that annoy you, when papa huayro is nice with chilli sauce?]

To refer to an Andean person as a potato could hardly be more pointed: rural, stuck in the soil, unsophisticated, mute. The woman's words are rather moving; and who would not wish for such a kindly and thoughtful aunt? But in the unforgiving sociolinguistic environment of shantytown Lima, her attempts to rationalize language use will in the end be vain: the boy will almost certainly grow up considering himself a Spanish speaker, and almost certainly suppress any knowledge of Quechua or, to the best of his ability, any traces of Quechua accent (*moteo*) that he had. To suppose otherwise would be to wish human nature to be other than it is.

5. Language and the Self-Image of the Migrant

Somos estudiantes/somos del Perú./Somos profesores/para nuestra niñez,/ médicos seremos/para la orfandad./Somos ingenieros/para nuestro país/ arquitectos somos/de nuestro destino.[45]

(From "*Somos Estudiantes*" by Los Shapis.)

There could scarcely be a more emphatic and confident statement of individual self-belief and self-reliance than this. The migrant's thirst for progress and pragmatic orientation toward the future, noted particularly by commentators such as Franco and Cosamalón,[46] are remarked upon time and again by observers of and participants in the social changes taking place in Peru. It would be strange if this did not have a linguistic dimension, and it would be strange if Peru were unique; and indeed, Edwards, having reviewed a body of situations of language shift around the world, duly notes an element common to almost all, namely: "a powerful concern for linguistic practicality, communicative efficiency, social mobility and economic advancement."[47]

Practicality, then, in language as in everything else. The migrant's mindset is pragmatic, opportunist, unsentimental, with a strong sense of personal responsibility for one's fate. "*Arquitectos somos/de nuestro destino*" sounds like the authentic voice of the migrant to Lima (of the fund-raising shantytown *pollada*, the self-help building group, the night school, the soup kitchen or *olla común*) and it does not sound like the voice of people who are easily pressured or traduced into losing their cultural identity.

Loss of Quechua, seen through this lens, looks merely like a pragmatic cultural adaptation. And to adapt or dispense with parts of one's culture is not necessarily or simply (*pace* Ojeda y Ojeda, Weber, and others) a sign of cultural subjugation or poor self-image. Change may be willed; particularly, one might feel, by "economic" migrants to Lima, fired by their "deseo de cambio y progreso" ("desire for change and progress").[48] And when culture changes—as in these circumstances it must—language, as an inherent part of the culture, automatically becomes available for reexamination and renegotiation.

> Participationist pluralism—in which some ethnic "content" is lost or altered—should not be seen as some blind turning away from roots, under pressure from an overarching majority. There is every indication that groups desire change (or, at least, the advantages which they hope it will bring).[49]

This leads us to a further, crucial point, which has serious implications for those who wish to see maintenance or revitalization of Quechua in Peru. It is best encapsulated in Fishman's insight that language shift is actually a late-order phenomenon, and cultural attrition does not so much accompany it as exist as a necessary condition for it.[50] In other words, the shift in self-identity which leads to language loss has already taken place by the time the language loss is noted (that is to say, it probably happens *before* migration): and this means that campaigners for language maintenance find themselves forced into the position of arguing for the continued use of something which is viewed as essentially outmoded and antimodern.

This is undoubtedly the case for Quechua, as the words of the speakers cited throughout this piece have already suggested. And it is therefore not the case that migrant speakers of the language simply feel *vergüenza* (shame, embarrassment) in using it in public (or to put it another way: they do not avoid speaking the language simply because of the hegemonic dominant language and its speakers)—for they do not tend to use it much in private either, except in the most circumscribed and often symbolic of domains.[51] They do not use it for it no longer fits their identity: their sense of who they are, or who they want to be.

Most important of all in the context of the possibility of reversing language shift, the adventure of migration tends to be seen as a once-only, one-way event. Migrants in Lima talk nostalgically about their land (the *tierra* or the *chacra*), but they do not often—if ever—intend to return to live there. The irreversible movement in space represented by migration is paralleled by a feeling of irreversible movement in life experience itself: it would be foolish and undesirable, indeed impossible, to try to turn back the clock by returning to the "old" ways; and this is as true of language as it is of anything else. Hence a long-time Lima resident, a native speaker of Quechua from Ancash, musing on his own mutation into a Spanish speaker, stated simply: *"Ya no podemos regresar al quechua."* We can't go back to Quechua now. The "*regresar*" tells us everything.

6. Conclusion

Once we approach the question of language choice from the point of view of the speakers themselves in creating their own self-image, it becomes clear that *vergüenza* as an explanation of the shift to Spanish among migrants[52] is only partially convincing: it does not seem to sit easily with the marked self-belief and confidence that characterizes migrant culture. Rather, the preference for Spanish might as validly be interpreted as representing a refusal to allow the *limeños* to dictate the terms of the argument; a defiant appropriation by migrants of Bourdieu's *langue légitime*[53] and an assertion that it belongs to them as much as to anybody. In this way, the "conquest" of Spanish, the reinvention of oneself as a Spanish speaker, can be seen as in a way analogous to the thousands of Peruvian national flags which festoon the shacks of the *pueblos jóvenes* of Lima: a claim for inclusion in the national polity; an insistence that the Andean migrant be incorporated into the national discourse.

Los Mojarras, a rock/*chicha* group from the Lima district of El Agustino, summarized the feelings of first and second generation migrants in a stirring and affectionate address to what is emphatically now *their* city, too:

Ahí va la generación de pueblos de inmigrantes,/que vivieron un mundo diferente al de sus padres, al de sus abuelos.../Lima limeña, Lima provinciana, Lima tu presente, somos tu futuro.[54] (From "Nostalgia Provinciana" by Los Mojarras)

The association of Quechua with the past stands in direct opposition to the migrants' impatience with the "old" ways of doing things and their clear-eyed orientation toward the present and future. As the song explicitly states, a fundamental element of the migrants' self-image is their very sense of living in a different way to that of their forebears, of constructing a new world. As Franco has it, the migrants "...eligieron el futuro" ("chose the future".)[55]

Even allowing for the various and unpredictable relationships that language bears to culture and lifestyle, it should be rather clear that those who choose the national (or even global), the modern, the progressive, the untraditional in almost every field of their life are unlikely to wish to hold on to a language which holds associations of precisely the reverse. Even less are they likely to be keen to pass the language on to their children.

Remaking themselves with such effort, why should they then wish to cast the new generation in an outdated mold? Where Quechua is represented as belonging to the past, and migrants see themselves as committed to the future, a fundamental opposition is constructed which is almost guaranteed to produce a negative outcome for the maintenance of the language. This dual feature of Peruvian language shift, forming the context within which all other pressures toward shift or maintenance are experienced, is of the very first importance in explaining how and why Quechua is lost.

We have been discussing here mainly, of course, language shift in the large urban areas. However, and without wishing to push the argument further than it can reasonably go, it is clear that there are implications here for the long-term survival of Quechua in the country as a whole. Not all Andean people migrate; not all want to; not all are impatient to instigate change, especially if it comes at a cultural cost, or with unpredictable side-effects. A great many Andean people are thoroughly committed to, immersed in, a Quechua-speaking culture, and would wish to see future generations brought up in it. But the bundle of associations that Quechua holds, associations that are necessarily damaging to it in the long run, are held not just among migrants but very widely indeed throughout Peru; and no speaker or community of speakers can be entirely isolated from the prevailing discourse. Given the Peruvian context of recurrent social and political upheaval, mass migration and a pressing need and desire for rural economic, infrastructural, and educational development, I personally suspect that language shift to Spanish is only likely to continue, and probably increase, for the foreseeable future.

That is not to say that Quechua is necessarily doomed. The essence of the problem, as was noted above, is that advocates of minority language maintenance can often find themselves arguing for something which is seen as obsolete and antimodern. We can therefore describe what is admittedly a hugely difficult challenge in a satisfyingly simple way: the task for Quechua maintenance campaigners is to find ways of being modern in and through Quechua.

This should not be impossible, especially if they proceed from the assumption that people's views about their own lives are usually well-founded, and should be taken on their own terms. That is to say, it is important to recognize that migrant (and other) speech communities undergoing language shift do not tend in general to regard themselves as victims of cultural oppression; rather, shift to Spanish may be viewed by its subjects as a positive and empowering element of the transformation of the self. While it is possible to see the loss of Quechua as a capitulation to dominant social and linguistic norms, to see it solely in these terms is to underestimate the complexity and dynamism of migrant culture in Peru, and to deny the capacity of speakers to make meaningful decisions about their own lives.

Notes

1. Nancy H. Hornberger and Serafín M. Coronel-Molina, "Quechua Language Shift, Maintenance, and Revitalization in the Andes: The Case for Language Planning," *International Journal of the Sociology of Language* 167 (2004), 9–67, see 25–30.
2. Ibid., p. 29.
3. Joshua A. Fishman, *Reversing Language Shift* (Clevedon: Multilingual Matters, 1991), p. 65.
4. Robert Le Page and Andrée Tabouret-Keller, *Acts of Identity: Creole-based Approaches to Language and Ethnicity* (Cambridge: Cambridge University Press, 1985).
5. David Graddol, *English Next* (London: The British Council, 2006), p. 56.
6. Ibid., p. 56.
7. Joseph Lo Bianco, "Globalisation and National Communities of Communication," *Language Problems and Language Planning* 29:2 (2005), 109–35, see 117.
8. Hornberger and Coronel-Molina, "Quechua Language Shift, Maintenance, and Revitalization," p. 25.
9. See for example, Sarah K. Myers, *Language Shift among Migrants to Lima, Peru* (Chicago: University of Chicago, Department of Geography, 1973), and cf. Stewart Adams, *The Emergence of a Quechua Sub-Culture in the City of Arequipa as the Result of the Phenomenon of Internal Migration from Rural Areas to Urban Areas within Peru* (St. Andrews: University of St. Andrews, 1976).
10. For a detailed account of the way in which Quechua has influenced Spanish in Andean speech, see J. Clancy Clements, *The Linguistic Legacy of Spanish and Portuguese: Colonial Expansion and Language Change* (Cambridge and New York: Cambridge University Press, 2009), pp. 158–89.
11. Eva Gugenberger, "Migración y desplazamiento lingüístico en Arequipa," in Rodolfo Cerrón-Palomino and Gustavo Solís Fonseca (eds.), *Temas de Lingüística Amerindia* (Lima: CONCYTEC, 1989), pp. 181–92.
12. Marilyn Manley, "Quechua Language Attitudes and Maintenance in Cuzco, Peru," *Language Policy* 7:4 (Dec. 2008), 323–44.
13. Rosaleen Howard, "Quechua in Tantamayo (Peru): Toward a 'Social Archaeology' of Language," *International Journal of the Sociology of Language* 167 (2004), 95–118, see 103.
14. See for example, Pierre Bourdieu (John B. Thompson, ed.), *Language and Symbolic Power* (Cambridge: Polity Press. 1991).
15. Monica Heller, "Code-switching and the Politics of Language," in Li Wei (ed.), *The Bilingualism Reader* 2nd ed. (London and New York: Routledge, 2007), pp. 163–76, see p. 165.
16. Ibid., p. 175.

17. Linguistic Minorities Project, *The Other Languages of England* (London: Routledge Kegan Paul, 1985), p. 117.

18. Bourdieu, *Language and Symbolic Power.*

19. Rodolfo Cerrón-Palomino, "Language Policy in Peru: A Historical Overview," *International Journal of the Sociology of Language 77* (1989), 11–33.

20. See for example, Nancy H. Hornberger, "Bilingual Education Success but Policy Failure," *Language in Society* 16:2 (1987), 205–26.

21. Nancy H. Hornberger and Kendall A. King, "Reversing Quechua Language Shift in South America," in Joshua A. Fishman (ed.), *Can Threatened Languages be Saved? Reversing Language Shift Revisited* (Clevedon: Multilingual Matters, 2001), pp. 166–94, see pp. 178–85.

22. Ibid., p. 167.

23. Diana Weber, "Mother Tongue Education in Quechua," in Peter Cole, Gabriella Hermon, and Mario Daniel Martín (eds.), *Language in the Andes* (Newark: University of Delaware, 1994), pp. 90–115, see p. 98.

24. See for example, John Edwards, "Language, Diversity and Identity," in John Edwards (ed), *Linguistic Minorities, Policies, and Pluralism* (London: Academic Press, 1984), pp. 277–310, see pp. 281–3; and the Peruvian situation had been discussed at some length by Hornberger, "Bilingual Education Success but Policy Failure."

25. Diana Weber, "El programa LEELA: Una alternativa para la educación bilingüe," in Luis Miranda (ed.), *Actas del 1er Congreso de Lenguas Indígenas de Sudamérica*, vol. 1 (Lima: Universidad Ricardo Palma, 2000), pp. 137–47.

26. "I believe, if I can put forward a very personal opinion, that so-called 'female illiteracy' is one of the bulwarks of indigenous Peruvian cultural resistance to Western cultural invasion. To have considered it purely as a deficiency to be overcome does not do justice to the problem in its entirety". Ludolfo Ojeda y Ojeda, "El maestro y el quechua: En torno a la ley de oficialización del quechua en la Región Inka," in Juan Carlos Godenzzi (ed.), *El quechua en debate: Ideología, normalización y enseñanza* (Cuzco: Centro de Estudios Regionales Andinos "Bartolomé de las Casas," 1992), pp. 245–61, see p. 249.

27. "A Spencerian conception of cultures as 'organisms' that are able to preserve their integrity independently of history or society". César Itier, "'Cuzqueñistas' y 'Foráneos': Las resistencias a la normalización de la escritura del quechua," in Juan Carlos Godenzzi (ed.), *El quechua en debate: Ideología, normalización y enseñanza* (Cuzco: Centro de Estudios Regionales Andinos "Bartolomé de las Casas," 1992), pp. 85–93, see p. 90.

28. John Edwards, "Irish: Planning and Preservation," *Journal of Multilingual and Multicultural Development* 5 (1984), 267–75, see 270.

29. Fishman, *Reversing Language Shift*, p. 64.
30. Nancy C. Dorian, "Linguistic and Ethnographic Fieldwork," in Joshua A. Fishman (ed.), *Handbook of Language and Ethnic Identity* (New York and Oxford: Oxford University Press, 1999), pp. 25–41, see p. 34.
31. Jerzy J. Smolicz, "Minority Languages as Core Values of Ethnic Cultures," in Willem Fase, Koen Jaspaert, and Sjaak Kroon (eds.), *Maintenance and Loss of Minority Languages* (Amsterdam and Philadelphia: John Benjamins, 1992), pp. 277–305, see p. 281.
32. Lo Bianco, "Globalisation and National Communities of Communication," p. 117.
33. Victor Ginsburgh, Ignacio Ortuño-Ortín, and Shlomo Weber, *Learning Foreign Languages. Theoretical and Empirical Implications of the Selten and Pool Model* (London: Centre for Economic Policy Research, 2005).
34. Hornberger and King, "Reversing Quechua Language Shift," pp. 170–1.
35. See Fishman, *Reversing Language Shift*; Joshua A. Fishman (ed.), *Can Threatened Languages be Saved?* (Clevedon: Multilingual Matters, 2001).
36. Hornberger and King, "Reversing Quechua Language Shift," p. 167.
37. *Insight Guide Peru* (London: APA Publications: 2007), p. 261.
38. Meanwhile, "ordinary" speakers' own confidence in their quality of Quechua, or pride in their local variety, can also be undermined by the Academia's routine disregard for anything other than the supposedly "high" variety—the *qhapaq simi*— typically spoken by its own officials and members: Tim Marr, "Language Ideology, Ownership and Maintenance: The Discourse of the Academia Mayor de la Lengua Quechua," in Li Wei, Jean-Marc Dewaele, and Alex Housen (eds.), *Opportunities and Challenges of Bilingualism* (Berlin: Mouton de Gruyter, 2002), pp. 199–219. Hornberger and King, "Reversing Quechua Language Shift," pp. 172–3, rightly praise the Quechua revitalization efforts of the Academia's late Faustino Navarro. Unfortunately, however, the fact that he was, and even still is, often referred to in Cuzco as "el Inca" (the part he played in the annual Inti Raymi festival) testifies to the extent to which the language has tended to be promoted in terms of past glories—what Joshua A. Fishman, *Language and Nationalism* (Rowley, MA: Newbury House, 1972), p. 44, calls the "link with the glorious past")—rather than of present-day utility.
39. See Marr, "Language Ideology, Ownership and Maintenance"; Mercedes Niño-Murcia, "Linguistic Purism in Cuzco, Peru: A Historical Perspective," *Language Problems and Language Planning* 21:2 (1997), 134–61.

40. "I'm a boy from the provinces/I get up very early in the morning/ to go with my brothers ayayayay to work./I don't have a father or mother/not even a dog to bark at me./All I have is the hope ayayayay of getting on in life."

41. Jane Hill and Kenneth Hill, "Language Death and Relexification in Tlaxcalan Nahuatl," *International Journal of the Sociology of Language* 12 (1977), 55–70, see 59.

42. See Carlos Franco, *Imágenes de la sociedad peruana: La "otra" modernidad* (Lima: CEDEP, 1991), pp. 79–109, for a useful discussion of migrant perceptions.

43. See for example, Ben Rampton, *Crossing: Language and Ethnicity among Adolescents* 2nd ed. (Manchester: St. Jerome Press, 2005).

44. *Papa huayro* and *papa seca* are types of Andean potato. Note the heavy Quechua influence in this speaker's (rather rudimentary) Spanish.

45. "We are students /we are from Peru. /We are teachers/for our children, /we will be doctors/for the orphans. /We are engineers /for our country /we are architects /of our destiny."

46. Franco, *Imágenes de la sociedad peruana*; Ana Lucía Cosamalón, "El lado oculto de lo cholo. Presencia de rasgos culturales y afirmación de una identidad," *Allpanchis* 25:41 (1993), 211–26.

47. John Edwards, *Language, Society, and Identity* (Oxford: Blackwell, 1985), p. 85.

48. Cosamalón, "El lado oculto de lo cholo," p. 214.

49. John Edwards, *Language, Society, and Identity*, pp. 107–8.

50. Fishman (ed.), *Can Threatened Languages be Saved?*

51. Tim Marr, "The Language Left at Ticlio: Social and Cultural Perspectives on Quechua Language Loss in Lima, Peru," unpublished Ph.D. dissertation, University of Liverpool, 1998.

52. Hornberger and King, "Reversing Quechua Language Shift"; Hornberger and Coronel-Molina, "Quechua Language Shift"; Cerrón-Palomino, "Language Policy in Peru."

53. Cf. Penelope Harvey, "Lenguaje y relaciones de poder: Consecuencias para una política lingüística," *Allpanchis* 19:29/30 (1987), pp. 105–31, see p. 121, who refers to the desire to "adquirir o por lo menos neutralizar el poder por la apropiación de sus símbolos."

54. "There goes the generation of migrants, /who lived in a world different to that of their parents and grandparents. /Traditional Lima, provincial Lima, Lima your present, /we are your future."

55. Franco, *Imágenes de la sociedad peruana*, p. 8

Glossary

Terms are from Spanish unless otherwise specified. Those which entered Spanish from Quechua are indicated by [Q.]. Where traditional Spanish spelling departs from modern standard orthography for Southern Quechua, we also give the correct Quechua spelling.

Acllacuna [Q. aklla *chosen* + plural suffix –kuna] *Chosen women who served the Inca and state cult.*

arancel eclesiástico *Fees charged for sacraments by the Catholic Church.*

asiento *Contract, often between royal authorities and a private individual or corporation, regarding a commercial concession or the exploitation of a given resource.*

Audiencia *Royal Court; the highest legal tribunal in the Spanish colonies, also with a legislative role.*

ayllu [Q.] *Andean kin group based on common descent.*

cabildo *Municipal council.*

cacique *Native Andean chief; synonymous with* curaca.

campesino *Subsistence farmer,* "*peasant.*"

castellanización *Castilianisation, i.e., Hispanicisation, in broad cultural terms, or specifically the shift from speaking indigenous languages to speaking Spanish.*

cédula *Royal decree.*

chacra [Q. chakra] *Field, plot of land.*

Chanca *Ethnic group in fifteenth-century Peru, centred on Andahuaylas; enemies of the Inca.*

chicha *Fermented maize beer; see also* cultura chicha.

civilista, civilismo *Relating to the* Partido Civil, *a political party active in Peru in the late nineteenth and early twentieth centuries.*

corregidor *Magistrate in charge of a province, combining administrative and judicial roles.*

Cortes *Spanish parliament.*

criollo(s) *White(s), generally of Spanish descent and often of elite status.*

cultura chicha *Modern urban culture created by mass Andean immigration, esp. to Lima.*

curaca [Q. kura(ka)q? *elder*] *Native Andean chief; synonymous with* cacique.

curacazgo *Role or jurisdiction of a* cacique; *chieftaincy.*

doctrina de indios *Parish in an indigenous district administered by members of the secular or regular clergy.*

encomendero *Holder of an* encomienda.

encomienda *Grant of native labour to an individual, institution, or corporation; functionally synonymous with* repartimiento.

forastero *Lit. "foreigner" or "outsider": an indigenous person not native to their community of residence, a status inherited by their descendants. Contrasts with* originario.

gamonales *Local landed potentates; petty tyrant landlords.*

hacendado *Owner of a* hacienda.

hacienda *Great landed estate.*

huaca [Q. waka] *Any object or place imbued with religious significance or numinosity.*

indígena *Indigenous person; Indian.*

indigenismo *Intellectual current, at its peak in the early twentieth century, which sought a greater social and political role and rights for native peoples in Spanish America.*

(indio) ladino *Hispanicized Indian, especially one who spoke Spanish.*

lengua general *An indigenous language adopted or adapted for state purposes across a wide area, as for evangelisation. In the Peruvian context, particularly "la lengua general del Inga," i.e., Quechua as used for official purposes in the early Spanish colony.*

llaccta [Q. llaqta]*Ancestral and/or ethnic community; in the Spanish period, adapted to equate to Spanish concepts of* (home) town, region *or* nation; *see chapter 7.*

malqui [Q. mallki]*Mummy of an ancestor, an object of veneration for communities descended from.*

mestizo *Person of mixed white and Indian descent.*

mita [Q. mit'a, lit. a (rolling or recurrent) *season, time,* or *turn of duty*] *Forced labour draft, usually for large public projects, especially in mining.*

mita de plaza Mita *at the service of a municipality or its leading citizens.*

mitayo [Q. mit'a + suffix –yuq: "one whose turn it is"]*Draft labourer; one forced to serve in a* mita.

mitma (also Hispanicized plural **mitimaes**) [Q. mitma, *outsider, new-comer*, in modern terms effectively *(im)migrant*] *Member of a group forcibly resettled under the Inca for purposes of state, often far from their original homeland.*

montonero *Guerrilla, fighter in a* montonera, *a guerrilla movement or irregular military force, usually in the Andean highlands.*

moteo, motoseo *An accent in Spanish that reveals that the speaker's mother tongue is an Andean language, especially Quechua. Most notably, pronouncing* i *for* e, *and* u *for* o *(or, in hypercorrection, vice versa).*

originario *Indigenous person native to his or her community of residence; "originary." Contrasts with* forastero.

principal *Chief or high-ranking member of an indigenous community.*

pueblo joven *Modern term, especially in Peru, for a new shanty-town, mushrooming around a city (*lit. *young town).*

puna *High-altitude grassy plains above the treeline (c. 3500m+), especially in the Central and Southern Andes.*

quebrada *Lit.* gorge, ravine, gully*; in the Andes often used to refer specifi-cally to agriculturally productive mid–altitude stretches of river–valleys, as they descend swiftly from high–altitude plateaus such as the Bolivian* Altiplano.

quipu [Q. khipu, *knot*] *Inca accounting and record–keeping system using knotted strings .*

quipucamayoc [Q. *khipu* kamayuq, "one who has command of the *khipu*"] *Inca official with expertise in composing and reading quipus.*

Real Audiencia *See* Audiencia.

reducción *Village where native peoples were forcibly resettled and concen-trated, in the decades following the Conquest.*

repartimiento *Grant of native labour to an individual, institution, or corporation; functionally synonymous with* encomienda.

revisita *Official inspection of a native village or province, usually to fiscal ends.*

señorío *Lordship or chiefdom; the jurisdiction of a lord or chief, or the condition of being one.*

sierra *Mountain range, highlands; here, the Andes.*

tlacuilo [Nahuatl] *Scribe and painter of Aztec codices.*

tratado *Treaty or treatise.*

vecino *Spanish resident, often a male head of household.*

visita *Inspection of a village or region by a royal official.*

visitador *Royal official undertaking a* visita.

visita general *Large-scale* visita, *as of an entire viceroyalty such as Peru.*

visitador general *Royal official undertaking a* visita general.

yanacona [Q. yana + plural suffix –kuna] *Native retainers or dependents.*

yunka [Q.] *Warm valley at low altitude—especially the moist and densely vegetated eastward descents from the Andes to Amazonia, though also used of the rainforest in general, and of irrigated valleys westwards to the Pacific coast. Also, an inhabitant of such a zone.*

Bibliography

Primary Sources, Early Dictionaries, and Government Publications

Alvarez, Bartolomé (María del Carmen Martín Rubio, Juan J. R. Villarías Robles, and Fermín del Pino Díaz, eds.), *De las costumbres y conversión de los indios del Perú. Memorial a Felipe II* (1588; Madrid: Ediciones Polifemo, 1998).

Anchorena, José Dionisio, *Traducción al quechua de la ley orgánica de municipalidades en lo relativo a los concejos de distrito* (Lima: Imprenta del Estado, 1873).

———, *Gramática quechua ó del idioma del imperio de los incas* (Lima: Imprenta del Estado, 1874).

Anonymous, *Memoria que el Ministro de Estado en el Despacho de Instrucción, Culto, Justicia y Beneficencia presenta al Congreso Nacional de 1874* (Lima: Imprenta del Universo, 1874).

Asamblea Constituyente, *Nueva Constitución Política del Estado* (La Paz: Asamblea Constituyente, 2007).

Ávila, Francisco de, *Tratado de los evangelios, que nuestra madre la iglesia propone en todo el año…*, vol. 1 (Lima: Jorge López de Herrera, 1646).

———, *Segundo tomo de los sermones de todo el año, en lengva indica, y Castellana, para la enseñanza de los Indios, y extirpacion de sus Idolatrias*, vol. 2 (Lima: Jorge López de Herrera, 1648).

Bertonio, Ludovico, *Arte de la lengua Aymara* (1612; Leipzig: B. G. Teubner, 1879).

———, *Vocabulario de la lengua Aymara* (1612; Cochabamba: Centro de Estudios de la Realidad Económica y Social, 1984).

———, *Vocabulario de la lengua Aymara* (1612; La Paz: Radio San Gabriel, 1993).

Botmiliau, Adolfo de, "La feria de Vilque en el Collao, 1846," in Estuardo Núñez (ed.), *El Perú visto por viajeros* 2 vols. (Lima: Ediciones Peisa, 1974–1975), vol. 2, pp. 69–76.

Bromley, Juan (ed.), *Libros de Cabildo de Lima* 23 vols. (Lima: Imprenta Torres Aguirre, 1935–1964).

Bustamante, Juan, *Los indios del Perú. Compilación hecha por Juan Bustamante* (Lima: J. M. Monterola, 1867).

Cabello Valboa, Miguel, *Miscelánea Antártica. Una historia del Perú antiguo* (Lima: Universidad Nacional Mayor de San Marcos, 1951).

Calancha, Antonio de la, *Corónica moralizada del orden de San Agustín* 6 vols. (1638; Lima: Ignacio Prado Pastor, 1974).

Cobo, Bernabé, *Historia del Nuevo Mundo* (1653; Madrid: Atlas, 1964).

Contreras, Miguel de (Noble David Cook, ed.), *Padrón de los indios de Lima en 1613* (Lima: Universidad Nacional Mayor de San Marcos, 1968).

Cordero, Luis, *Diccionario quichua-español español-quichua* (1892; Cuenca: Universidad de Cuenca, 1967).

Dávila Brizeño, Diego, "Descripción y relación de la provincia de los yauyos [1586]," in Marcos Jiménez de la Espada (ed.), *Relaciones Geográficas de Indias* (Madrid: Ediciones Atlas, 1965), vol. 1, pp. 155–65.

Enock, Reginald, *The Andes and the Amazon: Life and Travel in Peru* (London: T. Fisher Unwin, 1907).

Espinosa Medrano, Juan de (César Itier, crit. ed.), *El robo de Proserpina y sueño de Endimión. Auto sacramental en Quechua* (Lima: Instituto Riva-Agüero, 2010).

Esquivel y Navia, Diego de (Félix Denegri Luna, ed.), *Noticias Cronológicas de la Gran Ciudad del Cuzco* 2 vols. (Lima: Fundación Augusto N. Wiese, 1980).

Fernández Nodal, José, *Elementos de gramática quichua ó idioma de los yncas* (Aylesbury and London: Watson and Hazell, [1873]).

Gago, Vicente, "Proclama del Dr. Vicente Gago, capellán del hospital militar de Santa Ana, a sus paisanos los habitantes de la provincia de Jauja, en su lengua nativa y peculiar" (Lima: Imprenta de Rio, 1822).

Garcilaso de la Vega, "El Inca" (Aurelio Miró Quesada, ed.), *Comentarios Reales de los Incas* (1609; Caracas: Biblioteca Ayacucho, 1976).

———, "El Inca" (A. Rosenblat, ed.), *Comentarios Reales de los Incas* 2 vols. (1609; Buenos Aires: Emecé, 1945).

González Holguín, Diego, *Gramatica y arte nveva de la lengva general de todo el Peru, llamada lengua Qquichua, o lengua del Inca* (Lima: Francisco del Canto, 1607).

———, *Gramática y arte nueva de la lengua general de todo el Perú, llamada lengua Quichua, o lengua del Inca* (1607; Heppenheim: Frany Wolf, 1975).

———, *Vocabvlario de la lengva general de todo el Perv llamada Qquichua, o del Inca* (Lima: Francisco del Canto, 1608).

——— (intr. Ramiro Matos Mendieta and prol. Raúl Porras Barrenechea), *Vocabulario de la lengua general de todo el Perú llamada lengua quichua o del Inca* (1608; Lima: Universidad Nacional de San Marcos, 1989).

Government of Peru, *Ley Orgánica de Municipalidades* (Lima: Imprenta del Estado, 1873).

Guinness, Geraldine, *Peru: Its Story, People, and Religion...* (London: Morgan & Scott, 1909).

Herndon, W. M. Lewis, *Exploration of the Valley of the Amazon* (Washington: Taylor & Maury, 1854).

Hill, S. S., *Travels in Peru and Mexico* 2 vols. (London: Longman, Green, Longman, & Roberts, 1860).

Jiménez de la Espada, Marcos, *Relaciones Geográficas de Indias. Perú* 3 vols. (Madrid: Ediciones Atlas, 1965).

Liñán y Cisneros, Melchor de, "Relación de gobierno," 1681, in Lewis Hanke (ed.), *Los virreyes españoles en América durante el gobierno de la casa de Austria: Perú* 7 vols. (Madrid: Ediciones Atlas, 1978–1980), vol. 5, pp. 180–273.

Lissón Chávez, Emilio, *La Iglesia de España en el Perú. Colección de documentos para la historia de la iglesia en el Perú* 5 vols. (Seville: Dimisionario de Lima, 1943–1956).

Loayza, Francisco A. (ed.), *Fray Calixto Túpak Inka: documentos originales y, en su mayoría, totalmente desconocidos, auténticos, de este apóstol indio, valiente defensor de su raza, desde el año 1746 a 1760* (Lima: Pequeños grandes libros de historia de América, 1948).

López de Caravantes, Francisco (Guillermo Lohmann Villena and Marie Helmer, eds.), *Noticia General del Perú* 6 vols. (1630; Madrid, 1985–1989).

Marcoy, Paul, *Travels in South America. From the Pacific Ocean to the Atlantic Ocean*, vol. 1 (New York: Scribner, Armstrong, & Co, 1875).

Markham, Clements R., *Cuzco: A Journey to the Ancient Capital of Peru* (London: Chapman and Hall, 1856).

——— (Peter Blanchard, ed.), *Markham in Peru: The Travels of Clements R. Markham, 1852–1853* (Austin: University of Texas Press, 1991).

Middendorf, E. W., *Dramatische und lyrische dichtungen der keshua-sprache* (Leipzig: F. A. Brockhaus, 1891).

Middendorf, E. W., *Perú: Observaciones y estudios del pais y sus habitantes durante una permanencia de 25 años* 3 vols. (1893–1895; Lima: Universidad Nacional Mayor de San Marcos, 1973).

Ministerio del Interior, *Comisión Honoraria de Reducciones de Indios, Publicación N0 1. La situación actual de los indios argentinos frente a los decretos . . .* (Buenos Aires: Ministerio del Interior, 1935).

Pacheco Zegarra, Gavino, *Ollantai. Drame en vers quechua du temps des incas* (Paris: Maisonneuve, 1878).

Paz Soldán, Mateo, and Mariano Felipe Paz Soldán, *Geografía del Perú* (Paris: Fermin Didot, 1862).

Pérez Bocanegra, Juan, *Ritval formvlario e institvcion de cvras* (Lima: Geronymo de Contreras, 1631).

Poeppig, Eduardo, *Viaje al Perú y al Río Amazonas, 1827–1832* (Iquitos: CETA, 2003).

Ramírez, Balthasar, "Description del Reyno del Piru . . .," in H. Trimborn (ed.), *Quellen zur Kulturgeschichte des präkolumbischen Amerika. Fuentes de la historia cultural de la América precolombina* (1597; Stuttgart: Strecker und Schröder, 1936).

Republic of Bolivia, *Nueva Constitución Política del Estado* (2009).

Republic of Ecuador, *Constitución Política de la República del Ecuador* (2008).

Republic of Peru, *Constitución Política del Perú* (1993).

Rivera Serna, Raúl (ed.), *Libro del Cabildo de la Ciudad de San Juan de la Frontera de Huamanga—1539–1547 . . .* (Lima: Casa de la Cultura del Perú, 1966).

Salomon, Frank, and George Urioste (ed. and trans.), *The Huarochirí Manuscript, a Testament of Ancient and Colonial Andean Religion* (Austin: University of Texas Press, 1991).

Santo Tomás, Domingo de, *Lexicon, o Vocabulario de la lengua general del Perv*, facs. ed. (1560; Madrid: Ediciones de Cultura Hispánica—Agencia Española de Cooperación Internacional, 1994).

Smyth, W., *Narrative of a Journey from Lima to Para . . .* (London: John Murray, 1836).

Solórzano y Pereyra, Juan de, *Política Indiana* (1647; reprinted Madrid and Buenos Aires: Compañía Ibero-Americana, 1930).

Squier, Ephraim George, *Peru. Incidents of Travel and Exploration in the Land of the Incas* (1877; New York: AMS, 1973).

Taylor, Gerald (ed.), *Ritos y tradiciones de Huarochirí*, second revised ed. (Lima: Instituto Francés de Estudios Andinos / Banco Central de Reserva del Perú / Universidad Particular Ricardo Palma, 1999).

Tercer Concilio de Lima, *Doctrina Christiana, y catecismo para instrvccion de los Indios...* (Lima: Antonio Ricardo, 1584).

Toledo, Francisco de (María Justina Sarabia Viejo, ed.), *Disposiciones gubernativas para el virreinato del Perú*, 2 vols. (1569–1580; Seville: Escuela de Estudios Hispanoamericanos, 1986–1989).

Torres Saldamando, Enrique, Pablo Patrón, and Nicanor Boloña (eds.), *Libro primero de cabildos de Lima* 3 vols. (Paris: Paul Dupont, 1888).

Tschiffely, Aimé Félix, *Tschiffely's Ride* (1933; London: 1952).

Villar, Leonardo, "Informe del Dr. Leonardo Villar, sobre la Gramática Quechua del Dr. José D. Anchorena," *Boletín de la Sociedad Geográfica de Lima* 11:11 (1901), 175–83.

Witt, Heinrich, *Diario 1824–1890: Un testamento personal sobre el Perú del siglo XIX* 2 vols. (Lima: Banco Mercantil, 1992).

Wrigley, G. M., "Fairs of the Central Andes," *Geographical Review* 7:2 (Feb. 1919), 65–80.

Secondary Works

Adams, Stewart, *The Emergence of a Quechua Sub-Culture in the City of Arequipa as the Result of the Phenomenon of Internal Migration from Rural Areas to Urban Areas within Peru* (St. Andrews: University of St. Andrews, 1976).

Adelaar, Willem F. H., *Morfología del Quechua de Pacaraos* (Lima: Universidad Nacional Mayor de San Marcos, 1987).

———, "En pos de la lengua culle," in Rodolfo Cerrón-Palomino and Gustavo Solís Fonseca (eds.), *Temas de lingüística amerindia: Primer congreso nacional de investigaciones lingüística-filológicas* (Lima: CONCYTEC, 1989), pp. 83–105.

———, "La procedencia dialectal del manuscrito de Huarochirí en base a sus características lingüísticas," *Revista Andina* 12:1 (1994), 137–54.

———, "Comentario a las ponencias de J. C. Godenzzi y C. Itier," in César Itier (ed.), *Del siglo de oro al siglo de las luces. Lenguaje y sociedad en los Andes del siglo XVIII* (Cuzco: Centro de Estudios Rurales Andinos "Bartolomé de las Casas," 1995), pp. 113–16.

———, "Unprotected Languages: The Silent Death of the Languages of Northern Peru," in Anita Herzfeld and Yolanda Lastra (eds.), *Las causas sociales de la desaparición y del mantenimiento de las lenguas en las naciones de América* (Hermosillo: Universidad de Sonora, 1999), pp. 205–22.

Adelaar, Willem F. H., with Pieter C. Muysken, *The Languages of the Andes* (Cambridge and New York: Cambridge University Press, 2004).

Adelaar, Willem F. H., and Jorge Trigoso Pérez, "Un documento colonial quechua de Cajamarca," in S. Dedenbach-Salazar Sáenz, C. Arellano Hoffmann, E. König, and H. Prümers (eds.), *50 Years of Americanist Studies at the University of Bonn. New Contributions to the Archaeology, Ethnohistory, Ethnolinguistics and Ethnography of the Americas* vol. 2 (Bonn: Bonner Amerikanistische Studien, 1998), pp. 641–51.

Adorno, Rolena, "Images of *Indios Ladinos* in Early Colonial Peru," in Kenneth J. Andrien and Rolena Adorno (eds.), *Transatlantic Encounters: Europeans and Andeans in the Sixteenth Century* (Berkeley and Los Angeles: University of California Press, 1991), pp. 232–70.

Alaperrine-Bouyer, Monique, *La educación de las elites indígenas en el Perú colonial* (Lima: Instituto Francés de Estudios Andinos, 2007).

Albó, Xavier, *Los mil rostros del quechua. Sociolingüística de Cochabamba* (Lima: Instituto de Estudios Peruanos, 1974).

———, *Bolivia plurilingüe. Guía para planificadores y educadores* (La Paz: UNICEF-CIPCA, 1995).

Albó, Xavier, *Educando en la diferencia: Hacia unas políticas interculturales y lingüísticas para el sistema educativo* (La Paz: Ministerio de Educación / UNICEF / CIPCA, 2002).

———, "El futuro del quechua visto desde una perspectiva boliviana," *International Journal of the Sociology of Language* 167 (2004), 119–30.

Alderetes, Jorge R., and Lelia Inés Albarracín, "El quechua en Argentina: El caso de Santiago del Estero," *International Journal of the Sociology of Language* 167 (2004), 83–93.

Andrade Ciudad, Luis, "Las lenguas indígenas del presente," in Luis Andrade Ciudad and Jorge Iván Pérez Silva (eds.), *Las lenguas del Perú* (Lima: Pontificia Universidad Católica del Perú, 2009), pp. 36–79.

Andrien, Kenneth J., "The *Noticias Secretas de América* and the Construction of a Governing Ideology for the Spanish American Empire," *Colonial Latin American Review* 7:2 (1998), 175–92.

———, *Andean Worlds: Indigenous History, Culture, and Consciousness under Spanish Rule, 1532–1825* (Albuquerque: University of New Mexico Press, 2001).

———, "The Coming of Enlightened Reform in Bourbon Peru: Secularization of the *Doctrinas de Indios*, 1746–1773," in Gabriel Pacquette (ed.), *Enlightened Reform in Southern Europe and its Atlantic Colonies, c. 1750–1830* (Farnham: Ashgate, 2009), pp. 183–202.

Animato, Carlo, Paolo A. Rossi, and Clara Miccinelli (eds.), *Quipu: Il nodo parlante dei misteriosi Incas* (Genoa: Edizioni Culturali Internazionali, 1989).

Ares Queija, Berta, "'Un borracho de chicha y vino'. La construcción social del mestizo (Perú, s. XVI)," in Gregorio Salinero (ed.), *Mezclado y sospechoso. Movilidad e identidades, España y América (siglos XVI–XVIII)* (Madrid: Casa de Velázquez, 2005), pp. 121–44.

Austin Alchon, Suzanne, *Native Society and Disease in Colonial Ecuador* (Cambridge and New York: Cambridge University Press, 1991).

Ballón Aguirre, Enrique, "La dentera multilingüe e intercultural en las sociedades andinas (conflictos de lengua, habla y escritura)," *Revista Andina* 49 (2009), 135–64.

Basadre, Jorge, *Introducción a las bases documentales para la historia de la república del Perú con algunas reflexiones*, vol. 2 (Lima: Ediciones P. L. Villanueva, 1971).

Basto Girón, Luis J., "Las mitas de Huamanga y Huancavelica," *Publicaciones del Instituto de Etnología*, 8 (Lima, 1954); also published as "Las mitas de Huamanga y Huancavelica," *Perú Indígena* 5:13 (Dec. 1954), 215–42.

Belanger, Brian, "Secularization and the Laity in Colonial Mexico: Querétaro, 1598–1821," unpublished Ph.D. dissertation, Tulane University, 1990.

Benson, Susan, "Injurious Names: Naming, Disavowal, and Recuperation in Contexts of Slavery and Emancipation," in Gabriele Vom Bruck and Barbara Bodenhorn (eds.), *The Anthropology of Names and Naming* (Cambridge: Cambridge University Press, 2006), pp. 178–99.

Beresford-Jones, David G., and Paul Heggarty, "Broadening our Horizons: A New Methodology and Cross-Disciplinary Hypothesis for Andean Prehistory," in Paul Heggarty and David G. Beresford-Jones (eds.), *Archaeology and Language in the Andes* (London and Oxford: British Academy / Oxford University Press, forthcoming).

Bourdieu, Pierre (John B. Thompson, ed.), *Language and Symbolic Power* (Cambridge: Polity Press, 1991).

Bowser, Frederick P., *The African Slave in Colonial Peru, 1524–1650* (Stanford: Stanford University Press, 1974).

Bradby, Barbara, "The 'Black Legend' of Huancavelica: The Mita Debates and Opposition to Wage-Labour in the Colonial Mercury Mine," in Julio Sánchez Gómez and Guillermo Mira Delli-Zotti (eds.), *Hombres, Técnica, Plata. Minería y Sociedad en Europa y América, Siglos XVI–XIX* (Seville: Aconcagua, 2000), pp. 227–57.

Brading, David A., "Tridentine Catholicism and Enlightened Despotism in Bourbon Mexico," *Journal of Latin American Studies* 15:1 (May 1983), 1–22.

———, *Church and State in Bourbon Mexico: The Diocese of Michoacán, 1749–1818* (Cambridge: Cambridge University Press, 1994).

Brown, Kendall W., "Workers' Health and Colonial Mercury Mining at Huancavelica, Peru," *The Americas* 57:4 (Apr. 2001), 467–96.

Burger, R. L., "Central Andean language expansion and the Chavín sphere of interaction," in P. Heggarty and D. Beresford-Jones (eds.) *Archaeology and Language in the Andes* (London and Oxford: British Academy / Oxford University Press, forthcoming).

Cameron, Deborah, *Verbal Hygiene* (London: Routledge, 1995).

Cerrón-Palomino, Rodolfo, *Diccionario quechua de Junín-Huanca-Castellano y vice versa* (Lima: Ministerio de Educación, 1976).

———, "Lengua y sociedad en el Valle del Mantaro: Primera parte: Quechua fronterizo," *Amerindia* 12 (1987), 33–93.

———, *Lingüística Quechua* (Cuzco: Centro de Estudios Regionales Andinos "Bartolomé de las Casas," 1987; reprinted 2003).

———, "Unidad y diferenciación lingüística en el mundo andino," *Lexis: Revista de lingüística y literatura* 11:1 (1987), 71–104.

———, "Language Policy in Peru: A Historical Overview," *International Journal of the Sociology of Language* 77 (1989), 11–33.

———, "Reconsideración del llamado 'quechua costeño'," *Revista Andina*, 16 (1990), 335–409.

———, *La lengua de Naimlap. Reconstrucción y obsolescencia del mochica* (Lima: Pontificia Universidad Católica del Perú, 1995).

———, "Tras las huellas del aimara cuzqueño," *Revista Andina* 33 (1999), 137–61.

———, *Lingüística Aimara* (Lima: Centro de Estudios Regionales Andinos "Bartolomé de las Casas," 2000).

———, *Castellano andino. Aspectos sociolingüísticos, pedagógicos y gramaticales* (Lima: Pontificia Universidad Católica del Perú, 2003).

———, "Reconstrucción del proto-uro: fonología," *Lexis*, XXXI (2007), 47–104.

———, "Collana, Payan, y Cayao: Los clasificadores de los ceques," in *Voces del Ande. Ensayos sobre onomástica andina* (Lima: Pontificia Universidad Católica del Perú, 2008), pp. 245–59.

Charles, John Duffy, "Indios Ladinos: Colonial Andean Testimony and Ecclesiastical Institutions, 1583–1650," unpublished Ph.D. dissertation, Yale University, 2003.

Charney, Paul, *Indian Society in the Valley of Lima, Peru, 1532–1824* (Lanham, MD: University Press of America, 2001).

Chiodi, F. (ed.), *La educación indígena en América Latina*, 2 vols. (Santiago and Quito: OREALC / GTZ / Abya Yala, 1990).

Chirinos Rivera, Andrés, "Las lenguas indígenas peruanas más allá del año 2000," *Revista Andina* 32 (1998), 453–79.

———(trans.), *Perumanta hatun kamachina, 1993. Constitución Política del Perú* (Lima: Fondo Editorial del Congreso de la República Peruana, 1999).

———, *Atlas etnolingüístico del Perú* (Cuzco: Centro de Estudios Regionales Andinos "Bartolomé de las Casas," 2001).

Clements, J. Clancy, *The Linguistic Legacy of Spanish and Portuguese: Colonial Expansion and Language Change* (Cambridge and New York: Cambridge University Press, 2009).

Cohen, Ronald, *The Kanuri of Bornu* (New York: Holt, Rinehart and Winston 1967).

Cole, Jeffrey A., "An Abolitionism Born of Frustration: The Conde de Lemos and the Potosí Mita, 1667–1673," *Hispanic American Historical Review* 63:2 (May 1983), 307–33.

Comisión de la Verdad y Reconciliación del Perú, *Informe Final* (2003). Online at www.cverdad.org.pe.

Contreras, Carlos, *La ciudad del mercurio: Huancavelica, 1570–1700* (Lima: Instituto de Estudios Peruanos, 1982).

Cook, Noble David, *Demographic Collapse: Indian Peru, 1520–1620* (Cambridge: Cambridge University Press, 1981).

Coordinadora Permanente de los Pueblos Indígenas del Perú (COPPIP), *Correo indígena*, October 13, 2003.

Cornejo Guerrero, Miguel Antonio, "Arqueología de santuarios inkas en la Guaranga de Sisicaya, valle de Lurín," *Tawantinsuyu: Una revista internacional de estudios inkas* 1 (1995), 18–28.

———, "Pachacamac y el canal de Guatca en el Bajo Rímac," *Bulletin de l'Institut Français d'Études Andines* 33:3 (2004), 783–814.

Coronel-Molina, Serafín M., "Functional Domains of the Quechua Language in Peru: Issues of Status Planning," *International Journal of Bilingual Education and Bilingualism* 2:3 (1999), 166–80.

———, "Language Ideologies of the High Academy of the Quechua Language in Cuzco, Peru," *Latin American and Caribbean Ethnic Studies* 3:3 (Nov. 2008), 319–40.

Cosamalón, Ana Lucía, "El lado oculto de lo cholo. Presencia de rasgos culturales y afirmación de una identidad," *Allpanchis* 25:41 (1993), 211–26.

Covey, R. Alan, *How the Incas Built Their Heartland: State Formation and the Innovation of Imperial Strategies in the Sacred Valley, Peru* (Ann Arbor: University of Michigan Press, 2006).

Covey, R. Alan, and Christina M. Elson, "Ethnicity, Demography, and Estate Management in Sixteenth-Century Yucay," *Ethnohistory* 54:2 (Spring 2007), 303–35.

Cusihuamán G., Antonio, *Diccionario quechua, Cuzco-Collao* (Lima: Ministerio de Educación, 1976).

Davies, Thomas Mockett, "Indian Integration in Peru: A Half Century of Experience, 1900–1948," unpublished Ph.D. dissertation, University of New Mexico, 1970.

De Granda, Germán, *Estudios de lingüística andina* (Lima: Pontificia Universidad Católica del Perú, 2001).

De la Cadena, Marisol, *Indigenous Mestizos. The Politics of Race and Culture in Cuzco, Peru, 1919–1991* (Durham, NC: Duke University Press, 2000).

De la Puente Brunke, José, *Encomiendas y encomenderos en el Perú. Estudio social y político de una institución colonial* (Seville: Excelentísima Diputación Provincial de Sevilla, 1992).

Deustua, José, "Routes, Roads, and Silver Trade in Cerro de Pasco, 1820–1860: The Internal Market in Nineteenth-Century Peru," *Hispanic American Historical Review* 74:1 (Feb. 1994), 1–31.

Dorian, Nancy C., "Linguistic and Ethnographic Fieldwork," in Joshua A. Fishman (ed.), *Handbook of Language and Ethnic Identity* (New York and Oxford: Oxford University Press, 1999), pp. 25–41.

Durston, Alan, "La escritura del quechua por indígenas en el siglo XVII. Nuevas evidencias en el Archivo Arzobispal de Lima (estudio preliminar y edición de textos)," *Revista Andina* 37 (2003), 207–36.

———, *Pastoral Quechua: The History of Christian Translation in Colonial Peru, 1550–1650* (Notre Dame, IN: University of Notre Dame Press, 2007).

———, "Native Language Literacy in Colonial Peru: The Question of Mundane Quechua Writing Revisited," *Hispanic American Historical Review* 88:1 (Feb. 2008), 41–70.

Duviols, Pierre, "Huari y Llacuaz: Agricultores y pastores, un dualismo prehispánico de oposición y complementariedad," *Revista del Museo Nacional* 39 (1973), 153–91.

———, "Sumaq T'ika. La Princesse du village sans eau," *Journal de la Société des Américanistes* 63 (1974–1976), 153–98.

Earle, Rebecca, *The Return of the Native: Indians and Myth-Making in Spanish America, 1810–1930* (Durham, NC: Duke University Press, 2007).

Edwards, John, "Language, Diversity and Identity," in John Edwards (ed.), *Linguistic Minorities, Policies, and Pluralism* (London: Academic Press, 1984), pp. 277–310.

———, "Irish: Planning and Preservation," *Journal of Multilingual and Multicultural Development* 5 (1984), 267–75.

———, *Language, Society, and Identity* (Oxford: Blackwell, 1985).

Eeckhout, Peter, *Pachacamac durant l'Intermédiaire récent. Étude d'un site monumental préhispanique de la Côte centrale du Pérou* (Oxford: BAR International Series, 1999).

Elliott, John H., "A Europe of Composite Monarchies," *Past and Present* 137 (Nov. 1992), 48–71.

Espino Relucé, Gonzalo, *Adolfo Vienrich. La inclusión andina y la literatura quechua* (Lima: Universidad Ricardo Palma, 2004).

Espinoza Soriano, Waldemar, "Los mitmas yungas de Collique en Cajamarca, siglos XVI y XVII," *Revista del Museo Nacional* 36 (1970), 9–57.

———, "Agua y riego en tres ayllus de Huarochirí, siglo XV y XVI," *Actas y memorias del XXXIV Congreso Internacional de Americanistas* (Lima: Pontificia Universidad Católica del Perú, 1981), vol. 3, pp. 147–66.

———, "Los fundamentos lingüísticos de la etnohistoria andina y comentarios en torno al Anónimo de Charcas de 1604," in Rodolfo Cerrón-Palomino (ed.), *Aula quechua* (Lima: Signo, 1982), pp. 163–202.

———, "Los señoríos de Yaucha y Picoy en el abra del medio y alto Rímac. Siglos XV y XVI. El testimonio de la etnohistoria," *Revista Histórica* 34 (1984), 157–279.

———, "Huarochirí y el Estado Inca," in V. Thatar A. (ed.), *Huarochirí: Ocho mil años de historia* (Santa Eulalia: Municipalidad de Santa Eulalia de Acopaya, 1992), vol. 1, pp. 117–94.

Estenssoro Fuchs, Juan Carlos, *Del paganismo a la santidad. La incorporación de los indios del Perú al catolicismo, 1532–1750* (Lima: Instituto Francés de Estudios Andinos / Pontificia Universidad Católica del Perú / Instituto Riva-Agüero, 2003).

Favre, Henri, "Relaciones sociales y procesos culturales: Los fenómenos de indianización en Huancavelica durante los siglos XIX y XX," in J. P. Deler and Y. Saint-Geours (eds.), *Estados y naciones en los Andes: Hacia una historia comparativa: Bolivia—Colombia—Ecuador—Perú* 2 vols. (Lima: Instituto de Estudios Peruanos, Instituto Francés de Estudios Andinos, 1986), vol. 1, pp. 323–24.

———, *El indigenismo* (1996; Mexico City: Fondo de Cultura Económica, 1998).

Feltham, Patricia Jane, "The Lurín Valley Project. Some Results for the Late Intermediate and Late Horizon," in A. Kendall (ed.), *Current Archaeological Projects in the Central Andes* (Oxford: British Archaeological Reports, International Series 210, 1984), pp. 45–73.

Fennell, Christopher C., *Crossroads and Cosmologies: Diasporas and Ethnogenesis in the New World* (Gainesville: University Press of Florida, 2007).

Fishman, Joshua A., "Bilingualism With and Without Diglossia; Diglossia With and Without Bilingualism," *Journal of Social Issues* 23:2 (Apr. 1967), 29–38.

———, *Language and Nationalism* (Rowley, MA: Newbury House, 1972).

———, *Reversing Language Shift* (Clevedon: Multilingual Matters, 1991).

——— (ed.), *Can Threatened Languages be Saved?* (Clevedon: Multilingual Matters, 2001).

Flores Galindo, Alberto, *Arequipa y el sur andino: Ensayo de historia regional (siglos XVIII–XX)* (Lima: Editorial Horizonte, 1977).

———, *Aristocracia y plebe: Lima, 1760–1830* (Lima: Mosca Azul, 1984).

Franco, Carlos, *Imágenes de la sociedad peruana: La "otra" modernidad* (Lima: CEDEP, 1991).

García, Manuel Andrés, *De peruanos e Indios: La figura del indígena en la intelectualidad y política criollas (Perú: siglos XVIII—XIX)* (Huelva: Universidad Internacional de Andalucía, 2007).

Garrett, David T., *Shadows of Empire: The Indian Nobility of Cusco, 1750–1825* (Cambridge and New York: Cambridge University Press, 2005).

Ginsburgh, Victor, Ignacio Ortuño-Ortín, and Shlomo Weber, *Learning Foreign Languages. Theoretical and Empirical Implications of the Selten and Pool Model* (London: Centre for Economic Policy Research, 2005).

Glave, Luis Miguel, *La república instalada. Formación nacional y prensa en el Cuzco, 1825–1839* (Lima: Instituto de Estudios Peruanos, 2004).

Godenzzi, Juan Carlos, "Literacy and Modernization among the Quechua-Speaking Population of Peru," in Nancy H. Hornberger (ed.), *Indigenous Literacies in the Americas: Language Planning from the Bottom Up* (Berlin: Mouton de Gruyter, 1997), pp. 237–49.

Gómez Rendón, J., *Typological and Social Constraints on Language Contact* (Amsterdam: Netherlands Graduate School of Linguistics, 2008).

Gonzales, Michael J., "Neo-Colonialism and Indian Unrest in Southern Peru, 1867–1898," *Bulletin of Latin American Research* 6:1 (1987), 1–26.

Gootenberg, Paul, *Between Silver and Guano: Commercial Policy and the State in Postindependence Peru* (Princeton, NJ: Princeton University Press, 1989).

———, "Population and Ethnicity in Early Republican Peru: Some Revisions," *Latin American Research Review* 26:3 (1991), 109–57.

Graddol, David, *English Next* (London: The British Council, 2006).

Graubart, Karen B., *With Our Labor and Sweat: Indigenous Women and the Formation of Colonial Society in Peru, 1550–1700* (Stanford: Stanford University Press, 2007).

Grieshaber, Erwin P., "Survival of Indian Communities in Nineteenth-Century Bolivia: A Regional Comparison," *Journal of Latin American Studies* 12:2 (Nov. 1980), 223–69.

Griffiths, Nicholas, *The Cross and the Serpent: Religious Repression and Resurgence in Colonial Peru* (Norman: University of Oklahoma Press, 1996).

Gugenberger, Eva, "Migración y desplazamiento lingüístico en Arequipa," in Rodolfo Cerrón-Palomino and Gustavo Solís Fonseca (eds.), *Temas de Lingüística Amerindia* (Lima: CONCYTEC, 1989), pp. 181–92.

Haboud, Marleen, *Quichua y castellano en los Andes ecuatorianos. Los efectos de un contacto prolongado* (Quito: Abya-Yala, 1998).

———, "Quichua Language Vitality: An Ecuadorian Perspective," *International Journal of the Sociology of Language* 167 (2004), 69–81.

Harris, Olivia, "Ethnic Identity and Market Relations: Indians and Mestizos in the Andes," in Brooke Larson and Olivia Harris (eds.), *Ethnicity, Markets, and Migration in the Andes: At the Crossroads of History and Anthropology* (Durham, NC: Duke University Press, 1995), pp. 351–90.

Harrison, Regina, *"True" Confessions: Quechua and Spanish Cultural Encounters in the Viceroyalty of Peru* (College Park: University of Maryland, Latin American Studies Center, 1992).

Harvey, Penelope, "Lenguaje y relaciones de poder: Consecuencias para una política lingüística," *Allpanchis* 19:29/30 (1987), 105–31.

Harvey, Penelope, "Women Who Won't Speak Spanish," in Pauline Burton, Ketaki Kushari Dyson, and Shirley Ardener (eds.), *Bilingual Women: Anthropological Approaches to Second Language Use* (Oxford: Berg, 1994), pp. 44–64.

Heggarty, Paul, "Enigmas en el origen de las lenguas andinas: Aplicando nuevas técnicas a las incógnitas por resolver," *Revista Andina* 40 (2005), 9–57, 70–80.

———, "Linguistics for Archaeologists: Principles, Methods and the Case of the Incas," *Cambridge Archaeological Journal* 17:3 (2007), 311–40.

Heller, Monica, "Code-switching and the Politics of Language," in Li Wei (ed.), *The Bilingualism Reader* 2nd ed. (London and New York: Routledge, 2007), pp. 163–76.

Hemming, John, *The Conquest of the Incas (New York: Harcourt, Brace & Company, 1970*).

Herrera, Sajid Alfredo, "Primary Education in Bourbon San Salvador and Sonsonate, 1750–1808," in Jordana Dym and Christophe Belaubre (eds.), *Politics, Economy, and Society in Bourbon Central America, 1759–1821* (Boulder: University of Colorado Press, 2007), pp. 17–45.

Hill, Jane, and Kenneth Hill, "Language Death and Relexification in Tlaxcalan Nahuatl," *International Journal of the Sociology of Language* 12 (1977), 55–70.

Hill, Jonathan D. (ed.), *History, Power, and Identity: Ethnogenesis in the Americas, 1492–1992* (Iowa City: University of Iowa Press, 1996).

Hobsbawm, Eric J., *Nations and Nationalism since 1780: Programme, Myth, Reality* (Cambridge: Cambridge University Press, 1990).

Hornberger, Nancy H., "Bilingual Education Success but Policy Failure," *Language in Society* 16:2 (1987), 205–26.

———, "Five Vowels or Three? Linguistics and Politics in Quechua Language Planning in Peru," in James Tollefson (ed.), *Power and Inequality in Language Education* (Cambridge: Cambridge University Press, 1995), pp. 187–205.

——— (ed.), *Indigenous Literacies in the Americas: Language Planning from the Bottom Up* (Berlin: Mouton de Gruyter, 1997).

Hornberger, Nancy H., and Serafín M. Coronel-Molina, "Quechua Language Shift, Maintenance, and Revitalization in the Andes: The Case for Language Planning," *International Journal of the Sociology of Language* 167 (2004), 9–67.

Hornberger, Nancy H., and Kendall A. King, "Reversing Quechua Language Shift in South America," in Joshua A. Fishman (ed.), *Can Threatened Languages be Saved? Reversing Language Shift Revisited* (Clevedon: Multilingual Matters, 2001), pp. 166–94.

Howard, Rosaleen, "Quechua in Tantamayo (Peru): Toward a "Social Archaeology" of Language," *International Journal of the Sociology of Language* 167 (2004), 95–118.

———, *Por los linderos de la lengua. Ideologías lingüísticas en los Andes* (Lima: Instituto de Estudios Peruanos / Instituto Francés de Estudios Andinos / Pontificia Universidad Católica del Perú, 2007).

———, "Beyond the Lexicon of Difference: Discursive Performance of Identity in the Andes," *Latin American and Caribbean Ethnic Studies* 4:1 (2009), 17–46.

———, "Education Reform, Indigenous Politics, and Decolonisation in the Bolivia of Evo Morales," *International Journal of Educational Development* 29:6 (2009), 583–93.

———, "Language, Signs, and the Performance of Power: The Discursive Struggle over Decolonization in the Bolivia of Evo Morales," *Latin American Perspectives* 37:3 (2010), 176–94.

———, "'Why Do They Steal Our Phonemes?' Inventing the Survival of the Cañari Language (Ecuador)," in Eithne B. Carlin and Simon van de Kerke (eds.), *Linguistics and Archaeology in the Americas: The Historicization of Language and Society* (Leiden: Brill, 2010), pp. 123–45.

Howard-Malverde, Rosaleen, "'Pachamama is a Spanish word': Linguistic Tension between Aymara, Quechua and Spanish in Northern Potosí (Bolivia)," *Anthropological Linguistics* 37:2 (Summer 1995), 141–68.

Huertas Vallejo, Lorenzo, "Poblaciones indígenas en Huamanga colonial," in Amalia Castelli, Marcia Koth de Paredes, and Mariana Mould de Pease (eds.), *Etnohistoria y antropología andina* (Lima: Museo Nacional de Historia, 1981), pp. 131–144.

Hühnefeldt, Christine, *Lucha por la tierra y protesta indígena: Las comunidades indígenas entre colonia y república, 1800–1830* (Bonn: University of Bonn, 1982).

Isbell, William H., *Mummies and Mortuary Monuments. A Postprocessual Prehistory of Central Andean Social Organization* (Austin, TX: University of Texas Press, 1997).

Itier, César, "Lengua general y comunicación escrita: Cinco cartas en quechua de Cotahuasi—1616," *Revista Andina*, 17 (1991), 65–107.

———, "'Cuzqueñistas' y 'Foráneos': Las resistencias a la normalización de la escritura del quechua," in Juan Carlos Godenzzi (ed.), *El quechua en debate: Ideología, normalización y enseñanza* (Cuzco: Centro de Estudios Regionales Andinos "Bartolomé de las Casas," 1992), pp. 85–93.

———, "Un nuevo documento colonial escrito por indígenas en quechua general: La petición de los caciques de Uyupacha al obispo de Huamanga (hacia 1670)," *Lexis: revista de lingüística y literatura* 16:1 (1992), 1–21.

———, *El teatro quechua en el Cuzco*, vol. 1 (Lima: Instituto Francés de Estudios Andinos / Centro de Estudios Regionales Andinos "Bartolomé de Las Casas," 1995); vol. 2 (Lima: Instituto Francés de Estudios Andinos / Centro de Estudios Regionales Andinos "Bartolomé de Las Casas," 2000).

———, "Quechua y cultura en el Cuzco del siglo XVIII: De la 'lengua general' al 'idioma del imperio de los incas'," in César Itier (ed.), *Del siglo de oro al siglo de las luces. Lenguaje y sociedad en los Andes del siglo XVIII* (Cuzco: Centro de Estudios Regionales Andinos "Bartolomé de Las Casas," 1995), pp. 89–111.

———, "Lengua general y quechua cuzqueño en los siglos XVI y XVII,' in Luis Millones, Hiroyasu Tomoeda, and Tatsuhiko Fujii (eds.), *Desde afuera y desde adentro. Ensayos de etnografía e historia del Cuzco y Apurímac* (Osaka: National Museum of Ethnology, 2000), pp. 47–59.

Itier, César, "La propagation de la langue générale dans le sud du Pérou," in *Le savoir, pouvoir des élites dans l'empire espagnol d'Amérique* (Paris: Université de la Sorbonne Nouvelle Paris III, 2001), pp. 63–74.

———, "Quechua, Aymara and Other Andean Languages: Historical, Linguistic and Socio-Linguistic Aspects," paper presented at the Maison de l'Amérique Latine, Paris, Jan. 16, 2002.

———, "Las cartas en quechua de Cotahuasi. El pensamiento político de un cacique de inicios del siglo XVII," in Bernard Lavallé (ed.), *Máscaras, tretas y rodeos del discurso colonial en los Andes* (Lima: Instituto Francés de Estudios Andinos / Instituto Riva-Agüero, 2005), pp. 41–71.

Jacobsen, Nils, "Civilization and its Barbarism: The Inevitability of Juan Bustamante's Failure," in Judith Ewell and William H. Beezley (eds.), *The Human Tradition in Latin America: The Nineteenth Century* (Wilmington, DEL.: SR Books, 1989), pp. 82–101.

———, *Mirages of Transition: The Peruvian Altiplano, 1780–1930* (Berkeley: University of California Press 1993).

———, "Liberalism and Indian Communities in Peru, 1821–1920," in Robert H. Jackson (ed.), *Liberals, the Church, and Indian Peasants: Corporate Lands and the Challenge of Reform in Nineteenth-Century Spanish America* (Albuquerque: University of New Mexico Press, 1997), pp. 123–70.

Klarén, Peter F., *Peru: Society and Nationhood in the Andes* (New York: Oxford University Press, 2000).

Kubler, George, *The Indian Caste of Peru, 1795–1940: A Population Study based upon Tax Records and Census Reports* (Washington, D.C.: Smithsonian Institution, 1952).

Landerman, Peter N., "Quechua Dialects and their Classification," unpublished Ph.D. dissertation, University of California at Los Angeles, 1991.

Langer, Erick D., "Indian Trade and Ethnic Economies in the Andes, 1780–1880," *Estudios Interdisciplinarios de América Latina y el Caribe* 15:1 (Jan.–June 2004), 9–33.

———, "Bringing the Economic Back In: Andean Indians and the Construction of the Nation-State in Nineteenth-Century Bolivia," *Journal of Latin American Studies* 41:3 (Aug. 2009), 527–51.

———, and Robert H. Jackson, "Liberalism and the Land Question in Bolivia, 1825–1920," in Robert H. Jackson (ed.), *Liberals, the Church, and Indian Peasants: Corporate Lands and the Challenge of Reform in Nineteenth-Century Spanish America* (Albuquerque: University of New Mexico Press, 1997), pp. 171–92.

Larson, Brooke, "Andean Highland Peasants and the Trials of Nation-Making during the Nineteenth Century," in Frank Salomon and Stuart Schwartz (eds.), *The Cambridge History of the Native Peoples of the Americas*, vol. 3 *South America* (Cambridge: Cambridge University Press, 2000), part 2, pp. 558–703.

———, *Trials of Nation-Making: Liberalism, Race and Modernity in the Andes, 1810–1910* (Cambridge: Cambridge University Press, 2004).

Lastra, Yolanda, *Cochabamba Quechua Syntax* (The Hague: Mouton, 1968).

Laughlin, Robert M., *Beware the Great Horned Serpent! Chiapas Under the Threat of Napoleon* (Albany, NY: Institute for Mesoamerican Studies, 2003).

Laurencich Minelli, Laura (ed.), *"Exsul Immeritus Blas Valera Populo Suo" e*

"Historia et Rudimenta Linguae Piruanorum": *Indios, gesuiti, e spagnoli in due documenti segreti sul Perú del XVII secolo* (Bologna: CLUEB, 2007).

Laurie, Nina, R. Andolina, and S. Radcliffe, "Indigenous Professionalization: Transnational Social Reproduction in the Andes," *Antipode* 35:3 (2003), 463–90.

Lavallé, Bernard, *Le marquis et le marchand: Les luttes de pouvoir au Cuzco (1700–1730)* (Paris: CNRS, 1987).

Le Page, Robert, and Andrée Tabouret-Keller, *Acts of Identity: Creole-based Approaches to Language and Ethnicity* (Cambridge: Cambridge University Press, 1985).

Levillier, Roberto, *Don Francisco de Toledo, supremo organizador del Perú. Su vida, su obra, 1515–1582* (Madrid: Espasa-Calpe, 1935).

Levinsohn, Stephen H., *The Inga Language* (The Hague and Paris: Mouton, 1976).

Linguistic Minorities Project, *The Other Languages of England* (London: Routledge Kegan Paul, 1985).

Lo Bianco, Joseph, "Globalisation and National Communities of Communication," *Language Problems and Language Planning* 29:2 (2005), 109–35.

Lockhart, James, "Trunk Lines and Feeder Lines: The Spanish Reaction to American Resources," in Kenneth J. Andrien and Rolena Adorno (eds.), *Transatlantic Encounters: Europeans and Andeans in the Sixteenth Century* (Berkeley and Los Angeles: University of California Press, 1991), pp. 90–120.

Lodge, R. Anthony, *French: From Dialect to Standard* (London: Routledge, 1993).

Lohmann Villena, Guillermo, *Las minas de Huancavelica en los siglos XVI y XVII* (Seville: Escuela de Estudios Hispano-Americanos, 1949).

López-Hurtado Q., Luis Enrique, *De resquicios a boquerones. La educación intercultural bilingüe en Bolivia* (La Paz: PROEIB Andes / Plural, 2005).

Lynch, John, *Bourbon Spain, 1700–1808* (Oxford: Basil Blackwell, 1989).

Luykx, Aurolyn, "The Future of Quechua and the Quechua of the Future: Language Ideologies and Language Planning in Bolivia," *International Journal of the Sociology of Language* 167 (2004), 147–58.

Majluf, Natalia, "De la rebelión al museo: Genealogías y retratos de los incas, 1781–1900," in Thomas B. F. Cummins (ed.), *Los incas, reyes del Perú* (Lima: Banco de Crédito, 2005), pp. 253–319.

Mallon, Florencia, *The Defense of Community in Peru's Central Highlands: Peasant Struggle and Capitalist Transition, 1860–1940* (Princeton: Princeton University Press, 1983).

Manley, Marilyn, "Quechua Language Attitudes and Maintenance in Cuzco, Peru," *Language Policy* 7:4 (Dec. 2008), 323–44.

Mannheim, Bruce, *The Language of the Inka since the European Invasion* (Austin: University of Texas Press, 1991).

Manrique, Nelson, *Yawar mayu: Sociedades terratenientes serranas, 1879–1910* (Lima: Instituto Francés de Estudios Andinos, 1988).

Marcus, Joyce, and Jorge E. Silva, "The Chillón Valley 'Coca Lands': Archaeological Background and Environmental Context,'" in María Rostworowski de Diez Canseco (ed.), *Conflicts over Coca Fields in XVIth-*

Century Peru (Ann Arbor: University of Michigan, 1988), pp. 1–32.

Marr, Tim, "The Language Left at Ticlio: Social and Cultural Perspectives on Quechua Language Loss in Lima, Peru," unpublished Ph.D. dissertation, University of Liverpool, 1998.

———, "Neither the State nor the Grass Roots: Language Maintenance and the Discourse of the Academia Mayor de la Lengua Quechua," *International Journal of Bilingual Education and Bilingualism* 2:3 (1999), 181–97.

———, "Language Ideology, Ownership and Maintenance: The Discourse of the Academia Mayor de la Lengua Quechua," in Li Wei, Jean-Marc Dewaele, and Alex Housen (eds.), *Opportunities and Challenges of Bilingualism* (Berlin: Mouton de Gruyter, 2002), pp. 199–219.

Mazet, Claude, "Population et société à Lima aux XVIe et XVIIe siècles: La paroisse San Sebastián (1562–1689)," *Cahiers des Amériques Latines* 13–14 (1976), 53–100.

Méndez, Cecilia, "Incas Si, Indios No: Notes on Peruvian Creole Nationalism and Its Contemporary Crisis," *Journal of Latin American Studies* 28:1 (1996), 197–225.

———, *The Plebeian Republic. The Huanta Rebellion and the Making of the Peruvian State, 1820–1850* (Durham, NC: Duke University Press, 2005).

Mendoza, Zoila S., *Creating Our Own: Folklore, Performance, and Identity in Cuzco, Peru* (Durham, N. C.: Duke University Press, 2008).

Miller, Jay, "Delaware Personhood," *Northeast Anthropology* 42 (Fall 1991), 17–27.

Mills, Kenneth, *Idolatry and Its Enemies: Colonial Andean Religion and Extirpation, 1640–1750* (Princeton: Princeton University Press, 1997).

Molina B., Ramiro, and Xavier Albó, *Gama étnica y lingüística de la población boliviana* (La Paz: Programa de la Naciones Unidas para el Desarrollo, 2006).

Monsalve, Martín, "Civil(ized) Society and the Public Sphere in Multiethnic Societies: Struggles over Citizenship in Lima, Peru (1850–1880)," unpublished Ph.D. dissertation, State University of New York, Stony Brook, 2005.

Morales Valerio, Francisco, "Secularización de doctrinas: Fin de un modelo evangelizador en la Nueva España?" *Archivo Ibero-Americano: Revista Franciscana e Estudios Históricos* 52: 205–208 (1992), 465–96.

Muecke, Ulrich, *Political Culture in Nineteenth-Century Peru: The Rise of the Partido Civil* (Pittsburgh: University of Pittsburgh Press, 2004).

Mujica, Elías, "*Altiplano*-Coast Relationships in the South-Central Andes: From Indirect to Direct Complementarity," in Izumi Shimada, Craig Morris, and Shozo Masuda (eds.), *Andean Ecology and Civilization: An Interdisciplinary Perspective on Andean Ecological Complementarity* (Tokyo: University of Tokyo Press, 1985), pp. 103–40.

Mumford, Jeremy Ravi, "Vertical Empire: The Struggle for Andean Space in the Sixteenth Century," unpublished Ph.D. dissertation, Yale University, 2005.

Murra, John V., "El control vertical de un máximo de pisos ecológicos en la economía de las sociedades andinas," in John V. Murra, *Formaciones económicas y políticas del mundo andino* (Lima: Instituto de Estudios Peruanos, 1975), pp. 59–115.

Muysken, Pieter, "Media lengua," in Sarah G. Thomason (ed.), *Contact Languages:*

a Wider Perspective (Amsterdam: John Benjamins, 1997), pp. 365–425.

Myers, Sarah K., *Language Shift among Migrants to Lima, Peru* (Chicago: University of Chicago, Department of Geography, 1973).

Niño-Murcia, Mercedes, "Linguistic Purism in Cuzco, Peru: A Historical Perspective," *Language Problems and Language Planning* 21:2 (1997), 134–61.

Ojeda y Ojeda, Ludolfo, "El maestro y el quechua: En torno a la ley de oficialización del quechua en la Región Inka," in Juan Carlos Godenzzi (ed.), *El Quechua en debate: Ideología, normalización y enseñanza* (Cuzco: Centro de Estudios Regionales Andinos "Bartolomé de las Casas," 1992), pp. 245–61.

Onuki, Yoshio, "The *Yunga* Zone in the Prehistory of the Central Andes: Vertical and Horizontal Dimensions in Andean Ecological and Cultural Processes," in Izumi Shimada, Craig Morris, and Shozo Masuda (eds.), *Andean Ecology and Civilization: An Interdisciplinary Perspective on Andean Ecological Complementarity* (Tokyo: University of Tokyo Press, 1985), pp. 339–356.

Parker, Gary J., "Falacias y verdades acerca del quechua," in Alberto Escobar (ed.), *El reto del multilingüismo en el Perú* (Lima, Instituto de Estudios Peruanos, 1972), pp. 111–21.

Pearce, Adrian J. , "Huancavelica 1700–1759: Administrative Reform of the Mercury Industry in Early Bourbon Peru," *Hispanic American Historical Review* 79:4 (Nov. 1999), 669–702.

———"The Peruvian Population Census of 1725–1740," *Latin American Research Review* 36:3 (Oct. 2001), 69–104.

Pearson, Chris, "Birth-order Names in Japan and Papua New Guinea," *Far Outliers* blog, March 15, 2007, at http://faroutliers.wordpress.com/2007/03/15/birth-order-names-in-japan-and-papua-new-guinea

Piel, Jean, "The Place of the Peasantry in the National Life of Peru in the Nineteenth Century," *Past & Present* 46 (Feb. 1970), 108–33.

Piho, Virve, *La secularización de las parroquias en la Nueva España y su repercusión en San Andrés Calpan* (México: Instituto Nacional de Antropología e Historia, 1981).

Pike, Frederick B., *The Modern History of Peru* (New York: Frederick A. Praeger, 1967).

Platt, Tristan, *Estado boliviano y ayllu andino: Tierra y tributo en el norte de Potosí* (Lima: Instituto de Estudios Peruanos, 1982).

———, Thérèse Bouysse-Cassagne, and Olivia Harris, *Qaraqara-Charka: Mallku, Inka Y Rey En La Provincia De Charcas, Siglos XV-XVII*, Travaux de l'Institut Français d'Études Andines, 174 (La Paz: Institut Français d'Études Andines, 2006).

Plaza Martínez, Pedro, "Quechua," in Mily Crevels and Pieter Muysken (eds.), *Lenguas de Bolivia* vol. 1, *Ambito andino* (La Paz: Plural Editores, 2009), pp. 215–84.

Porras Barrenechea, Raul, *Fuentes históricas peruanas (apuntes de un curso universitario)* (Lima: Instituto Raul Porras Barrenechea, 1963).

Presta, Ana María, "Undressing the *Coya* and Dressing the Indian Woman: Market Economy, Clothing, and Identities in the Colonial Andes, La Plata (Charcas), Late Sixteenth and Early Seventeenth Centuries," *Hispanic American Historical Review* 90:1 (2010), 41–74.

Quilter, Jeffrey, and Gary Urton (eds.), *Narrative Threads: Accounting and Recounting in Andean Khipu* (Austin: University of Texas Press, 2002).

Radin, Paul, *The Winnebago Tribe* (1923; Lincoln: University of Nebraska Press, 1970).

Ramírez, Susan E., "To Serve God and King: The Origins of Public Schools for Native Children in Eighteenth-century Peru," *Colonial Latin American Review*, 17:1 (June 2008), 73–99.

Ramos, Gabriela, "Diezmos, comercio y conflictos sociales a inicios del siglo XVII (Arzobispado de Lima): 1600–1630," in Gabriela Ramos (ed.), *La venida del reino: religión, evangelización y cultura en América, siglos XVI–XX* (Cuzco: Centro de Estudios Regionales Andinos "Bartolomé de las Casas," 1994), pp. 229–81.

———, "Muerte, conversión e identidad en los Andes peruanos. Lima y Cuzco, 1532–1670," unpublished Ph.D. dissertation, University of Pennsylvania, 2001.

———, *Death and Conversion in the Andes. Lima and Cuzco, 1532–1670* (Notre Dame, IN: Notre Dame University Press, 2010).

———, "Los tejidos y la sociedad colonial andina," *Colonial Latin American Review* 19:1 (Apr. 2010), 115–49.

Rampton, Ben, *Crossing: Language and Ethnicity among Adolescents* 2nd ed. (Manchester: St. Jerome Press, 2005).

Restall, Matthew, "A History of the New Philology and the New Philology in History," *Latin American Research Review* 38:1 (Feb. 2003), 113–34.

Rivet, Paul, and Georges de Créqui-Montfort, *Bibliographie des langues aymará et kichua,* 4 vols. (Paris: Institut d'Ethnologie, 1951–56).

Rodríguez O., Jaime E., *The Independence of Spanish America* (Cambridge and New York: Cambridge University Press, 1998).

Rosaldo, Renato, "Ilongot Naming: The Play of Associations," in E. Tooker and H. Conklin (eds.), *Naming Systems* (Washington, DC: American Ethnological Society, 1984), pp. 11–24.

Rostworowski de Diez Canseco, María, "Plantaciones prehispánicas de coca en la vertiente del pacífico," in María Rostworowski de Diez Canseco, *Etnia y sociedad: Costa peruana prehispánica* (Lima: Instituto de Estudios Peruanos, 1977), pp. 155–95.

———, "El avance de los Yauyos hacia la costa en tiempos míticos," in María Rostworowski de Diez Canseco, *Señoríos indígenas de Lima y Canta* (Lima: Instituto de Estudios Peruanos, 1978), pp. 31–44.

———, "Los Yauyos coloniales y el nexo con el mito," in María Rostworowski de Diez Canseco, *Señoríos indígenas de Lima y Canta* (Lima: Instituto de Estudios Peruanos, 1978), pp. 109–122.

——— (ed.), *Conflicts over Coca Fields in XVIth-Century Peru* (Ann Arbor: University of Michigan, 1988).

——— (ed.), *El señorío de Pachacamac: El informe de Rodrigo Cantos de Andrade de 1573* (Lima, Instituto de Estudios Peruanos / Banco Central de Reserva del Perú, 1999).

———, *Pachacamac* (Lima: Instituto de Estudios Peruanos, 2002).

Salles-Reese, Veronica, *From Viracocha to the Virgin of Copacabana: Representation of the Sacred at Lake Titicaca* (Austin: University of Texas Press, 1997).

Salomon, Frank, *The Cordkeepers: Khipus and Cultural Life in a Peruvian Village* (Durham, NC: Duke University Press, 2004).

Salomon, Frank, and Sue Grosboll, "Names and Peoples in Incaic Quito: Retrieving Undocumented Historic Processes through Anthroponymy and Statistics," *American Anthropologist* 88:2 (June 1986), 387–99.

Sánchez Santiró, Ernest, "El nuevo orden parroquial de la ciudad de México: Población, etnia, y territorio (1768–1777)," *Estudios de Historia Novohispana* 30 (Jan.–June 2004), 63–92.

Shimada, Izumi, *Pachacamac Archaeology: Retrospect and Prospect* (Philadelphia: University Museum Press, 1991).

Sichra, Inge, *La vitalidad del quechua. Lengua y sociedad en dos provincias de Cochabamba* (La Paz: PROEIB Andes / Plural, 2003).

———, "Trascendiendo o fortaleciendo el valor emblemático del quechua: Identidad de la lengua en la ciudad de Cochabamba," in Serafín M. Coronel-Molina and L. L. Grabner-Coronel (eds.), *Lenguas e identidades en los Andes. Perspectivas ideológicas y culturales* (Quito: Abya Yala, 2005), pp. 211–50.

Smolicz, Jerzy J., "Minority Languages as Core Values of Ethnic Cultures," in Willem Fase, Koen Jaspaert, and Sjaak Kroon (eds.), *Maintenance and Loss of Minority Languages* (Amsterdam and Philadelphia: John Benjamins, 1992), pp. 277–305.

Spalding, Karen, *Huarochirí: An Andean Society under Inca and Spanish Rule* (Stanford: Stanford University Press, 1984).

Stern, Steve J., *Los pueblos indígenas del Perú y el desafío de la conquista española* (Madrid: Alianza Editorial, 1986).

Tanck de Estrada, Dorothy, *Pueblos de Indios y educación en el México colonial, 1750–1821* (México: El Colegio de México, 1999).

Taylor, Gerald, "Lengua general y lenguas particulares en la antigua provincia de Yauyos (Perú)," *Revista de Indias* 43:171 (1983), 265–89.

———, "Yauyos, un microcosmo dialectal quechua," *Revista Andina* 3 (1984), 121–46.

———, "Un documento quechua de Huarochirí—1607," *Revista Andina* 5 (1985), 157–85.

———, "Algunos datos nuevos sobre el quechua de Yauyos (Vitis y Huancaya)," *Revista Andina* 9 (1987), 253–65.

———, *Estudios de dialectología quechua (Chachapoyas, Ferreñafe, Yauyos)* (Lima: Universidad Nacional de Educación Enrique Guzmán y Valle, 1994).

———, "Dos mapas del pueblo de Cocha-Laraos (1595, 1597)," *Amerindia* 19–20 (1995), 151–62.

———, *Estudios lingüísticos sobre Chachapoyas* (Lima: Instituto Francés de Estudios Andinos / Universidad Nacional Mayor de San Marcos, 2000).

———, "Camac, camay y camasca en el manuscrito quechua de Huarochirí," in Gerald Taylor, *Camac, camay y camasca y otros ensayos sobre Huarochirí y Yauyos* (Lima: Instituto Francés de Estudios Andinos, 2000), pp. 1–17.

Taylor, William B., *Magistrates of the Sacred: Priests and Parishioners in Eighteenth-Century Mexico* (Stanford: Stanford University Press, 1996).

Thurner, Mark, *From Two Republics to One Divided: Contradictions of Post-colonial Nationmaking in Andean Peru* (Durham, NC: Duke University Press, 1997).

Torero, Alfredo, "Los dialectos quechuas," *Anales Científicos de la Universidad Agraria* 2 (1964), 446–78.

———, "Lingüística e historia de la sociedad andina," in A. Escobar (ed.), *El reto del multilingüismo en el Perú* (Lima: Instituto de Estudios Peruanos, 1972), pp. 51–106.

———, *El quechua y la historia social andina* (Lima: Universidad Ricardo Palma, 1974).

———, "Lingüística e historia de la sociedad andina," in *Lingüística e indigenismo moderno de América* (Trabajos presentados al XXXIX Congreso Internacional de Americanistas), vol. 5. (Lima: Instituto de Estudios Peruanos, 1975), pp. 221–259.

———, "El comercio lejano y la difusión del quechua. El caso del Ecuador," *Revista Andina* 4 (1984), 367–89.

———, "Lenguas y pueblos altiplánicos en torno al siglo XVI," *Revista Andina* 10 (1987), 329–405.

———, "Acerca de la lengua Chinchaysuyo," in César Itier (ed.), *Del Siglo de Oro al Siglo de las Luces: Lenguaje y sociedad en los Andes del siglo XVIII* (Cuzco: Centro de Estudios Regionales Andinos "Bartolomé de Las Casas," 1995), pp. 13–31.

———, *Idiomas de los Andes. Lingüística e historia* (Lima: Instituto Francés de Estudios Andinos / Horizonte, 2002); 2nd ed. (2005).

Urrutia, Jaime, *Huamanga: Región e historia, 1536–1770* (Huamanga: Universidad Nacional de San Cristóbal, 1985).

Urton, Gary, "From Knots to Narratives: Reconstructing the Art of Historical Record Keeping in the Andes from Spanish Transcriptions of Inka *Khipus*," *Ethnohistory* 45:3 (Summer 1998), 409–38.

———, *Signs of the Inka Khipu: Binary Coding in the Andean Knotted String Records* (Austin: University of Texas Press, 2003).

Van Beek, Walter E. A., "Becoming Human in Dogon, Mali," in Göran Aijmer (ed.), *Coming Into Existence: Birth and Metaphors of Birth* (Gothenburg: University of Gothenburg, 1992), pp. 47–70.

Van Young, Eric, "The New Cultural History Comes to Old Mexico," *Hispanic American Historical Review,* 79: 2 (May 1999), 211–47.

Vieira Powers, Karen, *Andean Journeys: Migration, Ethnogenesis and the State in Colonial Quito* (Albuquerque: University of New Mexico Press, 1995).

Vienrich, Adolfo, *Azucenas quechuas / Fábulas quechuas* (1905–1906; Lima: Ediciones Lux, 1999).

Von Gleich, Utta, *Educación primaria bilingüe intercultural en América Latina* (Eschborn: Deutsche Gesellschaft für Zusamenarbeit, 1989).

———, "New Quechua Literacies in Bolivia," *International Journal of the Sociology of Language* 167 (2004), pp. 131–46.

Walker, Charles F., "Los indios en la transición de colonia a república: Base social de la modernización política?" in Henrique Urbano (ed.), *Tradición y modernidad en los Andes* 2nd ed. (Cuzco: Centro de Estudios Regionales Andinos "Bartolomé de las Casas," 1997), pp. 1–14.

Walker, Charles F., *Smoldering Ashes. Cuzco and the Creation of Republican Peru, 1780–1840* (Durham, NC: Duke University Press, 1999).

Weber, Diana, "Mother Tongue Education in Quechua," in Peter Cole, Gabriella

Hermon, and Mario Daniel Martín (eds,), *Language in the Andes* (Newark, DE: University of Delaware, 1994), pp. 90–115.

———, "El programa LEELA: Una alternativa para la educación bilingüe," in Luis Miranda (ed.), *Actas del 1er Congreso de Lenguas Indígenas de Sudamérica*, vol. 1 (Lima: Universidad Ricardo Palma, 2000), pp. 137–47.

Whitaker, Arthur Preston, *The Huancavelica Mercury Mine: A Contribution to the History of the Bourbon Renaissance in the Spanish Empire* (Cambridge, MASS.: Harvard University Press, 1941).

Wightman, Ann, *Indigenous Migration and Social Change: The Forasteros of Cuzco, 1570–1720* (Durham, NC: Duke University Press, 1990).

Wölck, Wolfgang, "Las lenguas mayores del Perú y sus hablantes," in Alberto Escobar (ed.), *El reto del multilingüismo en el Perú* (Lima: Instituto de Estudios Peruanos, 1972), pp. 189–216.

Woolard, Kathryn A., "Language Convergence and Language Death as Social Processes," in Nancy Dorian (ed.), *Investigating Obsolescence. Studies in Language Contraction and Death* (Cambridge: Cambridge University Press, 1989), pp. 355–67.

Index

Please note: This book follows a chronological sequence through its various chapters. Where an index entry contains a large number of page references, then, it is helpful to bear in mind that those pages typically pertain to **progressively later time-periods**, from the Conquest through to the present day, as follows: